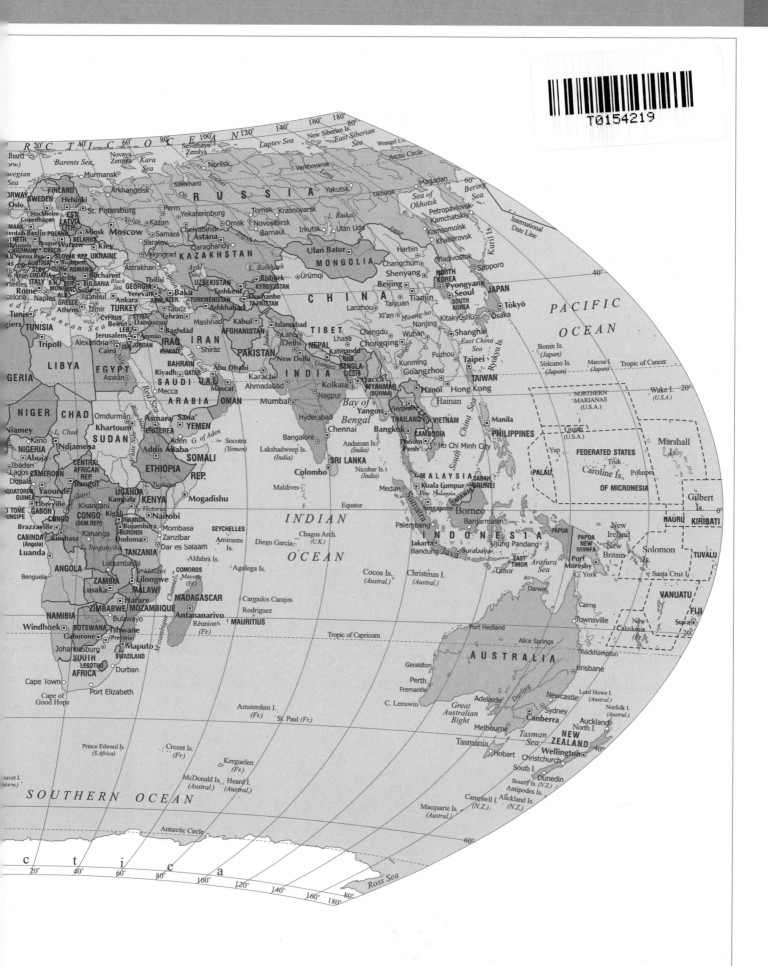

Scale 1:104 500 000

Modern World University Atlas

ANTHEM PRESS

Anthem Press
A division of Wimbledon Publishing Company Limited
www.anthempress.com

This edition first published in the UK and the USA in 2009
by Anthem Press
75–76 Blackfriars Road, London SE1 8HA, UK
& PO Box 9779, London SW19 7ZG, UK
& 244 Madison Avenue #116, New York, NY 10016, USA

British Library Cataloguing in Publication Data
A catalogue record for this book is available from the British Library.

Library of Congress Cataloging in Publication Data
A catalog record for this book has been requested.

ISBN-13: 978 1 84331 306 9 (Hbk)
ISBN-10: 1 84331 306 5 (Hbk)

ISBN-13: 978 1 84331 319 9 (Ebk)
ISBN-10: 1 84331 319 7 (Ebk)

1 3 5 7 9 10 8 6 4 2

Printed in India

THEMATIC INDEX

MAP SYMBOLS

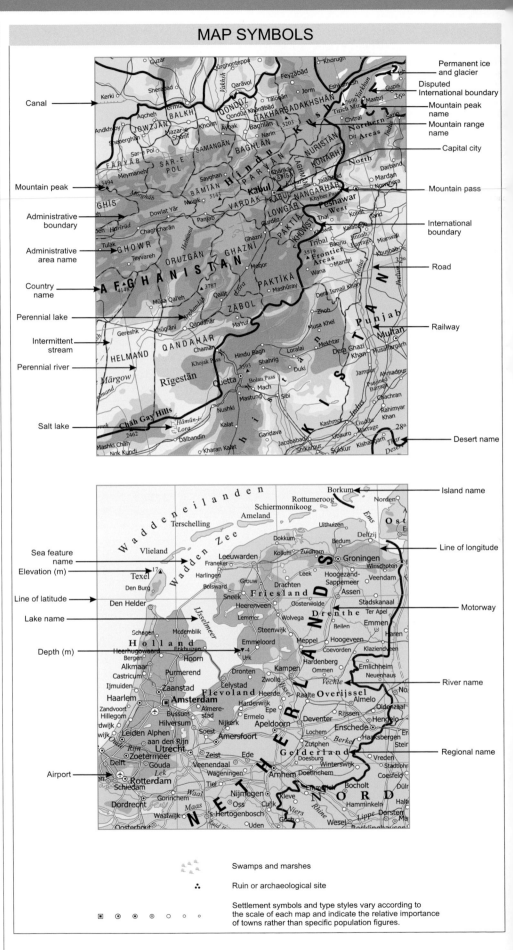

Swamps and marshes

Ruin or archaeological site

Settlement symbols and type styles vary according to the scale of each map and indicate the relative importance of towns rather than specific population figures.

SCALE

The scale of a map is the relationship between two points shown on the map and the distance between the same two points on the Earth's surface. Scale can be expressed in four ways: as a ratio, in words, as a fraction, and as a graphic (bar) scale.

A scale expressed as a ratio of say 1:50,000 means that one unit on the map represents 50,000 units on the ground; for instance, 1 centimetre represents 50,000 centimetres (50 metres). The statement "one centimetre represents 50 metres" is an expression of this scale in words.

Scale expressed as a fraction, 1/50,000, means that any distance on the map is 1/50,000th of the distance on the ground. The bottom part of the fraction is called the 'scale denominator'.

Due to depicting the curvature of Earth's surface on a flat, two-dimensional map surface, scale varies from place to place. Thus a 'representative fraction' is stated for scale that is correct at the centre of the map but varies elsewhere. While called a 'representative fraction', it really is a representative ratio. The expression of scale as 1:50,000, 1:300 000 and so on is the 'representative fraction'.

A bar scale is a ruler with ground distances added. A graphic scale is used to measure distances on the map. A distance between two places on the map can be marked on the edge of a sheet of paper, which is then placed besides the bar scale and the distance gauged.

Maps are usually produced at standard scales, such as 1:50,000, 1:100,000, and so on. The distance on the ground equals the distance measured on the map multiplied by the scale denominator. Calculation: Measure 3 cm on a map with scale 1:12 400 000;

x 12,400,000 = 37,200,000 cm = 37,200 metres = 37.2 kilometres.

The map extracts to the right show New York and its surrounding area at different scales. The representative fraction is given at top right of each map. Map 1 (1:50 000) is a large-scale map. Most of the streets are named and major landmarks marked, but the map only covers part of central New York. Maps with a ratio of 1:50,000 to 1:250,000 are considered medium scale. Map 2 (1:3000 000) is a small-scale map and enables us to see the whole of central New York. Maps 3 and 4 show how greater areas can be depicted as the map scale decreases. Map 5 (1:35 000 000) is at such a small scale that New York is represented by a city symbol and we can see a large part of north-east United States and north-east Canada.

Map scales must be used with care as large distances on small-scale maps can be represented by 1 or 2 centimetres. As a general rule, the larger the map scale, the more accurate and reliable will be the distance measured.

LATITUDE AND LONGITUDE

The geometric system of latitudes and longitudes are used for the accurate positioning of individual points on the Earth's surface. Latitude parallels are drawn west-east around the Earth, parallel to the Equator, decreasing in diameter from the Equator until they become a point at the poles.

Latitude is the distance of a point north or south of the Equator measured at an angle with the centre of the Earth, whereby the Equator is latitude 0 degree, the North Pole is 90 degrees north and the South Pole 90 degrees south. The Tropic of Cancer is at 23 degrees 30 minutes North and the Tropic of Capricorn is at 23 degrees 30 minutes South. The Arctic Circle is at 66 degrees 30 minutes North and the Antarctic Circle is at 66 degrees 30 minutes South. On the maps in the atlas, the lines of latitude and longitudes are represented by blue lines running across the map, with the degree figures in black at the sides of the maps. The degree interval depends on the scale of the map.

Line of longitude are meridians drawn north-south, cutting the lines of latitude at right angles on the Earth's surface and intersecting with one another at the poles. Longitude is measured by an angle at the centre of the Earth from the Prime Meridian (0 degree), which passes through Greenwich in London. It is given as a measurement east or west of the Greenwich Meridian from 0 to 180 degrees. On the atlas maps, we have given the degree figures of latitude in black at the top and bottom margins of the map.

In the index each place name is followed by its map page number, and then its latitude and longitude. The unit of measurement is the degree, which is subdivided into 60 minutes. An index entry states the position of a place in degrees and minutes. The latitude is followed by N (north) or S (south) and the longitude E (east) or W (west).

For Example:
Salem, U.S.A.   142   44 56N 123 2W
Salem is on map page 142, and 44 degrees 56 minutes north of the Equator and 123 degrees 2 minutes west of Greenwich.

The Map on the left shows how to estimate the required distance from the nearest line of latitude or longitude on the map page, in order to locate a place or feature listed in the index such as Berlin in Germany. Berlin lies between 52° and 53° latitude and between 13° and 14° longitude. The distance between 13° longitude and the location of Berlin is 11.1 mm (25 minutes) and the distance between 52° and the location of Berlin is 21.5mm (30 minutes). So the exact location of Berlin is 52 30N 13 25E.

Map 1   Scale 1 : 50 000

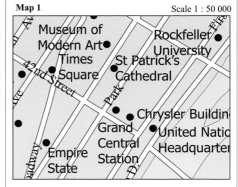

Map 2   Scale 1: 300 000

Map 3   Scale:1: 2 000 000

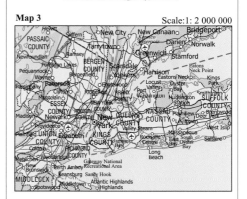

Map 4   Scale:1:12 400 000

Map 5   Scale 1:35 000 000

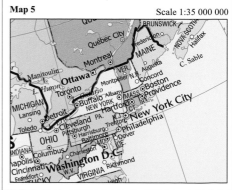

Maps are drawn on a flat surface and represent a part or whole of the Earth's surface. The spherical shape of the earth is represented on the plane surface by devising geometrical and mathematical methods to derive a network of latitudes and longitudes upon which an accurate depiction of the earth is made. This process of transformation is known as projection.

A projection can be derived by projecting light through a globe made of glass with graticules marked on it, onto any developable surface and is called a perspective projection. But if meridians and parallels are modified with the aid of mathematics, or if the map projection acquires certain other particular properties it is called a non-perspective projection.

Correct Area: An equal area map projection aims at preserving the ratio of mapped area to the corresponding earth area. Since area is a product of both length and breadth, we can increase one and diminish the other. Projections with this property are called Equal Area or Equivalent Projection.

Correct Shape: The conformal or orthomorphic projection aims at maintaining the shape of the map surface at any point to the shape of the corresponding point on the earth. The scale should be same at any point in all directions, and the angle at which the parallels intersect the meridians governs the shape of areas. But no projection can provide true shape to large areas like continents.

Correct Distance: The scale is correct in these projections and the azimuthal projections present true bearings. They are called Equidistant Projections. There are three types of projections according to the area used for transferring the graticule:
(1) Zenithal projections, (2) Conical projections, (3) Cylindrical projections.

ZENITHAL PROJECTIONS

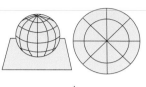

These projections are constructed by placing a plane tangent to the globe and light is focussed on it from various positions to produce an image of the parallels and meridians on the plane. The plane can be tangent to a globe and can occupy several positions either at one of the poles, or at any point on the equator or at any other point. In these projections the directions of all points from the centre of the map remain correct, and therefore it is also called Azimuthal Projection. Zenithal projections can be divided into three types based on the position of light.

Gnomonic: The light is placed at the centre of the globe.

Stereographic: The light is placed at a point diametrically opposite to the point where the plane touches the globe.

Orthographic: The light is at infinity so that the rays of light are parallel.

Each of these three types of zenithal projections can be further sub-divided with reference to the position of the plane surface on the globe. They are:

(1) Polar: Plane surface is a tangent to one of the poles. (2) Equatorial: Plane surface is a tangent to any point on the equator. (3) Oblique: Plane surface is a tangent to any other point.

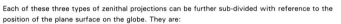

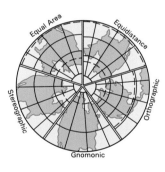

Polar: It is simple to construct, and the five different methods comparing area, distortion and so on, are shown left.

Equatorial: In this Lambert Azimuthal equal area projection, both equal area and bearing is true from the centre.

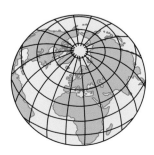

Oblique: This projection is calculated from a selected central point such as the poles and it retains equal area properties. It is a good projection to show large continental masses.

CONICAL PROJECTIONS

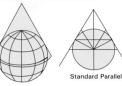
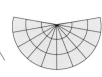

Standard Parallel

Conical projections are constructed by projecting part of the globe on to a cone which just touches a circle on the globe. The parallel latitude, around which the cone is tangent to the globe is known as the standard parallel, and it is correctly represented on a projection. Other points on the globe are casting their shadows on the cone. When this cone is developed into a flat surface it is a conical projection.

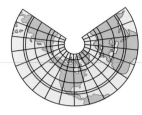

Polyconic:
This projection is derived by considering the number of cones placed over a globe. Each of these cones is in tangent to its corresponding latitude, thereby making each parallel a standard parallel. The scale is true along every parallel. Countries with large latitudinal and limited longitudinal extent in the mid-latitudes can be shown satisfactorily using this projection.

Bonne:
This projection is a modified version of the simple conic projection. It has only one standard parallel, but each parallel is truly divided and so it is an equal area projection. The distance between any two given parallels along the central meridians is true and constant, but the shape is distorted at the edges.

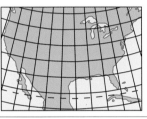

Conical Projection with Two Standard Parallels:
In the simple conical projections there is only one standard parallel, and the area of a country with a large land mass cannot be shown correctly. However it can be represented more correctly with two standard parallels and it is constructed with the cone bisecting the surface of the globe. This projection is suitable for larger countries like Canada, USA, etc.

CYLINDRICAL PROJECTIONS

Cylindrical projections are constructed by projecting the surface of the globe on to a cylinder just touching the globe in which the light is supposed to be placed at the centre of the globe. The scale is correct only along the equator.

Winkel Equal Area/Winkel Triple Projections:
In this projection the world can be shown on a map with the correct relative size and area.

Mercator: The latitudes are drawn parallel to the equator. The areas away from the equator are very much exaggerated. The pole (which is actually a point), is represented by a line equal to the equator.

The meridians are perpendicular to the equator and parallel to each other.

Conventional Projection: Some projections can be constructed purely by mathematical computation. These projections meet our special requirements and are called conventional projections. They are: 1. Globular, 2. Mollweide's, 3. Interrupted Molleweide's, 4. Sinusoidal, 5. Interrupted Sinusoidal, 6. Hammer's.

Mollweide: This is an equal area projection, and the shape is well maintained in the equatorial, tropical and mid-latitude areas.

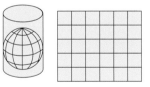

Simple Cylindrical

Two Standard Parallels

Landsat 7 satellite

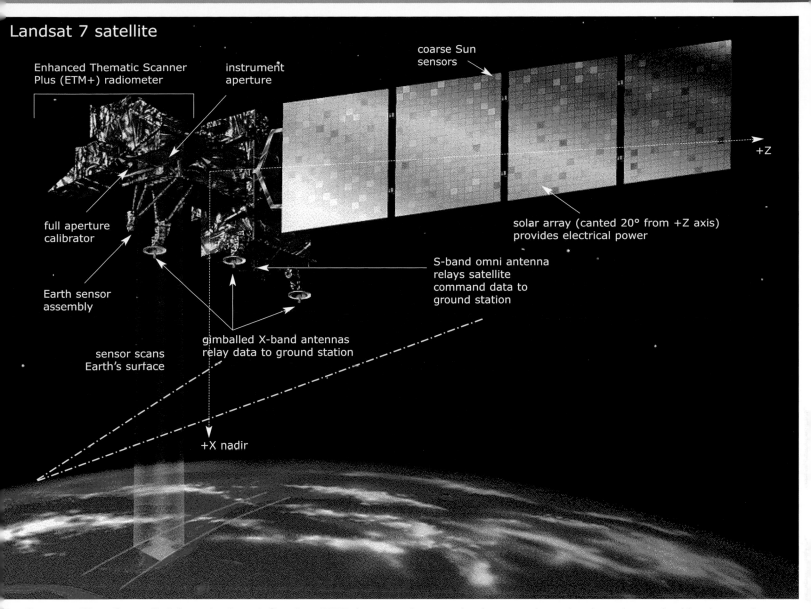

Enhanced Thematic Scanner Plus (ETM+) radiometer

instrument aperture

coarse Sun sensors

+Z

solar array (canted 20° from +Z axis) provides electrical power

full aperture calibrator

S-band omni antenna relays satellite command data to ground station

Earth sensor assembly

gimballed X-band antennas relay data to ground station

sensor scans Earth's surface

+X nadir

The first satellite, *Sputnik 1*, launched on 4 October 1957. It signalled the beginning of a revolution in our ability to survey and map the Earth. TIROS-1 (Television Infrared Observation Satellite) was the first successful weather satellite. Launched on 1 April 1960, for 79 days it provided television images of Earth's weather patterns from a circular orbit about 700–750 km (435–470 miles) above the Earth. **Landsat-1**, the first Earth resources satellite, launched on 23 July 1972. **Landsat-5**, launched on 1 March 1984, has provided images of Earth for nearly 25 years. **Landsat-7**, the most recent in the series, launched on 15 April 1999. It continues to function despite a faulty scan line corrector.

Today, there are nearly 2,500 satellites orbiting Earth. Sophisticated digital sensors scan Earth's surface and atmosphere day and night, collecting and transmitting to ground stations huge volumes of data on Earth's physical, chemical and biological systems, which is then processed, analysed and stored by computers. This 'remote sensing' makes it possible to collect data on dangerous or remote areas. It also is more rapid and less intrusive than data collection on the ground, ensuring that fragile areas remain undisturbed.

Remote sensing enables us to monitor and assess the state of, and changes in, the natural and man-made environment. It is becoming more important due to the dramatic impact that modern human civilisation is having on our planet. It helps us to minimise

the negative impacts through adaptation and mitigation, and provides us with observational information to improve life on Earth.

Types of remote sensing

There are two types of remote sensing. **Passive sensors** detect natural energy (radiation) that is emitted or reflected by the object or surrounding area being observed. Reflected sunlight is the most common source of radiation measured by passive sensors. Examples of passive remote sensors include film photography, infra-red, charge-coupled devices and radiometers. **Active sensors**, on the other hand, emit energy in order to scan objects and areas. A passive sensor then detects and measures the radiation that is reflected or scattered from the target. For instance, **Synthetic Aperture Radar (SAR)** sensors send out a microwave signal and create an image from the radiation reflected back. SAR signals penetrate cloud cover and do not require sunlight. SAR is used to produce precise digital elevation models of large-scale terrain.

Radiometers and photometers are the most common remote sensing instruments, collecting reflected and emitted radiation in a wide range of frequencies. The most common are visible and infra-red sensors, followed by microwave, gamma ray and rarely, ultraviolet. They may also be used to detect the emission spectra of various chemicals, providing data on chemical concentrations in Earth's atmosphere.

Thematic scanners

Thematic scanners have been in use since the 1970s. They are usually found on earth observation satellites such as the Landsat series and IKONOS. Thematic scanners record data from many bands of the electromagnetic spectrum at the same time. Visible sensors provide data on the visible bands, consisting of the three primary colours (red, green and blue). An image composed from a non-visible band, such as infra-red or microwave, is called a 'false-colour composite'.

The choice of waveband depends on the purpose of the final image: geology, hydrology and agronomy have different best combinations of wavebands. Whatever waveband is chosen, each scanner records data of constant width but potentially several thousand kilometres in length. Once the data has been relayed to a ground station, it is usually split into approximately square sections or scenes for distrubution.

Maps of land cover and land use from thematic mapping can be used to locate mineral deposits, detect or monitor land usage and deforestation, and monitor the health of plants and crops.

Resolutions

The quality of remote sensing data consists of its spatial, spectral, radiometric and temporal resolutions. **Spatial resolution** refers to the size of a pixel that is recorded in a raster image - typically pixels may correspond to square areas ranging in side length from 1 to 1000 metres. **Spectral resolution** refers to the number of different frequency bands recorded - usually, this is the number of sensors carried by the satellite. Current Landsat satellites have seven bands, including several in the infra-red spectrum. The MODIS satellites are the highest resolving at 31 bands. **Radiometric resolution** refers to the number of different intensities of radiation the sensor is able to distinguish. Typically, this ranges from 8 to 14 bits in each band, corresponding to 256 levels of the grey scale and up to 16,384 intensities or 'shades' of colour. The **temporal resolution** is simply the frequency of flyovers by the satellite or plane, and is only relevant in time-series studies or those requiring an averaged or mosaic image such as in monitoring of deforestation.

Uluru (Ayers Rock), Central Australia, captured by Space Imaging's IKONOS satellite. IKONOS is a commercial earth observation satellite, and was the first to collect publicly available high-resolution imagery at 1- and 4-metre resolution. It launched on 24 September 1999.

Satellite orbits

Most **earth observation satellites**, including the Landsat series, are in a near-polar, Sun-synchronous, Low Earth Orbit (LEO). At altitudes of between 700 km and 900 km (430–460 miles), the satellites revolve around the Earth at about 27,400 km/h (8 km/s), making one complete revolution around the Earth in about 100 minutes and on each orbit cross a particular line of latitude at the same local (solar) time. This ensures that the satellite scans most of the globe, repeating its coverage every two to three weeks. More recent satellites have sensors that can be titled sideways from the orbital path, thus potentially reducing the coverage time for a particular segment of the globe to a few days.

A network of **meteorological satellites**, including GOES and Meteosat, provide visible and infra-red images of Earth's surface and atmosphere from **geostationery orbits** directly above Earth's equator. These satellites are at an altitude of about 35,800 km (22,250 miles) and revolve around the Earth every 24 hours. Each satellite remains above the same point on the Equator. These satellites monitor the weather and climate of the Earth, but also provide other vital information on phenomena such as city lights, fires, pollution, ocean currents, snow cover, and volcanic activity.

In addition, there are around 31 **Global Positioning System (GPS** navigational satellites in Medium Earth Orbit (MEO), at an altitude of about 20,200 km (12,550 miles). These circle the Earth in six different orbital planes, transmitting microwave signals that enable us to determine our location (longitude, latitude, altitude) to within a few metres. Originally developed by the US Department of Defense in 1978, GPS is now available to individuals through hand-held electronic receivers and in-car satellite navigation systems.

Earth Observing System

NASA's Earth Observing System (EOS) is a coordinated series of satellites for long-term global observations of Earth's land surface, biosphere, atmosphere, and oceans. The LDCM program seeks to continue Landsat's unique and vital legacy in earth science.

NASA's Earth Observing System

Satellite	Study area	Launch date
SeaWiFS	ocean colour	1 August 1997
TRIMM	tropical rainfall	27 November 1997
Landsat-7	various	15 April 1999
QuikSCAT	sea winds	19 June 1999
Terra (ASTER, CERES, (MISR, MODIS, MOPITT)	various	18 December 1999
ACRIMSAT	solar radiation	20 December 1999
EO-1	various	21 November 2000
Jason	ocean surface	7 December 2001
Meteor-3M (SAGE III)	atmosphere	10 December 2001
GRACE	gravity field	17 March 2002
Aqua	water cycle	4 May 2002
ADEOS II (SeaWinds)	solar panel failed	12 December 2002
ICESat	ice sheet/sea ice	12 January 2003
SORCE	solar variability	25 January 2003
Aura	atmosphere	15 July 2004
CloudSat	clouds	27 April 2006
CALIPSO	aerosols & clouds	27 April 2006
OSTM	ocean surface	May 2008
Glory	aerosols, clouds	due December 2008
OCO	carbon dioxide	due December 2008
Aquarius	sea salinity	due September 2009
NPP	various	due September 2009
LDCM	Landsat continuity	due July 2011

ORLD, CONTINENTS, OCEANS

	km^2	miles^2	%
orld	509,450,000	196,672,000	–
ater	360,000,000	138,984,000	70.7
d	149,450,000	57,688,000	29.3
cific Ocean	155,557,000	60,061,000	43.2
antic Ocean	76,762,000	29,638,000	21.3
dian Ocean	68,556,000	26,470,000	19.0
uthern Ocean	20,327,000	7,848,000	5.6
ctic Ocean	14,056,000	5,427,000	3.9
ia	44,500,000	17,177,000	29.8
rica	30,302,000	11,697,000	20.3
rth America	24,241,000	9,357,000	16.2
uth America	17,793,000	6,868,000	11.9
tarctica	14,100,000	5,443,000	9.4
rope	9,957,000	3,843,000	6.7
stralia & Oceania	8,557,000	3,303,000	5.7

OUNTAINS

World's top 30 mountains are in Asia.

ia	country	metres	feet
erest	*China/Nepal*	8,850	29,035
(Godwin Austen)	*China/Kashmir*	8,611	28,251
nchenjunga	*India/Nepal*	8,598	28,208
otse	*China/Nepal*	8,516	27,939
akalu	*China/Nepal*	8,481	27,824
o Oyu	*China/Nepal*	8,201	26,906
aulagari	*Nepal*	8,167	26,795
anaslu	*Nepal*	8,156	26,758
nga Parbat	*Kashmir*	8,126	26,660
napurna	*Nepal*	8,078	26,502
asherbrum	*China/Kashmir*	8,068	26,470
xabangma	*China*	8,012	26,286
ngbachen	*India/Nepal*	7,902	25,925
vor	*Pakistan*	7,720	25,328
Kommunizma	*Tajikistan*	7,495	24,590
emavend	*Iran*	5,604	18,386
arat	*Turkey*	5,165	16,495
nong Kinabalu	*Malaysia (Borneo)*	4,101	13,455
ji-San	*Japan*	3,776	12,388

rica	country	metres	feet
imanjaro	*Tanzania*	5,895	19,340
Kenya	*Kenya*	5,199	17,057
wenzori	*Uganda/D.R. Congo*	5,109	16,762
s Dashen	*Ethiopia*	4,620	15,157
eru	*Kenya*	4,565	14,977
risimbi	*Rwanda/D.R. Congo*	4,507	14,787
Elgon	*Kenya/Uganda*	4,321	14,176
tu	*Ethiopia*	4,307	14,130
ubkal	*Morocco*	4,165	13,665
t Cameroon	*Cameroon*	4,070	13,353

rth America	country	metres	feet
McKinley (Denali)	*USA (Alaska)*	6,194	20,321
t Logan	*Canada*	5,959	19,551
co de Orizaba	*Mexico*	5,610	18,405
t St Elias	*USA/Canada*	5,489	18,008
pcatépetl	*Mexico*	5,452	17,887
t Foraker	*USA (Alaska)*	5,304	17,401
accihuatl	*Mexico*	5,286	17,342
cania	*Canada*	5,226	17,146
Steele	*Canada*	5,073	16,644
t Bona	*USA (Alaska)*	5,005	16,420
t Whitney	*USA (California)*	4,418	14,495
jumulco	*Guatemala*	4,220	13,845
irripó Grande	*Costa Rica*	3,837	12,589
co Duarte	*Dominican Rep.*	3,175	10,417

uth America	country	metres	feet
concagua	*Argentina*	6,962	22,841
onete	*Argentina*	6,872	22,546
os de Salado	*Argentina/Chile*	6,863	22,516
ssis	*Argentina*	6,779	22,241
ercedario	*Argentina/Chile*	6,770	22,211
ascarán	*Peru*	6,768	22,204
llaillaco	*Argentina/Chile*	6,723	22,057
do de Cachi	*Argentina*	6,720	22,047
rupaja	*Peru*	6,632	21,758
jama	*Bolivia*	6,520	21,391
imborazo	*Ecuador*	6,267	20,561
co Cristóbal Colón	*Colombia*	5,800	19,029
co Bolívar	*Venezuela*	5,007	16,427

tarctica		metres	feet
nson Massif		4,897	16,066
t Kirkpatrick		4,528	14,855

rope	country	metres	feet
brus	*Russia*	5,642	18,510
ont Blanc	*France/Italy*	4,808	15,774
onte Rosa	*Italy/Switzerland*	4,634	15,203
om	*Switzerland*	4,545	14,911
skamm	*Switzerland*	4,527	14,852
eisshorn	*Switzerland*	4,505	14,780
schorn	*Switzerland*	4,490	14,730
atterhorn/Cervino	*Italy/Switzerland*	4,528	14,855
ont Maudit	*France/Italy*	4,465	14,649
ent Blanche	*Switzerland*	4,356	14,291
adelhorn	*Switzerland*	4,327	14,196
> Grandes Jorasses	*France/Italy*	4,208	13,806
Jungfrau	*Switzerland*	4,158	13,642
Grossglockner	*Austria*	3,797	12,457
Mulhacén	*Spain*	3,478	11,411
Zugspitze	*Germany*	2,962	9,718
Olympus	*Greece*	2,917	9,570
Triglav	*Slovenia*	2,863	9,393
Gerlachovsky	*Slovak Republic*	2,655	8,711
Galdhøppigen	*Norway*	2,469	8,100
Kebnekaise	*Sweden*	2,117	6,946
Ben Nevis	*UK*	1,342	4,403

Australia & Oceania	country	metres	feet
Puncak Jaya	*Indonesia*	4,884	16,023
Puncak Trikora	*Indonesia*	4,730	15,518
Puncak Mandala	*Indonesia*	4,640	15,427
Mt Wilhelm	*Papua New Guinea*	4,508	14,790
> Mauna Kea	*USA (Hawaii)*	4,205	13,796
Mauna Loa	*USA (Hawaii)*	4,169	13,678
Aoraki Mt Cook	*New Zealand*	3,753	12,313
Mt Kosciuszko	*Australia*	2,230	7,316

RIVERS

Asia	mouth	kilometres	miles
Yangtze [3]	*Pacific Ocean*	6,380	3,960
Yenisey–Angara [5]	*Arctic Ocean*	5,550	3,445
Huang He [6]	*Pacific Ocean*	5,464	3,395
Ob–Irtysh [7]	*Arctic Ocean*	5,410	3,360
Mekong [9]	*Pacific Ocean*	4,500	2,795
Amur [10]	*Pacific Ocean*	4,442	2,760
Lena	*Arctic Ocean*	4,402	2,735
Irtysh	*Ob*	4,250	2,640
Yenisey	*Arctic Ocean*	4,090	2,540
Ob	*Arctic Ocean*	3,680	2,285
Indus	*Indian Ocean*	3,100	1,925
Brahmaputra	*Indian Ocean*	2,900	1,800
Syrdarya	*Aral Sea*	2,860	1,775
Salween	*Indian Ocean*	2,800	1,740
Euphrates	*Indian Ocean*	2,700	1,675
> Amudarya	*Aral Sea*	2,540	1,575

Africa	mouth	kilometres	miles
Nile [1]	*Mediterranean*	6,670	4,140
Congo [8]	*Atlantic Ocean*	4,670	2,900
Niger	*Atlantic Ocean*	4,180	2,595
Zambezi	*Indian Ocean*	3,540	2,200
Oubangi/Uele	*Congo*	2,250	1,400
Kasai	*Congo*	1,950	1,210
Shabelle	*Indian Ocean*	1,930	1,200
Orange	*Atlantic Ocean*	1,860	1,155
Cubango	*Okavango Delta*	1,800	1,120
Limpopo	*Indian Ocean*	1,770	1,100
> Senegal	*Atlantic Ocean*	1,640	1,020

North America	mouth	kilometres	miles
Mississippi–Missouri [4]	*Gulf of Mexico*	5,971	3,710
Mackenzie	*Arctic Ocean*	4,240	2,630
Missouri	*Mississippi*	3,780	2,350
Mississippi	*Gulf of Mexico*	3,780	2,350
Yukon	*Pacific Ocean*	3,185	1,980
Rio Grande	*Gulf of Mexico*	3,030	1,880
Arkansas	*Mississippi*	2,340	1,450
Colorado	*Pacific Ocean*	2,330	1,445
Red	*Mississippi*	2,040	1,445
Columbia	*Pacific Ocean*	1,950	1,210
Saskatchewan	*Lake Winnipeg*	1,940	1,205

South America	mouth	kilometres	miles
Amazon [2]	*Atlantic Ocean*	6,450	4,010
Paraná–Plate	*Atlantic Ocean*	4,500	2,800
Purus	*Amazon*	3,350	2,080
Madeira	*Amazon*	3,200	1,990
São Francisco	*Atlantic Ocean*	2,900	1,800
Paraná	*Plate*	2,800	1,740
Tocantins	*Atlantic Ocean*	2,750	1,710
Paraguay	*Paraná*	2,550	1,580
Orinoco	*Atlantic Ocean*	2,500	1,550
Pilcomayo	*Paraná*	2,500	1,550
Araguaia	*Tocantins*	2,250	1,400

Europe	mouth	kilometres	miles
Volga	*Caspian Sea*	3,700	2,300
Danube	*Black Sea*	2,850	1,770
Ural	*Caspian Sea*	2,535	1,575
Dnepr (Dnipro)	*Black Sea*	2,285	1,420
Kama	*Volga*	2,030	1,260
Don	*Volga*	1,990	1,240
Petchora	*Arctic Ocean*	1,790	1,110
Oka	*Volga*	1,480	920
Belaya	*Kama*	1,420	880
Dnister (Dniester)	*Black Sea*	1,400	870
Vyatka	*Kama*	1,370	850
Rhine	*North Sea*	1,320	820
> N. Dvina	*Arctic Ocean*	1,290	800
Elbe	*North Sea*	1,145	710

Australia & Oceania	mouth	kilometres	miles
Murray	*Southern Ocean*	2,520	1,565
Murrumbidgee	*Murray*	1,575	980
Darling	*Murray*	1,390	865
Lachlan	*Murrumbidgee*	1,370	850

LAKES

Asia	country	km^2	miles^2
Caspian Sea [1]	*Asia*	371,000	143,000
Lake Baikal [8]	*Russia*	30,500	11,780
Aral Sea [10]	*Kazakhstan/Uzbekistan*	28,687	11,086
Tonlé Sap	*Cambodia*	20,000	7,700
Lake Balqash	*Kazakhstan*	18,500	7,100

Africa	country	km^2	miles^2
Lake Victoria [3]	*East Africa*	68,000	26,000
Lake Tanganyika [6]	*Central Africa*	33,000	13,000
Lake Malawi/Nyasa [9]	*East Africa*	29,600	11,430
Lake Chad	*Central Africa*	25,000	9,700
Lake Turkana	*Ethiopia/Kenya*	8,500	3,290
Lake Volta	*Ghana*	8,480	3,270

North America	location	km^2	miles^2
Lake Superior [2]	*Canada/USA*	82,350	31,800
Lake Huron [4]	*Canada/USA*	59,600	23,010
Lake Michigan [5]	*USA*	58,000	22,400
Great Bear Lake [7]	*Canada*	31,800	12,280
Great Slave Lake	*Canada*	28,500	11,000
Lake Erie	*Canada/USA*	25,700	9,900
Lake Winnipeg	*Canada*	24,400	9,400
Lake Ontario	*Canada/USA*	19,500	7,500
Lake Nicaragua	*Nicaragua*	8,200	3,200

South America	country	km^2	miles^2
Lake Titicaca	*Bolivia/Peru*	8,300	3,200
Lake Poopo	*Bolivia*	2,800	1,100

Europe	country	km^2	miles^2
Lake Ladoga	*Russia*	17,700	6,800
Lake Onega	*Russia*	9,700	3,700
Saimaa system	*Finland*	8,000	3,100
Vänern	*Sweden*	3,500	2,100

Australia & Oceania	country	km^2	miles^2
Lake Eyre	*Australia*	8,900	3,400
Lake Torrens	*Australia*	5,800	2,200
Lake Gairdner	*Australia*	4,800	1,900

ISLANDS

Asia	location	km^2	miles^2
Borneo [3]	*South-East Asia*	744,360	287,400
Sumatra [6]	*Indonesia*	473,600	182,860
Honshu [7]	*Japan*	230,500	88,980
Celebes	*Indonesia*	189,000	73,000
Java	*Indonesia*	126,700	48,900
Luzon	*Phillipines*	104,700	40,400
Hokkaido	*Japan*	78,400	30,300

Africa	location	km^2	miles^2
Madagascar [4]	*Indian Ocean*	587,040	226,660
Socotra	*Indian Ocean*	3,600	1,400
Réunion	*Indian Ocean*	2,500	965

North America	location	km^2	miles^2
Greenland [1]	*Atlantic Ocean*	2,175,600	839,800
Baffin Island [5]	*Canada*	508,000	196,100
Victoria Island [9]	*Canada*	212,200	81,900
Ellesmere Island [10]	*Canada*	212,000	81,800
Cuba	*Caribbean Sea*	110,860	42,800
Hispaniola	*Dominican Rep./Haiti*	76,200	29,400
Jamaica	*Caribbean Sea*	11,400	4,400
Puerto Rico	*Atlantic Ocean*	8,900	3,400

South America	location	km^2	miles^2
Tierra del Fuego	*Argentina/Chile*	47,000	18,100

Europe	location	km^2	miles^2
Great Britain	*UK*	229,880	88,700
Iceland	*Atlantic Ocean*	103,000	39,800
Ireland	*Ireland/UK*	84,400	32,600
Novaya Zemlya	*Russia*	48,200	18,600
Sicily	*Italy*	25,500	9,800
Corsica	*France*	8,700	3,400

Australia & Oceania	location	km^2	miles^2
New Guinea [2]	*Indonesia/Papua N.G.*	821,030	317,000
New Zealand (S.)	*Pacific Ocean*	150,500	58,100
New Zealand (N.)	*Pacific Ocean*	114,700	44,300
Tasmania	*Australia*	67,800	26,200
Hawaii	*Pacific Ocean*	10,450	4,000

OCEAN DEPTHS

	ocean	metres	feet
Mariana Trench	*Pacific Ocean*	11,022	36,161
Tonga Trench	*Pacific Ocean*	10,882	35,702
Japan Trench	*Pacific Ocean*	10,554	34,626
Kuril Trench	*Pacific Ocean*	10,542	34,587
Puerto Rico Deep	*Atlantic Ocean*	9,220	30,249
Cayman Trench	*Atlantic Ocean*	7,680	25,197
Java Trench	*Indian Ocean*	7,450	24,442
Molloy Deep	*Arctic Ocean*	5,608	18,399
Gulf of Mexico	*Atlantic Ocean*	5,203	17,070
Mediterranean Sea	*Atlantic Ocean*	5,121	16,801
Red Sea	*Indian Ocean*	2,635	8,454
Black Sea	*Atlantic Ocean*	2,211	7,254

Items are listed in order of size by continent up to this mark > items after this mark are selective

The world top ten are shown in brackets [x]

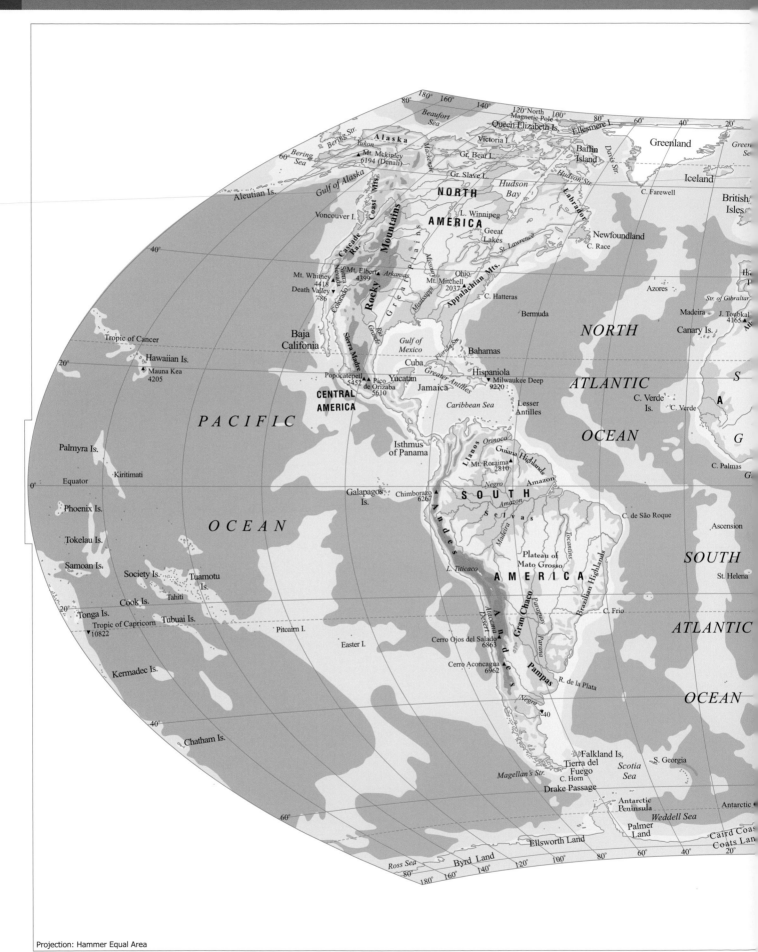

Projection: Hammer Equal Area

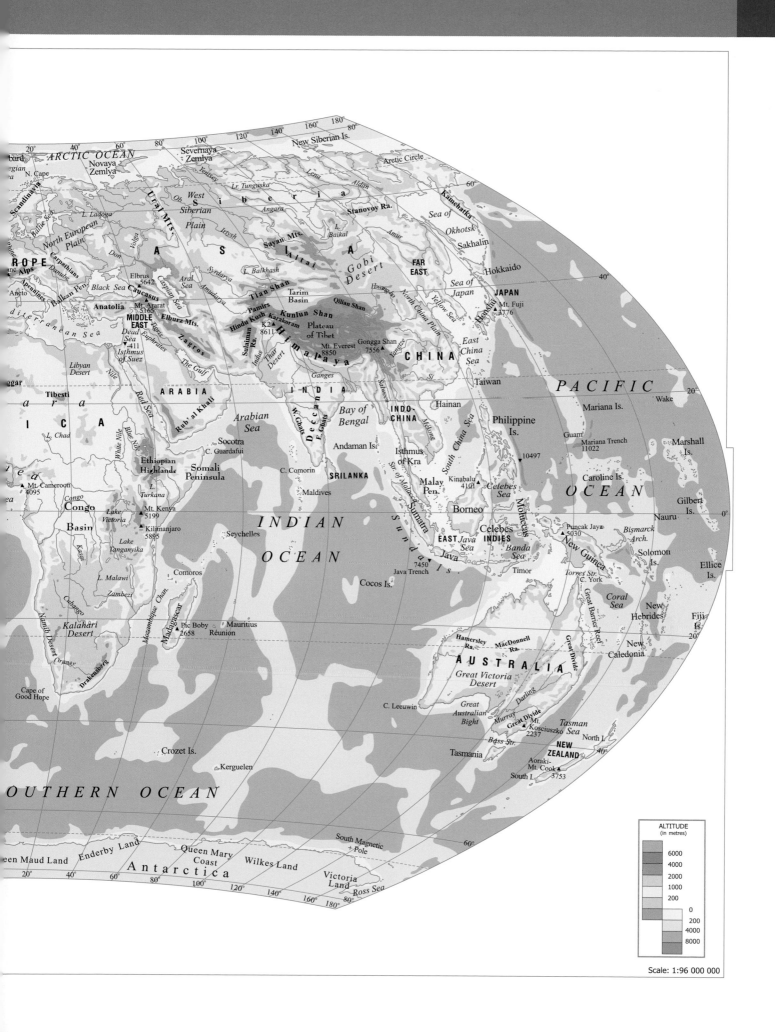

ARCTIC OCEAN
N. Cape
Spitsbergen
Novaya
Zemlya
Severnaya
Zemlya
New Siberian Is.
Arctic Circle

Scandinavia
Baltic Sea
North European Plain
L. Ladoga
Ural Mts.
West Siberian Plain
Ob
Yenisey
Lr. Tunguska
Lena
Aldan
Angara
Kamchatka

EUROPE
Alps
Apennines
Carpathians
Danube
Don
Volga
ASIA
Irtysh
L. Balkhash
Sayan Mts.
Altai
Baikal
Stanovoy Ra.
Amur
Sea of Okhotsk
Sakhalin
FAR EAST

Aneto
Balkan Pen.
Black Sea
Caucasus
Elbrus 5642
Caspian Sea
Aral Sea
Sirdarya
Amudarya
Tian Shan
Tarim Basin
Qilian Shan
Gobi Desert
Hokkaido
Sea of Japan
JAPAN
Mt. Fuji 3776

Mediterranean Sea
Anatolia
MIDDLE EAST
Mt. Ararat 5165
Elburz Mts.
Zagros
Pamirs
Hindu Kush
K2 8611
Karakoram
Kunlun Shan
Plateau of Tibet
Honshu
North China Plain
Yellow Sea

Libyan Desert
Dead Sea -411
Isthmus of Suez
Tigris
Euphrates
The Gulf
Sulaiman Ra.
Indus
Thar Desert
Himalaya
Mt. Everest 8850
Gongga Shan 7556
CHINA
Yangtze
Si
East China Sea

Tibesti
AFRICA
Nile
Red Sea
ARABIA
Ganges
INDIA
Salween
Mekong
Taiwan
PACIFIC

a
L. Chad
White Nile
Blue Nile
Rub' al Khali
Arabian Sea
Socotra
C. Guardafui
W. Ghats
Deccan
E. Ghats
Bay of Bengal
Andaman Is.
INDO-CHINA
Hainan
Mariana Is.
Wake

Mt. Cameroon 4095
Congo
Ethiopian Highlands
Somali Peninsula
C. Comorin
SRILANKA
Isthmus of Kra
Malay Pen.
Kinabalu 4101
Guam
Mariana Trench 11022
Marshall Is.

ea
Congo Basin
Kasai
L. Turkana
Lake Victoria
Mt. Kenya 5199
Maldives
INDIAN
Sumatra
Borneo
Celebes Sea
Caroline Is.
OCEAN

Lake Tanganyika
Kilimanjaro 5895
Seychelles
OCEAN
EAST INDIES
Java Sea
Celebes
Banda Sea
Puncak Jaya 5030
New Guinea
Bismarck Arch.
Solomon Is.
Nauru
Gilbert Is.

Cobango
L. Malawi
Zambezi
Comoros
Java
Timor
Moluccas
Ellice Is.

Namib Desert
Kalahari Desert
Orange
Madagascar
Pic Boby 2658
Mauritius
Réunion
Cocos Is.
Java Trench 7450
Sunda Is.
Torres Str.
C. York
Great Barrier Reef
Coral Sea
New Hebrides
Fiji Is.

Drakensberg
Hamersley Ra.
MacDonnell Ra.
Great Divide
New Caledonia

Cape of Good Hope
AUSTRALIA
Great Victoria Desert

Crozet Is.
C. Leeuwin
Great Australian Bight
Murray
Darling
Great Divide
Mt. Kosciuszko 2237
Tasman Sea
North I.

Kerguelen
Bass Str.
Tasmania
NEW ZEALAND
Aoraki-Mt. Cook 3753
South I.

SOUTHERN OCEAN
South Magnetic Pole

Queen Maud Land
Enderby Land
Queen Mary Coast
Wilkes Land
Antarctica
Victoria Land
Ross Sea

ALTITUDE
(in metres)
6000
4000
2000
1000
200
0
200
4000
8000

Scale: 1:96 000 000

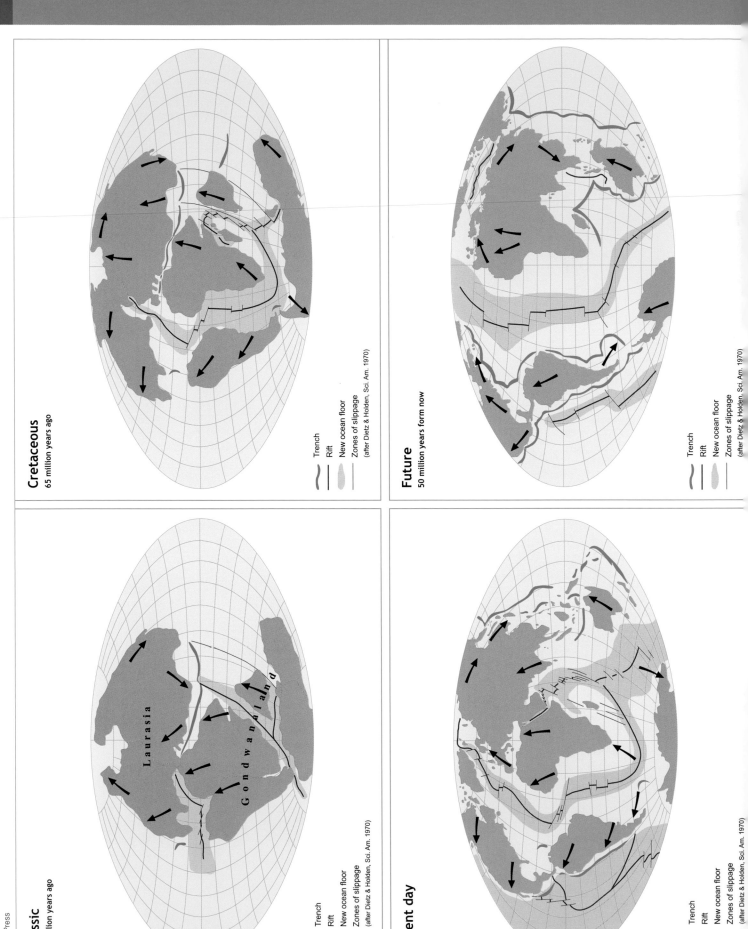

Cretaceous
65 million years ago

Trench
Rift
New ocean floor
Zones of slippage
(after Dietz & Holden, Sci. Am. 1970)

Future
50 million years form now

Trench
Rift
New ocean floor
Zones of slippage
(after Dietz & Holden, Sci. Am. 1970)

Jurassic
180 million years ago

Laurasia

Gondwanaland

Trench
Rift
New ocean floor
Zones of slippage
(after Dietz & Holden, Sci. Am. 1970)

Present day

Trench
Rift
New ocean floor
Zones of slippage
(after Dietz & Holden, Sci. Am. 1970)

In 1915, Alfred Wegener (1880–1930) published the theory of continental drift. Continents move over the Earth's surface at a rate of a few centimetres per year, adding up to thousands of kilometres over geological time. About 180 million years ago, the giant supercontinent Panagea began to break up, forming Gondwanaland and Laurasia.

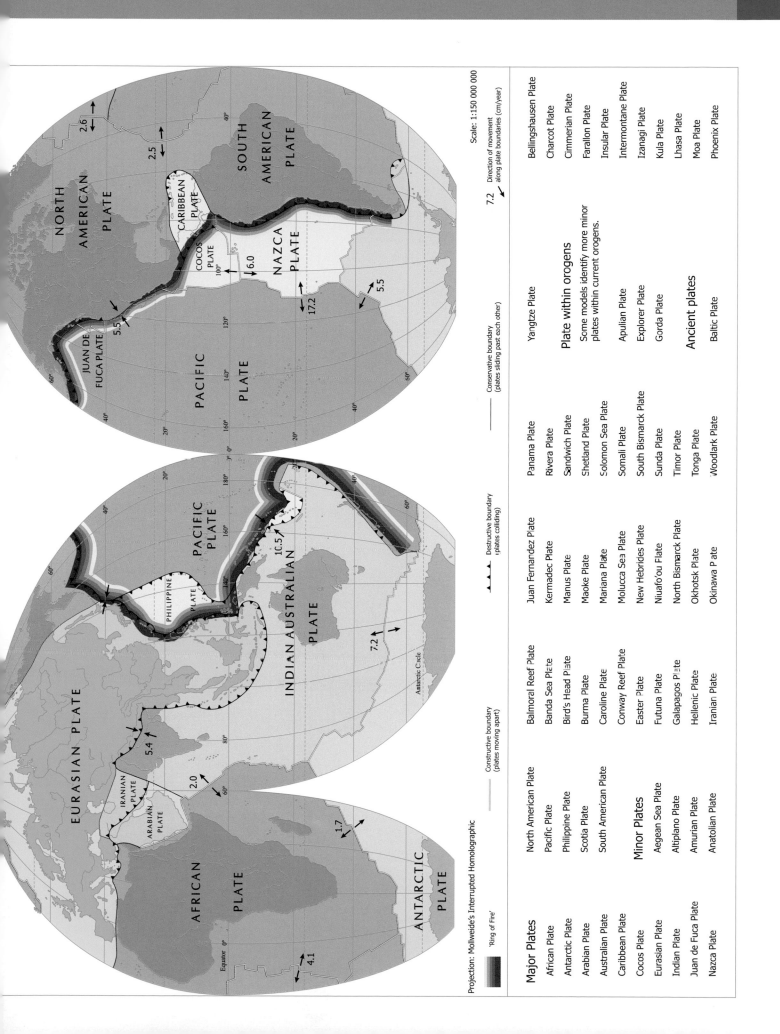

Projection: Mollweide's Interrupted Homolographic

Scale: 1:150 000 000

'Ring of Fire'

——— Constructive boundary
(plates moving apart)

▲▲▲ Destructive boundary
(plates colliding)

——— Conservative boundary
(plates sliding past each other)

7.2 → Direction of movement
along plate boundaries (cm/year)

Major Plates

African Plate	North American Plate	Balmoral Reef Plate
Antarctic Plate	Pacific Plate	Banda Sea Plate
Arabian Plate	Philippine Plate	Bird's Head Plate
Australian Plate	Scotia Plate	Burma Plate
Caribbean Plate	South American Plate	Caroline Plate
Cocos Plate		Conway Reef Plate
Eurasian Plate	**Minor Plates**	Easter Plate
Indian Plate	Aegean Sea Plate	Futuna Plate
Juan de Fuca Plate	Altiplano Plate	Galapagos Plate
Nazca Plate	Amurian Plate	Hellenic Plate
	Anatolian Plate	Iranian Plate

Juan Fernandez Plate	Panama Plate	Yangtze Plate
Kermadec Plate	Rivera Plate	
Manus Plate	Sandwich Plate	**Plate within orogens**
Maoke Plate	Shetland Plate	Some models identify more minor
Mariana Plate	Solomon Sea Plate	plates within current orogens.
Molucca Sea Plate	Somali Plate	
New Hebrides Plate	South Bismarck Plate	Apulian Plate
Niuafo'ou Plate	Sunda Plate	Explorer Plate
North Bismarck Plate	Timor Plate	Gorda Plate
Okhotsk Plate	Tonga Plate	
Okinawa Plate	Woodlark Plate	**Ancient plates**

Bellingshausen Plate	
Charcot Plate	
Cimmerian Plate	
Farallon Plate	
Insular Plate	
Intermontane Plate	
Izanagi Plate	
Kula Plate	
Lhasa Plate	
Moa Plate	
Phoenix Plate	
Baltic Plate	

Earthquakes

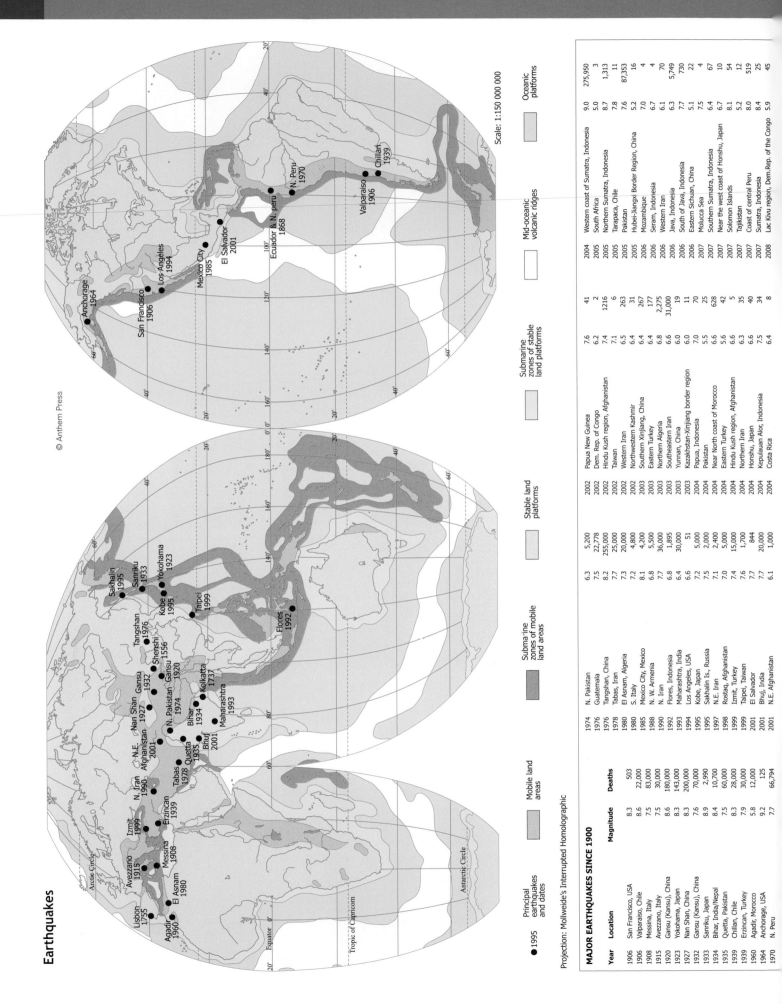

© Anthem Press

Scale: 1:150 000 000

Projection: Mollweide's Interrupted Homolographic

Legend:
- 1995 ● Principal earthquakes and dates
- Mobile land areas
- Submarine zones of mobile land areas
- Stable land platforms
- Submarine zones of stable land platforms
- Mid-oceanic volcanic ridges
- Oceanic platforms

MAJOR EARTHQUAKES SINCE 1900

Year	Location	Magnitude	Deaths
1906	San Francisco, USA	8.3	503
1906	Valparaiso, Chile	8.6	22,000
1908	Messina, Italy	7.5	83,000
1915	Avezzano, Italy	7.5	30,000
1920	Gansu (Kansu), China	8.6	180,000
1923	Yokohama, Japan	8.3	143,000
1927	Nan Shan, China	8.3	200,000
1932	Gansu (Kansu), China	7.6	70,000
1933	Sanriku, Japan	8.9	2,990
1934	Bihar, India/Nepal	8.4	10,700
1935	Quetta, Pakistan	7.5	60,000
1939	Chillan, Chile	8.3	28,000
1939	Erzincan, Turkey	7.9	30,000
1960	Agadir, Morocco	5.8	12,000
1964	Anchorage, USA	9.2	125
1970	N. Peru	7.7	66,794
1974	N. Pakistan	6.3	5,200
1976	Guatemala	7.5	22,778
1976	Tangshan, China	8.2	255,000
1978	Tabas, Iran	7.7	25,000
1980	El Asnam, Algeria	7.3	20,000
1985	Mexico City, Mexico	8.1	4,800
1988	N.W. Armenia	6.8	4,200
1990	N. Iran	7.7	36,000
1992	Flores, Indonesia	6.8	1,895
1993	Maharashtra, India	6.4	30,000
1994	Los Angeles, USA	6.6	51
1995	Kobe, Japan	7.2	5,000
1995	Sakhalin Is., Russia	7.5	2,000
1997	N.E. Iran	7.1	2,400
1998	Rostaq, Afghanistan	7.0	5,000
1999	Izmit, Turkey	7.4	15,000
1999	Taipei, Taiwan	7.6	1,700
2001	El Salvador	6.3	35
2001	Bhuj, India	7.7	20,000
2001	N.E. Afghanistan	6.1	1,000
2002	Papua New Guinea	7.6	41
2002	Dem. Rep. of Congo	6.2	2
2002	Hindu Kush region, Afghanistan	7.4	1216
2002	Taiwan	7.1	6
2003	Western Iran	6.5	263
2003	Northwestern Kashmir	6.4	31
2003	Southern Xinjiang, China	6.4	267
2003	Eastern Turkey	6.8	177
2003	Northern Algeria	7.7	2,275
2003	Southeastern Iran	6.6	31,000
2003	Yunnan, China	6.4	19
2003	Kazakhstan-Xinjiang border region	6.0	11
2004	Papua, Indonesia	7.0	70
2004	Pakistan	5.5	25
2004	Near North coast of Morocco	6.6	628
2004	Eastern Turkey	5.6	42
2004	Hindu Kush region, Afghanistan	6.6	5
2004	Northern Iran	6.3	35
2004	Honshu, Japan	6.6	40
2004	Kepulauan Alor, Indonesia	7.5	34
2004	Costa Rica	6.4	8
2004	Western coast of Sumatra, Indonesia	9.0	275,950
2005	South Africa	5.0	3
2005	Northern Sumatra, Indonesia	8.7	1,313
2005	Tarapaca, Chile	7.8	11
2005	Hubei-Jiangxi Border Region, China	7.6	87,353
2006	Mozambique	5.2	16
2006	Seram, Indonesia	7.0	4
2006	Western Iran	6.7	4
2006	Java, Indonesia	6.1	70
2006	South of Java, Indonesia	6.3	5,749
2006	Eastern Sichuan, China	7.7	730
2007	Molucca Sea	5.1	22
2007	Southern Sumatra, Indonesia	7.5	4
2007	Near the west coast of Honshu, Japan	6.4	67
2007	Solomon Islands	6.7	10
2007	Tajikistan	8.1	54
2007	Coast of central Peru	5.2	12
2007	Sumatra, Indonesia	8.0	519
2008	Lac Kivu region, Dem.Rep. of the Congo	8.4	25
		5.9	45

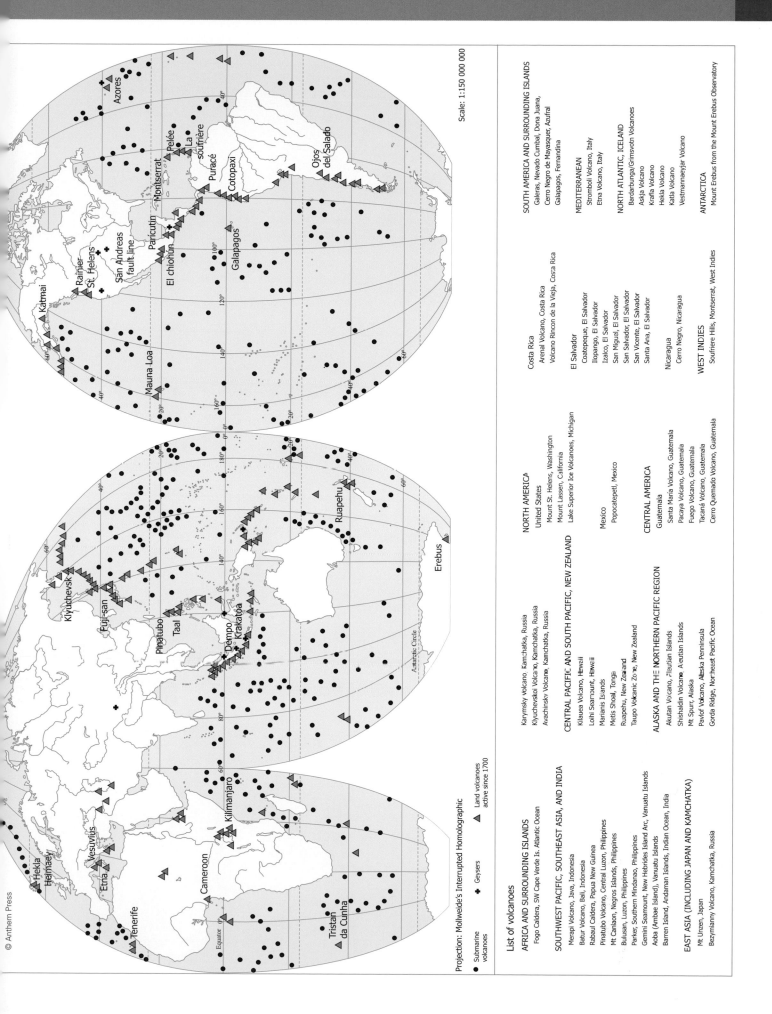

Projection: Mollweide's Interrupted Homolographic

Scale: 1:150 000 000

Key:
- • Submarine volcanoes
- + Geysers
- ▲ Land volcanoes active since 1700

List of volcanoes

AFRICA AND SURROUNDING ISLANDS
Fogo Caldera, SW Cape Verde Is. Atlantic Ocean

SOUTHWEST PACIFIC, SOUTHEAST ASIA, AND INDIA
Merapi Volcano, Java, Indonesia
Batur Volcano, Bali, Indonesia
Rabaul Caldera, Papua New Guinea
Pinatubo Volcano, Central Luzon, Philippines
Mt Canlaon, Negros Islands, Philippines
Bulusan, Luzon, Philippines
Parker, Southern Mindanao, Philippines
Gemini Seamount, New Hebrides Island Arc, Vanuatu Islands
Aoba (Ambae Island), Vanuatu Islands
Barren Island, Andaman Islands, Indian Ocean, India

EAST ASIA (INCLUDING JAPAN AND KAMCHATKA)
Mt Unzen, Japan
Bezymianny Volcano, Kamchatka, Russia
Karymsky Volcano, Kamchatka, Russia
Klyuchevskoi Volcano, Kamchatka, Russia
Avachinsky Volcano, Kamchatka, Russia

CENTRAL PACIFIC AND SOUTH PACIFIC, NEW ZEALAND
Kilauea Volcano, Hawaii
Loihi Seamount, Hawaii
Marianas Islands
Metis Shoal, Tonga
Ruapehu, New Zealand
Taupo Volcanic Zone, New Zealand

ALASKA AND THE NORTHERN PACIFIC REGION
Akutan Volcano, Aleutian Islands
Shishaldin Volcano, Aleutian Islands
Mt Spurr, Alaska
Pavlof Volcano, Alaska Peninsula
Gorda Ridge, Northeast Pacific Ocean

NORTH AMERICA
United States
Mount St. Helens, Washington
Mount Lassen, California
Lake Superior Ice Volcanoes, Michigan

Mexico
Popocatepetl, Mexico

CENTRAL AMERICA
Guatemala
Santa Maria Volcano, Guatemala
Pacaya Volcano, Guatemala
Fuego Volcano, Guatemala
Tacaná Volcano, Guatemala
Cerro Quemado Volcano, Guatemala

Costa Rica
Arenal Volcano, Costa Rica
Volcano Rincon de la Vieja, Costa Rica

El Salvador
Coatepeque, El Salvador
Ilopango, El Salvador
Izalco, El Salvador
San Miguel, El Salvador
San Salvador, El Salvador
San Vicente, El Salvador
Santa Ana, El Salvador

Nicaragua
Cerro Negro, Nicaragua

WEST INDIES
Soufriere Hills, Montserrat, West Indies

SOUTH AMERICA AND SURROUNDING ISLANDS
Galeras, Nevado Cumbal, Dona Juana,
Cerro Negro de Mayasquer, Azufral
Galapagos, Fernandina

MEDITERRANEAN
Stromboli Volcano, Italy
Etna Volcano, Italy

NORTH ATLANTIC, ICELAND
Bardarbunga/Grimsvotn Volcanoes
Askja Volcano
Krafla Volcano
Hekla Volcano
Katla Volcano
Vestmannaeyjar Volcano

ANTARCTICA
Mount Erebus from the Mount Erebus Observatory

Geological timescale
(millions of years)

Quaternary
Neogene
Palaeogene
Cretaceous
Jurassic
Triassic
Permian
Pennsylvanian
Mississippian
Devonian
Silurian
Ordovician
Cambrian
Late Proterozoic
Middle Proterozoic
Early Proterozoic
Late Archean
Middle Archean
Early Archean

Glacial ice
Age unknown

Cenozoic
Mesozoic
Paleozoic
Precambrian

Mesozoic & Cenozoic
Paleozoic & Mesozoic
Precambrian & Paleozoic

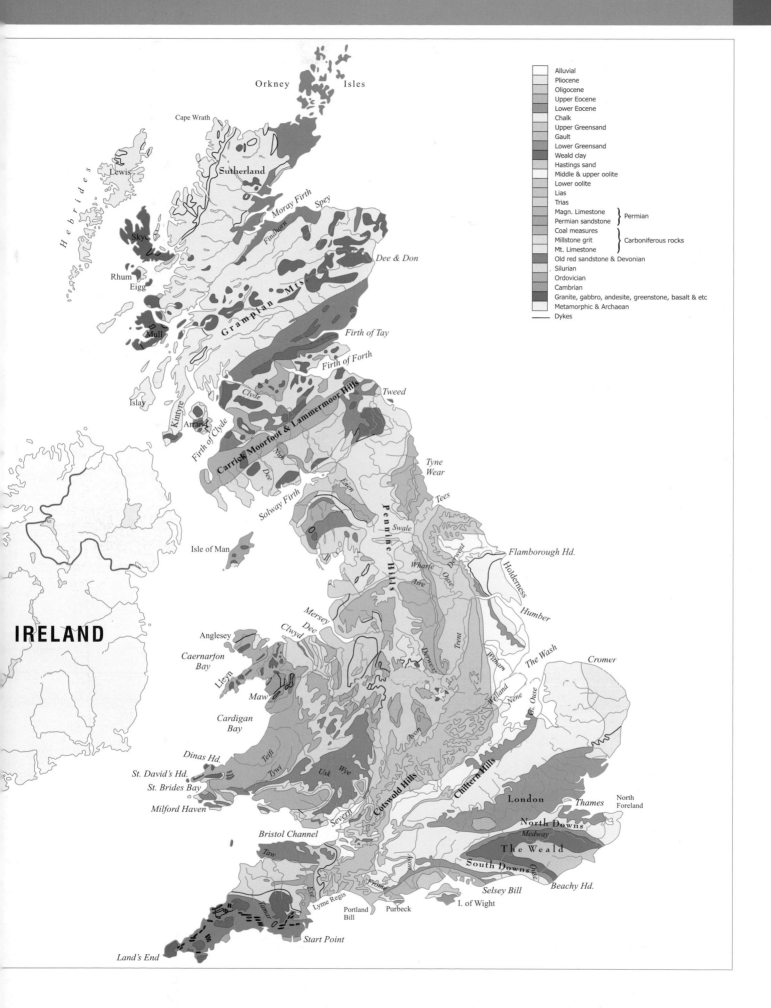

Legend:
- Alluvial
- Pliocene
- Oligocene
- Upper Eocene
- Lower Eocene
- Chalk
- Upper Greensand
- Gault
- Lower Greensand
- Weald clay
- Hastings sand
- Middle & upper oolite
- Lower oolite
- Lias
- Trias
- Magn. Limestone } Permian
- Permian sandstone }
- Coal measures } Carboniferous rocks
- Millstone grit }
- Mt. Limestone }
- Old red sandstone & Devonian
- Silurian
- Ordovician
- Cambrian
- Granite, gabbro, andesite, greenstone, basalt & etc
- Metamorphic & Archaean
- —— Dykes

Labels on map:

Orkney Isles
Cape Wrath
Sutherland
Hebrides
Lewis
Moray Firth
Spey
Findhorn
Skye
Dee & Don
Rhum
Eigg
Grampian Mts.
Mull
Firth of Tay
Islay
Firth of Forth
Kintyre
Arran
Tweed
Firth of Clyde
Clyde
Carrick Moorfoot & Lammermoor Hills
Nith
Dee
Tyne
Wear
Solway Firth
Eden
Tees
Pennine Hills
Swale
Flamborough Hd.
Isle of Man
Wharfe
Derwent
Holderness
Aire
Ouse
Humber
Mersey
Dee
Trent
Clwyd
Anglesey
Derwent
The Wash
Cromer
Caernarfon Bay
Witham
Lleyn
Welland
Nene
Maw
G. Ouse
Cardigan Bay
Avon
Dinas Hd.
Teifi
Wye
Chiltern Hills
St. David's Hd.
Tywi
Usk
London
Thames
North Foreland
St. Brides Bay
Cotswold Hills
Milford Haven
Severn
North Downs
Bristol Channel
Medway
The Weald
Taw
South Downs
Ouse
Avon
Beachy Hd.
Exe
Frome
Selsey Bill
Lyme Regis
Portland Bill
Purbeck
I. of Wight
Tamar
Start Point
Land's End

IRELAND

▲ Bcharre, Lebanon

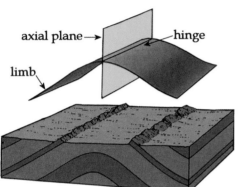

anticline a geologic fold where the rock strata incline downward from the central axis

▲ Barstow, California, US

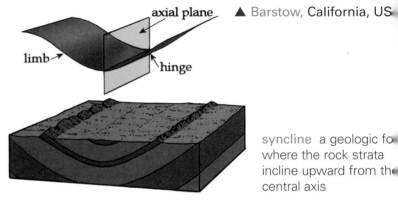

syncline a geologic fo[ld] where the rock strata incline upward from th[e] central axis

Zagros Mountains, **western Iran**, were formed as the Eurasian and Arabian tectonic plates collided. The collision caused extensive folding of the area's sedimentary rocks. The Zagros are a huge anticline of limestone and sandstone. The tile-like patterns seen here are gigantic V-shaped ridges that extend for hundreds of miles.

Anti-Atlas Mountains, **south-west Morocco**, were formed when the Eurasian and African plates collided, starting about 80 million years ago. The collision caused a massive upheaval of sandstone and limestone rock, which buckled and uplifted to form the fold structures seen here.

Aletsch Glacier, **southern Switzerland**, is the largest glacier in the Alps. Dark medial moraine, close to the middle of the glacier, runs in two bands along the whole length of the glacier to its toe. This medial moraine is collected from the ice of three large ice fields.

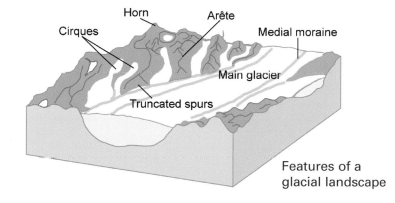

Horn
Arête
Cirques
Medial moraine
Main glacier
Truncated spurs

Features of a glacial landscape

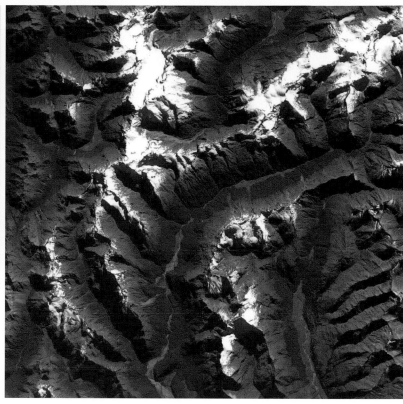

Mount Aspiring National Park, **South Island, New Zealand**, is a spectacular glacial landscape. This satellite image shows a U-shaped valley: a typical feature of alpine landscape. Most U-shaped valleys started as V-shaped before glaciers carved them out wider and deeper.

Malispina Glacier, **southern Alaska**, is a classic example of a piedmont glacier. It is fed by glaciers flowing from ice fields in the Saint Elias Mountains. Piedmont glaciers are glacial fans formed where confined valley glaciers emerge from mountains. Piedmont glaciers dominate and flatten the landscape through scouring. Alpine glaciers develop in mountainous regions and steepen the landscape.

Seward Glacier

Agassiz Glacier

Malaspina Glacier

interlobate moraine

folded moraine resulting from flow compression

recessional moraines

end moraine

San Andreas Fault Zone —

— Hayward Fault

San Francisco

11.5

Slip amount (ft) — 12.8

9.8

San Andreas Fault, California. The Pacific plate and the North America plate meet at the San Andreas Fault. Intense pressure builds up along the fault as the two plates grind against each other. On 18 April 1906, the pressure resulted in a massive earthquake across coastal California. The ground on either side of the fault line slipped more than 20 feet away from each other in some places. The quake set off a catastrophic fire that devastated San Francisco, killing about 700 people and leaving half the population homeless.

San Andreas Fault, California, is one of the longest faults in North America, stretching 1,200 kilometres (800 miles). The fault is the linear feature to the right of the Temblor mountains. To the right of the fault is the Carrizo Plain. Dry conditions on the plain have helped preserve the surface trace of the fault.

Great Kanto earthquake, Honshu, Japan. On 1 September 1923, a massive earthquake occurred off the east coast of Japan. The earthquake killed about 105,000 people and destroyed or damaged 600,000 buildings. Tokyo, at the time the world's third largest city, was devastated by the earthquake.

San Andreas Fault

DEADLIEST EARTHQUAKES OF THE LAST 100 YEARS			
1. Tangshan, Chn (28 July 1976)	255,000 dead	6. Kanto, Jpn (1 September 1923)	105,000
2. Indian Ocean (26 December 2004)	225,000	7. South Asia (8 October 2005)	75,000
3. Xining, Chn (22 May 1927)	200,000	8. Gansu, Chn (25 December 1932)	70,000
4. Gansu, Chn (16 December 1920)	180,000	9. Ancash, Peru (31 May 1944)	66,000
5. Ashgabat, Tur (6 October 1948)	110,000	10. Messina, Ita (28 December 1908)	60,000

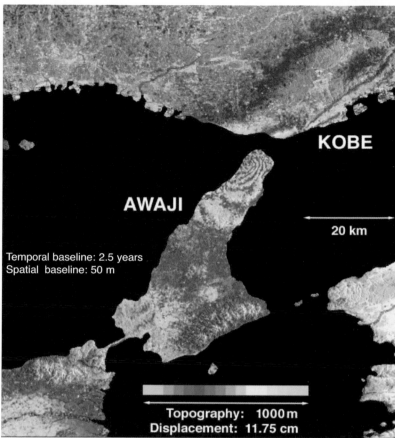

Bam, south-east Iran. On 27 December 2003, a huge earthquake struck Bam, killing more than 25,000 people and destroying 70 per cent of buildings. The 2,000-year-old mud citdael (shown at centre) crumbled. Many people were buried under their mud-brick homes.

Izmit, north-west Turkey. On 18 August 1999, an earthquake struck the city of Izmit, killing 45,000 people and leaving half-a-million homeless. This interferogram shows the shifts in the Earth's surface. The North Anatolian Fault moved more than 2.5 metres (8 feet). Thin red lines show the locations of faults. The thick black lines mark the fault rupture indicated by the satellite data.

Kobe earthquake, Honshu, Japan. On 17 January, an earthquake killed 5,100 people, injured 27,000 and caused US $200 billion in damages. The interferogram shows the the deformation of the Earth's surface near the coast of Honshu.

Japan earthquakes (1961–94) showing magnitude and color coded according to earthquake depth. The 1995 Kobe earthquake occurred on a strike-slip fault off the Median Tectonic Line. The map also shows the 1944 and 1946 earthquakes.

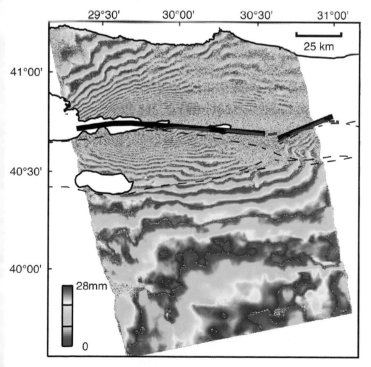

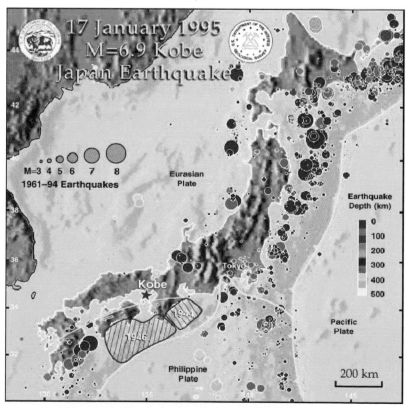

A **volcano** is a landform that develops over a fissure or vent in the Earth's crust through which magma (molten rock), ash and gases are or have been expelled.

Central vent volcanoes, where eruption occurs from a single pipe, typically form cones or domes. Fissure volcanoes, where magma is expelled from a linear fracture in the Earth's crust, usually build plains or plateaux.

More than 80 per cent of Earth's surface comes from volcanoes. There are over 500 'active' volcanoes in the world. More than half of these volcanoes are in the Pacific 'Ring of Fire' (see page 15). Volcanoes are mostly found at the edges of Earth's tectonic plates, but some occur above hotspots within plate interiors. Many of the most violently explosive volcanoes (such as Mount St Helens, Popocatapétl, and Soufrière Hills) occur where plates collide (destructive margins).

Mauna Loa, **Hawaii**, is the world's largest active volcano. It has an estimated volume of 75,000 km³ (18,000 miles³). Its peak rises more than 8 kilometres (5 miles) above the ocean floor. Mauna Loa has erupted more than 35 times since Captain James Cook visited in 1778, the first European sighting. The most recent eruption was in 1984. This picture shows how remote imaging can map lava flows and other volcanic structures. Mokuaweoweo Caldera, the large summit crater, is visible near the centre of the image. Leading away from the caldera (towards top right and lower centre) are the two main rift zones, shown in orange. Rift zones are areas of weakness within the upper part of a volcano that are ripped open as magma approaches the surface at the start of an eruption.

Taal, **Luzon, northern Philippines**, is sometimes known as the 'killer volcano' of the Philippines. In 1911, a violent eruption killed more than 1,300 people. Lake Taal (black area at centre) nearly fills the 30-kilometre-diameter (18-mile) caldera. Volcano Island, the island in Lake Taal, itself contains a crater lake. The bright yellow patch on the southwest side of the island marks the site of an explosion crater that formed during the last major eruption of Taal in 1965. The 1965 eruption killed several hundred people.

Despite the fact that Taal has witnessed 32 massive eruptions since the first documented eruption in 1752, the area is being developed for tourism.

DEADLIEST VOLCANOES OF THE LAST 100 YEARS			
1. Mount Pelée, Mtq (8 May 1902)	30,000 dead	6. Santiaguito, Gtm (1929)	5,000
2. Nevado del Ruiz, Col (13 November 1985)	22,800	7. Mount Lamington, Png (15 January 1951)	3,000
3. Santa Maria, Gtm (24 October 1902)	6,000	8. Nyos, Cmr (21 August 1986)	1,746
4. Mount Kelud, Idn (1909)	5,500	9. Mount Agung, Idn (3 January 1963)	1,584
5. Mount Kelud, Idn (May 1919)	5,000	10. Mount Soufrière (7 May 1902)	1,565

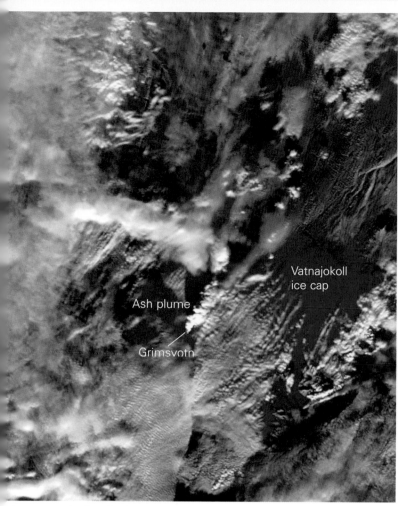

rimsvotn, **Iceland**, sits below the Vatnajokull ice cap, Europe's rgest glacier. Grimsvotn is Iceland's most active volcano. This satellite nage captures an eruption in November 2004. Ice appears as bright d in this false-colour image. As the plume is blown north, steam om the melting ice dissipates, and dark ash is more visible.

Ruapehu, **North Island, New Zealand**, is one of New Zealand's most active volcanoes, with ten eruptions since 1861. In 1953, a lahar (volcanic mudflow) killed more than 150 people. The lahars originate from a lake seen here nestled at the top of the volcano's caldera. Lahars have left deep carvings in the flank of Ruapehu.

ount St Helens, **Washington, USA**, erupted catastrophically on 3 May 1980, killing 57 people. This image from 4 October 2004 aptures the volcano rumbling back to life as a new volcanic dome ses out of the crater formed by the 1980 eruption. In just two eeks, the new dome grew 110 metres (360 feet).

Mount Pelée, **Martinique**, is the location of the deadliest volcano of the 20th century. This photograph captures the obliteration of the town of St Pierre on 8 May 1902. The eruption produced low-lying clouds of incandescent ash and gas known as *nuées ardentes* or pyroclastic flows that engulfed St Pierre, killing 30,000 people.

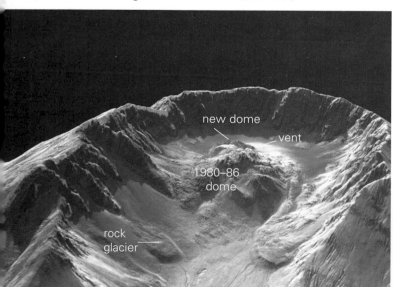

A tsunami is a long and large wave or series of waves caused by an underwater earthquake, submarine volcanic eruption or landslide on the ocean bed.

Tsunami are often incorrectly called 'tidal waves', but their formation is unconnected to the tides. It is the wavelength of a tsunami (distance from crest to crest) that gives tsunami such monstrous speed and energy. When a tsunami strikes a coastline, people close to the shore typically see the sea-level rise above high tide, then suddenly retreat far below low tide. Next, a wave rears up and strikes with great ferocity and massive volume.

On 26 December 2004, a massive earthquake with a magnitude of between 9.1 and 9.3 occurred off the west coast of Sumatra, Indonesia. The earthquake triggered a tsunami across coastal areas of the Indian Ocean, killing 225,000 people in 11 countries.

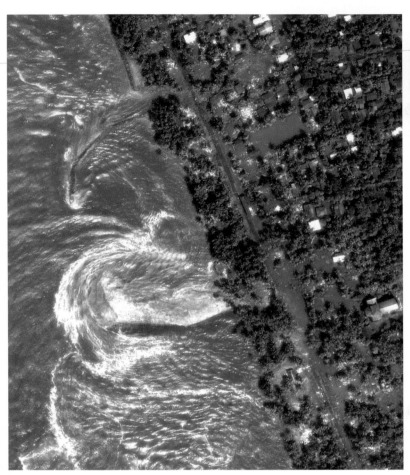

Kalutara, south-west Sri Lanka, is struck by the huge tsunami of 26 December 2004. After Indonesia, Sri Lanka suffered the most fatalities, as more than 35,000 people lost their lives.

Sumatra, Indonesia, suffered great loss of life and widespread destruction from the tsunami of 26 December 2004. An estimated 168,000 people died as a result of the tsunami in Indonesia.

Asian Tsunami (26 December 2004): arrival time of first wave (hrs)

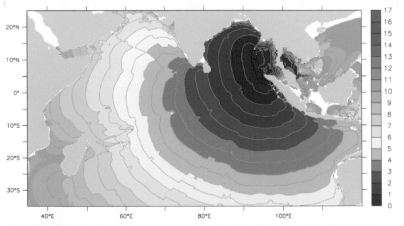

Asian Tsunami (26 December 2004): maximum wave height (cm)

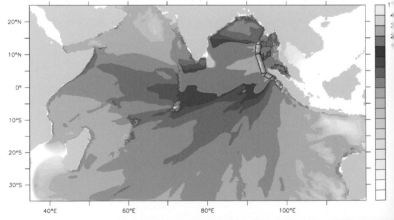

DEADLIEST TSUNAMI OF THE LAST 100 YEARS

1. INDIAN OCEAN (26 DECEMBER 2004)	225,000 DEAD	
2. MORO GULF, PHL (16 AUGUST 1976)	8,000	
3. SANRIKU, JPN (24 OCTOBER 1902)	3,000	
4. PAPUA NEW GUINEA (17 JULY 1998)	2,180	
5. TOKAIDO, JPN (1 SEPTEMBER 1923)	2,144	
6. NANKAIDO, JPN (20 DECEMBER 1946)	1,997	
7. SOUTHERN CHILE (22 MAY 1960)	1,260	
8. FLORES, IDN (12 DECEMBER 1992)	1,000	
9. RYUKYU ISLANDS, JPN (7 DECEMBER 1944)	998	
10. SULAWESI, IDN (23 FEBRUARY 1923)	600	

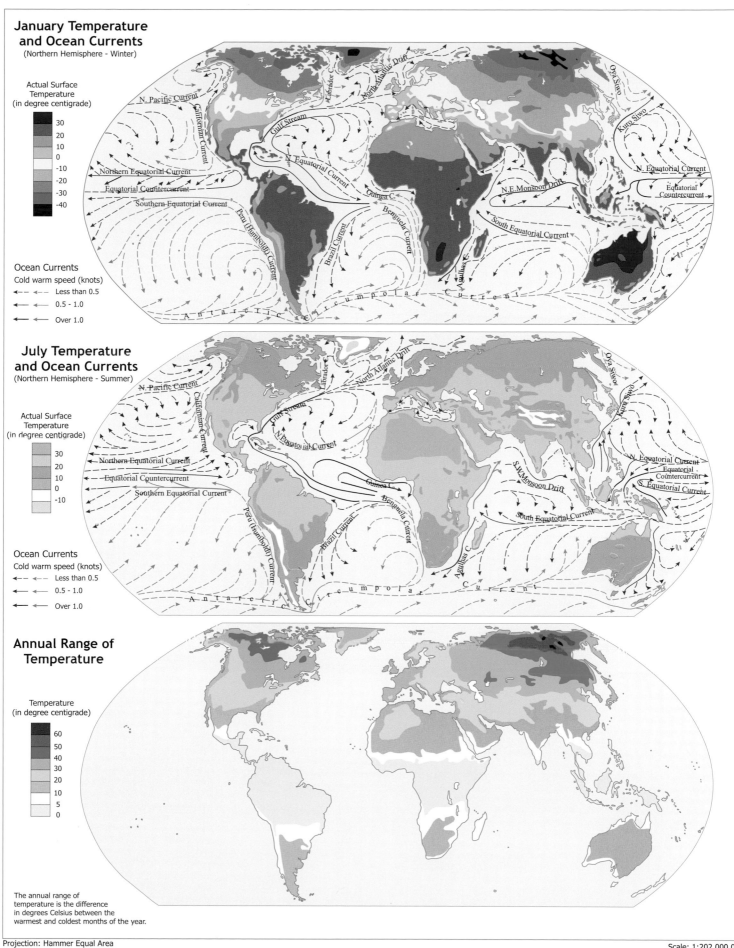

January Temperature and Ocean Currents

(Northern Hemisphere - Winter)

Actual Surface
Temperature
(in degree centigrade)

- 30
- 20
- 10
- 0
- -10
- -20
- -30
- -40

Ocean Currents
Cold warm speed (knots)
- Less than 0.5
- 0.5 - 1.0
- Over 1.0

July Temperature and Ocean Currents

(Northern Hemisphere - Summer)

Actual Surface
Temperature
(in degree centigrade)

- 30
- 20
- 10
- 0
- -10

Ocean Currents
Cold warm speed (knots)
- Less than 0.5
- 0.5 - 1.0
- Over 1.0

Annual Range of Temperature

Temperature
(in degree centigrade)

- 60
- 50
- 40
- 30
- 20
- 10
- 5
- 0

The annual range of
temperature is the difference
in degrees Celsius between the
warmest and coldest months of the year.

Projection: Hammer Equal Area

Scale: 1:202 000 000

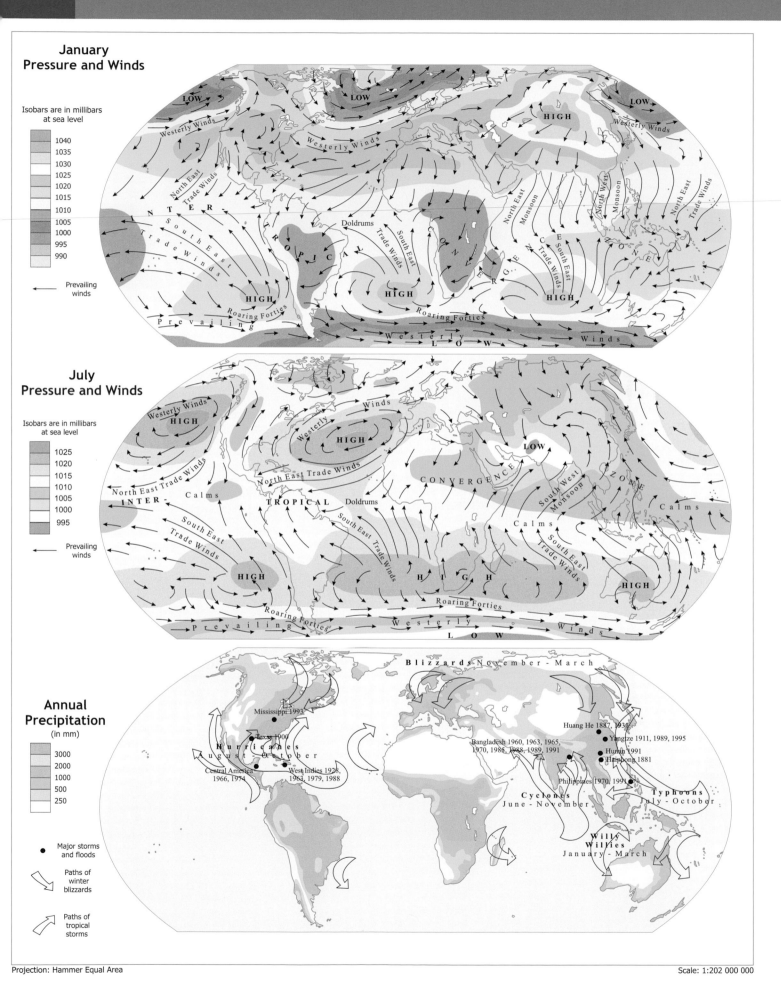

January
Pressure and Winds

Isobars are in millibars
at sea level

1040
1035
1030
1025
1020
1015
1010
1005
1000
995
990

→ Prevailing
winds

LOW
LOW
HIGH
LOW
Westerly Winds
Westerly Winds
Westerly Winds
North East Trade Winds
North West Monsoon
North East Monsoon
North East Trade Winds
I N T E R
S outh East Trade Winds
T R O P I C A L
Doldrums
South East Trade Winds
C O N V E R G E N C E
South East Trade Winds
Z O N E
HIGH
HIGH
HIGH
Roaring Forties
Roaring Forties
Prevailing
Westerly
Winds
L O W

July
Pressure and Winds

Isobars are in millibars
at sea level

1025
1020
1015
1010
1005
1000
995

→ Prevailing
winds

Westerly Winds
HIGH
Winds
Westerly
HIGH
LOW
North East Trade Winds
North East Trade Winds
Calms
I N T E R -
C O N V E R G E N C E
Z O N E
South East Trade Winds
TROPICAL
Doldrums
South East Trade Winds
South West Monsoon
Calms
Calms
Calms
South East Trade Winds
HIGH
H I G H
HIGH
Roaring Forties
Roaring Forties
Prevailing
Westerly
Winds
L O W

Annual
Precipitation
(in mm)

3000
2000
1000
500
250

● Major storms
and floods

⇨ Paths of
winter
blizzards

⇨ Paths of
tropical
storms

B l i z z a r d s November - March
Mississippi 1993
Huang He 1887, 1931
Yangtze 1911, 1989, 1995
Texas 1900
Bangladesh 1960, 1963, 1965, 1970, 1985, 1988, 1989, 1991
Hunan 1991
Haiphong 1881
H u r r i c a n e s
A u g u s t - O c t o b e r
Central America 1966, 1974
West Indies 1928, 1963, 1979, 1988
Philippines 1970, 1991
T y p h o o n s
July - October
C y c l o n e s
June - November
W i l l y
W i l l i e s
January - March

Projection: Hammer Equal Area

Scale: 1:202 000 000

urricane Andrew was the costliest natural disaster to strike the nited States prior to Hurricane Katrina. On 23 August 1992, Andrew ade landfall at Dade County, south-east Florida, narrowly missing owntown Miami. With wind speeds of 220 kilometres per hour 40 miles per hour), Andrew left about 250,000 people homeless in orida. It later moved across the Gulf of Mexico to Louisiana.

Hurricane Katrina made landfall over southeast Louisiana and southern Mississippi early on 29 August 2005. With wind speeds of 217 kilometres per hour (135 miles per hour), Katrina pounded the U.S. Gulf Coast. The eye of the storm was due east of New Orleans, Louisiana. Katrina claimed more than 1,800 lives and caused more than US $81 billion of damage.

urricane Katrina caused storm surges that flooded 80 per cent the city of New Orleans. New Orleans is about 2 metres (6.6 et) below sea level and the storm surges breached a network of vees designed to protect the city. The floods also inundated the astal marshes to the southeast of the city.

Louisiana Superdome, New Orleans, became an emergency shelter for more than 25,000 people unable to evacuate before the arrival of Hurricane Katrina. The stadium (bottom centre) itself was damaged and surrounded by flood water as captured by this detailed satellite image from 31 August 2005.

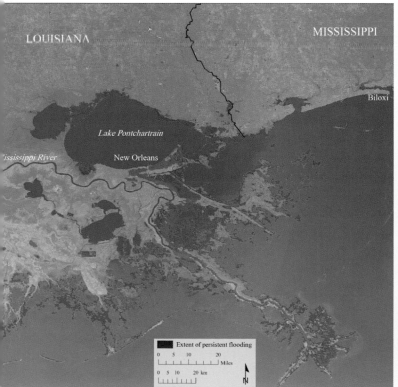

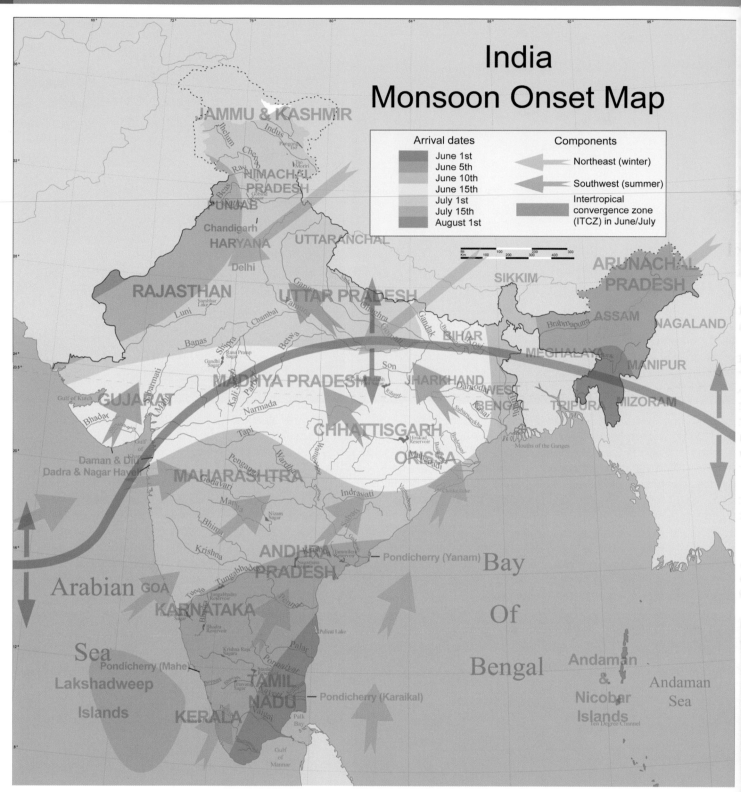

India
Monsoon Onset Map

Arrival dates
June 1st
June 5th
June 10th
June 15th
July 1st
July 15th
August 1st

Components
Northeast (winter)
Southwest (summer)
Intertropical convergence zone (ITCZ) in June/July

Summer monsoon, India, occurs from June through September. Northern and central India heat up during the summer, which causes a low-pressure area over the northern and central Indian subcontinent. To fill this void, moisture-laden winds from the Indian Ocean rush in. These winds are drawn towards the Himalayas, which acts like a high wall and stops the winds passing into Central Asia, forcing them to rise. With the gain in altitude of the clouds, the temperature drops and precipitation occurs. Some areas of the subcontinent receive up to 10 metres (33 ft) of rain. The topology of southern India causes the monsoon winds to divide into the Arabian Sea branch and the Bay of Bengal branch.

WEATHER RECORDS

Highest temperature
Al 'Aziziyah, Libya, 57.7°C (135.9°F), 13 September 1923

Lowest temperature (outside poles)
Verkhoyansk, Russia, -67.8°C (-93.6°F), 15 January 1892

Highest pressure
Tosontsengel, Mongolia, 1,085.6 mb, 19 December 2001

Lowest pressure
Manchester, South Dakota, USA, 850 mb, 24 June 2003 in F-4 tornado

Wettest place
Lloro, Colombia, averages 13 m (40 ft) of rainfall per year

Driest place
Arica, Chile, averages 0.76 mm (0.03 in) of rainfall per year

Jet streams

Trade winds

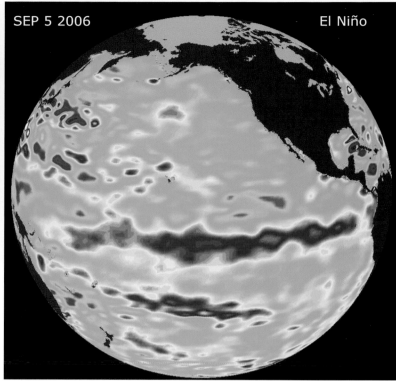

SEP 5 2006   El Niño

Niño, **Pacific Ocean**. El Niño was named by Peruvian fisherman ter baby Jesus because warm waters appeared in the eastern cific Ocean off the coast of Peru usually just before Christmas. Niño occurs every 4 to 12 years and can greatly affect global eather patterns. The phenomenon is thought to be triggered nen the steady westward blowing trade winds weaken and even verse direction. This change in the winds allows a large mass of arm water that is normally located near Australia to move east ong the equator until it reaches the coast of South America. In ly 1997, the area of high sea level exceeded one-and-one-half nes the area of the continental U.S. Warmer water evaporates at higher rate and the resulting warm moist air rises and forms tall oud towers. In the tropics, the warm water and the resulting tall oud towers typically produce large amounts of rain and alters the oical jet stream patterns around the world.

an El Niño year, the lack of cold nutrient-rich water rising to the irface off the coast of Peru leads to a decline in the production of ytoplankton and thus a reduction in fish stocks. In the El Niño of 082–83, for instance, the catch of anchovies fell by 600 per cent.

La Niña is essentially the opposite of El Niño, where the trade winds are stronger than normal and the cold water that normally exists along the coast of South America extends to the central equatorial Pacific. A La Niña event also changes global weather patterns, and is associated with less moisture in the air resulting in less rain along the coasts of North and South America.

On our globes, the white and red areas indicate unusual patterns of heat storage; in the white areas, the sea surface is between 14 and 32 centimetres (6 to 13 inches) above normal; in the red areas, it's about 10 centimetres (4 inches) above normal. The green areas indicate normal conditions, while purple signifies at least 18 centimetres (7 inches) below normal sea level.

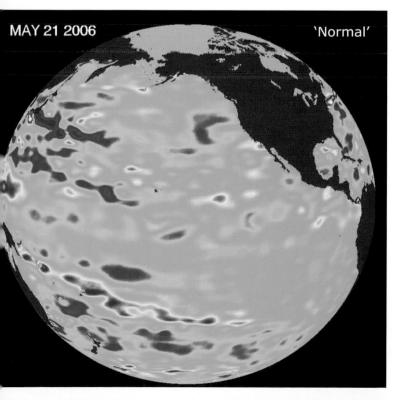

MAY 21 2006   'Normal'

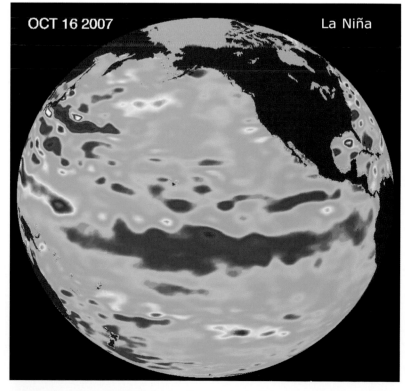

OCT 16 2007   La Niña

Addis Ababa, Ethiopia 2,410m	
Temperature Daily max °C	Average monthly maximum temperature in degrees Celsius
Daily min °C	Average monthly minimum temperature in degrees Celsius
Average monthly °C	Average monthly temperature in degrees Celsius
Rainfall Monthly total mm	Average monthly precipitation in millimetres
Sunshine Hours per day	Average daily duration of bright sunshine per month in hours

Altitude of meterological station in metres

Figures in blue show the month with the:
- highest average maximum temperature
- lowest average minimum temperature
- highest monthly temperature
- highest monthly precipitation
- most hours of sunshine.

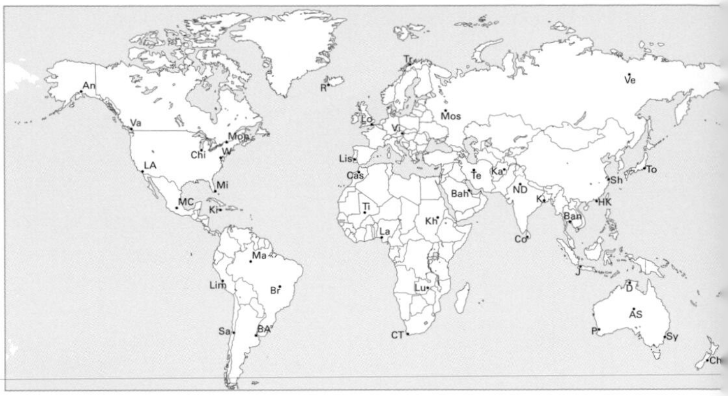

Addis Ababa, Ethiopia 2,410m	Jan	Feb	Mar	Apr	May	June	July	Aug	Sept	Oct	Nov	Dec	Year
Temperature Daily max °C	23	24	25	24	25	23	20	20	21	22	23	22	23
Daily min °C	6	7	9	10	9	10	11	11	10	7	5	5	8
Average monthly °C	14	15	17	17	17	16	16	15	15	15	14	14	15
Rainfall Monthly total mm	13	35	67	91	81	117	247	255	167	29	8	5	1,115
Sunshine Hours per day	8.7	8.2	7.6	8.1	6.5	4.8	2.8	3.2	5.2	7.6	6.7	7	6.4

Alice Springs, Australia 580m	Jan	Feb	Mar	Apr	May	June	July	Aug	Sept	Oct	Nov	Dec	Year
Temperature Daily max °C	35	35	32	27	23	19	19	23	27	31	33	35	28
Daily min °C	21	20	17	12	8	5	4	6	10	15	18	20	13
Average monthly °C	28	27	25	20	15	12	12	14	18	23	25	27	21
Rainfall Monthly total mm	44	33	27	10	15	13	7	8	7	18	29	38	249
Sunshine Hours per day	10.3	10.4	9.3	9.2	8	8	8.9	9.8	10	9.7	10.1	10	9.5

Anchorage, USA 183m	Jan	Feb	Mar	Apr	May	June	July	Aug	Sept	Oct	Nov	Dec	Year
Temperature Daily max °C	-7	-3	0	7	13	18	19	17	13	6	-2	-6	-6
Daily min °C	-15	-12	-9	-2	4	8	10	9	5	-2	-9	-14	-2
Average monthly °C	-11	-7	-4	3	9	13	15	13	9	2	-5	-10	-4
Rainfall Monthly total mm	20	18	13	11	13	25	47	64	64	47	28	24	374
Sunshine Hours per day	2.4	4.1	6.6	8.3	8.3	9.2	8.5	6	4.4	3.1	2.6	1.6	5.4

Athens, Greece 107m	Jan	Feb	Mar	Apr	May	June	July	Aug	Sept	Oct	Nov	Dec	Year
Temperature Daily max °C	13	14	16	20	25	30	33	33	29	24	19	15	23
Daily min °C	6	7	8	11	16	20	23	23	19	15	12	8	14
Average monthly °C	10	10	12	16	20	25	28	28	24	20	15	11	18
Rainfall Monthly total mm	62	37	37	23	23	14	6	7	15	51	56	71	402
Sunshine Hours per day	3.9	5.2	5.8	7.7	8.9	10.7	11.9	11.5	9.4	6.8	4.8	3.8	7.3

Bahrain City, Bahrain 2m	Jan	Feb	Mar	Apr	May	June	July	Aug	Sept	Oct	Nov	Dec	Year
Temperature Daily max °C	20	21	25	29	33	36	37	38	36	32	27	22	30
Daily min °C	14	15	18	22	25	29	31	32	29	25	22	16	23
Average monthly °C	17	18	21	25	29	32	34	35	32	29	25	19	26
Rainfall Monthly total mm	18	12	10	9	2	0	0	0	0	0.4	3	16	70
Sunshine Hours per day	5.9	6.9	7.9	8.8	10.6	13.2	12.1	12	12	10.3	7.7	6.4	9.5

Bangkok, Thailand 10m	Jan	Feb	Mar	Apr	May	June	July	Aug	Sept	Oct	Nov	Dec	Year
Temperature Daily max °C	32	33	34	35	34	33	32	32	32	31	31	31	33
Daily min °C	20	23	24	26	25	25	25	24	24	24	23	20	24
Average monthly °C	26	28	29	30	30	29	28	28	28	28	27	26	28
Rainfall Monthly total mm	9	30	36	82	165	153	168	183	310	239	55	8	1,438
Sunshine Hours per day	8.2	8	8	10	7.5	6.1	4.7	5.2	5.2	6.1	7.3	7.8	7

Brasília, Brazil 910m	Jan	Feb	Mar	Apr	May	June	July	Aug	Sept	Oct	Nov	Dec	Year
Temperature Daily max °C	32	33	34	35	34	33	32	32	32	31	31	31	33
Daily min °C	18	18	18	17	15	13	13	14	16	18	18	18	16
Average monthly °C	23	23	23	22	21	20	20	21	23	24	23	22	22
Rainfall Monthly total mm	252	204	227	93	17	3	6	3	30	127	255	343	1,560
Sunshine Hours per day	5.8	5.7	6	7.4	8.7	9.3	9.6	9.8	7.9	6.5	4.8	4.4	7.2

Buenos Aires, Argentina 25m	Jan	Feb	Mar	Apr	May	June	July	Aug	Sept	Oct	Nov	Dec	Year
Temperature Daily max °C	30	29	26	22	18	14	14	16	18	21	25	28	22
Daily min °C	17	17	16	12	9	5	6	6	8	10	14	16	11
Average monthly °C	23	23	21	17	13	10	10	11	13	15	19	22	16
Rainfall Monthly total mm	79	71	109	89	76	61	56	61	79	86	84	99	950
Sunshine Hours per day	9.2	8.5	7.5	6.8	4.9	3.5	3.8	5.2	6	6.8	8.1	8.5	6.6

Cairo, Egypt 75m	Jan	Feb	Mar	Apr	May	June	July	Aug	Sept	Oct	Nov	Dec	Year
Temperature Daily max °C	19	21	24	28	32	35	35	35	33	30	26	21	28
Daily min °C	9	9	12	14	18	20	22	22	20	18	14	10	16
Average monthly °C	4	4	3	1	2	1	0	0	1	1	3	7	27
Rainfall Monthly total mm	12	19	17	42	67	98	68	76	36	45	12	13	505
Sunshine Hours per day	6.9	8.4	8.7	9.7	10.5	11.9	11.7	11.3	10.4	9.4	8.3	6.4	9.5

Cape Town, South Africa 44m	Jan	Feb	Mar	Apr	May	June	July	Aug	Sept	Oct	Nov	Dec	Year
Temperature Daily max °C	26	26	25	23	20	18	17	18	19	21	24	25	22
Daily min °C	15	15	14	11	9	7	7	7	8	10	13	15	11
Average monthly °C	21	20	20	17	14	13	12	12	14	16	18	20	16
Rainfall Monthly total mm	12	19	17	42	67	98	68	76	36	45	12	13	505
Sunshine Hours per day	11.4	10.2	9.4	7.7	6.1	5.7	6.4	6.6	7.6	8.6	10.2	10.9	8.4

Casablanca, Morocco 59m	Jan	Feb	Mar	Apr	May	June	July	Aug	Sept	Oct	Nov	Dec	Year
Temperature Daily max °C	17	18	20	21	22	24	26	26	26	24	21	18	22
Daily min °C	8	9	11	12	15	18	19	20	18	15	12	10	14
Average monthly °C	13	13	15	16	18	21	23	23	22	20	17	14	18
Rainfall Monthly total mm	78	61	54	37	20	3	0	1	6	28	58	94	440
Sunshine Hours per day	5.2	6.3	7.3	9	9.4	9.7	10.2	9.7	9.1	7.4	5.9	5.3	7.9

Chicago, USA 186m	Jan	Feb	Mar	Apr	May	June	July	Aug	Sept	Oct	Nov	Dec	Year
Temperature Daily max °C	1	2	6	14	21	26	29	28	24	17	8	2	
Daily min °C	-7	-6	-2	5	11	16	20	19	14	8	0	-5	
Average monthly °C	-3	-2	2	9	16	21	24	23	19	13	4	-2	
Rainfall Monthly total mm	47	41	70	77	96	103	86	80	69	71	56	48	8
Sunshine Hours per day	4	5	6.6	6.9	8.9	10.2	10	9.2	8.2	6.9	4.5	3.7	

Christchurch, New Zealand 5m	Jan	Feb	Mar	Apr	May	June	July	Aug	Sept	Oct	Nov	Dec	Year
Temperature Daily max °C	21	21	19	17	13	11	10	11	14	17	19	21	
Daily min °C	12	12	10	7	4	2	1	3	5	7	8	11	
Average monthly °C	16	16	15	12	9	6	6	7	9	12	13	16	
Rainfall Monthly total mm	56	46	43	46	76	69	61	58	51	51	51	61	6
Sunshine Hours per day	7	6.5	5.6	4.7	4.3	3.9	4.1	4.7	5.6	6.1	6.9	6.3	5

Colombo, Sri Lanka 10m	Jan	Feb	Mar	Apr	May	June	July	Aug	Sept	Oct	Nov	Dec	Year
Temperature Daily max °C	30	31	31	31	30	30	29	29	30	29	29	30	
Daily min °C	22	22	23	24	25	25	25	25	25	24	23	22	
Average monthly °C	26	26	27	28	28	27	27	27	27	27	26	26	
Rainfall Monthly total mm	101	66	118	230	394	220	140	102	174	348	333	142	2,3
Sunshine Hours per day	7.9	9	8.1	7.2	6.4	5.4	6.1	6.3	6.2	6.5	6.4	7.8	6

Darwin, Australia 30m	Jan	Feb	Mar	Apr	May	June	July	Aug	Sept	Oct	Nov	Dec	Year
Temperature Daily max °C	32	32	33	33	33	31	31	32	33	34	34	33	
Daily min °C	25	25	25	24	23	21	19	21	23	25	26	26	
Average monthly °C	29	29	29	29	28	26	25	26	28	29	30	29	
Rainfall Monthly total mm	405	309	279	77	8	2	0	1	15	48	108	214	1,4
Sunshine Hours per day	5.8	5.8	6.6	9.8	9.3	10	9.9	10.4	10.1	9.4	9.6	6.8	8

Harbin, China 175m	Jan	Feb	Mar	Apr	May	June	July	Aug	Sept	Oct	Nov	Dec	Year
Temperature Daily max °C	-14	-9	0	12	21	26	29	27	20	12	-1	-11	
Daily min °C	-26	-23	-12	-1	7	14	18	16	8	0	-12	-22	
Average monthly °C	-20	-16	-6	6	14	20	23	22	14	6	-7	-17	
Rainfall Monthly total mm	4	6	17	23	44	92	167	119	52	36	12	5	5
Sunshine Hours per day	6.4	7.8	8	7.8	8.3	8.6	8.6	8.2	7.2	6.9	6.1	5.7	7

Hong Kong, China 35m	Jan	Feb	Mar	Apr	May	June	July	Aug	Sept	Oct	Nov	Dec	Year
Temperature Daily max °C	18	18	20	24	28	30	31	31	30	27	24	20	
Daily min °C	13	13	16	19	23	26	26	26	25	23	19	15	
Average monthly °C	16	15	18	22	25	28	28	28	27	25	21	17	
Rainfall Monthly total mm	30	60	70	133	332	479	286	415	364	33	46	17	2,2
Sunshine Hours per day	4.7	3.5	3.1	3.8	5	5.4	6.8	6.5	6.6	7	6.2	5.5	5

Honolulu, Hawaii 5m	Jan	Feb	Mar	Apr	May	June	July	Aug	Sept	Oct	Nov	Dec	Year
Temperature Daily max °C	26	26	26	27	28	29	29	29	30	29	28	26	
Daily min °C	19	19	19	20	21	22	23	23	23	22	21	20	
Average monthly °C	23	22	23	23	24	26	26	26	26	26	24	23	
Rainfall Monthly total mm	96	84	73	33	25	8	11	23	25	47	55	76	55
Sunshine Hours per day	7.3	7.7	8.3	8.6	8.8	9.1	9.4	9.3	9.2	8.3	7.5	6.2	8

Jakarta, Indonesia 10m	Jan	Feb	Mar	Apr	May	June	July	Aug	Sept	Oct	Nov	Dec	Year
Temperature Daily max °C	29	29	30	31	31	31	31	31	31	31	30	29	
Daily min °C	23	23	23	24	24	23	23	23	23	23	23	23	
Average monthly °C	26	26	27	27	27	27	27	27	27	27	27	26	
Rainfall Monthly total mm	7.3	7.7	8.3	8.6	8.8	9.1	9.4	9.3	9.2	8.3	7.5	6.2	8
Sunshine Hours per day													

Kabul, Afghanistan 1,791m	Jan	Feb	Mar	Apr	May	June	July	Aug	Sept	Oct	Nov	Dec	Year
Temperature Daily max °C	2	4	12	19	26	31	33	33	30	22	17	8	2
Daily min °C	-8	-6	1	6	11	13	16	15	11	6	1	-3	
Average monthly °C	-3	-1	6	13	18	22	25	24	20	14	9	3	1
Rainfall Monthly total mm	28	61	72	117	33	1	7	1	0	1	37	14	37
Sunshine Hours per day	5.9	6	5.7	6.8	10.1	11.5	11.4	11.2	9.8	9.4	7.8	6.1	8.

Khartoum, Sudan 380m	Jan	Feb	Mar	Apr	May	June	July	Aug	Sept	Oct	Nov	Dec	Year
Temperature Daily max °C	32	33	37	40	42	41	38	36	38	39	35	32	3
Daily min °C	16	17	20	23	26	27	26	25	25	25	21	17	2
Average monthly °C	24	25	28	32	34	34	32	30	32	32	28	25	3
Rainfall Monthly total mm	0	0	0	1	7	5	56	80	28	2	0	0	17
Sunshine Hours per day	10.6	11.2	10.4	10.8	10.4	10.1	8.6	8.6	9.6	10.3	10.8	1.6	10

Kingston, Jamaica 35m	Jan	Feb	Mar	Apr	May	June	July	Aug	Sept	Oct	Nov	Dec	Year
Temperature Daily max °C	30	30	30	31	31	32	32	32	32	31	31	31	3
Daily min °C	20	20	20	21	22	24	23	23	23	23	22	21	2
Average monthly °C	25	25	25	26	26	28	28	28	27	27	26	26	2
Rainfall Monthly total mm	23	15	23	31	102	89	38	91	99	180	74	36	80
Sunshine Hours per day	8.3	8.8	8.7	8.7	8.3	7.8	8.5	8.5	7.6	7.3	8.3	7.7	8

Kolkata (Calcutta), India 5m

		Jan	Feb	Mar	Apr	May	June	July	Aug	Sept	Oct	Nov	Dec	Year
Temperature	Daily max °C	27	29	34	36	35	35	32	32	32	32	29	26	31
	Daily min °C	13	15	21	24	25	26	26	26	26	23	18	13	21
	Average monthly °C	20	22	27	30	30	30	29	29	29	28	23	20	26
Rainfall	Monthly total mm	10	30	34	44	140	297	325	332	253	114	20	5	1,604
Sunshine	Hours per day	8.6	8.7	8.9	9	8.7	5.4	4.1	4.1	5.1	6.5	8.3	8.4	7.1

Lagos, Nigeria 40m

		Jan	Feb	Mar	Apr	May	June	July	Aug	Sept	Oct	Nov	Dec	Year
Temperature	Daily max °C	32	33	33	32	21	29	28	28	29	30	31	32	31
	Daily min °C	22	23	23	23	23	22	22	21	22	22	23	22	22
	Average monthly °C	27	28	28	28	27	26	25	24	25	26	27	27	26
Rainfall	Monthly total mm	28	41	99	99	203	300	180	56	180	190	63	25	1,464
Sunshine	Hours per day	5.9	6.8	6.3	6.1	5.6	3.8	2.8	3.3	3	5.1	6.6	6.5	2.2

Lima, Peru 120m

		Jan	Feb	Mar	Apr	May	June	July	Aug	Sept	Oct	Nov	Dec	Year
Temperature	Daily max °C	28	29	29	27	24	20	20	19	20	22	24	26	24
	Daily min °C	19	20	19	17	16	15	14	14	14	15	16	17	16
	Average monthly °C	24	24	24	22	20	17	17	16	17	18	20	21	20
Rainfall	Monthly total mm	1	1	1	1	5	5	8	8	8	3	3	1	45
Sunshine	Hours per day	6.3	6.8	6.9	6.7	4	1.4	1.1	1	1.1	2.5	4.1	5	3.9

Lisbon, Portugal 77m

		Jan	Feb	Mar	Apr	May	June	July	Aug	Sept	Oct	Nov	Dec	Year
Temperature	Daily max °C	14	15	17	20	21	25	27	28	26	22	17	15	21
	Daily min °C	8	8	10	12	13	15	17	17	17	14	11	9	13
	Average monthly °C	11	12	14	16	17	20	22	23	21	18	14	12	17
Rainfall	Monthly total mm	111	76	109	54	44	16	3	4	33	62	93	103	708
Sunshine	Hours per day	4.7	5.9	6	8.3	9.1	10.6	11.4	10.7	8.4	6.7	5.2	4.6	7.7

London, UK 5m

		Jan	Feb	Mar	Apr	May	June	July	Aug	Sept	Oct	Nov	Dec	Year
Temperature	Daily max °C	6	7	10	13	17	20	22	21	19	14	10	7	14
	Daily min °C	2	2	3	6	8	12	14	13	11	8	5	4	7
	Average monthly °C	4	5	7	9	12	16	18	17	15	11	8	5	11
Rainfall	Monthly total mm	54	50	37	37	46	45	57	59	49	57	64	48	593
Sunshine	Hours per day	1.7	2.3	3.5	5.7	6.7	7	6.6	6	5	3.3	1.9	1.4	4.3

Los Angeles, USA 30m

		Jan	Feb	Mar	Apr	May	June	July	Aug	Sept	Oct	Nov	Dec	Year
Temperature	Daily max °C	18	18	18	19	20	22	24	24	24	23	22	19	21
	Daily min °C	7	8	9	11	13	15	17	17	16	14	11	9	12
	Average monthly °C	12	13	14	15	17	18	21	21	20	18	16	14	17
Rainfall	Monthly total mm	69	74	46	28	3	3	0	0	5	10	28	61	327
Sunshine	Hours per day	6.9	8.2	8.9	8.8	9.5	10.3	11.7	11	10.1	8.6	8.2	7.6	9.2

Lusaka, Zambia 1,154m

		Jan	Feb	Mar	Apr	May	June	July	Aug	Sept	Oct	Nov	Dec	Year
Temperature	Daily max °C	26	26	26	27	25	23	23	26	29	31	29	27	27
	Daily min °C	17	17	16	15	12	10	9	11	15	18	18	17	15
	Average monthly °C	22	22	21	21	10	17	16	19	22	25	23	22	21
Rainfall	Monthly total mm	224	173	90	19	3	1	0	1	1	17	85	196	810
Sunshine	Hours per day	5.1	5.4	6.9	8.9	9	9	9.1	9.6	9.5	9	7	5.5	7.8

Manaus, Brazil 45m

		Jan	Feb	Mar	Apr	May	June	July	Aug	Sept	Oct	Nov	Dec	Year
Temperature	Daily max °C	31	31	31	31	31	31	32	33	34	34	33	32	32
	Daily min °C	24	24	24	24	24	24	24	24	24	25	25	24	24
	Average monthly °C	28	28	28	27	28	28	28	29	29	29	29	28	28
Rainfall	Monthly total mm	278	278	300	287	193	99	61	41	62	112	165	220	2,096
Sunshine	Hours per day	3.9	4	3.6	3.9	5.4	6.9	7.9	8.2	7.5	6.6	5.9	4.9	5.7

Mexico City, Mexico 2,309m

		Jan	Feb	Mar	Apr	May	June	July	Aug	Sept	Oct	Nov	Dec	Year
Temperature	Daily max °C	21	23	26	27	26	25	23	24	23	22	21	21	24
	Daily min °C	5	6	7	9	10	11	11	11	11	9	6	5	8
	Average monthly °C	13	15	16	18	18	18	17	17	17	16	14	13	16
Rainfall	Monthly total mm	8	4	9	23	57	111	160	149	119	46	16	7	709
Sunshine	Hours per day	7.3	8.1	8.5	8.1	7.8	7	6.2	6.4	5.6	6.3	7	7.3	7.1

Miami, USA 2m

		Jan	Feb	Mar	Apr	May	June	July	Aug	Sept	Oct	Nov	Dec	Year
Temperature	Daily max °C	24	25	27	28	30	31	32	32	31	29	27	25	28
	Daily min °C	14	15	16	19	21	23	24	24	24	22	18	15	20
	Average monthly °C	19	20	21	23	25	27	28	28	27	25	22	20	24
Rainfall	Monthly total mm	51	48	58	99	163	188	170	178	241	208	71	43	1,518
Sunshine	Hours per day	7.7	8.3	8.7	9.4	8.9	8.5	8.7	8.4	7.1	6.5	7.5	7.1	8.1

Montreal, Canada 57m

		Jan	Feb	Mar	Apr	May	June	July	Aug	Sept	Oct	Nov	Dec	Year
Temperature	Daily max °C	-6	-4	2	11	18	23	26	25	20	14	5	-3	11
	Daily min °C	-13	-11	-5	2	9	14	17	16	11	6	0	-9	3
	Average monthly °C	-9	-8	-2	6	13	19	22	20	16	10	3	-6	7
Rainfall	Monthly total mm	87	76	86	83	81	91	98	87	96	84	89	89	1,047
Sunshine	Hours per day	2.8	3.4	4.5	5.2	6.7	7.7	8.2	7.7	5.6	4.3	2.4	2.2	5.1

Moscow, Russia 156m

		Jan	Feb	Mar	Apr	May	June	July	Aug	Sept	Oct	Nov	Dec	Year
Temperature	Daily max °C	-6	-4	1	9	18	22	24	22	17	10	1	-5	9
	Daily min °C	-14	-16	-11	-1	5	9	12	9	4	-2	-6	-12	-2
	Average monthly °C	-10	-10	-5	4	12	15	18	16	10	4	-2	-8	4
Rainfall	Monthly total mm	31	28	33	35	52	67	74	74	58	51	36	36	575
Sunshine	Hours per day	1	1.9	3.7	5.2	7.8	8.3	8.4	7.1	4.4	2.4	1	0.6	4.4

New Delhi, India 220m

		Jan	Feb	Mar	Apr	May	June	July	Aug	Sept	Oct	Nov	Dec	Year
Temperature	Daily max °C	21	24	29	36	41	39	35	34	34	34	28	23	32
	Daily min °C	6	10	14	20	26	28	27	26	24	17	11	7	18
	Average monthly °C	14	17	22	28	33	34	31	30	29	26	20	15	25
Rainfall	Monthly total mm	25	21	13	8	13	77	178	184	123	10	2	11	665
Sunshine	Hours per day	7.7	8.2	8.2	8.7	9.2	7.9	6	6.3	6.9	9.4	8.7	8.3	8

Perth, Australia 60m

		Jan	Feb	Mar	Apr	May	June	July	Aug	Sept	Oct	Nov	Dec	Year
Temperature	Daily max °C	29	30	27	25	21	18	17	18	19	21	25	27	23
	Daily min °C	17	18	16	14	12	10	9	9	10	11	14	16	13
	Average monthly °C	23	24	22	19	16	14	13	13	15	16	19	22	18
Rainfall	Monthly total mm	8	13	22	44	128	189	177	145	84	58	19	13	900
Sunshine	Hours per day	10.4	9.8	8.8	7.5	5.7	4.8	5.4	6	7.2	8.1	9.6	10.4	7.8

Reykjavík, Iceland 18m

		Jan	Feb	Mar	Apr	May	June	July	Aug	Sept	Oct	Nov	Dec	Year
Temperature	Daily max °C	2	3	5	6	10	13	15	14	12	8	5	4	8
	Daily min °C	-3	-3	-1	1	4	7	9	8	6	3	0	-2	3
	Average monthly °C	0	0	2	4	7	10	12	11	9	5	3	1	5
Rainfall	Monthly total mm	89	64	62	56	42	42	50	56	67	94	78	79	779
Sunshine	Hours per day	10.8	8.9	8.5	5.5	3.6	3.3	3.3	3.6	4.8	6.1	8.7	10.1	6.4

Santiago, Chile 520m

		Jan	Feb	Mar	Apr	May	June	July	Aug	Sept	Oct	Nov	Dec	Year
Temperature	Daily max °C	30	29	27	24	19	15	15	17	19	22	26	29	23
	Daily min °C	12	11	10	7	5	3	3	4	6	7	9	11	7
	Average monthly °C	21	20	18	15	12	9	9	10	12	15	17	20	15
Rainfall	Monthly total mm	3	3	5	13	64	84	76	56	31	15	8	5	363
Sunshine	Hours per day	10.8	8.9	8.5	5.5	3.6	3.3	3.3	3.6	4.8	6.1	8.7	10.1	6.4

Shanghai, China 5m

		Jan	Feb	Mar	Apr	May	June	July	Aug	Sept	Oct	Nov	Dec	Year
Temperature	Daily max °C	8	8	13	19	24	28	32	32	27	23	17	10	20
	Daily min °C	-1	0	4	9	14	19	23	23	19	13	7	2	11
	Average monthly °C	3	4	8	14	19	23	27	27	23	18	12	6	15
Rainfall	Monthly total mm	48	59	84	94	94	180	147	142	130	71	51	36	1,136
Sunshine	Hours per day	4	3.7	4.4	4.8	5.4	4.7	6.9	7.5	5.3	5.6	4.7	4.5	5.1

Sydney, Australia 40m

		Jan	Feb	Mar	Apr	May	June	July	Aug	Sept	Oct	Nov	Dec	Year
Temperature	Daily max °C	26	26	25	22	19	17	17	18	20	22	24	25	22
	Daily min °C	18	19	17	14	11	9	8	9	11	13	16	17	14
	Average monthly °C	22	22	21	18	15	13	12	13	16	18	20	21	18
Rainfall	Monthly total mm	89	101	127	135	127	117	117	76	74	71	74	74	1,182
Sunshine	Hours per day	7.5	7	6.4	6.1	5.7	5.3	6.1	7	7.3	7.5	7.5	7.5	6.8

Tehran, Iran 1,191m

		Jan	Feb	Mar	Apr	May	June	July	Aug	Sept	Oct	Nov	Dec	Year
Temperature	Daily max °C	9	11	16	21	29	30	37	36	29	24	16	11	22
	Daily min °C	1	1	4	10	16	20	23	23	18	12	6	1	11
	Average monthly °C	4	6	10	15	22	25	30	29	23	18	11	6	17
Rainfall	Monthly total mm	37	23	36	31	14	2	1	1	1	5	29	27	207
Sunshine	Hours per day	5.9	6.7	7.5	7.4	8.6	11.6	11.2	11	10.1	7.6	6.9	6.3	8.4

Timbuktu, Mali 269m

		Jan	Feb	Mar	Apr	May	June	July	Aug	Sept	Oct	Nov	Dec	Year
Temperature	Daily max °C	31	35	38	41	43	42	38	35	38	40	37	31	37
	Daily min °C	13	16	18	22	26	27	25	24	24	23	18	14	21
	Average monthly °C	22	25	28	31	34	34	32	30	31	31	28	23	29
Rainfall	Monthly total mm	0	0	0	1	4	20	54	93	31	3	0	0	206
Sunshine	Hours per day	9.1	9.6	9.6	9.7	9.8	9.4	9.6	9	9.3	9.5	9.5	8.9	9.4

Tokyo, Japan 5m

		Jan	Feb	Mar	Apr	May	June	July	Aug	Sept	Oct	Nov	Dec	Year
Temperature	Daily max °C	9	9	12	18	22	25	29	30	27	20	16	11	19
	Daily min °C	-1	-1	3	4	13	17	22	23	19	13	7	1	10
	Average monthly °C	4	4	8	11	18	21	25	26	23	17	11	6	14
Rainfall	Monthly total mm	48	73	101	135	131	182	146	147	217	220	101	61	1,562
Sunshine	Hours per day	6	5.9	5.7	6	6.2	5	5.8	6.6	4.5	4.4	4.8	5.4	5.5

Tromsø, Norway 100m

		Jan	Feb	Mar	Apr	May	June	July	Aug	Sept	Oct	Nov	Dec	Year
Temperature	Daily max °C	-2	-2	0	3	7	12	16	14	10	5	2	0	5
	Daily min °C	-6	-6	-5	-2	1	6	9	8	5	1	-2	-4	0
	Average monthly °C	-4	-4	-3	0	4	9	13	11	7	3	0	-2	3
Rainfall	Monthly total mm	96	79	91	65	61	59	56	80	109	115	88	95	994
Sunshine	Hours per day	0.1	1.6	2.9	6.1	5.7	6.9	7.9	4.8	3.5	1.7	0.3	0	3.5

Vancouver, Canada 5m

		Jan	Feb	Mar	Apr	May	June	July	Aug	Sept	Oct	Nov	Dec	Year
Temperature	Daily max °C	6	7	10	14	17	20	23	22	19	14	9	7	14
	Daily min °C	0	1	3	5	8	11	13	12	10	7	3	2	6
	Average monthly °C	3	4	6	9	13	16	18	17	14	10	6	4	10
Rainfall	Monthly total mm	214	161	151	90	69	65	39	44	83	172	198	243	1,529
Sunshine	Hours per day	1.6	3	3.8	5.9	7.5	7.4	9.5	8.2	6	3.7	2	1.4	5

Verkhoyansk, Russia 137m

		Jan	Feb	Mar	Apr	May	June	July	Aug	Sept	Oct	Nov	Dec	Year
Temperature	Daily max °C	-47	-40	-20	-1	11	21	24	21	12	-8	-33	-42	-8
	Daily min °C	-51	-48	-40	-25	-7	4	6	1	-6	-20	-39	-50	-23
	Average monthly °C	-49	-44	-30	-13	2	12	15	11	3	-14	-36	-46	-16
Rainfall	Monthly total mm	7	5	5	4	5	25	33	30	13	11	10	7	155
Sunshine	Hours per day	0	2.6	6.9	9.6	9.7	10	9.7	7.5	4.1	2.4	0.6	0	5.4

Vienna, Austria 209m

		Jan	Feb	Mar	Apr	May	June	July	Aug	Sept	Oct	Nov	Dec	Year
Temperature	Daily max °C	1	3	8	15	19	23	25	24	20	14	7	3	14
	Daily min °C	-4	-3	-1	6	10	14	15	15	11	7	3	-1	6
	Average monthly °C	-1	1	5	10	15	18	20	19	15	10	4	1	10
Rainfall	Monthly total mm	39	44	44	45	70	67	84	72	42	56	52	45	660
Sunshine	Hours per day	1.8	2.7	4.1	5.6	7.1	7.4	7.9	7.4	5.5	4.4	2.1	1.7	4.8

Washington, USA 22m

		Jan	Feb	Mar	Apr	May	June	July	Aug	Sept	Oct	Nov	Dec	Year
Temperature	Daily max °C	7	8	12	19	25	29	31	30	26	20	14	8	19
	Daily min °C	-1	-1	2	8	13	18	21	20	16	10	4	-1	9
	Average monthly °C	3	3	7	13	19	24	26	25	21	15	9	4	14
Rainfall	Monthly total mm	84	68	96	85	103	88	108	120	100	78	75	45	1,080
Sunshine	Hours per day	4.4	5.7	6.7	7.4	8.2	8.8	8.6	8.2	7.5	6.5	5.3	4.5	6.8

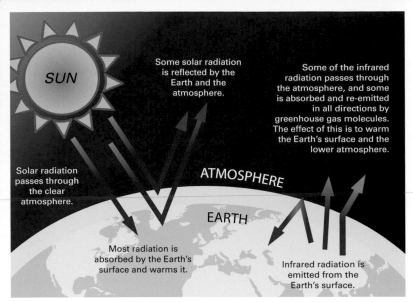

Without the greenhouse effect, Earth would be an uninhabitable frozen wasteland.

The term 'greenhouse effect' is confusing. Real greenhouses work by preventing convection (movement of air), while the greenhouse effect reduces radiation loss from the Earth. Earth receives energy from the Sun in the form of radiation. Earth's atmosphere has a natural supply of greenhouse gases, mainly water vapour, which trap the Sun's energy and recycle it, so that Earth's average surface temperature is 15 °C (59 °F) – about 33 ° (63 °F) warmer than it would be without the greenhouse effect.

Increased concentrations of the greenhouse gases carbon dioxid (CO_2) and methane (CH_4) in Earth's atmosphere have intensified the greenhouse effect and led to global warming, an increase in average temperature near the Earth's surface and in its oceans. The increased concentrations of CO_2 and CH_4 are the result of the burning of fossil fuels (natural gas, coal and oil) and of deforestation

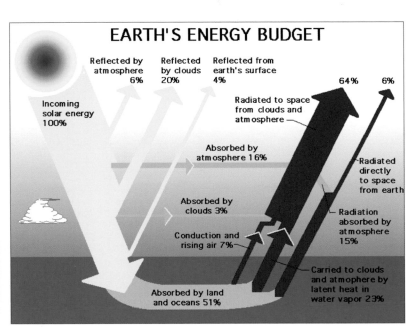

Under stable conditions, the total amount of radiation entering Earth's atmosphere balances the amount being radiated back into space, allowing Earth to maintain a constant average temperature This is called Earth's 'energy budget'. Energy returns to space from Earth in two ways: reflection and emission.

Part of the Sun's energy that comes to Earth is reflected back out to space in the same, short wavelengths in which it came. About 30 per cent of incoming solar radiation is reflected by Earth's atmosphere, cloud and Earth's surface. The percentage of solar energy that is reflected back to space is called the albedo.

The remaining 70 per cent is absorbed, warming Earth's surface, atmosphere and oceans. The solar energy absorbed by the Earth increases the planet's temperature. This energy is emitted back into space as long wave radiation (infra-red), creating a balance.

However, measurements indicate that Earth currently is absorbin more than it emits because CO_2 and CH_4 absorb infra-red radiatior

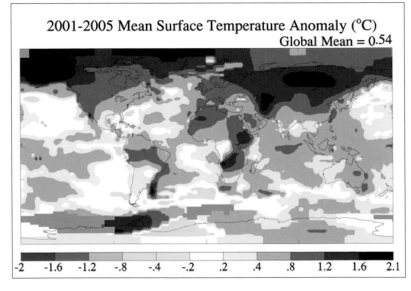

The global average temperature at the Earth's surface has risen 0.6 ± 0.2 °C (0.9 ± 0.4 °F) since the late 19th century, and 0.17 ° (0.31 °F) per decade in the last 30 years. This rapid global warmin has left Earth warmer than at any time in the last 12,000 years. Moreover, global temperatures are now within about 1 °C (1.8 °F) o the maximum estimated temperature during the past million years.

This colour-coded map shows average temperatures from 2001 to 2005, compared to a base period of temperatures from 1951–80. Dark red indicates the greatest warming and purple the greatest cooling. Global warming is greatest at high latitudes of the Northern Hemisphere. This is due to the melting of ice and snow, which decreases the percentage of sunlight reflected (albedo) and uncover the darker surfaces of ocean and land that absorb more sunlight and increase warming. Warming is less over the oceans than over land because of the great heat capacity of the deep ocean. The Eastern Pacific is warming slower than the Western Pacific because this region is cooled by deeper colder water rising to shallower depths.

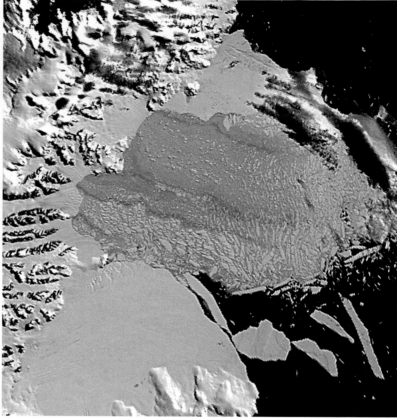

Larsen B ice shelf, **Antarctica**. These two images capture the disintegration of 3,250 square kilometres (1,250 square miles) of Larsen B in a 35-day period from 31 January (left) to 7 March (right) 2002. The ice within the collapsing shelf appears a vibrant blue in the right-hand image. The lost area of ice was greater than the US state of Rhode Island or the UK county of Gloucestershire. About 720 billion tonnes of ice collapsed and broke away from Antarctica, forming a plume of thousands of icebergs adrift in the Weddell Sea.

The Larsen B shelf on the eastern side of the Antarctic peninsula was about 220 metres (720 feet) thick. Scientists believe that the ice shelf has existed for at least 400 years and has probably been in existence since the end of the last major glaciation 12,000 years ago.

The 2002 collapse was the largest event in a sequence of retreats by ice shelves on the Antarctica peninsula over the last 30 years. During this period, Antarctica's seven ice shelves have declined by about 13,500 square kilometres (5,200 square miles). The retreats are due to strong climate warming in the region. The rate of warming is about 0.5 °C (0.9 °F) per decade, much greater than the average warming of planet Earth.

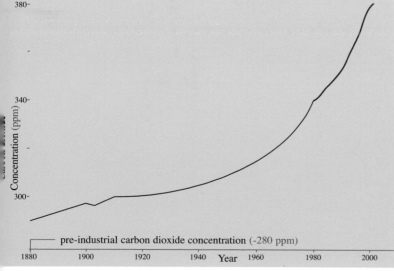

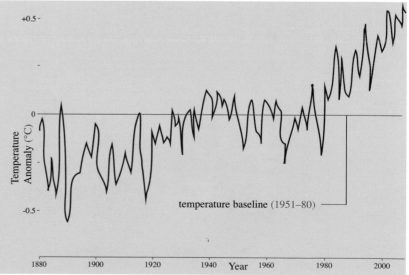

levels of carbon dioxide in Earth's atmosphere have been increasing since the start of the Industrial Revolution. Increasing combustion of fossil fuels has accelerated the trend since the mid-20th century. Eleven of the 12 warmest years since climate records began have occurred since 1995. The Intergovernmental Panel on Climate Change (IPCC) has concluded that as the world warms, storms, droughts and floods will intensify both in frequency and ferocity leading to rising sea levels and desertification. Many of the world's low-lying areas will disappear beneath the waves (see page 35). Global warming will reduce agricultural production and water supplies in many areas with the likelihood of increasing human conflict and migration.

sea ice minimum

1979–81

2003–0

Arctic sea ice, **Arctic Ocean**. This pair of images reveal the decline of sea ice in the Arctic Ocean over the past 25 years. The extent of the Arctic ice cap varies according to season and these images (based on a 3-year average) were taken in September, at the end of the summer melt season when Arctic sea ice is at a minimum.

Since 1979 there has been a decline of about 10 per cent per decade of September sea ice in the Arctic, or 72,000 square kilometres

(28,000 square miles) per year. Furthermore, the rate of decline is accelerating. In September 2007, the average sea ice extent was 4.28 million square kilometres (1.65 million square miles), shatterin the previous record low for the month (set in 2005) by 23 per cent

The shrinking of the Arctic ice cap is partly due to global warming. Satellite data collected from 1981 to 2001 show that some parts o the Arctic are warming faster than 2.5° C per decade.

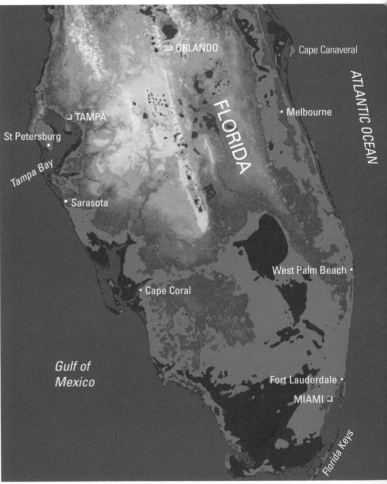

Melting ice sheet, **Greenland**. Greenland is fringed in red and orange, showing that the summer melt season was much longer than average in 2005 – up to 20 more melt days. Glaciers on Greenland's coast are sliding into the Atlantic. The melting could contribute around 4 centimetres to sea-level rise by 2100 (10 per cent of the total). This estimate could be too low since global warming doubled the rate of shrinking of Greenland's ice sheet between 1996 and 2005.

Sea-level rise, **Florida, USA**. Global sea level has risen an average o 3 mm (0.1 in) per year since 1993. About half of this rise is due to thermal expansion of the ocean and about half to melting ice. As Eart warms, melting will play a larger role and produce greater rises in sea level. Rising seas would devastate low-lying regions like Florida. Dark blue areas on the map are less than 5 m (16 ft) above sea level. The loss of Greenland's ice would produce a sea level rise of 7 m (23 ft).

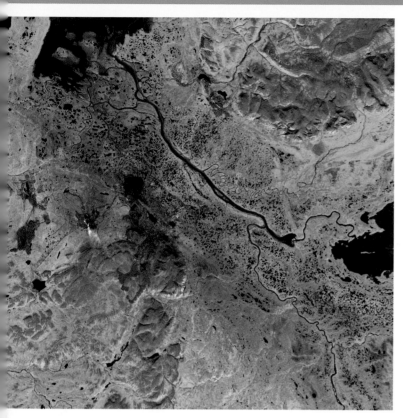

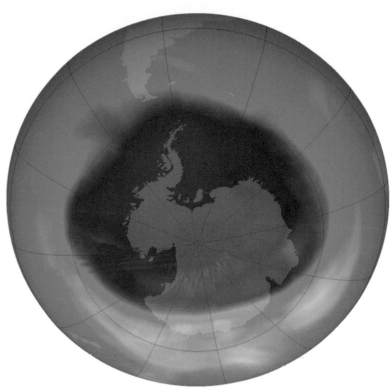

...rilsk, **north-east Siberia, Russia**. It has been estimated that ...per cent of the world's entire global emissions of sulphur dioxide ...mes from this Russian mining city, roughly 300 kilometres (180 ...les) north of the Arctic Circle. The release of sulphur dioxide, a ...urce of acid rain, has severly damaged the local ecosystem. When ...id rain falls on the ground, it dissolves and liberates heavy metals ...d aluminium which can kill plant and animal life. Blue-white plumes ...smoke (just left of centre) drift south-east from flue gas chimneys ...Norilsk. The deep and pale pinks downwind of the city, as well as ...e deep purple in the hillsides immediately outside Norilsk, indicate ...oderately to severely damaged ecosystems.

Ozone hole, Antarctica. Ozone acts as a crucial shield in Earth's atmosphere, absorbing harmful ultraviolet radiation from the Sun. In 1985 scientists discovered that the ozone layer had worn thin above Antarctica. The 'hole' had been caused by chemicals known as chlorofluorocarbons (CFCs), used in refrigeration and aerosols. CFCs contain high levels of chlorine, which breaks free in the bitter cold and darkness of Antarctic and Arctic winter and destroys ozone. The use of CFCs was restricted in 1987, but the ozone layer has been slow to recover. In this image from September 2005, the ozone hole (shown in deep blue) covers 27 million square kilometres. Scientists predict the ozone layer may recover by 2065.

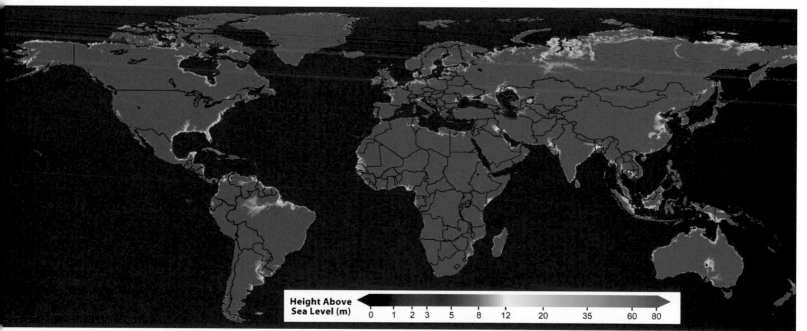

Height Above Sea Level (m)   0   1   2   3   5   8   12   20   35   60   80

...ea-level rise, **World**. Coastal areas on every continent are at risk ...om rising sea levels associated with global warming. In the UK, the ...ens are most at risk. Belgium, the Netherlands, northern Germany, ...ockholm and Helsinki are also under threat. A swathe of China's ...st coast from Shanghai to Jinxi faces peril. Singapore, Ho Chi Minh

City, Bangkok, Rangoon, much of Bangladesh, Chennai and Karachi could also sink beneath the waves. Low-lying coastal areas of West Africa are under threat. While in South America, Buenos Aires and Belém are at risk. In America, southern Florida, New Orleans, and much of the eastern seaboard and the Gulf coast are in harm's way.

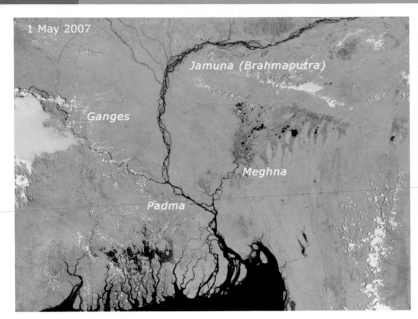

1 May 2007

Jamuna (Brahmaputra)

Ganges

Meghna

Padma

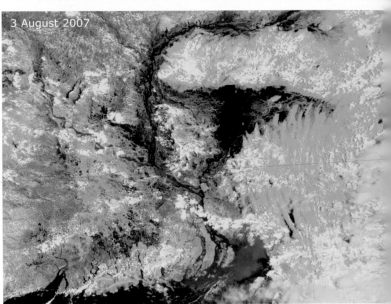

3 August 2007

▲ Ganges delta, **Bangladesh**. In July–August 2007, severe monsoon rains flooded parts of Bangladesh, India and Nepal, killing more than 1,000 people and displacing 20 million. These satellite images capture the extent of the flooding in the low-lying nation of Bangladesh. The image on the left shows the Ganges delta before the monsoon rains began; the course of each river clearly defined. The right-hand image shows the swollen River Jamuna, a flooded branch of which flows east into the overflowing River Meghna. The River Padma, formed by the convergence of the Ganges and Jamuna, is also flooded. The wetlands that surround the rivers are also denuded. More than 8 million Bangladeshis were affected by the floods.

▼ Gloucester, **England**. June and July 2007 brought torrential rain and devastating floods to England. One of the hardest hit regions was Gloucestershire, south-west England. The floods started in late June and continued throughout July. Floodwaters cover the land both sides of the River Severn north of the city of Gloucester. The entire city and surrounding areas were without mains water for 10–14 days.

▼ Mississippi, **USA**. This image of the Mississippi River in Mississippi, Arkansas, and Louisiana shows regions of the southern United States that are prone to flooding. There were two 'great Mississippi floods' in the 20th century – 1927 and 1993. The 1993 flood caused $15 billion in damages. The long, narrow lakes lying roughly parallel to the river are **oxbow lakes**. Oxbows are formed when a river changes course and the surrounding land dries out, forming isolated lakes. Oxbow lakes are common where rivers flow through generally flat terrain.

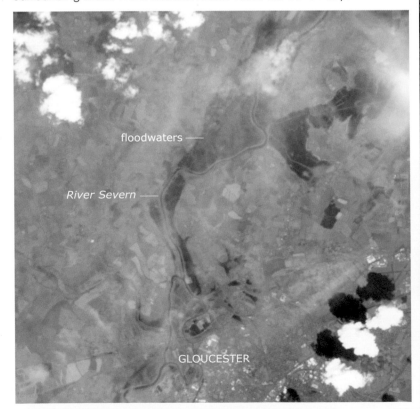

floodwaters —

River Severn —

GLOUCESTER

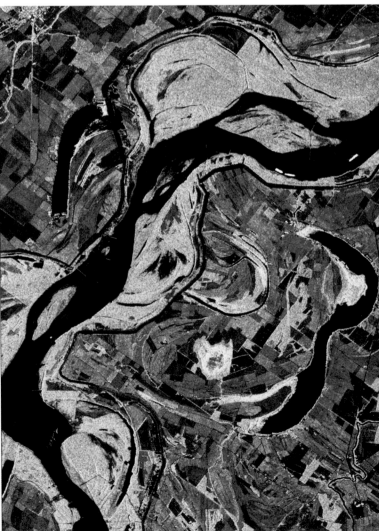

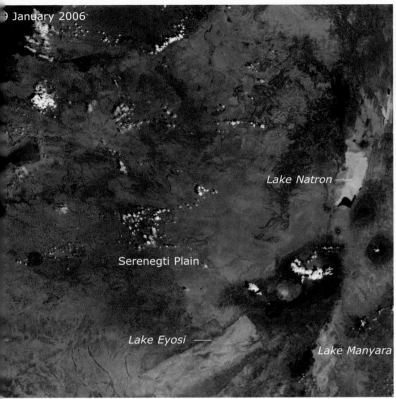

9 January 2006

Lake Natron —

Serenegti Plain

Lake Eyosi ——

Lake Manyara

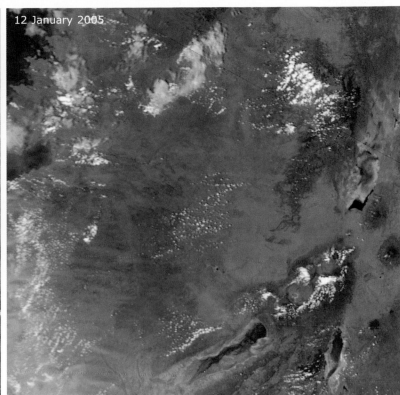

12 January 2005

Serengeti, **Tanzania**. By January 2006, widespread drought had withered the grass and other vegetation of the Serengeti plain in east Africa (left). The region appears parched compared to the green vegetation of the area in 2005 (right). Lakes Eyasi and Manyara appear to be completely dry. The rainy season should have begun

around October 2005, but failed to arrive. In 2005, the long season (March–May) and the short rainy season (October–December) failed across east Africa, causing crop failures, pasture degradation, water shortages and serious food security concerns.

▼ Lake Victoria area, **East Africa**. The failure of the rains in 2005 caused widespread drought in eastern Africa, with rainfall totals for the year only 20–60 per cent of normal. This satellite image shows the drought's impact on vegetation across southern Sudan and Ethiopia in the north, Kenya and Uganda in the centre and Tanzania in the south.

▼ Drought, **Australia**. In April 2007, most of Australia was in the grip of severe drought. April was one of the driest on record for parts of Australia. Reservoirs in the Snowy Mountain Hydroelectric Scheme, including Lake Eucumbene, were at 10 per cent capacity, the lowest in their 50-year history.

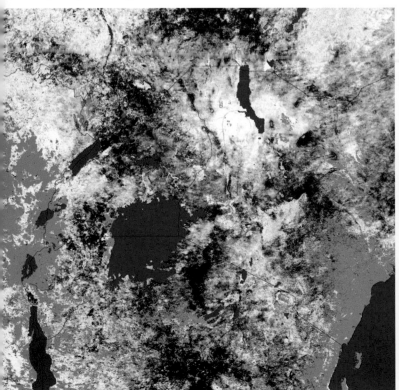

Deforestation is caused by humans clearing land for agriculture, timber, mining, settlement or hydroelectric power. Wind and rain then erodes the exposed topsoil, making regrowth unlikely.

About half of Earth's mature tropical rainforests (750–800 million hectares) have already been felled. Every month, we continue to lose about 1.1 million hectares (2.8 million acres) of the world's rainforests. By 2030, unless there is a major increase in efforts to preserve the rainforests, 80 per cent of the world's rainforest will have disappeared and another 10 per cent will be degraded.

Rainforests are home to two-thirds of all animal and plant life on Earth, and deforestation is causing the extinction of hundreds of thousands of species. The clearing of forests is also estimated to contribute to one-third of all greenhouse gas emissions, fuelling the process of global warming.

September 2000

September 2006

Rondônia, southern Brazil, is part of the "Arc of Deforestation" in the south of the Amazonian rainforest. Over a six-year period, these images reveal the almost complete cleareance of an area southwest of the Pacaás Novos National Park, southern Rondônia.

The deforestation of Rondônia is caused primarily by a huge influx of people, encouraged by cheap land offered by the Brazilian Government for agriculture. Since the 1980s, Brazil has lost more than 15,000 km² (9,000 miles²) of forest per year.

Tierras Bajas, Santa Cruz, Bolivia
Year Deforested
pre 1976   1987–1988   1993–1994
1976–1984   1989–1990   1995–1996
1985–1986   1991–1992   1997–1998

0   km   50

Tierras Bajas, Santa Cruz, Bolivia, has lost most of its forest to agriculture. Solid white lines indicate planned colonies, dashed lines show spontaneous colonies, and dotted lines show Mennonite colonies. Between 1990 and 2005, Bolivia lost more than 4 million hectares of forest (6.45% of total forested land).

Kalimantan, Borneo, Indonesia, was engulfed by fires caused by the 'slash and burn' of forests for wood and to clear land for crop growing. Red dots mark the location of the fires, which produced a toxic haze across Southeast Asia in 2006. Between 1990 and 2005, Indonesia cleared more than 28 million hectares of forest.

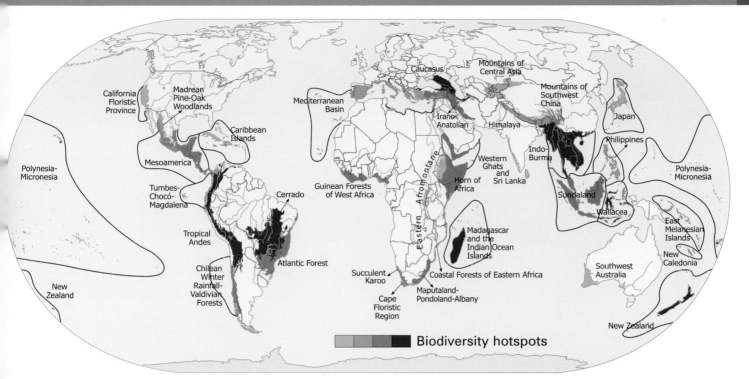

Biodiversity hotspots

Preservation of the biodiversity of species **was a major aim of the 1992 Earth Summit.** The 34 hotspots identified by Conservation International (see above) cover just 2.3% of Earth's surface but are home to 50% of the world's plants and 42% of the world's vertebrates. These hotspots have lost at least 70% of their original habitat. Many scientists believe that we are witnessing the sixth great mass extinction of life on Earth. The IUCN Red List is an evaluation of the species most at risk of extinction. The 2007 Red List reveals that one in five mammals, one in eight birds, and almost one third of all amphibians face extinction.

IUCN RED LIST	No. of described species	No. of species evaluated by 2007	No. of threatened species in 1996–98	No. of threatened species in 2000	No. of threatened species in 2002	No. of threatened species in 2003	No. of threatened species in 2004	No. of threatened species in 2006	No. of threatened species in 2007	No. threatened in 2007 as % of species described
Vertebrates										
Mammals	5,416	4,863	1,096	1,130	1,137	1,130	1,101	1,093	1,094	20%
Birds	9,956	9,956	1,107	1,183	1,192	1,194	1,213	1,206	1,217	12%
Reptiles	8,240	1,385	253	296	293	293	304	341	422	5%
Amphibians	6,199	5,915	124	146	157	157	1,770	1,811	1,808	29%
Fishes	30,000	3,119	734	752	742	750	800	1,171	1,201	4%
Subtotal	59,811	25,238	3,314	3,507	3,521	3,524	5,188	5,622	5,742	10%
Invertebrates										
Insects	950,000	1,255	537	555	557	553	559	623	623	0.07%
Molluscs	81,000	2,212	920	938	939	967	974	975	978	1.21%
Crustaceans	40,000	553	407	408	409	409	429	459	460	1.15%
Corals	2,175	13	-	-	-	-	-	-	5	0.23%
Others	130,200	83	27	27	27	30	30	44	42	0.03%
Subtotal	1,203,375	4,116	1,891	1,928	1,932	1,959	1,992	2,101	2,108	0.18%
Plants										
Mosses	15,000	92	-	80	80	80	80	80	79	0.53%
Ferns and allies	13,025	211	-	-	-	111	140	139	139	1%
Gymnosperms	980	909	142	141	142	304	305	306	321	33%
Dicotyledons	193,350	9,622	4,929	5,099	5,202	5,768	7,025	7,086	7,121	4%
Monocotyledons	59,300	1,149	257	291	290	511	771	779	778	1%
Green Algae	3,715	2	-	-	-	-	-	-	0	0.00%
Red Algae	5,956	58	-	-	-	-	-	-	9	0.15%
Subtotal	297,326	12,043	5,328	5,611	5,714	6,774	8,321	8,390	8,447	3%
Others										
Lichens	10,000	2	-	-	-	2	2	2	2	0.02%
Mushrooms	16,000	1	-	-	-	-	-	1	1	0.01%
Brown Algae	2,849	15	-	-	-	-	-	-	6	0.21%
Subtotal	28,849	18	-	-	-	2	2	3	9	0.03%
TOTAL	1,589,361	41,415	10,533	11,046	11,167	12,259	15,503	16,116	16,303	1%

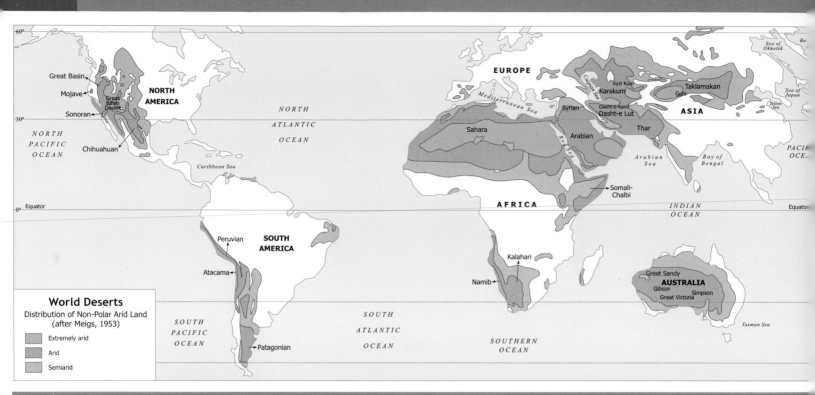

World Deserts
Distribution of Non-Polar Arid Land
(after Meigs, 1953)

- Extremely arid
- Arid
- Semiarid

WORLD'S DESERTS (AREA)

1. ANTARCTIC (14 million sq km)	7. GREAT BASIN (492,000 sq km)	13. TAKLAMAKAN (270,000 sq km)	19. SIMPSON (145,000 sq km)
2. SAHARA (9.1 million sq km)	8. CHIHUAHUAN (450,000 sq km)	14. KALAHARI (260,000 sq km)	20. ATACAMA (140,000 sq km)
3. ARABIAN (2.33 million sq km)	9. GREAT SANDY (400,000 sq km)	15. DASHT-E KAVIR (260,000 sq km)	21. NAMIB (135,000 sq km)
4. GOBI (1.3 million sq km)	10. KARAKUM (350,000 sq km)	16. SYRIAN (260,000 sq km)	22. MOJAVE (65,000 sq km)
5. PATAGONIAN (670,000 sq km)	11. SONORAN (310,000 sq km)	17. THAR (200,000 sq km)	
6. GREAT VICTORIA (647,000 sq km)	12. KYZYL KUM (300,000 sq km)	18. GIBSON (155,000 sq km)	

Taklamakan Desert, Xinjiang, north-west China. The Taklamakan is a cold desert with temperatures falling well below -20°C (-4°F) in winter. It covers most of the Tarim Basin, and is 1,000 km (600 miles) long and 400 km (250 miles) wide. Two branches of the Silk Road cross the Taklamakan's northern and southern edge.

Dasht-e Kavir, northern Iran. The Dasht-e Kavir (Great Salt Desert) is the largest desert in Iran. Temperatures can reach 50°C (122°F) in summer. Day and night temperatures can vary by up to 70°C. The heat cause extreme vaporization that creates salt marshes and salt mudflats, seen here in swirls of colour.

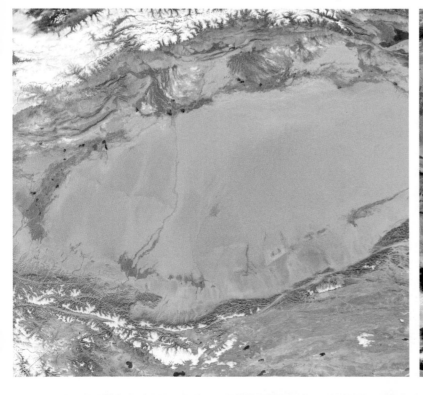

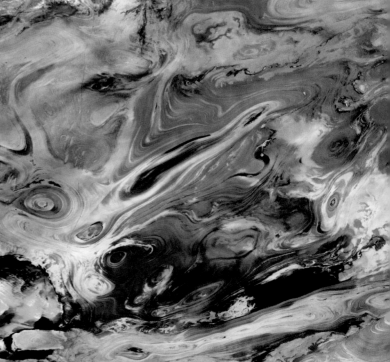

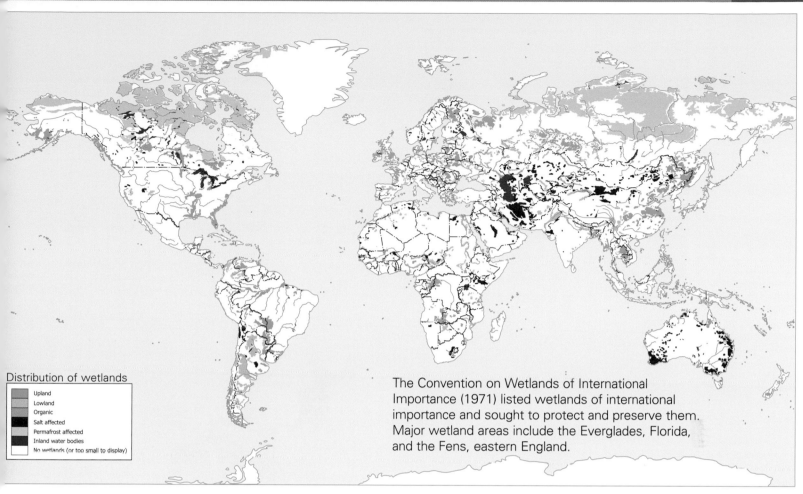

Distribution of wetlands
- Upland
- Lowland
- Organic
- Salt affected
- Permafrost affected
- Inland water bodies
- No wetlands (or too small to display)

The Convention on Wetlands of International Importance (1971) listed wetlands of international importance and sought to protect and preserve them. Major wetland areas include the Everglades, Florida, and the Fens, eastern England.

Wetlands are ecosystems where the water table lies close to the surface for much of the year. They are a transition zone between areas of land and water. Wetlands include bogs, marshes, swamps and fens. They are home to a rich diversity of flora and fauna, many of which are endemic. Wetlands are also ecologically valuable as regulators of flooding and the water cycle. They are under threat from the expansion of farmland and the built environment.

▼ Wetlands, **Gulf of Mexico**. These images capture the coastal wetlands of Louisiana, Mississippi, Alabama and part of the Florida panhandle. The reddish colour of the image at bottom indicates the profusion of vegetation. The red hues on the main image show aquatic vegetation. Cities appear gray, with New Orleans visible on the left of all images. Wetlands account for only 5% of the total land area of the United States, but over 30% of the nation's flora.

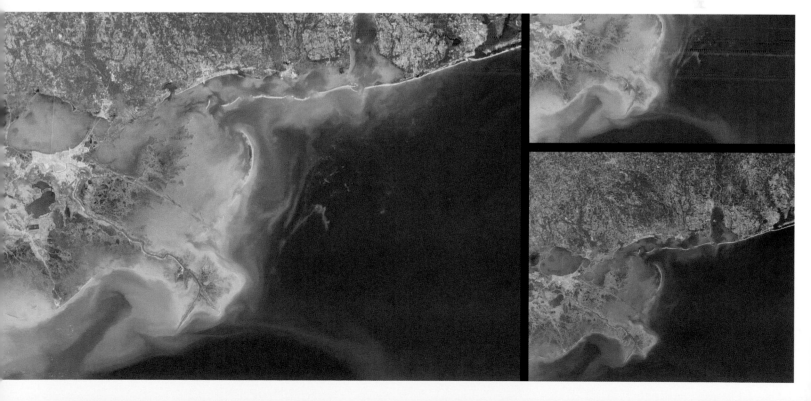

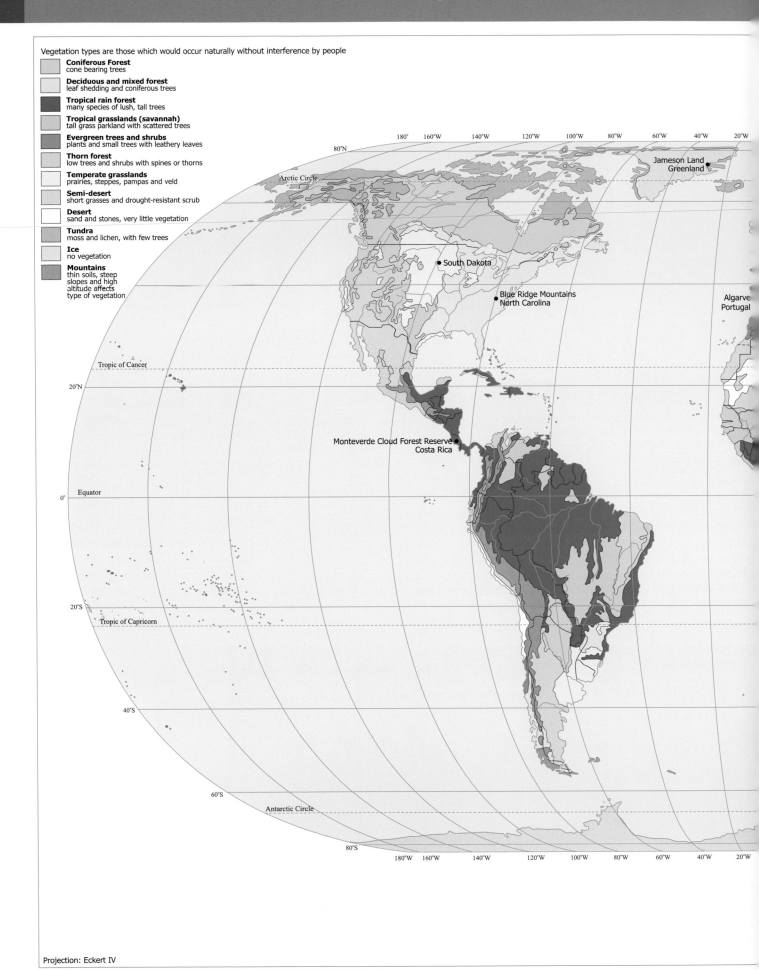

Vegetation types are those which would occur naturally without interference by people

Coniferous Forest
cone bearing trees

Deciduous and mixed forest
leaf shedding and coniferous trees

Tropical rain forest
many species of lush, tall trees

Tropical grasslands (savannah)
tall grass parkland with scattered trees

Evergreen trees and shrubs
plants and small trees with leathery leaves

Thorn forest
low trees and shrubs with spines or thorns

Temperate grasslands
prairies, steppes, pampas and veld

Semi-desert
short grasses and drought-resistant scrub

Desert
sand and stones, very little vegetation

Tundra
moss and lichen, with few trees

Ice
no vegetation

Mountains
thin soils, steep
slopes and high
altitude affects
type of vegetation

Jameson Land
Greenland

South Dakota

Blue Ridge Mountains
North Carolina

Algarve
Portugal

Monteverde Cloud Forest Reserve
Costa Rica

80°N

Arctic Circle

Tropic of Cancer

20°N

Equator

20°S

Tropic of Capricorn

40°S

60°S

Antarctic Circle

80°S

180° 160°W 140°W 120°W 100°W 80°W 60°W 40°W 20°W

Projection: Eckert IV

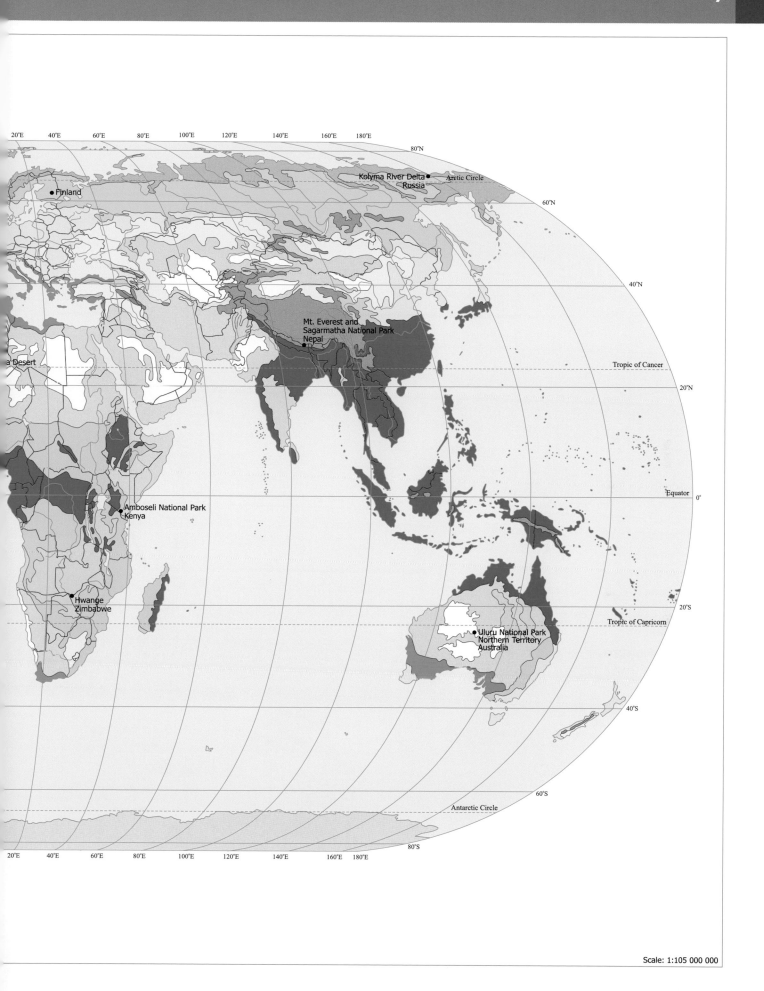

20°E 40°E 60°E 80°E 100°E 120°E 140°E 160°E 180°E

80°N

Kolyma River Delta •
Russia   Arctic Circle

• Finland

60°N

40°N

Mt. Everest and
Sagarmatha National Park
Nepal

Tropic of Cancer

20°N

a Desert

Amboseli National Park
Kenya

Equator   0°

Hwange
Zimbabwe

20°S

Uluru National Park
Northern Territory
Australia   Tropic of Capricorn

40°S

60°S

Antarctic Circle

80°S

20°E 40°E 60°E 80°E 100°E 120°E 140°E 160°E 180°E

Scale: 1:105 000 000

Land Use, Forestry and Fishing

Land Use

- Arable
- Arable and pasture
- Market gardening
- Woods and forest
- Rough grazing
- Pasture
- Savanna
- Non-productive
- Industrial areas

Forestry

- 5% of world production of coniferous wood
- 5% of world production of deciduous wood

Fishing

- Principal fishing grounds

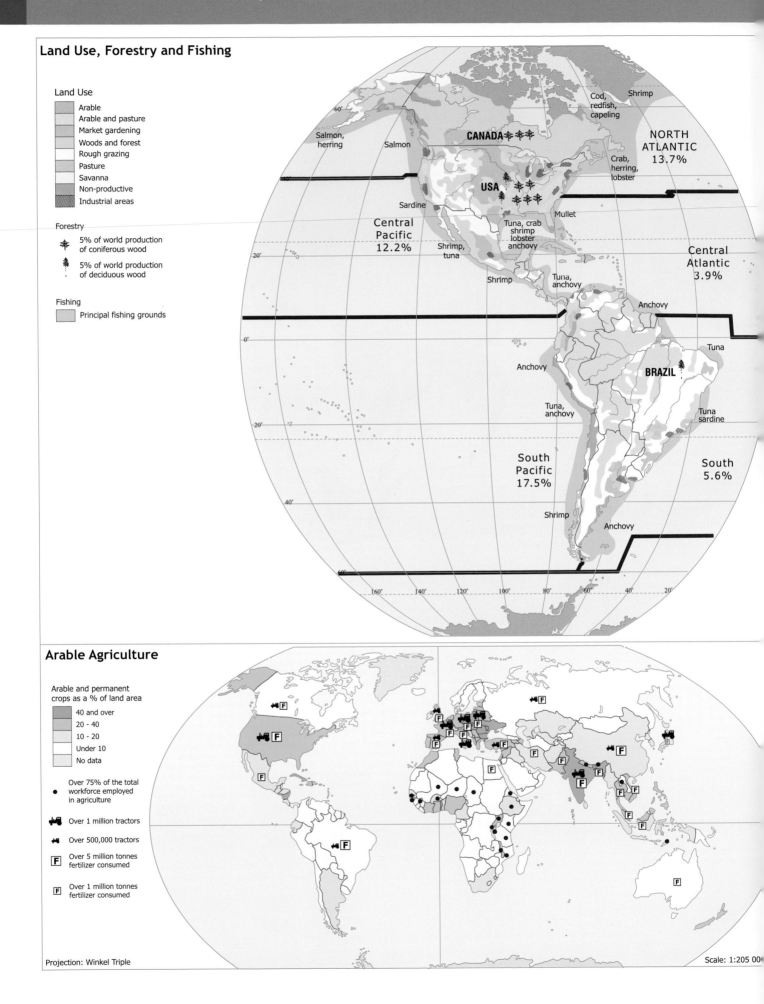

Salmon, herring

Salmon

CANADA

NORTH ATLANTIC 13.7%

Cod, redfish, capeling

Shrimp

Crab, herring, lobster

USA

Sardine

Central Pacific 12.2%

Tuna, crab shrimp lobster anchovy

Mullet

Shrimp, tuna

Central Atlantic 3.9%

Shrimp

Tuna, anchovy

Anchovy

Tuna

Anchovy

BRAZIL

Tuna, anchovy

Tuna sardine

South Pacific 17.5%

South 5.6%

Shrimp

Anchovy

Arable Agriculture

Arable and permanent crops as a % of land area

- 40 and over
- 20 - 40
- 10 - 20
- Under 10
- No data

- Over 75% of the total workforce employed in agriculture
- Over 1 million tractors
- Over 500,000 tractors
- [F] Over 5 million tonnes fertilizer consumed
- [F] Over 1 million tonnes fertilizer consumed

Projection: Winkel Triple

Scale: 1:205 00

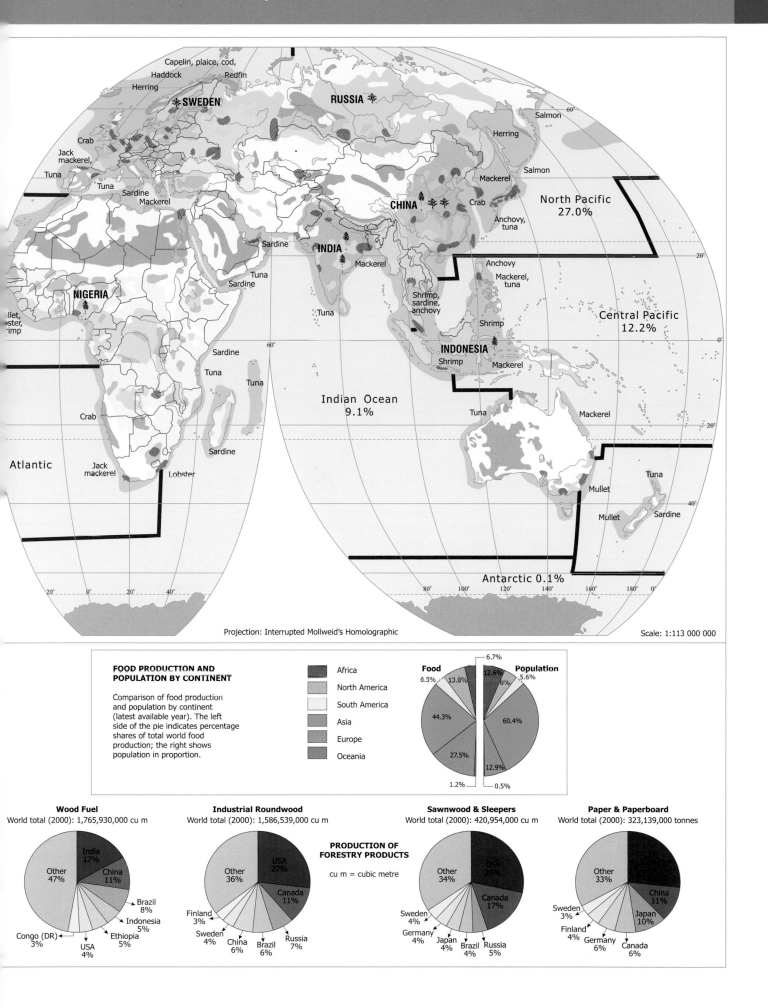

Capelin, plaice, cod,
Haddock   Redfin
Herring

☀ SWEDEN   RUSSIA ☀
                                    Salmon
Crab   Herring
Jack
mackerel,   Salmon
Tuna   Mackerel
        Tuna   CHINA ☀☀☀   Crab   North Pacific
        Sardine   27.0%
        Mackerel   INDIA ☀   Anchovy,
                                           tuna
        Sardine   Mackerel
                                    Anchovy
NIGERIA ☀   Tuna   Mackerel,
                       Sardine   tuna
llet,   Tuna   Central Pacific
ster,   Sardine   Shrimp,   12.2%
imp   sardine,   Shrimp
                Sardine   anchovy
                Tuna   INDONESIA ☀
                Tuna   Shrimp   Mackerel
                                           0°
Crab   Indian Ocean
                          9.1%   Tuna   Mackerel
Atlantic   Jack
                mackerel   Sardine   Tuna
                      Lobster   Mullet
                                                        Mullet Sardine
                                           Antarctic 0.1%

Projection: Interrupted Mollweid's Homolographic

Scale: 1:113 000 000

FOOD PRODUCTION AND POPULATION BY CONTINENT

Comparison of food production and population by continent (latest available year). The left side of the pie indicates percentage shares of total world food production; the right shows population in proportion.

- Africa
- North America
- South America
- Asia
- Europe
- Oceania

Food   **Population**
6.7%
6.5% 13.0% 12.6% 5.6%
44.3%   60.4%
27.5%   12.9%
1.2%   0.5%

Wood Fuel
World total (2000): 1,765,930,000 cu m

Other 47%
India 17%
China 11%
Brazil 8%
Indonesia 5%
Congo (DR) 3%
USA 4%
Ethiopia 5%

Industrial Roundwood
World total (2000): 1,586,539,000 cu m

Other 36%
USA 27%
Canada 11%
Finland 3%
Sweden 4%
China 6%
Brazil 6%
Russia 7%

PRODUCTION OF FORESTRY PRODUCTS

cu m = cubic metre

Sawnwood & Sleepers
World total (2000): 420,954,000 cu m

Other 34%
USA 29%
Canada 17%
Sweden 4%
Germany 4%
Japan 4%
Brazil 4%
Russia 5%

Paper & Paperboard
World total (2000): 323,139,000 tonnes

Other 33%
China 11%
Japan 10%
Sweden 3%
Finland 4%
Germany 6%
Canada 6%

Agriculture and Forestry

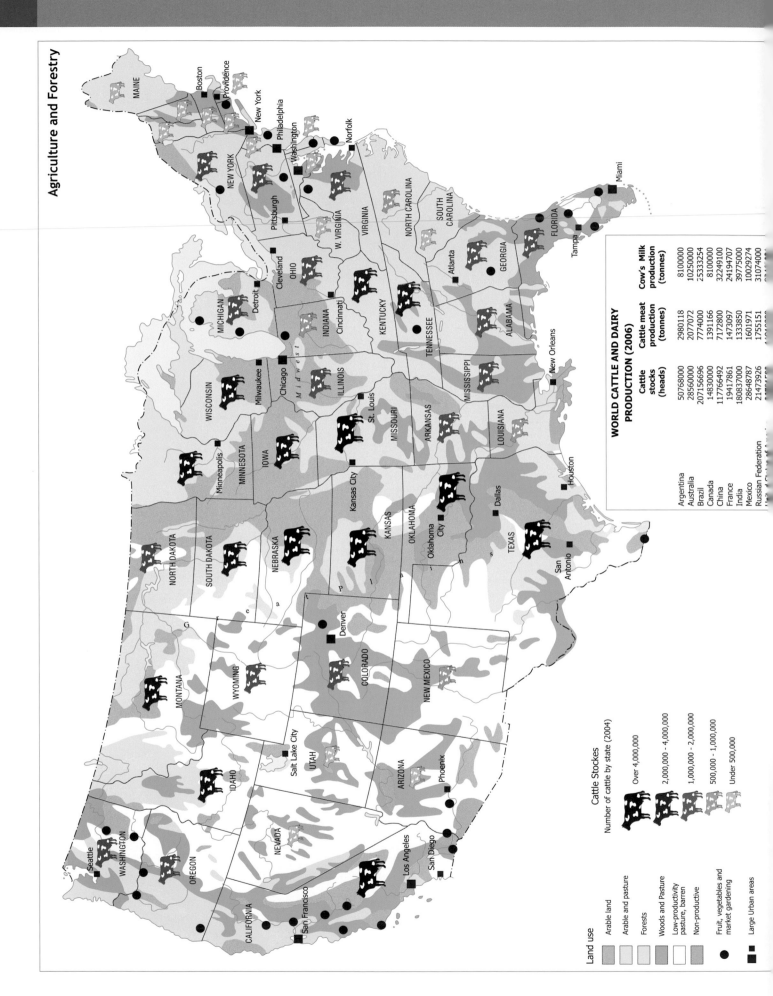

WORLD CATTLE AND DAIRY PRODUCTION (2006)			
	Cattle stocks (heads)	Cattle meat production (tonnes)	Cow's Milk production (tonnes)
Argentina	50768000	2980118	8100000
Australia	28560000	2077072	10250000
Brazil	207156696	7774000	25333254
Canada	14830000	1391166	8100000
China	117766492	7172800	32249100
France	19417861	1473097	24194707
India	180837000	1333850	39775000
Mexico	28648787	1601971	10029274
Russian Federation	21473926	1755151	31074000

Cattle Stockes

Number of cattle by state (2004)

Over 4,000,000

2,000,000 - 4,000,000

1,000,000 - 2,000,000

500,000 - 1,000,000

Under 500,000

● Fruit, vegetables and market gardening

■ Large Urban areas

Land use

Arable land

Arable and pasture

Forests

Woods and Pasture

Low-productivity pasture, barren

Non-productive

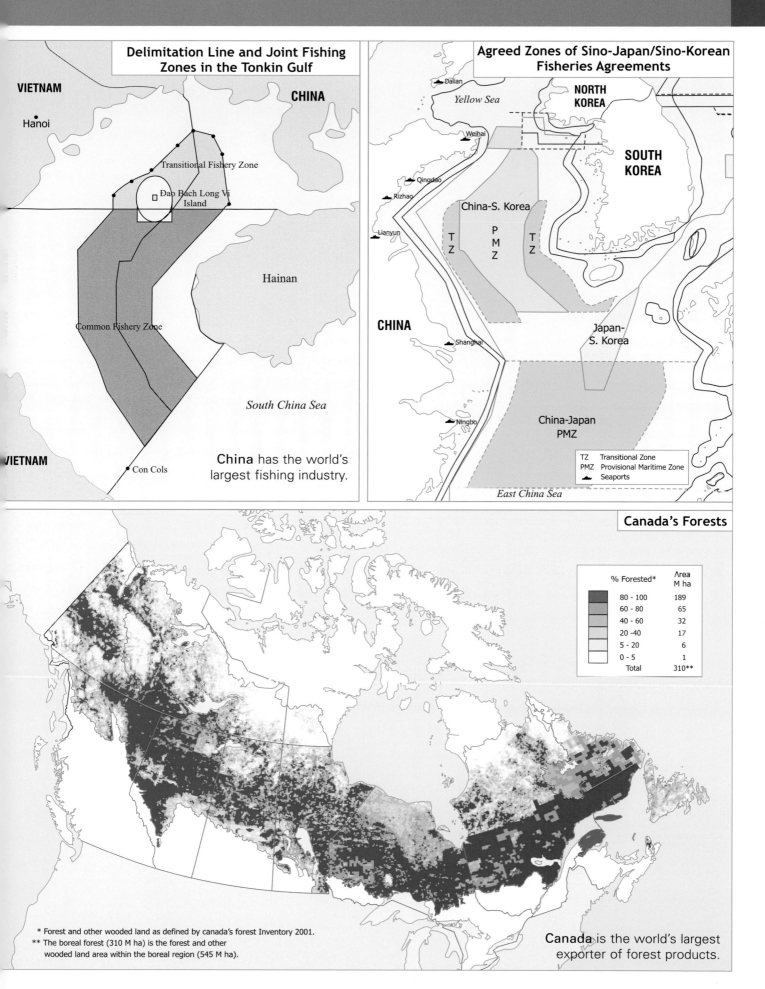

Delimitation Line and Joint Fishing Zones in the Tonkin Gulf

VIETNAM

Hanoi

CHINA

Transitional Fishery Zone

Đao Bach Long Vi
Island

Hainan

Common Fishery Zone

South China Sea

VIETNAM

Con Cols

China has the world's largest fishing industry.

Agreed Zones of Sino-Japan/Sino-Korean Fisheries Agreements

Dalian

Yellow Sea

NORTH KOREA

Weihai

SOUTH KOREA

Qingdao

Rizhao

China-S. Korea

Lianyun

T Z

P M Z

T Z

CHINA

Japan-
S. Korea

Shanghai

Ningbo

China-Japan
PMZ

TZ   Transitional Zone
PMZ   Provisional Maritime Zone
⏢   Seaports

East China Sea

Canada's Forests

% Forested*	Area M ha
80 - 100	189
60 - 80	65
40 - 60	32
20 -40	17
5 - 20	6
0 - 5	1
Total	310**

* Forest and other wooded land as defined by canada's forest Inventory 2001.

** The boreal forest (310 M ha) is the forest and other
   wooded land area within the boreal region (545 M ha).

Canada is the world's largest exporter of forest products.

Energy production

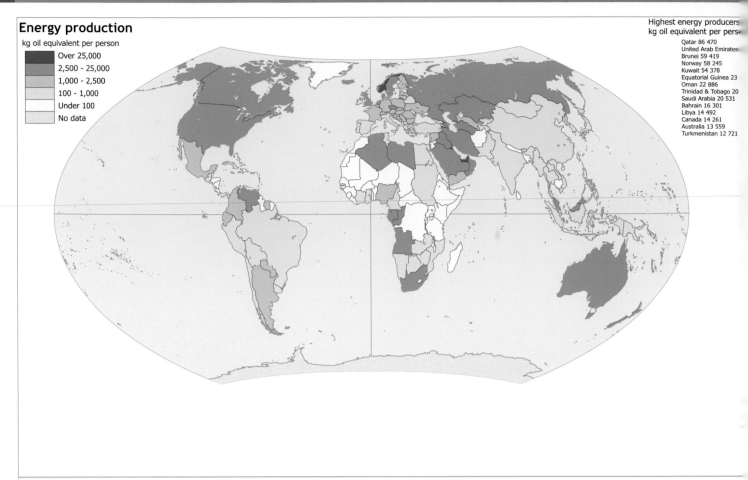

kg oil equivalent per person

- Over 25,000
- 2,500 - 25,000
- 1,000 - 2,500
- 100 - 1,000
- Under 100
- No data

Highest energy producers
kg oil equivalent per person

Qatar 86 470
United Arab Emirates
Brunei 59 419
Norway 58 245
Kuwait 54 378
Equatorial Guinea 23
Oman 22 886
Trinidad & Tobago 20
Saudi Arabia 20 531
Bahrain 16 301
Libya 14 492
Canada 14 261
Australia 13 559
Turkmenistan 12 721

Energy consumption

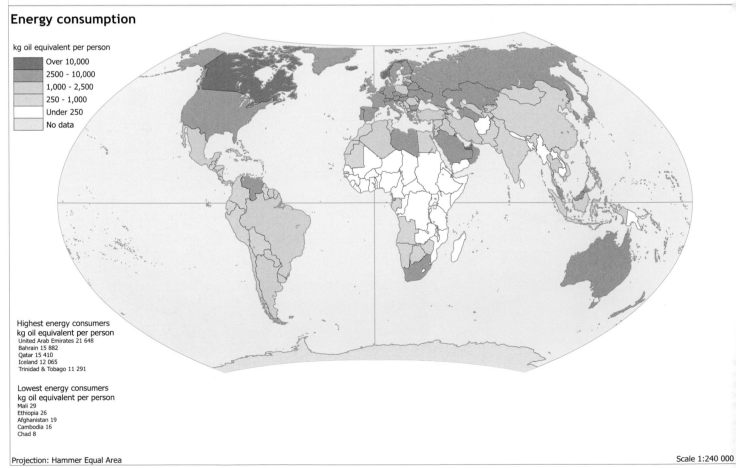

kg oil equivalent per person

- Over 10,000
- 2500 - 10,000
- 1,000 - 2,500
- 250 - 1,000
- Under 250
- No data

Highest energy consumers
kg oil equivalent per person
United Arab Emirates 21 648
Bahrain 15 882
Qatar 15 410
Iceland 12 065
Trinidad & Tobago 11 291

Lowest energy consumers
kg oil equivalent per person
Mali 29
Ethiopia 26
Afghanistan 19
Cambodia 16
Chad 8

Projection: Hammer Equal Area

Scale 1:240 000

Electricity Generation

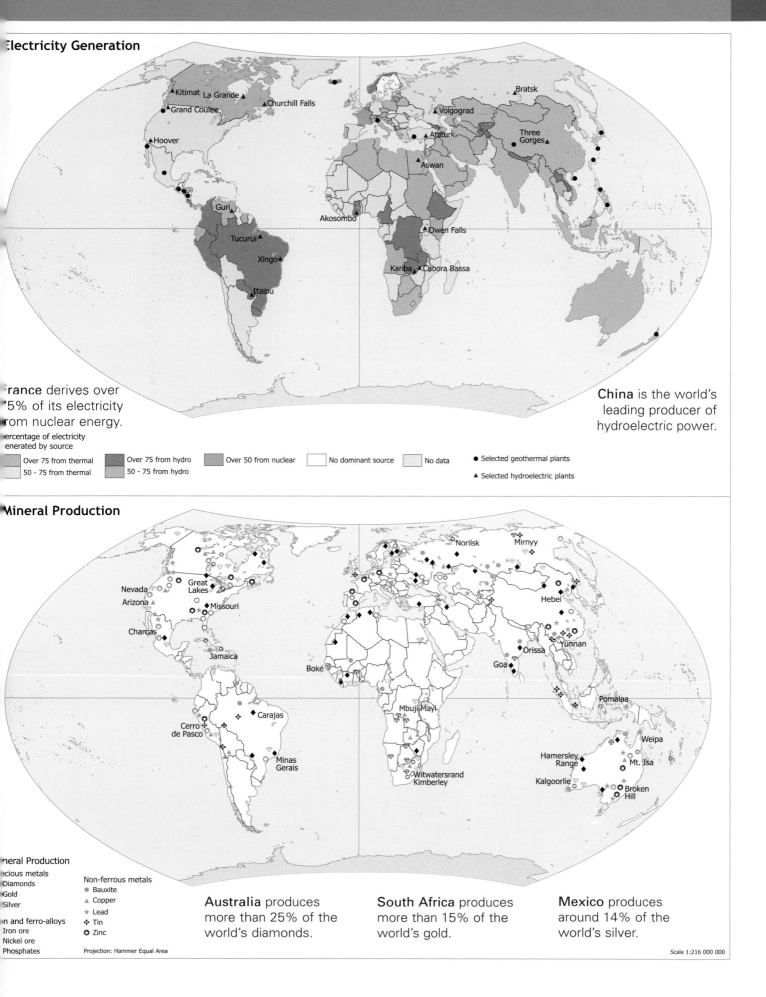

Kitimat La Grande Churchill Falls
Grand Coulee
Hoover
Bratsk
Volgograd
Ataturk
Three Gorges
Aswan
Guri
Akosombo
Owen Falls
Tucurui
Xingo
Kariba Cabora Bassa
Itaipu

France derives over 75% of its electricity from nuclear energy.

China is the world's leading producer of hydroelectric power.

Percentage of electricity generated by source

- Over 75 from thermal
- 50 - 75 from thermal
- Over 75 from hydro
- 50 - 75 from hydro
- Over 50 from nuclear
- No dominant source
- No data
- ● Selected geothermal plants
- ▲ Selected hydroelectric plants

Mineral Production

Norilsk Mirnyy
Great Lakes
Nevada
Arizona
Missouri
Hebei
Charcas
Jamaica
Yunnan
Boké
Orissa
Goa
Carajas
Mbuji Mayi
Cerro de Pasco
Pomalaa
Weipa
Minas Gerais
Hamersley Range Mt. Isa
Witwatersrand Kimberley
Kalgoorlie
Broken Hill

Mineral Production

Precious metals
- ◆ Diamonds
- Gold
- Silver

Iron and ferro-alloys
- Iron ore
- Nickel ore
- Phosphates

Non-ferrous metals
- ● Bauxite
- ▲ Copper
- ★ Lead
- ✣ Tin
- ✪ Zinc

Australia produces more than 25% of the world's diamonds.

South Africa produces more than 15% of the world's gold.

Mexico produces around 14% of the world's silver.

Projection: Hammer Equal Area

Scale 1:216 000 000

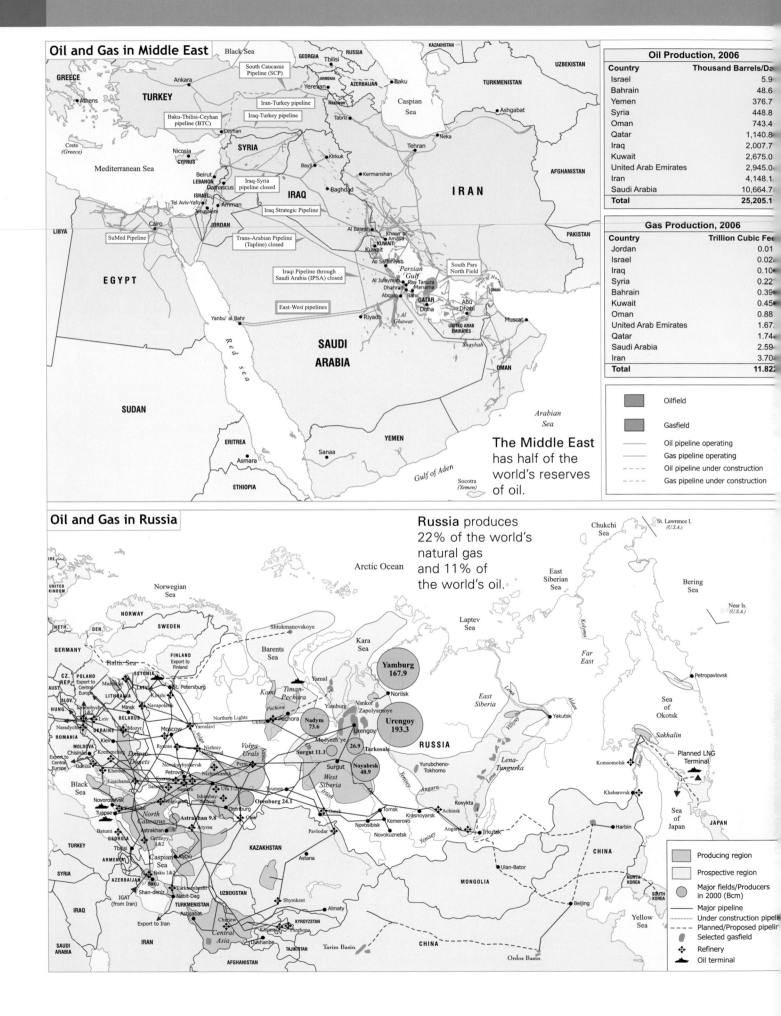

Oil and Gas in Middle East

The Middle East has half of the world's reserves of oil.

Oil Production, 2006	
Country	Thousand Barrels/Da
Israel	5.9
Bahrain	48.6
Yemen	376.7
Syria	448.8
Oman	743.4
Qatar	1,140.8
Iraq	2,007.7
Kuwait	2,675.0
United Arab Emirates	2,945.0
Iran	4,148.1
Saudi Arabia	10,664.7
Total	**25,205.1**

Gas Production, 2006	
Country	Trillion Cubic Fee
Jordan	0.01
Israel	0.02
Iraq	0.10
Syria	0.22
Bahrain	0.39
Kuwait	0.45
Oman	0.88
United Arab Emirates	1.67
Qatar	1.74
Saudi Arabia	2.59
Iran	3.70
Total	**11.82**

Legend:
- Oilfield
- Gasfield
- Oil pipeline operating
- Gas pipeline operating
- Oil pipeline under construction
- Gas pipeline under construction

Pipeline labels on map:
- South Caucasus Pipeline (SCP)
- Baku-Tbilisi-Ceyhan pipeline (BTC)
- Iran-Turkey pipeline
- Iraq-Turkey pipeline
- Iraq-Syria pipeline closed
- Iraq Strategic Pipeline
- SuMed Pipeline
- Trans-Arabian Pipeline (Tapline) closed
- Iraqi Pipeline through Saudi Arabia (IPSA) closed
- East-West pipelines

Oil and Gas in Russia

Russia produces 22% of the world's natural gas and 11% of the world's oil.

Major fields (Bcm):
- Yamburg 167.9
- Urengoy 193.3
- Nadym 73.6
- Noyabrsk 48.9
- Surgut 11.1
- Orenburg 24.1
- Astrakhan 9.8
- 26.9

Legend:
- Producing region
- Prospective region
- Major fields/Producers in 2000 (Bcm)
- Major pipeline
- Under construction pipeli
- Planned/Proposed pipeli
- Selected gasfield
- Refinery
- Oil terminal

Oil and Gas in Nigeria

Nigeria has the tenth largest natural gas reserves in the world. It is Africa's largest oil producer. The Gulf of Guinea has 10% of the world's oil reserves.

Texas oil reserves account for about 25% of total US oil reserves, and the state's natural gas reserves account for 30% of total natural gas reserves.

In 1975 the first British oil was brought ashore. Production peaked in the 1980s. North Sea oil production fell 10 % (230,000 barrels) in 2004, and a further 13% in 2005. Today, Britain is a net importer of crude oil. Two of the key centres are Great Yarmouth/Lowestoft and Aberdeen, regarded as the oil capital of Europe.

Australia is the world's largest exporter of coal (35% of total trade), iron ore, lead, diamonds, rutile, zinc and zirconium, second largest of gold and uranium, and third largest of aluminium. Mining contributes about 5.6% of Australia's total GDP.

Mining takes place in all Australia's istates and territories. Major mining areas include the Goldfields and Pilbara regions of Western Australia, the Hunter Valley in New South Wales, the Bowen Basin in Queensland, and the Latrobe Valley in Victoria. Major active mines in Australia include: the Olympic Dam in South Australia – the world's largest uranium resource – and Super Pit gold mine, near Kalgoorlie, Western Australia.

Brisbane
Gold Coast
Newcastle
Sydney
Canberra
Adelaide
Melbourne
Perth

Minerals

Precious metals & stones
- ♧ Diamond
- ● Gold
- ✿ Silver

Iron & ferro-alloys
- ✤ Iron\Manganese
- ◀ Nickel

Non-ferrous metal
- ● Bauxite
- ◀ Copper\Lead\Zinc
- ◀ Tin\Tungsten
- ✦ Uranium

Heavy minerals
- ✿ Mineral Sands

Energy
- ★ Coal

- ✦ Other Minerals

Projection : Lambert's Equivalent Azimuthal

Scale 1:20 000 000

Mining in South Africa

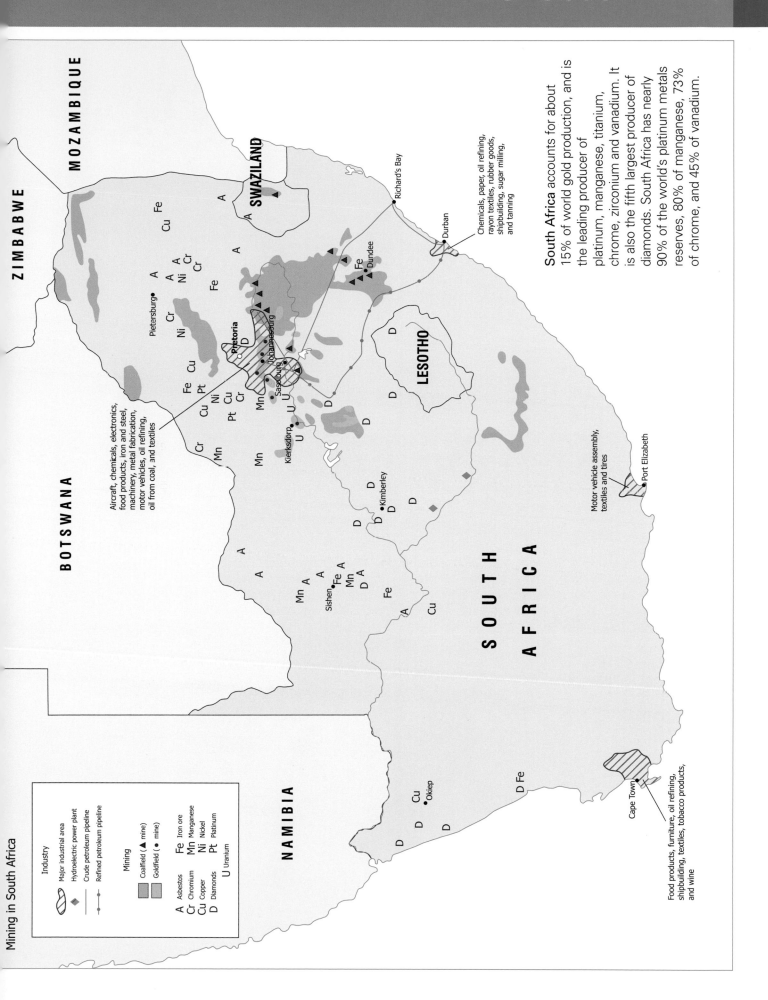

South Africa accounts for about 15% of world gold production, and is the leading producer of platinum, manganese, titanium, chrome, zirconium and vanadium. It is also the fifth largest producer of diamonds. South Africa has nearly 90% of the world's platinum metals reserves, 80% of manganese, 73% of chrome, and 45% of vanadium.

Chemicals, paper, oil refining, rayon textiles, rubber goods, shipbuilding, sugar milling, and tanning

Aircraft, chemicals, electronics, food products, iron and steel, machinery, metal fabrication, motor vehicles, oil refining, oil from coal, and textiles

Motor vehicle assembly, textiles and tires

Food products, furniture, oil refining, shipbuilding, textiles, tobacco products, and wine

ZIMBABWE

MOZAMBIQUE

BOTSWANA

NAMIBIA

SWAZILAND

LESOTHO

SOUTH AFRICA

Richard's Bay

Durban

Dundee

Pietersburg

Pretoria

Johannesburg

Sasolburg

Klerksdorp

Kimberley

Sishen

Okiep

Port Elizabeth

Cape Town

Industry

Major industrial area

Hydroelectric power plant

Crude petroleum pipeline

Refined petroleum pipeline

Mining

Coalfield (▲ mine)

Goldfield (● mine)

A Asbestos
Cr Chromium
Cu Copper
D Diamonds

Fe Iron ore
Mn Manganese
Ni Nickel
Pt Platinum

U Uranium

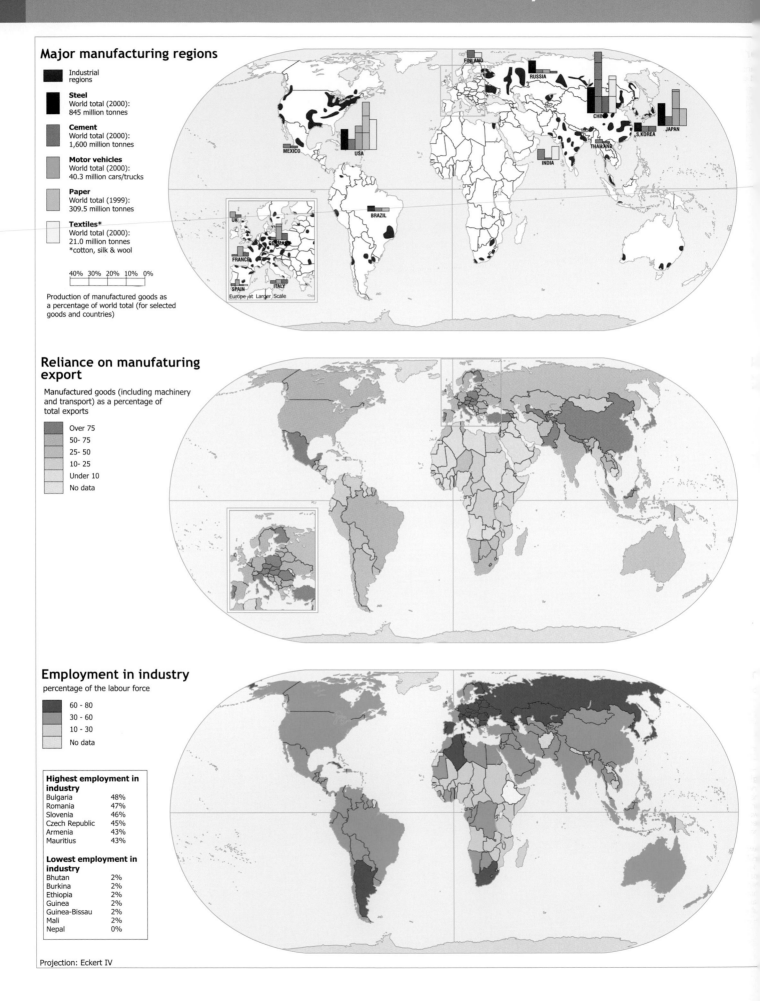

Major manufacturing regions

- Industrial regions
- **Steel** World total (2000): 845 million tonnes
- **Cement** World total (2000): 1,600 million tonnes
- **Motor vehicles** World total (2000): 40.3 million cars/trucks
- **Paper** World total (1999): 309.5 million tonnes
- **Textiles*** World total (2000): 21.0 million tonnes *cotton, silk & wool

40% 30% 20% 10% 0%

Production of manufactured goods as a percentage of world total (for selected goods and countries)

FINLAND · RUSSIA · CHINA · JAPAN · S.KOREA · THAILAND · INDIA · MEXICO · USA · BRAZIL

UK · GERMANY · FRANCE · SPAIN · ITALY
Europe at Larger Scale

Reliance on manufaturing export

Manufactured goods (including machinery and transport) as a percentage of total exports

- Over 75
- 50- 75
- 25- 50
- 10- 25
- Under 10
- No data

Employment in industry

percentage of the labour force

- 60 - 80
- 30 - 60
- 10 - 30
- No data

Highest employment in industry	
Bulgaria	48%
Romania	47%
Slovenia	46%
Czech Republic	45%
Armenia	43%
Mauritius	43%

Lowest employment in industry	
Bhutan	2%
Burkina	2%
Ethiopia	2%
Guinea	2%
Guinea-Bissau	2%
Mali	2%
Nepal	0%

Projection: Eckert IV

rld Trade

entage share of total
d exports by value

- Over 5
- 2.5 - 5
- 1 - 2.5
- 0.25 - 1
- 0.1 - 0.25
- Under 0.1
- No data

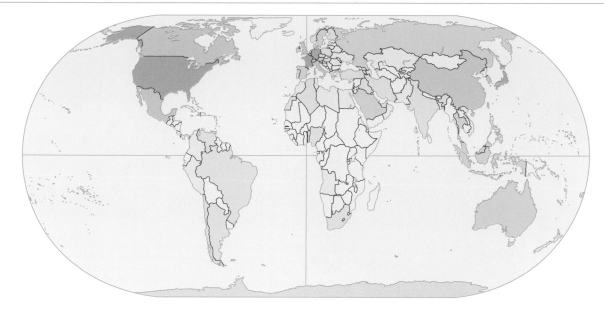

liance on trade

orts as a percentage
DP

- 50 and over
- 25- 50
- 10- 25
- 5- 10
- Under 5
- No data

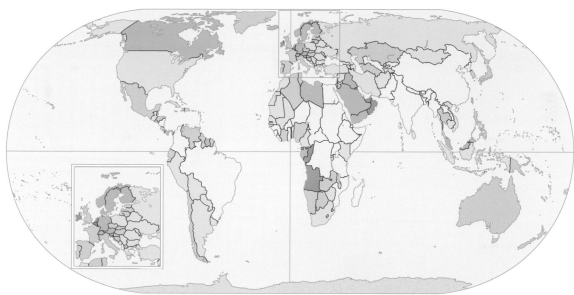

ployment in services

centage of the labour force

- 60 - 80
- 30 -60
- 10 - 30
- Under 10
- No data

ghest employment in services

hamas	79%
nei	74%
wait	74%
eden	74%
nada	72%

west employment in services

rkina	6%
pal	6%
er	6%
rundi	5%
anda	5%
utan	4%

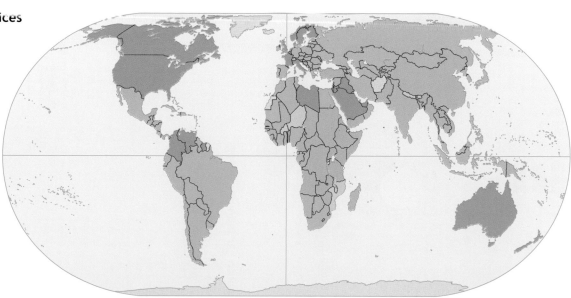

Scale: 1:262 000 000

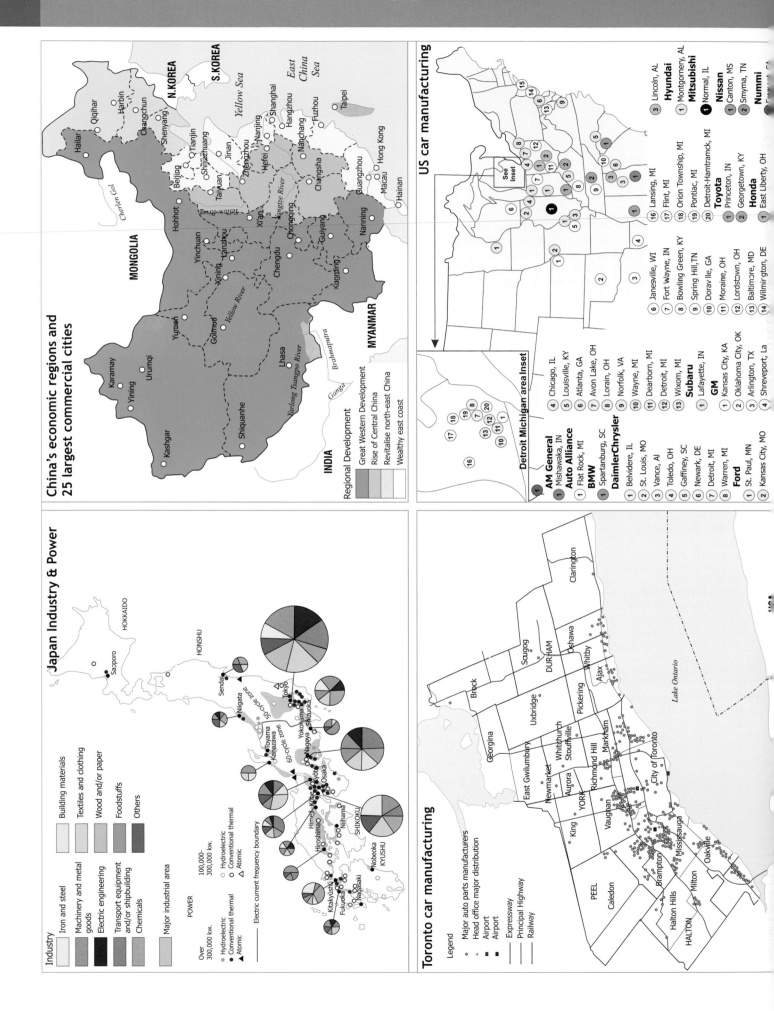

China's economic regions and 25 largest commercial cities

N.KOREA
S.KOREA

Qiqihar
Harbin
Hailar
Changchun
Shenyang
Yellow Sea
East China Sea

MONGOLIA

Hohhot
Beijing
Tianjin
Shijiazhuang
Taiyuan
Jinan
Zhengzhou
Nanjing
Shanghai
Hangzhou
Nanchang
Hefei
Fuzhou
Taipei

Yinchuan
Lanzhou
Xi'an
Chongqing
Changsha
Guangzhou
Macau
Hong Kong
Xining
Chengdu
Guiyang
Hainan
Kunming
Nanning

Yumen
Golmud
Yellow River
Lhasa
Yangtze River

Karamay
Urumqi
Yining
Yarlong Tsangpo River
Kashgar
Shiquanhe

Cherlen Gol
Tarim River
Brahmaputra
Ganga

INDIA
MYANMAR

Regional Development

Great Western Development
Rise of Central China
Revitalise north-east China
Wealthy east coast

US car manufacturing

See Inset

Detroit Michigan area Inset

AM General
(1) Mishawaka, IN
Auto Alliance
(1) Flat Rock, MI
BMW
(1) Spartanburg, SC
DaimlerChrysler
(1) Belvidere, IL
(2) St. Louis, MO
(3) Vance, Al
(4) Toledo, OH
(5) Gaffney, SC
(6) Newark, DE
(7) Detroit, MI
(8) Warren, MI
Ford
(1) St. Paul, MN
(2) Kansas City, MO

(3) Chicago, IL
(4) Louisville, KY
(5) Atlanta, GA
(6) Lorain, OH
(7) Avon Lake, OH
(8) Norfolk, VA
(9) Wayne, MI
(10) Dearborn, MI
(11) Detroit, MI
(12) Wixom, MI
(13) Lafayette, IN
GM
(1) Kansas City, KA
(2) Oklahoma City, OK
(3) Arlington, TX
(4) Shreveport, La

(5) Lansing, MI
(6) Janesville, WI
(7) Fort Wayne, IN
(8) Bowling Green, KY
(9) Spring Hill, TN
(10) Doraville, GA
(11) Moraine, OH
(12) Lordstown, OH
(13) Baltimore, MD
(14) Wilmington, DE
(15) Lincoln, AL
(16) Flint, MI
(17) Orion Township, MI
(18) Pontiac, MI
(19) Detroit-Hamtramck, MI
(20) Detroit-Hamtramck, MI

Hyundai
(3) Montgomery, AL
Toyota
(1) Princeton, IN
(2) Georgetown, KY
Honda
(1) East Liberty, OH

Mitsubishi
(1) Normal, IL
Nissan
(1) Canton, MS
(2) Smyrna, TN
Nummi
(1)

Japan Industry & Power

HOKKAIDO
Sapporo
HONSHU
Sendai
Niigata
50-cycle zone
60-cycle zone
Toyama
Takazawa
Yokohama
Shizuoka
Tokyo
Nagoya
Osaka
Kyoto
Kobe
Himeji
Hiroshima
Niihama
SHIKOKU
Kitakyushu
Fukuoka
Nagasaki
Nobeoka
KYUSHU

Industry

Iron and steel
Machinery and metal goods
Electric engineering
Transport equipment and/or shipbuilding
Chemicals
Major industrial area

Building materials
Textiles and clothing
Wood and/or paper
Foodstuffs
Others

POWER

Over 300,000 kw.
100,000–300,000 kw.

Hydroelectric
Conventional thermal
Atomic

○ Hydroelectric
○ Conventional thermal
△ Atomic

— Electric current frequency boundary

Toronto car manufacturing

Brock
Saugog
Scugog
Clarington
Oshawa
DURHAM
Whitby
Ajax
Uxbridge
Georgina
Whitchurch
Stouffville
Pickering
East Gwillumbury
Newmarket
Aurora
Richmond Hill
Markham
YORK
King
Vaughan
City of Toronto
Lake Ontario
Brampton
Caledon
PEEL
Mississauga
Milton
Oakville
Halton Hills
HALTON

Legend

Major auto parts manufacturers
Head office major distribution
Airport
Airport

Expressway
Principal Highway
Railway

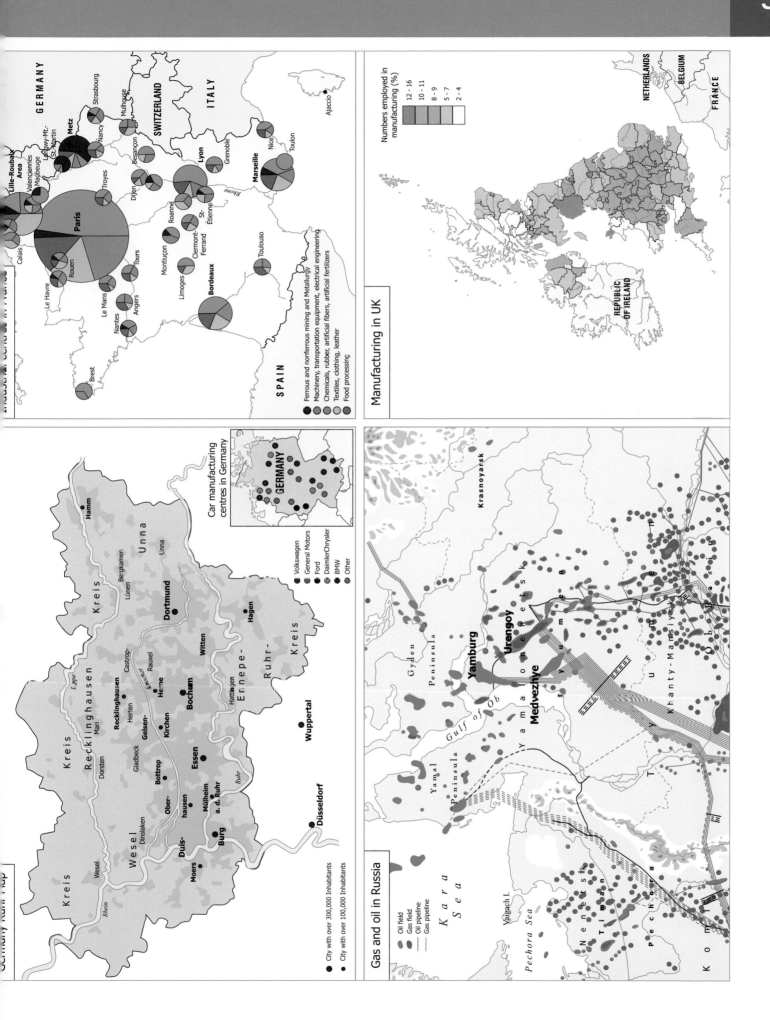

Industrial Centres in France

GERMANY

Lille-Roubaix Area
Calais
Valenciennes
Maubeuge
Longwy-Mt.-St.-Martin
Metz
Nancy
Strasbourg
Mulhouse
Le Havre
Rouen
Paris
Troyes
Dijon
Besançon
Brest
Le Mans
Angers
Nantes
Tours
Montluçon
Roanne
St-Étienne
Clermont-Ferrand
Lyon
Grenoble
Limoges
Toulouse
Bordeaux
Marseille
Nice
Toulon
Ajaccio

SWITZERLAND
ITALY
SPAIN

Rhône

- Ferrous and nonferrous mining and Metallurgy
- Machinery, transportation equipment, electrical engineering
- Chemicals, rubber, artificial fibers, artificial fertilizers
- Textiles, clothing, leather
- Food processing

Manufacturing in UK

Numbers employed in manufacturing (%)
- 12 - 16
- 10 - 11
- 8 - 9
- 5 - 7
- 2 - 4

NETHERLANDS
BELGIUM
FRANCE
REPUBLIC OF IRELAND

Germany Ruhr Map

GERMANY

Hamm
Kreis Unna
Bergkamen
Lünen
Unna
Dortmund
Hagen
Witten
Ennepe-Ruhr-Kreis
Hattingen
Herdecke
Kreis Recklinghausen
Dorsten
Marl
Recklinghausen
Herten
Gelsen-Kirchen
Herne
Castrop-Rauxel
Bochum
Gladbeck
Bottrop
Essen
Oberhausen
Mülheim a. d. Ruhr
Duis-Burg
Moers
Wesel
Dinslaken
Wuppertal
Düsseldorf

Lippe
Emscher
Ruhr
Rhein

Kreis Wesel
Kreis Recklinghausen

Car manufacturing centres in Germany
GERMANY
- Volkswagen
- General Motors
- Ford
- DaimlerChrysler
- BMW
- Other

● City with over 300,000 Inhabitants
• City with over 100,000 Inhabitants

Gas and oil in Russia

Krasnoyarsk

Gyden Peninsula
Yamburg
Urengoy
Medvezhye
Gulf of Ob
Yamal Peninsula
Yamalo-Nenetsk
Khanty-Mansiysk
Ob basin
Tyumen
Vaigach I.
Kara Sea
Pechora Sea
Nenetsk
Timan
Pechora
Komi

- Oil field
- Gas field
- Oil pipeline
- Gas pipeline

International organizations

- South Pacific Forum
- ASEAN Association of South East Asian Nations
- OAS Organization of American States
- Arab League
- OAU Organization of African Unity
- NATO North Atlantic Treaty Organization
- Council of Europe
- APEC Asia Pacific Economic Co-operation
- CIS Commonwealth of Independent States
- No data

Where more than one organization is involved the country is shown with interlocking shading

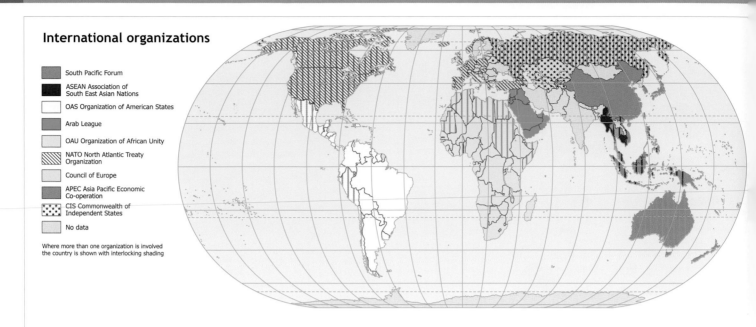

UNCTAD

United Nations Conference on Trade and Development

Almost all nations (191) are now members, Western Sahara is the only non-member

United Nations

The following countries are non-members
Northern Marianas
Taiwan
Vatican City
Western Sahara

Headquarters of selected World Organizations

Brussels:
The European Union
North Atlantic Treaty Organization (NATO)

The Hague:
International Court of Justice

New York:
United Nations

Paris:
United National Education, Scientific and Cultural Organization (UNESCO)

Organization for Economic Co-operation and Development (OECD)

Rome:
Food and Agricultural Organization of the United Nations (FAO)

Geneva:
World Health Organization (WHO)
World Trade Organization (WTO)

Washington:
Organization of American States (OAS)

Addis Ababa:
Organization of African Unity (OAU)

Cairo:
Arab League

Singapore:
Asia Pacific Economic Co-operation (APEC)

Strasbourg:
Council of Europe

European Parliament

Economic associations

- Colombo Plan
- OPEC Organization of Petroleum Exporting Countries
- OECD Organization for Economic Co-operation and Development
- CARICOM Caribbean Community and Common Market
- CACM Central American Common Market
- ALADI Latin American Integration Association
- Andean Community
- ECOWAS Economic Community of West African States
- UDEAC Central African Customs and Economic Union
- SADC Southern African Development Community
- No data

Where more than one organization is involved the country is shown with interlocking shading

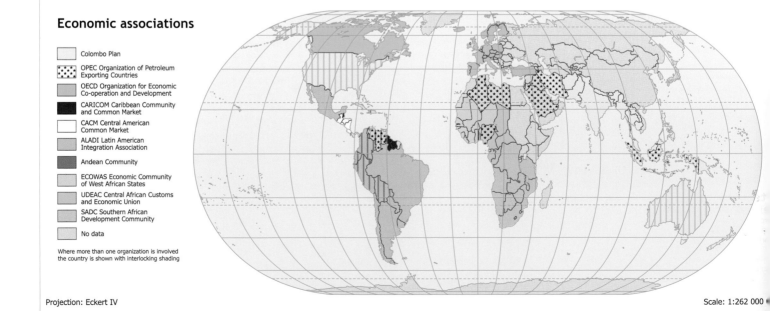

Projection: Eckert IV

Scale: 1:262 000

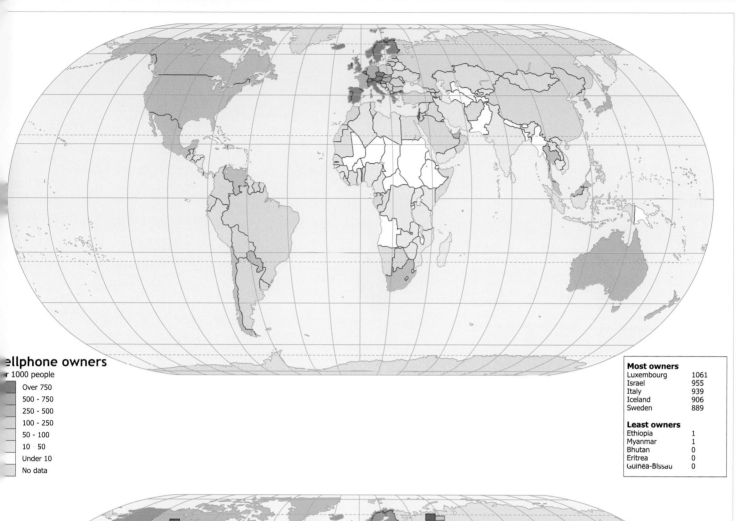

Cellphone owners
per 1000 people

- Over 750
- 500 - 750
- 250 - 500
- 100 - 250
- 50 - 100
- 10   50
- Under 10
- No data

Most owners	
Luxembourg	1061
Israel	955
Italy	939
Iceland	906
Sweden	889

Least owners	
Ethiopia	1
Myanmar	1
Bhutan	0
Eritrea	0
Guinea-Bissau	0

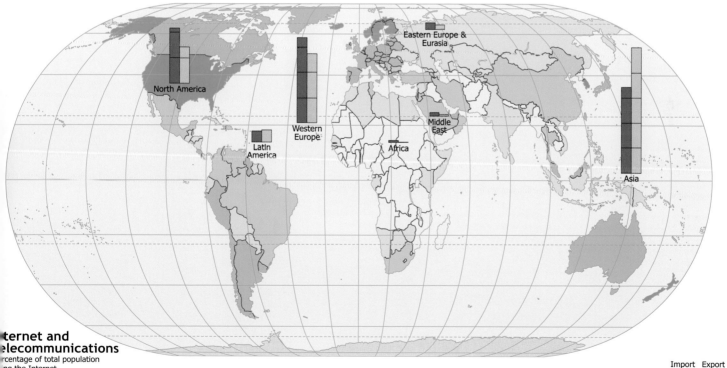

Internet and Telecommunications
Percentage of total population using the Internet
World total 1,604.1 million Internet users

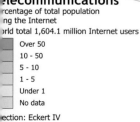

- Over 50
- 10 - 50
- 5 - 10
- 1 - 5
- Under 1
- No data

Projection: Eckert IV

Telecommunications

Trade in office machines and telecom equipment, percentage of world total

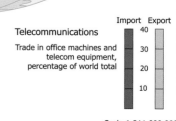

Scale 1:211 000 000

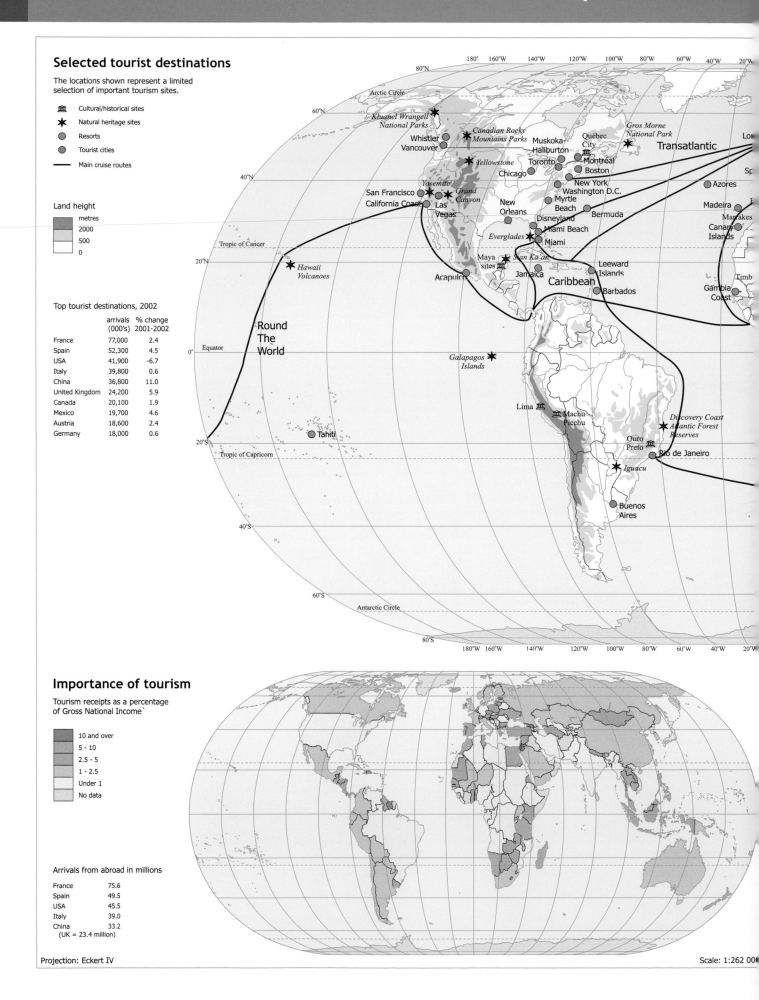

Selected tourist destinations

The locations shown represent a limited selection of important tourism sites.

- Cultural/historical sites
- Natural heritage sites
- Resorts
- Tourist cities
- Main cruise routes

Land height

metres
2000
500
0

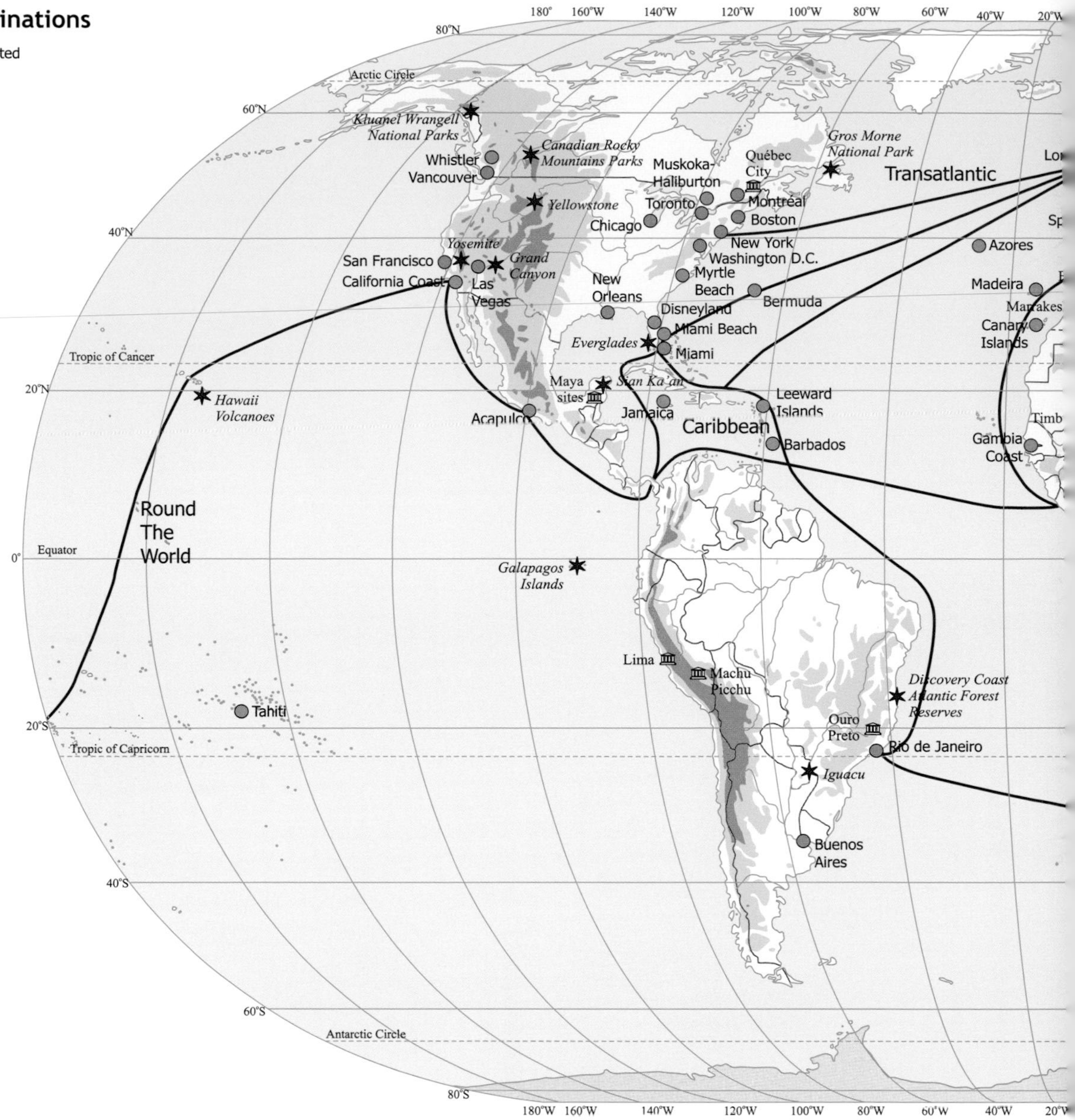

Arctic Circle
Tropic of Cancer
Equator
Tropic of Capricorn
Antarctic Circle
Kluanel Wrangell National Parks
Canadian Rocky Mountains Parks
Whistler
Vancouver
Yellowstone
Yosemite
San Francisco
California Coast
Las Vegas
Grand Canyon
Chicago
Toronto
Muskoka-Haliburton
Québec City
Montréal
Boston
New York
Washington D.C.
Myrtle Beach
Gros Morne National Park
Transatlantic
New Orleans
Disneyland
Miami Beach
Miami
Everglades
Bermuda
Azores
Madeira
Canary Islands
Gambia Coast
Maya sites
Sian Ka'an
Jamaica
Caribbean
Leeward Islands
Barbados
Acapulco
Hawaii Volcanoes
Round The World
Galapagos Islands
Tahiti
Lima
Machu Picchu
Discovery Coast Atlantic Forest Reserves
Ouro Preto
Rio de Janeiro
Iguacu
Buenos Aires

Top tourist destinations, 2002

	arrivals (000's)	% change 2001-2002
France	77,000	2.4
Spain	52,300	4.5
USA	41,900	-6.7
Italy	39,800	0.6
China	36,800	11.0
United Kingdom	24,200	5.9
Canada	20,100	1.9
Mexico	19,700	4.6
Austria	18,600	2.4
Germany	18,000	0.6

Importance of tourism

Tourism receipts as a percentage of Gross National Income`

- 10 and over
- 5 - 10
- 2.5 - 5
- 1 - 2.5
- Under 1
- No data

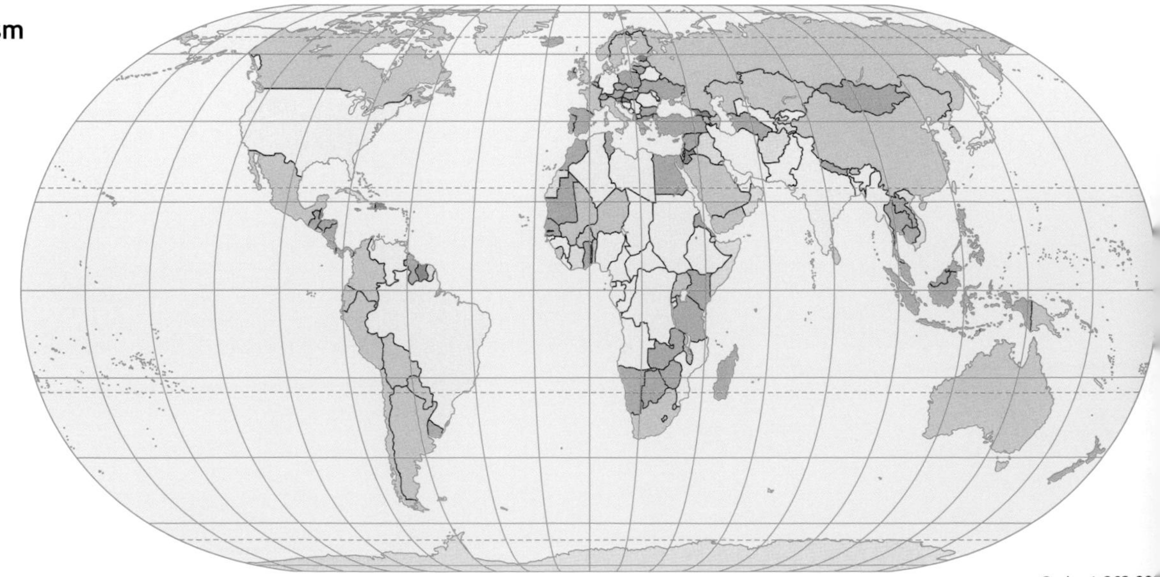

Arrivals from abroad in millions

France	75.6
Spain	49.5
USA	45.5
Italy	39.0
China	33.2

(UK = 23.4 million)

Projection: Eckert IV

Scale: 1:262 00

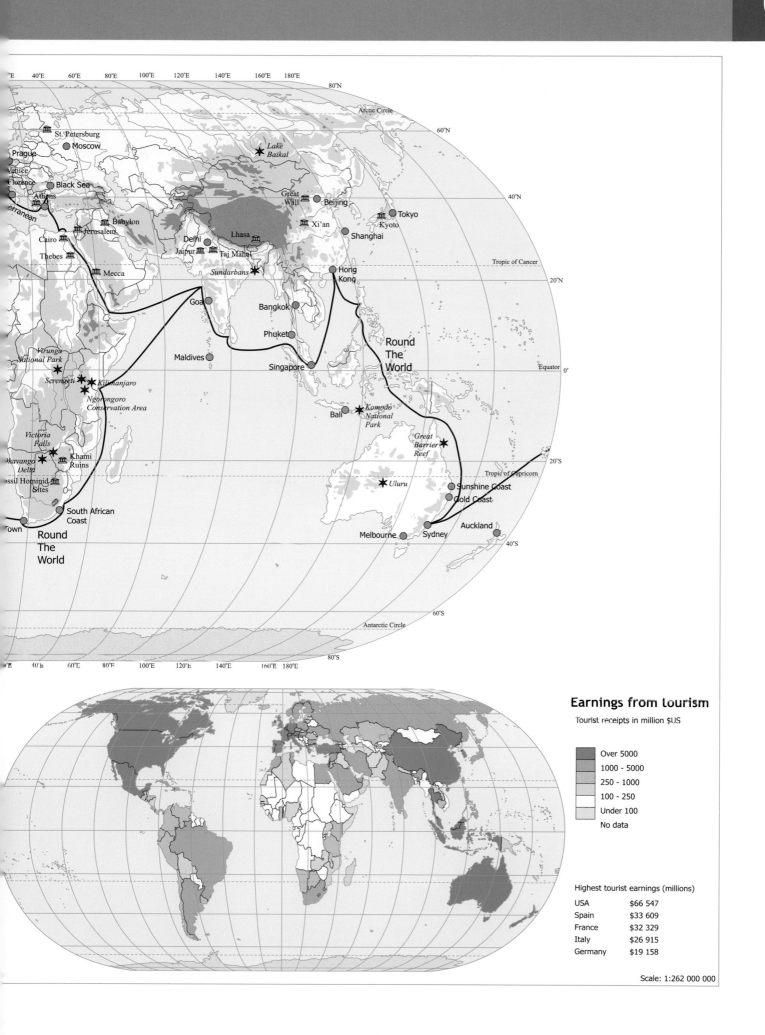

St. Petersburg
Moscow
Prague
Venice
Florence
Black Sea
Athens
terranean
Babylon
Jerusalem
Cairo
Thebes
Mecca

Lake Baikal
Great Wall
Beijing
Xi'an
Tokyo
Kyoto
Shanghai
Hong Kong

Delhi
Jaipur
Taj Mahal
Lhasa
Sundarbans

Goa
Bangkok
Phuket
Maldives
Singapore

Round The World

Virunga National Park
Serengeti
Kilimanjaro
Ngorongoro Conservation Area
Victoria Falls
kavango Delta
Khami Ruins
ssil Hominid Sites
South African Coast
Town
Round The World

Bali
Komodo National Park
Great Barrier Reef
Uluru
Sunshine Coast
Gold Coast
Melbourne
Sydney
Auckland

Arctic Circle
80°N
60°N
40°N
Tropic of Cancer
20°N
Equator   0°
Tropic of Capricorn
20°S
40°S
60°S
Antarctic Circle
80°S

40°E 60°E 80°E 100°E 120°E 140°E 160°E 180°E

Earnings from tourism

Tourist receipts in million $US

	Over 5000
	1000 - 5000
	250 - 1000
	100 - 250
	Under 100
	No data

Highest tourist earnings (millions)

USA	$66 547
Spain	$33 609
France	$32 329
Italy	$26 915
Germany	$19 158

Scale: 1:262 000 000

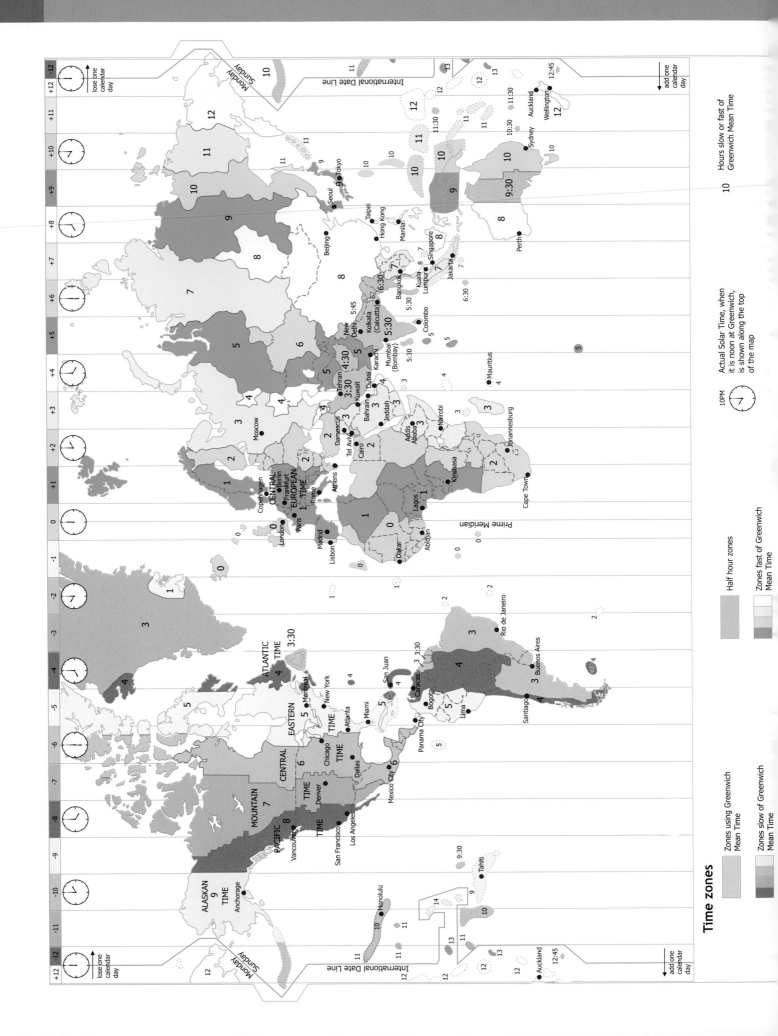

Time zones

Half hour zones — Zones using Greenwich Mean Time

Zones fast of Greenwich Mean Time

Zones slow of Greenwich Mean Time

10 — Hours slow or fast of Greenwich Mean Time

Actual Solar Time, when it is noon at Greenwich, is shown along the top of the map

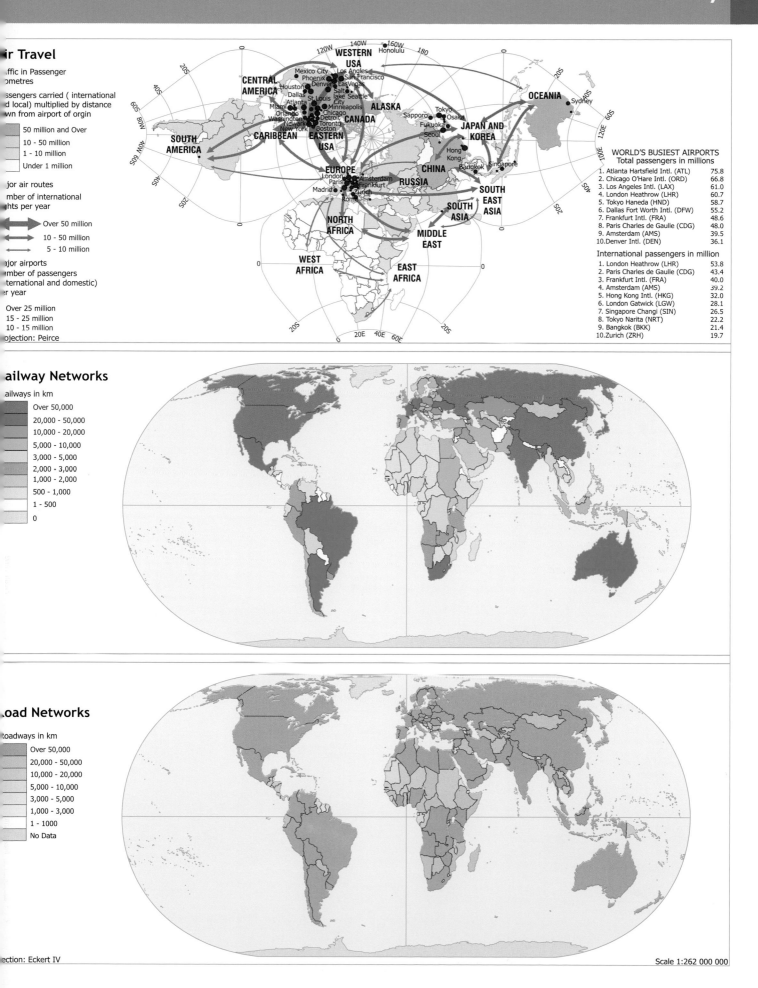

Air Travel

Traffic in Passenger Kilometres

Passengers carried (international and local) multiplied by distance flown from airport of orgin

- 50 million and Over
- 10 - 50 million
- 1 - 10 million
- Under 1 million

Major air routes
Number of international flights per year

- Over 50 million
- 10 - 50 million
- 5 - 10 million

Major airports
Number of passengers (international and domestic) per year

- Over 25 million
- 15 - 25 million
- 10 - 15 million

Projection: Peirce

WORLD'S BUSIEST AIRPORTS
Total passengers in millions

1. Atlanta Hartsfield Intl. (ATL)	75.8
2. Chicago O'Hare Intl. (ORD)	66.8
3. Los Angeles Intl. (LAX)	61.0
4. London Heathrow (LHR)	60.7
5. Tokyo Haneda (HND)	58.7
6. Dallas Fort Worth Intl. (DFW)	55.2
7. Frankfurt Intl. (FRA)	48.6
8. Paris Charles de Gaulle (CDG)	48.0
9. Amsterdam (AMS)	39.5
10.Denver Intl. (DEN)	36.1

International passengers in million

1. London Heathrow (LHR)	53.8
2. Paris Charles de Gaulle (CDG)	43.4
3. Frankfurt Intl. (FRA)	40.0
4. Amsterdam (AMS)	39.2
5. Hong Kong Intl. (HKG)	32.0
6. London Gatwick (LGW)	28.1
7. Singapore Changi (SIN)	26.5
8. Tokyo Narita (NRT)	22.2
9. Bangkok (BKK)	21.4
10.Zurich (ZRH)	19.7

Railway Networks

Railways in km

- Over 50,000
- 20,000 - 50,000
- 10,000 - 20,000
- 5,000 - 10,000
- 3,000 - 5,000
- 2,000 - 3,000
- 1,000 - 2,000
- 500 - 1,000
- 1 - 500
- 0

Road Networks

Roadways in km

- Over 50,000
- 20,000 - 50,000
- 10,000 - 20,000
- 5,000 - 10,000
- 3,000 - 5,000
- 1,000 - 3,000
- 1 - 1000
- No Data

Projection: Eckert IV

Scale 1:262 000 000

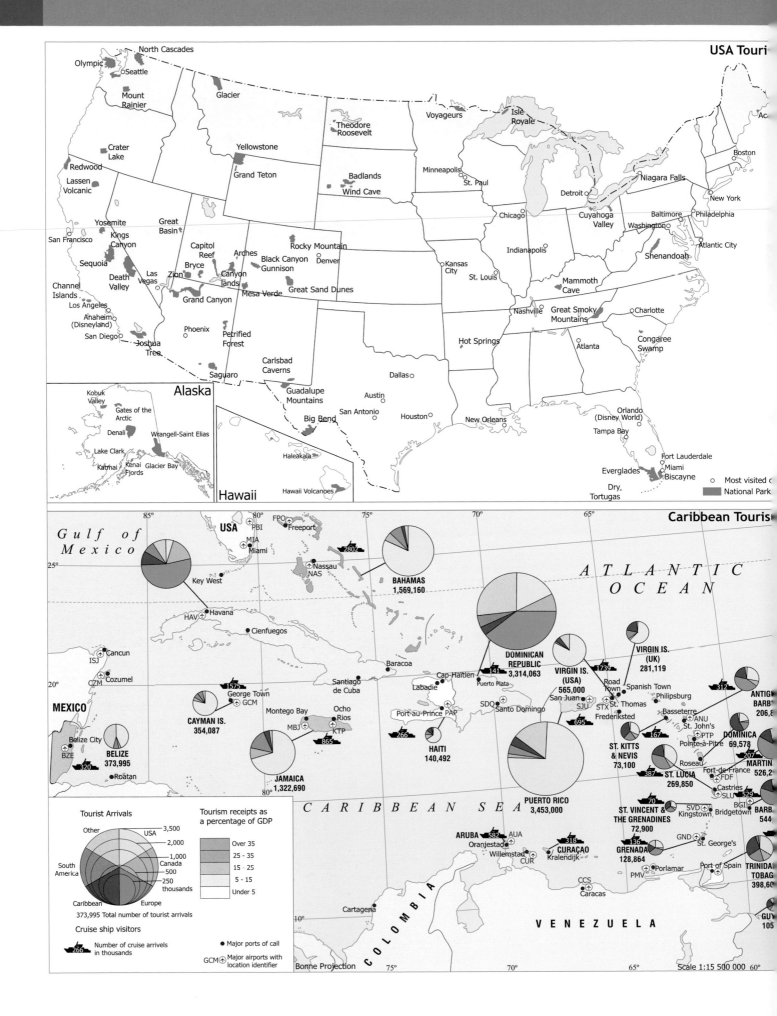

USA Touri

North Cascades
Olympic
Seattle
Mount Rainier
Glacier
Voyageurs
Isle Royale
Ac
Boston
Crater Lake
Redwood
Lassen Volcanic
Theodore Roosevelt
Yellowstone
Grand Teton
Badlands
Wind Cave
Minneapolis
St. Paul
Detroit
Niagara Falls
New York
Chicago
Cuyahoga Valley
Baltimore
Philadelphia
Washington
Atlantic City
Yosemite
Great Basin
Kings Canyon
San Francisco
Sequoia
Death Valley
Channel Islands
Los Angeles
Anaheim (Disneyland)
San Diego
Las Vegas
Zion
Bryce
Capitol Reef
Arches
Canyon lands
Mesa Verde
Rocky Mountain
Denver
Black Canyon Gunnison
Great Sand Dunes
Indianapolis
Kansas City
St. Louis
Mammoth Cave
Shenandoah
Nashville
Great Smoky Mountains
Charlotte
Congaree Swamp
Grand Canyon
Phoenix
Petrified Forest
Joshua Tree
Saguaro
Carlsbad Caverns
Guadalupe Mountains
Big Bend
Austin
San Antonio
Dallas
Houston
Hot Springs
Atlanta
New Orleans
Orlando (Disney World)
Tampa Bay
Fort Lauderdale
Miami
Biscayne
Everglades
Dry Tortugas

Alaska

Kobuk Valley
Gates of the Arctic
Denali
Wrangell-Saint Elias
Lake Clark
Katmai
Kenai Fjords
Glacier Bay

Haleakala

Hawaii

Hawaii Volcanoes

○ Most visited c
National Park

Caribbean Touris

Gulf of Mexico

USA
FPO ⊕ Freeport
PBI ⊕
MIA ⊕ Miami
Key West
🚢 280
Nassau
NAS ⊕
BAHAMAS
1,569,160

25°

A T L A N T I C O C E A N

HAV ⊕ Havana
Cienfuegos
Cancun
ISJ ⊕
CZM ⊕ Cozumel
Baracoa
Santiago de Cuba
Cap-Haïtien
🚢 141
Puerto Plata
DOMINICAN REPUBLIC
3,314,063
VIRGIN IS. (UK)
281,119
🚢 1739
Road Town
Spanish Town
Philipsburg

MEXICO

George Town ⊕ GCM
🚢 1575
CAYMAN IS.
354,087
Montego Bay
MBJ ⊕
🚢 865
Ocho Rios
KTP ⊕
Labadie
Port-au-Prince PAP ⊕
🚢 266
SDO ⊕
Santo Domingo
VIRGIN IS. (USA)
565,000
San Juan
SJU ⊕
🚢 695
St. Thomas
STX ⊕
Frederiksted
Basseterre
ANU ⊕
St. John's
🚢 312
ANTIG BARB
206,8

20°

Belize City
BZE ⊕
BELIZE
373,995
🚢 320
Roatan
JAMAICA
1,322,690
HAITI
140,492
🚢 387
🚢 167
PTP ⊕ Pointe-à-Pitre
DOMINICA
69,578
ST. KITTS & NEVIS
73,100
PUERTO RICO
3,453,000
ST. LUCIA
269,850
Roseau
🚢 207
MARTIN
526,2
FDF ⊕ Fort-de-France
Castries
SLU ⊕
🚢 529

80°

C A R I B B E A N   S E A

ST. VINCENT & THE GRENADINES
72,900
🚢 70
SVD ⊕
Kingstown
BGI ⊕ Bridgetown
BARB
544

ARUBA
AUA ⊕
🚢 582
Oranjestad
CURAÇAO
128,864
🚢 318
Willemstad
CUR ⊕
Kralendijk
GRENADA
🚢 136
GND ⊕
St. George's
Port of Spain
POS ⊕
TRINIDA TOBAG
398,6
PMV ⊕ Porlamar

10°

Cartagena

C O L O M B I A

CCS ⊕
Caracas

GU
105

V E N E Z U E L A

Tourist Arrivals

Other
USA
3,500
2,000
1,000
Canada
500
250 thousands
South America
Caribbean
Europe
373,995 Total number of tourist arrivals

Tourism receipts as a percentage of GDP

Over 35
25 - 35
15 - 25
5 - 15
Under 5

Cruise ship visitors

🚢 266   Number of cruise arrivals in thousands

● Major ports of call

GCM ⊕   Major airports with location identifier

Bonne Projection   75°   70°   65°   Scale 1:15 500 000   60°

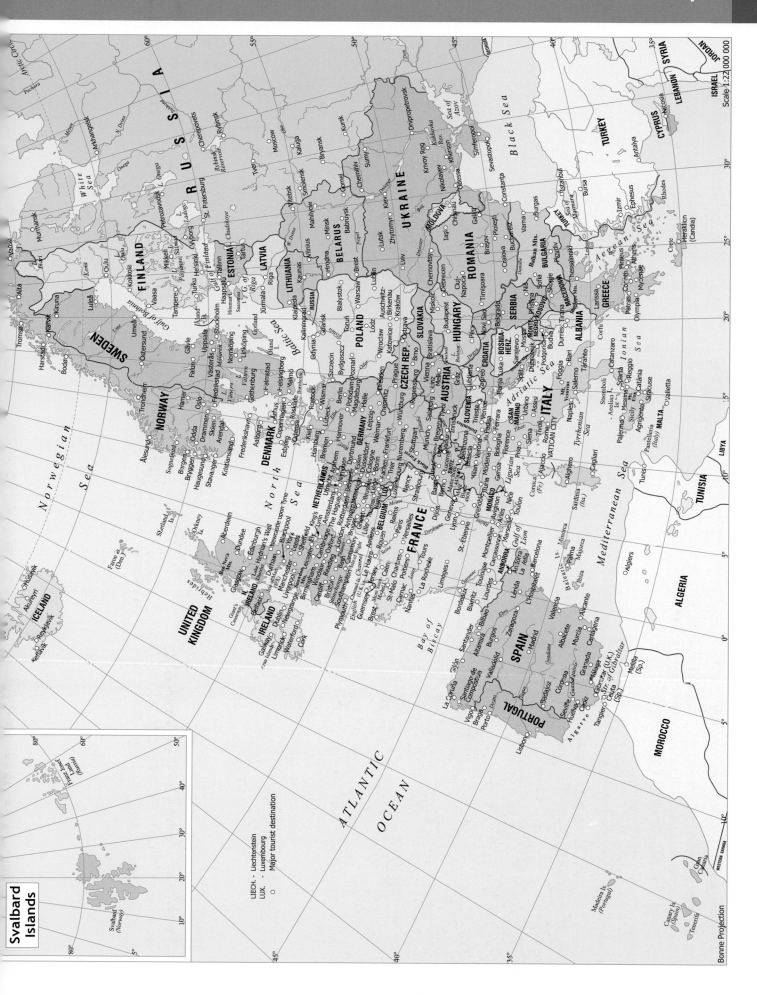

Scale 1:22 000 000

LIECH. - Liechtenstein
LUX. - Luxembourg
○ Major tourist destination

Svalbard Islands

Bonne Projection

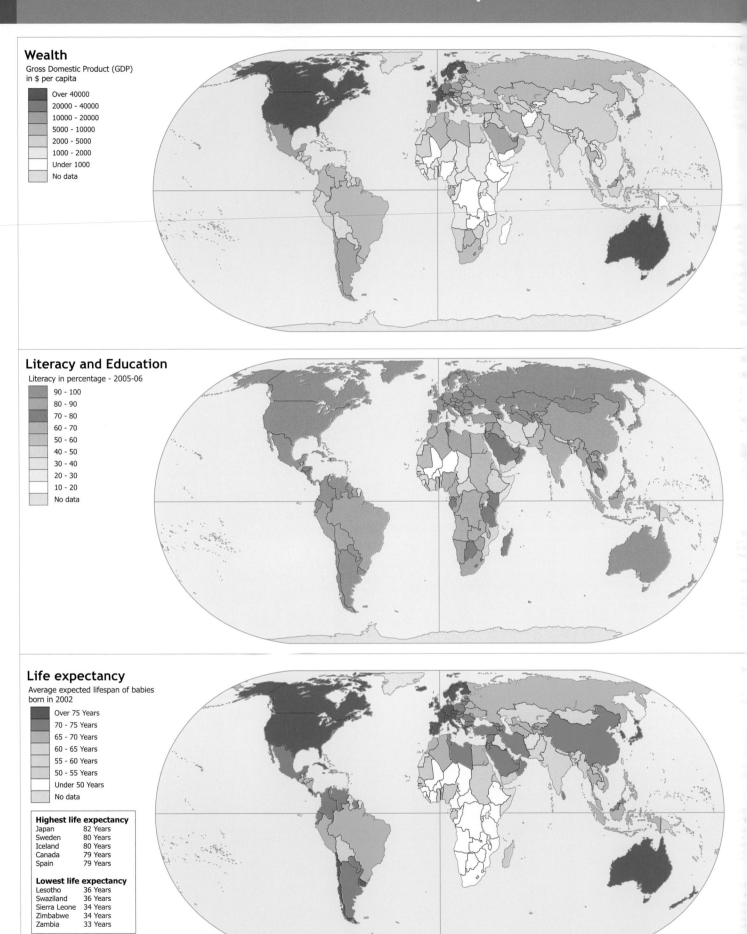

Wealth

Gross Domestic Product (GDP)
in $ per capita

- Over 40000
- 20000 - 40000
- 10000 - 20000
- 5000 - 10000
- 2000 - 5000
- 1000 - 2000
- Under 1000
- No data

Literacy and Education

Literacy in percentage - 2005-06

- 90 - 100
- 80 - 90
- 70 - 80
- 60 - 70
- 50 - 60
- 40 - 50
- 30 - 40
- 20 - 30
- 10 - 20
- No data

Life expectancy

Average expected lifespan of babies
born in 2002

- Over 75 Years
- 70 - 75 Years
- 65 - 70 Years
- 60 - 65 Years
- 55 - 60 Years
- 50 - 55 Years
- Under 50 Years
- No data

Highest life expectancy

Japan	82 Years
Sweden	80 Years
Iceland	80 Years
Canada	79 Years
Spain	79 Years

Lowest life expectancy

Lesotho	36 Years
Swaziland	36 Years
Sierra Leone	34 Years
Zimbabwe	34 Years
Zambia	33 Years

Projection: Eckert IV

Scale: 1:262 000

Human Development Index (HDI)

HDI (calculated by the UNDP) gives a value to countries using indicators of life expectancy, education and standards of living in 2000. Higher values show more developed countries

- 0.9 and Over
- 0.8 - 0.9
- 0.7 - 0.8
- 0.4 - 0.7
- Under 0.4
- No data

Highest values
Norway	0.942
Sweden	0.941
Canada	0.940
USA	0.939
Belgium	0.939

Lowest values
Sierra Leone	0.275
Niger	0.277
Burundi	0.313
Mozambique	0.322
Burkina Faso	0.325

(UK = 0.928)

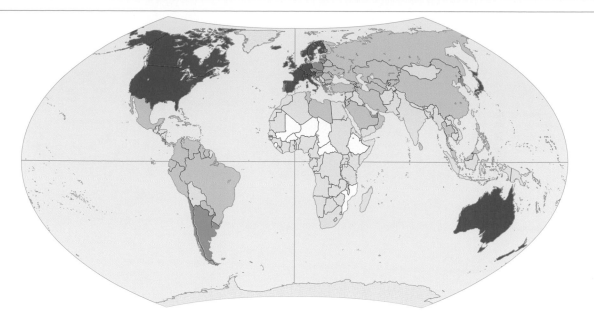

Gender Development Index (GDI)

GDI shows economic and social differences between men and women by using various UNDP indicators (2002). Countries with higher values of GDI have more equality between men and women

- 0.8 and Over
- 0.6 - 0.8
- 0.4 - 0.6
- Under 0.4
- No data

Highest values
Norway	0.941
Australia	0.938
Canada	0.938
USA	0.937
Sweden	0.936

Lowest values
Niger	0.263
Burundi	0.306
Mozambique	0.307
Burkina Faso	0.312
Ethiopia	0.313

(UK = 0.925)

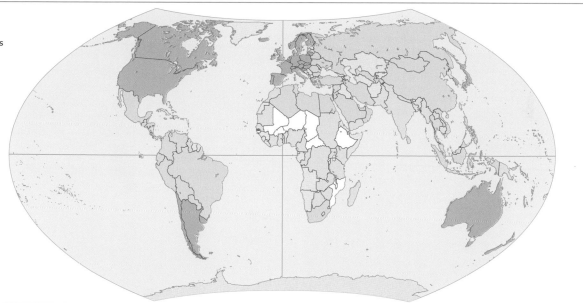

Health Care

Number of people per qualified doctor

- Over 15000
- 5000 - 15000
- 1000 - 5000
- 500 - 1000
- Under 500
- No data

Least number of people per qualified doctor
Italy	169
Saint Lucia	193
Belarus	219
Belgium	222
Estonia	223

Most number of people per qualified doctor
Tanzania	50,000
Malawi	50,000
Niger	50,000
Burundi	33,333
Ethiopia	33,333

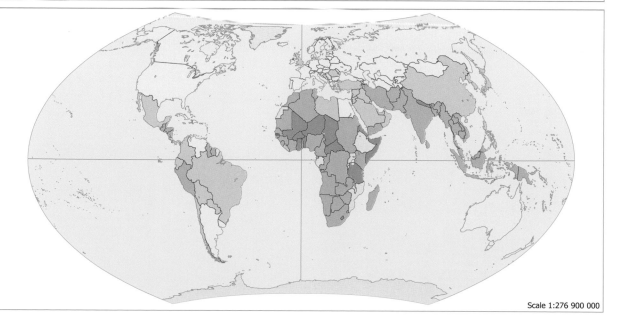

Scale 1:276 900 000

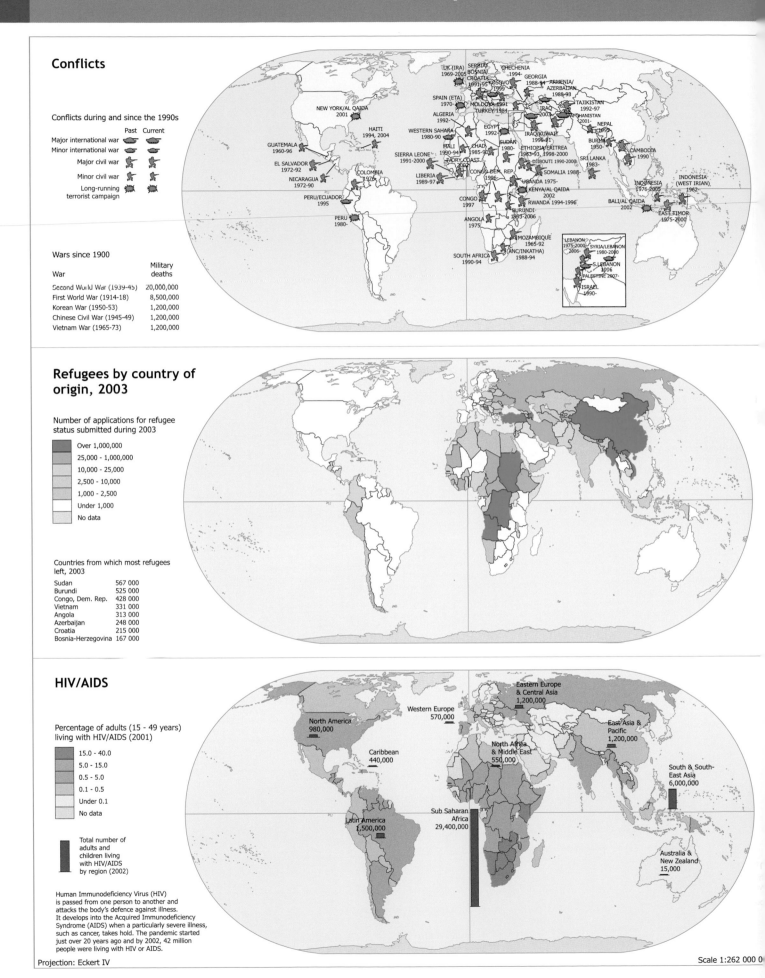

Conflicts

Conflicts during and since the 1990s

	Past	Current
Major international war		
Minor international war		
Major civil war		
Minor civil war		
Long-running terrorist campaign		

Wars since 1900

War	Military deaths
Second World War (1939-45)	20,000,000
First World War (1914-18)	8,500,000
Korean War (1950-53)	1,200,000
Chinese Civil War (1945-49)	1,200,000
Vietnam War (1965-73)	1,200,000

Map labels: NEW YORK/AL QAIDA 2001; UK (IRA) 1969-2005; SERBIA/BOSNIA/CROATIA 1991-95; KOSOVO 1999; CHECHENIA 1994; GEORGIA 1988-94; ARMENIA/AZERBAIJAN 1988-93; SPAIN (ETA) 1970-; MOLDOVA 1991; TURKEY 1984; IRAQ 2003; TAJIKISTAN 1992-97; AFGHANISTAN 2001-; NEPAL 1995; HAITI 1994, 2004; ALGERIA 1992; WESTERN SAHARA 1980-90; EGYPT 1992; IRAQ/KUWAIT 1990-91; BURMA 1950-; GUATEMALA 1960-96; MALI 1990-94; CHAD 1985-90; SUDAN 1980-; ETHIOPIA/ERITREA 1963-93, 1998-2000; SRI LANKA 1983-; CAMBODIA 1990; EL SALVADOR 1972-92; SIERRA LEONE 1991-2000; IVORY COAST 2002; DJIBOUTI 1990-2000; NICARAGUA 1972-90; COLOMBIA 1976-; LIBERIA 1989-97; CONGO, DEM. REP. 1996-; SOMALIA 1988-; UGANDA 1975-; INDONESIA 1976-2005; INDONESIA (WEST IRIAN) 1962-; PERU/ECUADOR 1995; KENYA/AL QAIDA 2002; BALI/AL QAIDA 2002; EAST TIMOR 1975-2000; PERU 1980-; CONGO 1997; RWANDA 1994-1996; BURUNDI 1993-2006; ANGOLA 1975; MOZAMBIQUE 1965-92; ANC/INKATHA 1988-94; SOUTH AFRICA 1990-94; LEBANON 1975-2000; SYRIA/LEBANON 1980-2000; S. LEBANON 1996; PALESTINE 2007-; ISRAEL 1990-

Refugees by country of origin, 2003

Number of applications for refugee status submitted during 2003

- Over 1,000,000
- 25,000 - 1,000,000
- 10,000 - 25,000
- 2,500 - 10,000
- 1,000 - 2,500
- Under 1,000
- No data

Countries from which most refugees left, 2003

Sudan	567 000
Burundi	525 000
Congo, Dem. Rep.	428 000
Vietnam	331 000
Angola	313 000
Azerbaijan	248 000
Croatia	215 000
Bosnia-Herzegovina	167 000

HIV/AIDS

Percentage of adults (15 - 49 years) living with HIV/AIDS (2001)

- 15.0 - 40.0
- 5.0 - 15.0
- 0.5 - 5.0
- 0.1 - 0.5
- Under 0.1
- No data

Total number of adults and children living with HIV/AIDS by region (2002)

Map labels: North America 980,000; Western Europe 570,000; Eastern Europe & Central Asia 1,200,000; East Asia & Pacific 1,200,000; Caribbean 440,000; North Africa & Middle East 550,000; South & South-East Asia 6,000,000; Latin America 1,500,000; Sub Saharan Africa 29,400,000; Australia & New Zealand 15,000

Human Immunodeficiency Virus (HIV) is passed from one person to another and attacks the body's defence against illness. It develops into the Acquired Immunodeficiency Syndrome (AIDS) when a particularly severe illness, such as cancer, takes hold. The pandemic started just over 20 years ago and by 2002, 42 million people were living with HIV or AIDS.

Projection: Eckert IV

Scale 1:262 000 0

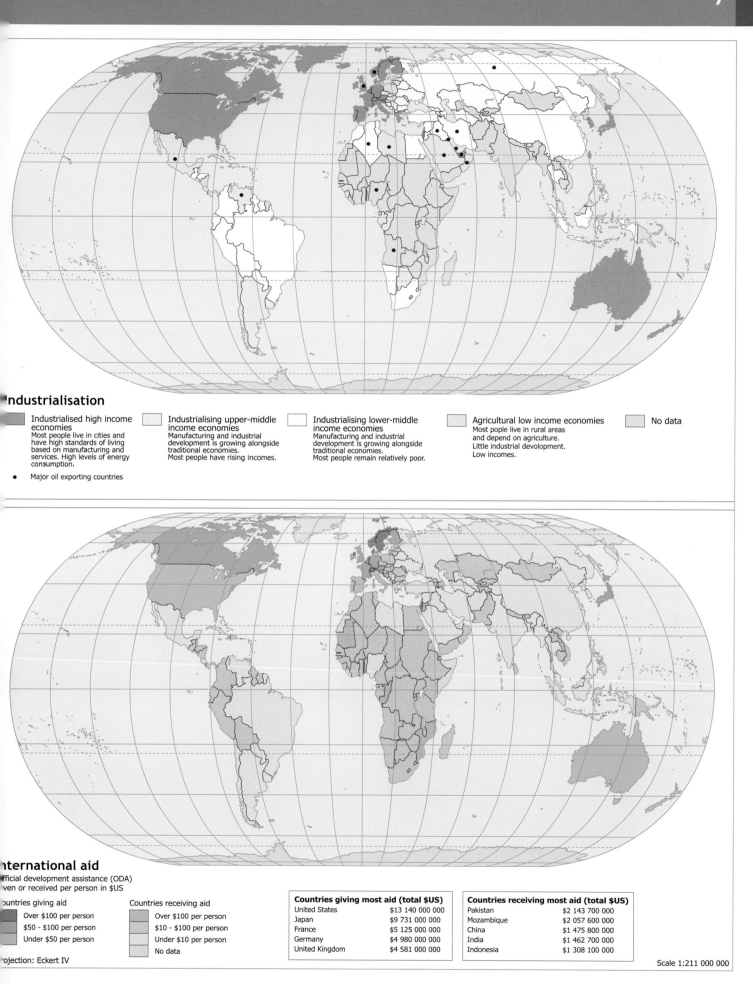

Industrialisation

■	**Industrialised high income economies** Most people live in cities and have high standards of living based on manufacturing and services. High levels of energy consumption.	**Industrialising upper-middle income economies** Manufacturing and industrial development is growing alongside traditional economies. Most people have rising incomes.	**Industrialising lower-middle income economies** Manufacturing and industrial development is growing alongside traditional economies. Most people remain relatively poor.	**Agricultural low income economies** Most people live in rural areas and depend on agriculture. Little industrial development. Low incomes.	**No data**

● Major oil exporting countries

International aid

Official development assistance (ODA)
given or received per person in $US

Countries giving aid
- Over $100 per person
- $50 - $100 per person
- Under $50 per person

Countries receiving aid
- Over $100 per person
- $10 - $100 per person
- Under $10 per person
- No data

Projection: Eckert IV

Countries giving most aid (total $US)	
United States	$13 140 000 000
Japan	$9 731 000 000
France	$5 125 000 000
Germany	$4 980 000 000
United Kingdom	$4 581 000 000

Countries receiving most aid (total $US)	
Pakistan	$2 143 700 000
Mozambique	$2 057 600 000
China	$1 475 800 000
India	$1 462 700 000
Indonesia	$1 308 100 000

Scale 1:211 000 000

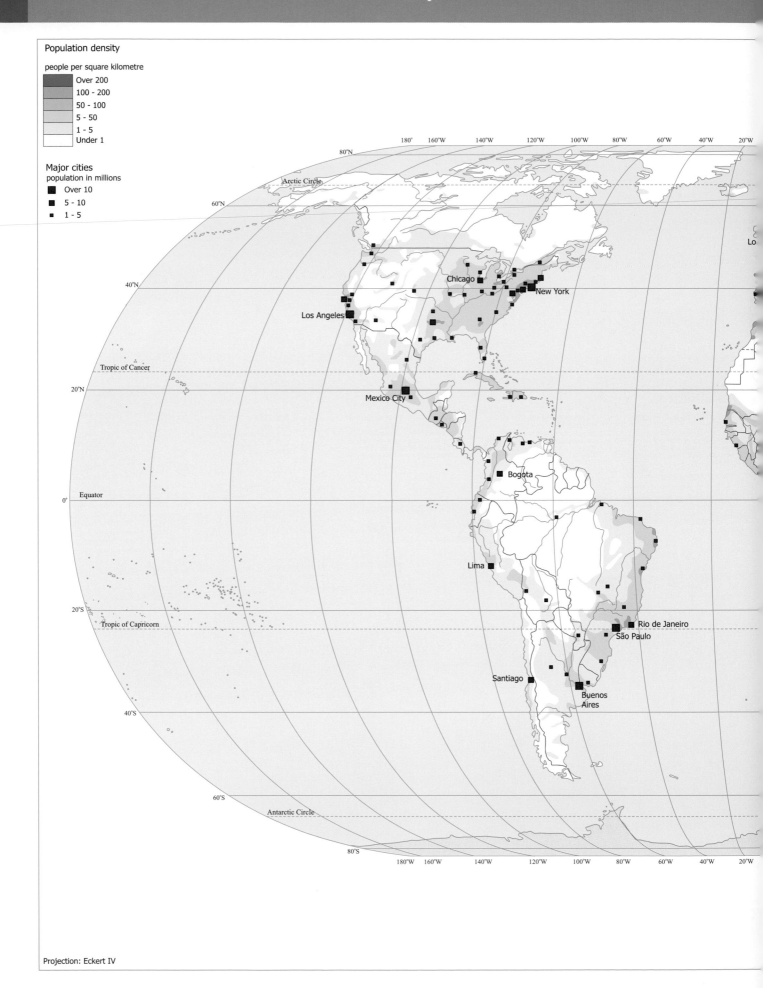

Population density

people per square kilometre

- Over 200
- 100 - 200
- 50 - 100
- 5 - 50
- 1 - 5
- Under 1

Major cities
population in millions

- Over 10
- 5 - 10
- 1 - 5

Projection: Eckert IV

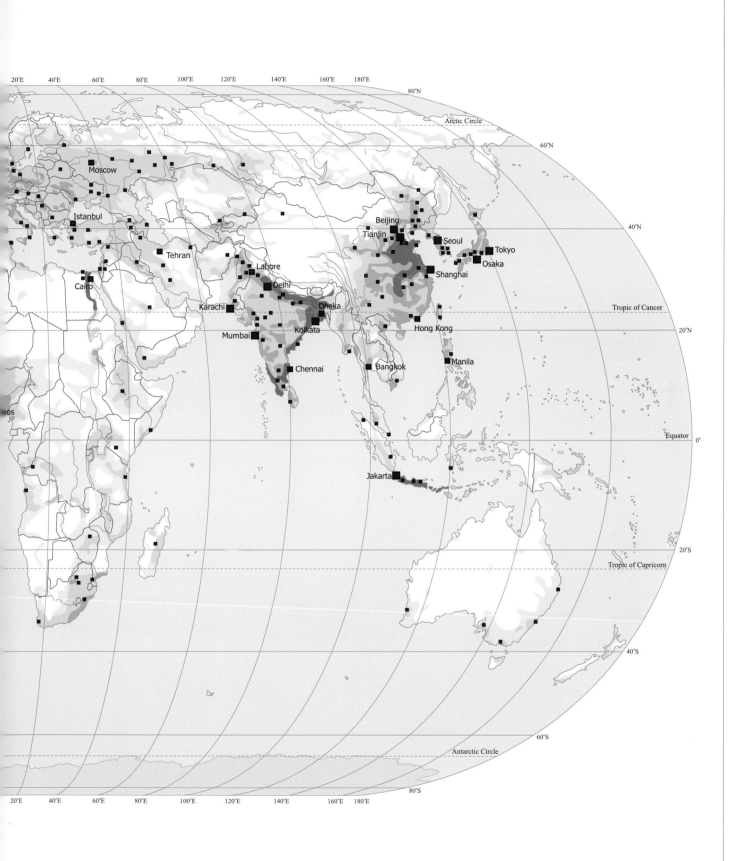

20°E 40°E 60°E 80°E 100°E 120°E 140°E 160°E 180°E

80°N

Arctic Circle

60°N

Moscow

40°N

Istanbul

Beijing

Tianjin

Seoul

Tokyo

Tehran

Osaka

Lahore

Shanghai

Delhi

Cairo

Tropic of Cancer

Karachi

Dhaka

20°N

Mumbai

Kolkata

Hong Kong

Chennai

Bangkok

Manila

Equator 0°

Jakarta

20°S

Tropic of Capricorn

40°S

60°S

Antarctic Circle

80°S

20°E 40°E 60°E 80°E 100°E 120°E 140°E 160°E 180°E

Scale: 1:105 000 000

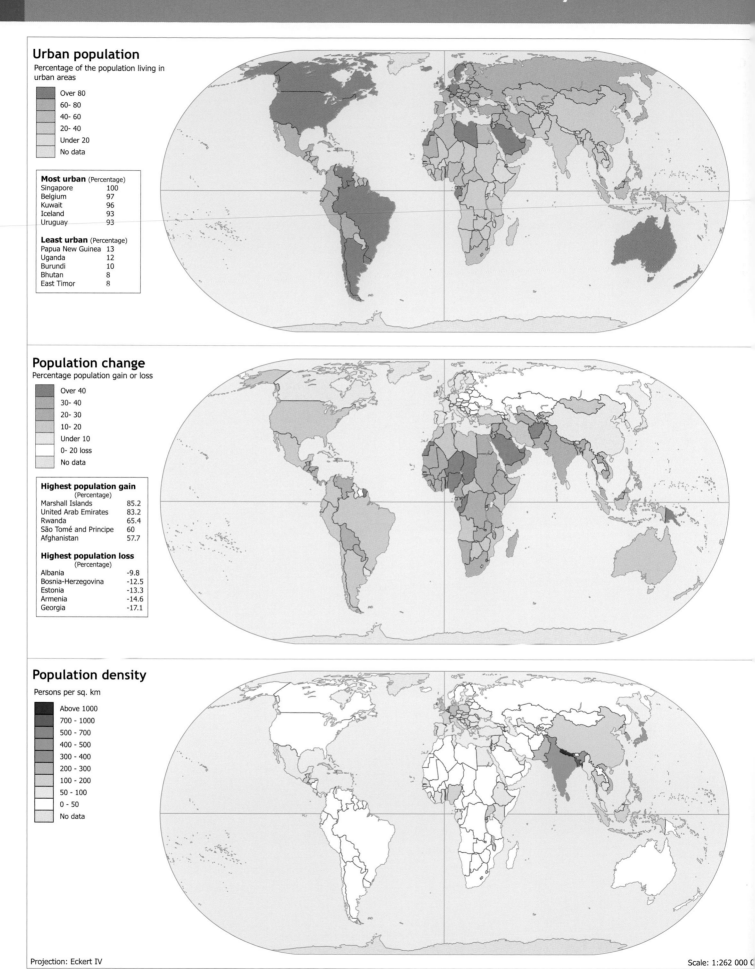

Urban population

Percentage of the population living in urban areas

- Over 80
- 60- 80
- 40- 60
- 20- 40
- Under 20
- No data

Most urban (Percentage)	
Singapore	100
Belgium	97
Kuwait	96
Iceland	93
Uruguay	93

Least urban (Percentage)	
Papua New Guinea	13
Uganda	12
Burundi	10
Bhutan	8
East Timor	8

Population change

Percentage population gain or loss

- Over 40
- 30- 40
- 20- 30
- 10- 20
- Under 10
- 0- 20 loss
- No data

Highest population gain (Percentage)	
Marshall Islands	85.2
United Arab Emirates	83.2
Rwanda	65.4
São Tomé and Principe	60
Afghanistan	57.7

Highest population loss (Percentage)	
Albania	-9.8
Bosnia-Herzegovina	-12.5
Estonia	-13.3
Armenia	-14.6
Georgia	-17.1

Population density

Persons per sq. km

- Above 1000
- 700 - 1000
- 500 - 700
- 400 - 500
- 300 - 400
- 200 - 300
- 100 - 200
- 50 - 100
- 0 - 50
- No data

Projection: Eckert IV

Scale: 1:262 000 0

Child Mortality

Death of children under 1 year old per 1000 live births

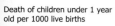

- 100 and Over
- 50 - 100
- 25 - 50
- 10 - 25
- Under 10
- No data

Countries with the highest and lowest child mortality

Highest values
Angola	194
Afghanistan	147
Sierra Leone	147
Mozambique	139
Liberia	132

Lowest values
Sweden	3
Iceland	4
Singapore	4
Finland	4
Japan	4

(UK = 6 deaths)

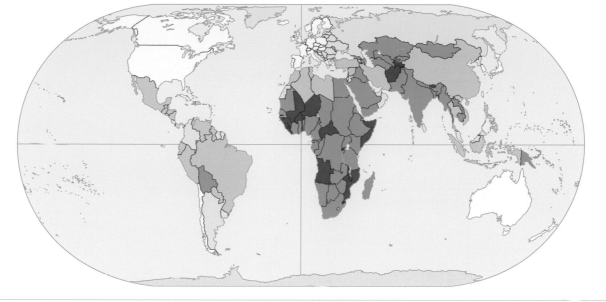

Family Size

Children born per woman

- More than 5
- 4 - 5
- 3 - 4
- 2 - 3
- 1 - 2
- No data

Countries with the largest and smallest family size

Largest
Somalia	7.1
Niger	7.1
Ethiopia	7.0
Yemen	7.0
Uganda	7.0

Smallest
Bulgaria	1.1
Latvia	1.2
Spain	1.2
Czech Rep.	1.2
Italy	1.2

(UK = 1.7 children)

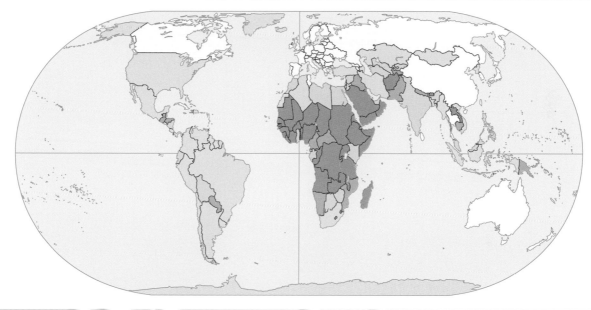

International migration

Percentage of total population foreign born

- Over 20
- 10 - 20
- 5 - 10
- 2 - 5
- Under 2
- No data

○ Countries where more than 20% of foreign earnings is sent home as payments from workers abroad

Highest percentage of foreign born
United Arab Emirates	90.2
Oman	33.6
Israel	30.9
Côte d' Ivoire	29.3
Jorden	26.4

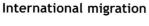

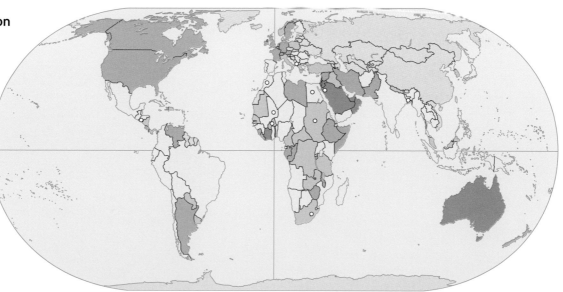

Projection: Eckert IV

Scale 1:262 000 000

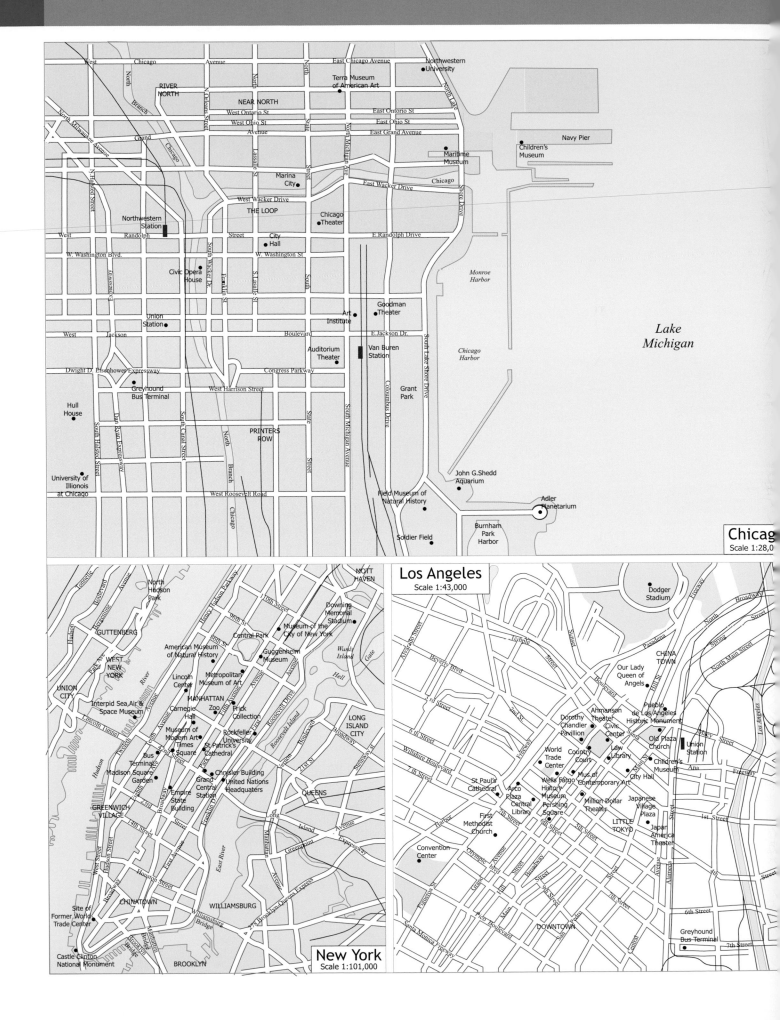

Chicago
Scale 1:28,0[00]

Los Angeles
Scale 1:43,000

New York
Scale 1:101,000

Lake Michigan

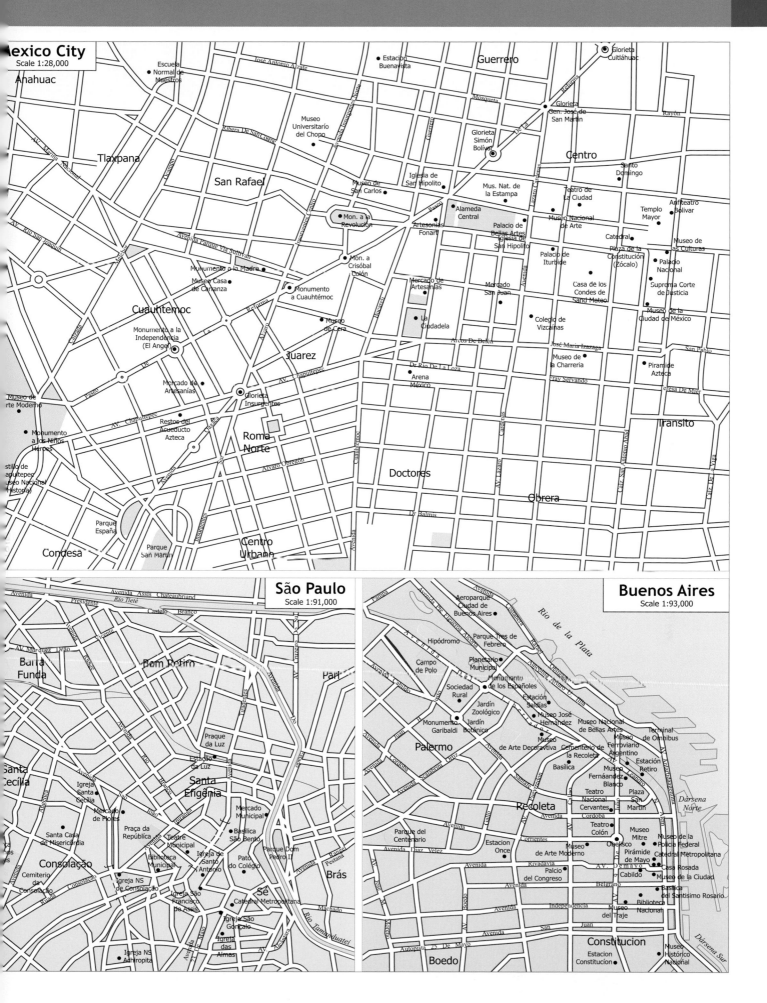

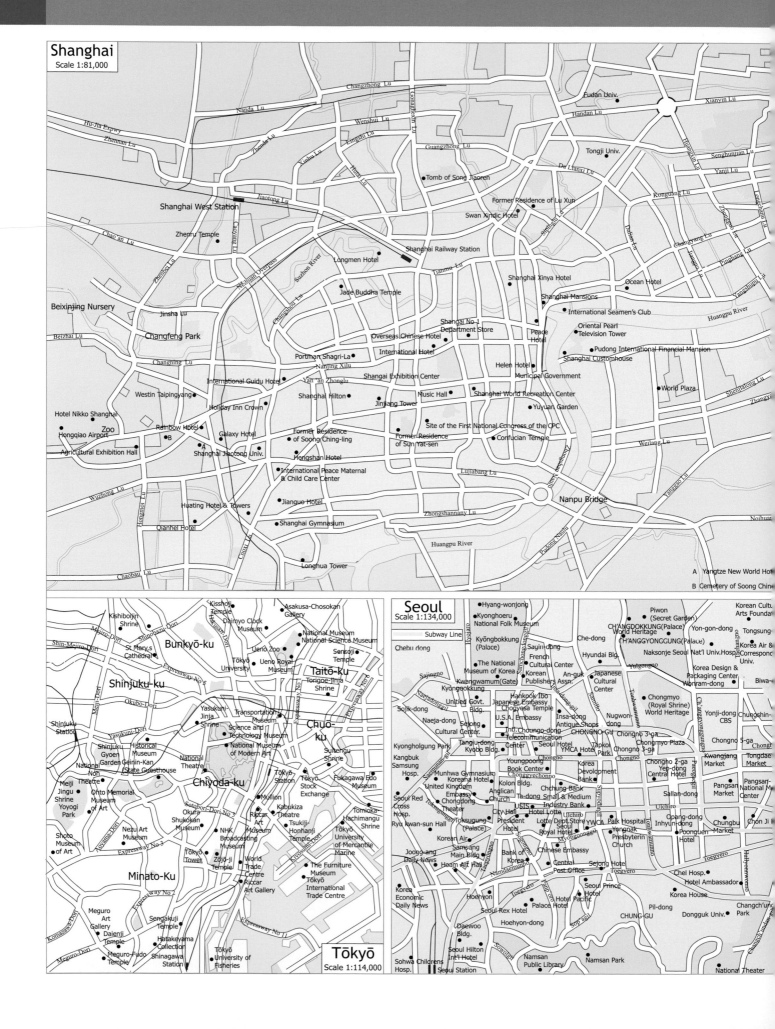

Shanghai
Scale 1:81,000

Changzhong Lu
Hu-Jia Expwy
Nanda Lu
Wenshui Lu
Zhennan Lu
Fudan Univ.
Xianyin Lu
Handan Lu
Guomao Lu
Yinshi Lu
Guangzhong Lu
Tongji Univ.
Yanji Lu
Jiaotong Lu
Shanghai West Station
Tomb of Song Jiaoren
Former Residence of Lu Xun
Senghunnian Lu
Chao an Lu
Zhenru Temple
Swan Xindic Hotel
Shanghai Railway Station
Longmen Hotel
Changyang Lu
Suzhou River
Jade Buddha Temple
Shanghai Xinya Hotel
Ocean Hotel
Beixinjing Nursery
Shanghai Mansions
International Seamen's Club
Huangpu River
Jinsha Lu
Changfeng Park
Shangai No 1 Department Store
Peace Hotel
Oriental Pearl Television Tower
Beizhai Lu
Overseas Chinese Hotel
International Hotel
Shanghai Customhouse
Pudong International Financial Mansion
Changning Lu
Portman Shagri-La
Nanjing Xilu
Shangai Exhibition Center
Helen Hotel
Municipal Government
International Guidu Hotel
Yan an Zhonglu
Westin Taipingyang
Shanghai Hilton
Music Hall
Shanghai World Recreation Center
World Plaza
Holiday Inn Crown
Jinjiang Tower
Yuyuan Garden
Hotel Nikko Shanghai
Rainbow Hotel
Site of the First National Congress of the CPC
Hongqiao Airport
Zoo
Galaxy Hotel
Former Residence of Soong Ching-ling
Former Residence of Sun Yat-sen
Confucian Temple
Agricultural Exhibition Hall
Shanghai Jiaotong Univ.
Hengshan Hotel
Weilang Lu
International Peace Maternal & Child Care Center
Wuzhong Lu
Lujiabang Lu
Jianguo Hotel
Nanpu Bridge
Huating Hotel & Towers
Zhongshannany Lu
Noihuar
Qianhel Hotel
Shanghai Gymnasium
Huangpu River
Chaobau Lu
Longhua Tower
A Yangtze New World Hot
B Cemetery of Soong Chine

Tōkyō
Scale 1:114,000

Kisshoji Temple
Asakusa-Chosokan Gallery
Kishibojin Shrine
Daimyo Clock Museum
National Museum
Shin-Mejiro-Dori
St Mary's Cathedral
Bunkyō-ku
National Science Museum
Ueno Zoo
Sensōji Temple
Tōkyō University
Ueno Royal Museum
Taitō-ku
Shinjuku-ku
Torigoe-Jima Shrine
Shinjuku Station
Yasukuni-Jinja Shrine
Transportation Museum
Chuō-ku
Science and Technology Museum
Suitengu Shrine
Shinjuku Gyoen
Historical Museum
National Museum of Modern Art
Garden Geinin-Kan (State Guesthouse)
Meiji Jingu
National Noh Theatre
National Theatre
Tōkyō Station
Tōkyō Stock Exchange
Fukagawa Edo Museum
Yoyogi Park
Ohto Memorial Museum of Art
Mullion
Kabukiza Theatre
Tomioka-Hachimangu Shrine
Nezu Art Museum
Riccar Art Museum
Tsukiji-Honhanji Temple
Shoto Museum of Art
Shukokan Museum
NHK Broadcasting Museum
Tōkyō University of Mercantile Marine
Tōkyō Tower
Zōjō-ji Temple
World Trade Centre
The Furniture Museum
Meguro Art Gallery
Riccar Art Gallery
Tōkyō International Trade Centre
Sengakuji Temple
Daienji Temple
Hatakeyama Collection
Minato-Ku
Meguro-Fudo Temple
Shinagawa Station
Tōkyō University of Fisheries

Seoul
Scale 1:134,000

Hyang-wonjong
Piwon (Secret Garden)
Korean Cultu Arts Foundat
Kyonghoeru
National Folk Museum
CH'ANGDOKKUNG(Palace) World Heritage
Yon-gon-dong
Tongsung
Subway Line
Chebu dong
Kyŏngbokkung (Palace)
Sayin-dong
Hyundai Bldg.
H'ANGGYONGGUNG(Palace)
Korea Air & Correspondenc Univ.
Sajingno
The National Museum of Korea
French Cultural Center
Japanese Cultural Center
Korea Design & Packaging Center
Kwangwamun(Gate)
An-guk
Korean Publishers Assn.
Wonram-dong
Kyŏngdokkung
Hankook Ibo
Japanese Embassy
Insa-dong Antique Shops
Chongmyo (Royal Shrine) World Heritage
Sojik-dong
Chogyesa Temple
Ind.Choungo-dong Telecommunication Center
CHONGNO-GU
Chongno 3-ga
Yonji-dong
CBS
Chongno 5-ga
Kyonghoiry Park
Tangju-dong
Seoul Hotel
Chongno Plaza
Tapkol Park
Chongno 3-ga
Kangbuk Samsung Hosp.
Kyobo Bldg.
YMCA Hotel
Kwangjang Market
Tongdae Market
Munhwa Gymnasium
Chonggyechonno
Korea Devolopment Bank
Chongno 2-ga
Yeb-dong Central Hotel
Pangsan Market
Koreana Hotel
United Kingdom
Kolon Bldg.
Chohung Bank
Sallan-dong
Pangsan-National Park
Seoul Red Cross Hosp.
Anglican Church
Ta-dong Small & Medium Industry Bank
Chongdong Theater
USIS
City Hall
Hotel Lotte
Lotte Dept.Store
Ulchiro
Ryu kwan-sun Hall
Toksugung (Palace)
President Hotel
Seoul Royal Hotel
YWCA
Paik Hospital
Opang-dong Inhyun-dong
Chungbu Market
Korean Air
Samsung Main Bldg.
Chinese Embassy
Myongdong
Yongnak Presbyterin Church
Poonguen Hotel
Chon Li
Joong-ang Daily News
Heam Art Hall
Bank of Korea
Central Post Office
Sejong Hotel
Chel Hosp.
Korea Economic Daily News
Namdaemun
Toegyero
Hotel Ambassador
Korea House
Hoehyon
Seoul Prince Hotel
Pil-dong
Changch'un Park
Seoul Rex Hotel
Hotel Pacific
CHUNG-GU
Dongguk Univ.
Hoehyon-dong
Daewoo Bldg.
Seoul Hilton Int'l Hotel
Namsan Public Library
Namsan Park
Sohwa Childrens Hosp.
Seoul Station
National Theater

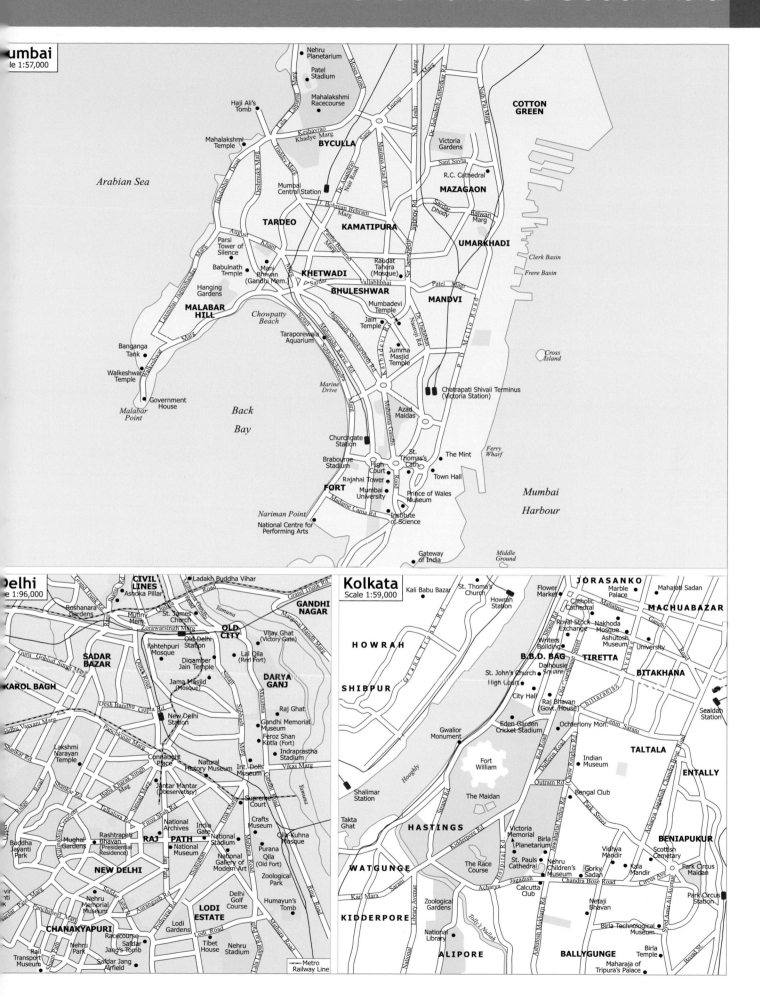

Mumbai
Scale 1:57,000

Arabian Sea

Nehru Planetarium
Patel Stadium
Haji Ali's Tomb
Mahalakshmi Racecourse
BYCULLA
COTTON GREEN
Mahalakshmi Temple
Keshavrao Khadye Marg
Victoria Gardens
R.C. Cathedral
Mumbai Central Station
J. Bohman Behram Marg
MAZAGAON
TARDEO
KAMATIPURA
UMARKHADI
Parsi Tower of Silence
Clerk Basin
Babulnath Temple
Mani Bhavan (Gandhi Mem.)
KHETWADI
Frere Basin
Hanging Gardens
BHULESHWAR
Raudat Tahera (Mosque)
MALABAR HILL
Chowpatty Beach
Mumbadevi Temple
MANDVI
Banganga Tank
Taraporewala Aquarium
Jain Temple
Walkeshwar Temple
Marine Drive
Jumma Masjid Temple
Cross Island
Government House
Back Bay
Chatrapati Shivaji Terminus (Victoria Station)
Malabar Point
Azad Maidas
Churchgate Station
Ferry Wharf
Mumbai Harbour
Brabourne Stadium
High Court
St. Thomas's Cath.
The Mint
Rajabai Tower
Town Hall
FORT
Mumbai University
Prince of Wales Museum
Nariman Point
National Centre for Performing Arts
Institute of Science
Gateway of India
Middle Ground

Delhi
Scale 1:96,000

CIVIL LINES
Ladakh Buddha Vihar
GANDHI NAGAR
Ashoka Pillar
Roshanara Gardens
Mutiny Mem.
St. James Church
Zorawarsingh Marg
OLD CITY
Vijay Ghat (Victory Gate)
Fahtehpuri Mosque
Old Delhi Station
SADAR BAZAR
Digamber Jain Temple
Lal Qila (Red Fort)
KAROL BAGH
Jama Masjid (Mosque)
DARYA GANJ
Desh Bandhu Gupta Rd
New Delhi Station
Raj Ghat
Lakshmi Narayan Temple
Gandhi Memorial Museum
Feroz Shan Kotla (Fort)
Connaught Place
Indraprastha Stadium
Natural History Museum
Int. Dolls Museum
Vikas Marg
Jantar Mantar (Observatory)
Crafts Museum
Supreme Court
National Archives
India Gate
Qila-Kuhna Mosque
Rashtrapati Bhavan (Presidential Residence)
National Stadium
Purana Qila (Old Fort)
RAJ PATH
National Museum
Buddha Jayanti Park
Mughal Gardens
National Gallery of Modern Art
NEW DELHI
Zoological Park
Nehru Memorial Museum
Delhi Golf Course
Humayun's Tomb
CHANAKYAPURI
Racecourse
LODI ESTATE
Safdar Jang's Tomb
Lodi Gardens
Rail Transport Museum
Safdar Jang Airfield
Nehru Park
Tibet House
Nehru Stadium

Kolkata
Scale 1:59,000

JORASANKO
Kali Babu Bazar
St. Thoma's Church
Flower Market
Marble Palace
Mahajati Sadan
Howrah Station
Catholic Cathedral
MACHUABAZAR
HOWRAH
Royal Stock Exchange
Nakhoda Mosque
Ashutosh Museum
University
Writers Building
St. John's Church
Dalhousie Square
TIRETTA
SHIBPUR
High Court
BITAKHANA
City Hall
Raj Bhavan (Govt. House)
Eden Garden Cricket Stadium
Ochterlony Mon.
Sealdah Station
Gwalior Monument
Lenin Sarani
TALTALA
Hooghly
Fort William
Indian Museum
ENTALLY
Shalimar Station
The Maidan
Bengal Club
Takta Ghat
HASTINGS
BENIAPUKUR
Victoria Memorial
Birla Planetarium
Vidhya Mandir
Scottish Cemetary
Nehru Children's Museum
Gorky Sadan
Kala Mandir
WATGUNGE
The Race Course
St. Pauls Cathedral
Chandra Bose Road
Park Circus Maidan
Zoological Gardens
Calcutta Club
Netaji Bhavan
Park Circus Station
KIDDERPORE
National Library
Birla Technological Museum
Birla Temple
ALIPORE
BALLYGUNGE
Maharaja of Tripura's Palace

Metro Railway Line

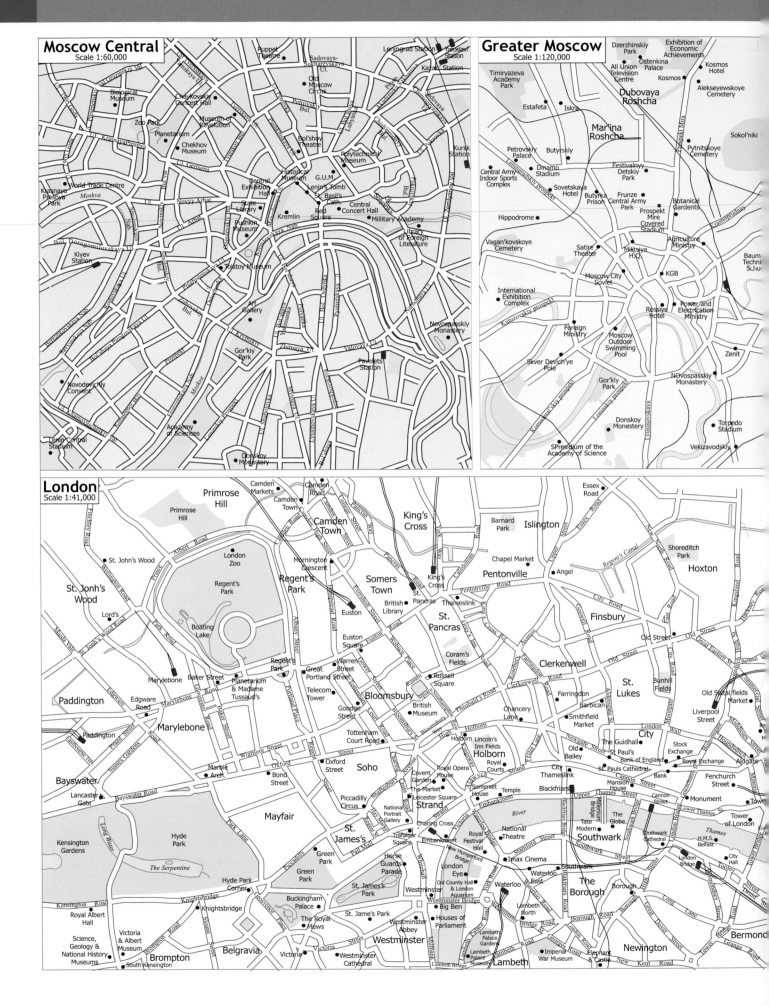

Moscow Central
Scale 1:60,000

Greater Moscow
Scale 1:120,000

London
Scale 1:41,000

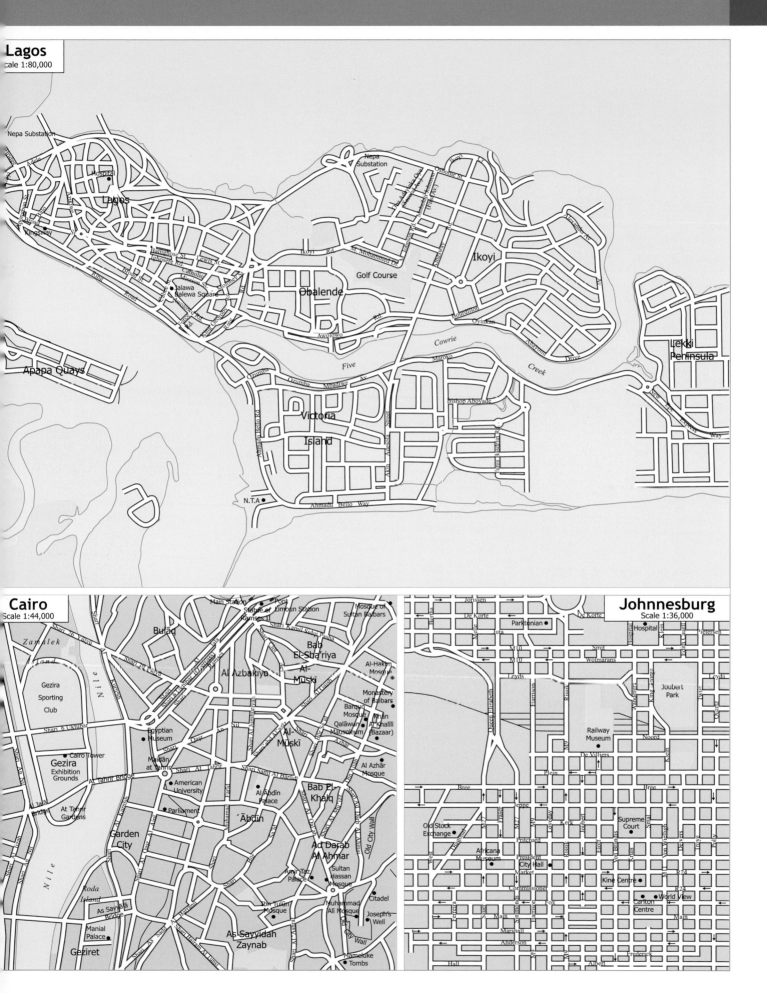

Lagos
Scale 1:80,000

Nepa Substation

Hospital

Lagos

Kingsway

Tinubu Sq.

Hospital

Nepa Substation

Osborne St.

Ikoyi

Ikoyi Rd.

Mt. Mohammed Dr.

Golf Course

Obalende

Awolowo

Bourdillon

Oyinkan

Cowrie

Maroko

Creek

Five

Lekki Peninsula

Apapa Quays

Ozumba

Ozumba Mbadiwe Av.

Akin Adesola Street

Bishop Aboyade

Victoria

Island

Point Road

N.T.A.

Ahmadu Bello Way

Cairo
Scale 1:44,000

Zamalek
Island

Shari 26 Yuliyu

Gezira
Sporting
Club

Nile

Main Station

Statue of
Ramses II

Limoun Station

Mosque of
Sultan Baibars

Shari Kamil Sidqi Pasha

Bulaq

Bab
El-Sha'riya

Al Azbakiyo

Al-
Muski

Al-Hakim
Mosque

Monastery
of Baibars

Barquq
Mosque

Khan
Al Khalili
(Bazaar)

Egyptian
Museum

Shari al Tahrir

Qalawun
Mausoleum

Cairo Tower

Gezira
Exhibition
Grounds

Maidan
at Tahrir

Al-
Muski

Shari Sami Al Barudi

Al Azhar

Al Azhar
Mosque

Al Tahrir Bridge

American
University

Al Jalal
Bridge

At Tahrir
Gardens

Parliament

Al Abdin
Palace

Bab El
Khalq

Garden
City

'Abdin

Ad Darab
Al Ahmar

Old City Wall

Amin Taz
Palace

Roda
Island

As Sayyida
Bridge

Ibn Tulun
Mosque

Muhammad
Ali Mosque

Sultan
Hassan
Mosque

Citadel

Joseph's
Well

Manial
Palace

As Sayyidah
Zaynab

City Wall

Geziret

Mameluke
Tombs

Johnnesburg
Scale 1:36,000

Jorissen

De Korte

Bertha

De Korte

Parktonian

Hospital

Petersen

M10

M10

Smit

Wolmarans

Leyds

Joubert
Park

Leyds

Railway
Museum

Noord

De Villiers

Plein

Bree

Bree

Jeppe

Old Stock
Exchange

Kerk

Supreme
Court

Africana
Museum

President

City Hall

Pritchard

Commissioner

Market

Kine Centre

R24

World View

Fox

R24

Carlton
Centre

Main

Marshall

Main

Anderson

Hall

Frederick

Albert

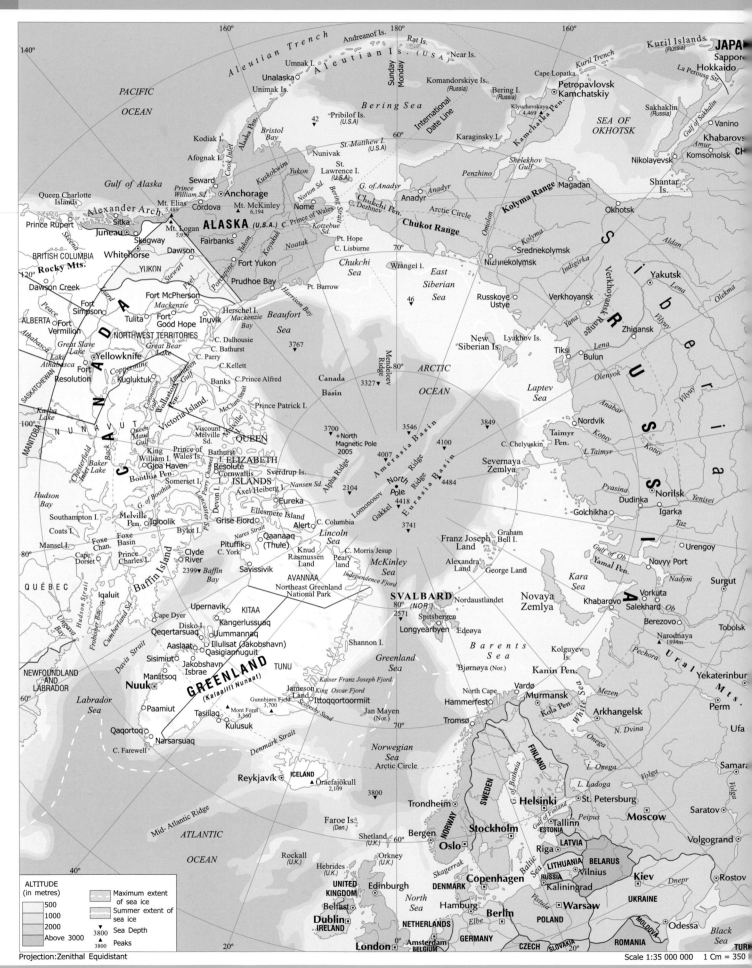

ALTITUDE
(in metres)
500
1000
2000
Above 3000

Maximum extent
of sea ice

Summer extent of
sea ice

▼ Sea Depth

▲ Peaks

Projection:Zenithal Equidistant

Scale 1:35 000 000   1 Cm = 350

The Arctic is the smallest and shallowest of Earth's oceans. Ice covers most of the Arctic year-round, although the floating Arctic ice cap is shrinking rapidly. In 1896 Fridtjof Nansen became the first person to cross the Arctic by boat, while in 1969 Wally Herbert was the first to walk to the North Pole. The Arctic's major ports are: Murmansk and Arkhangelsk (Russia); Church Manitoba (Canada); and Prudhoe Bay, Alaska (USA).

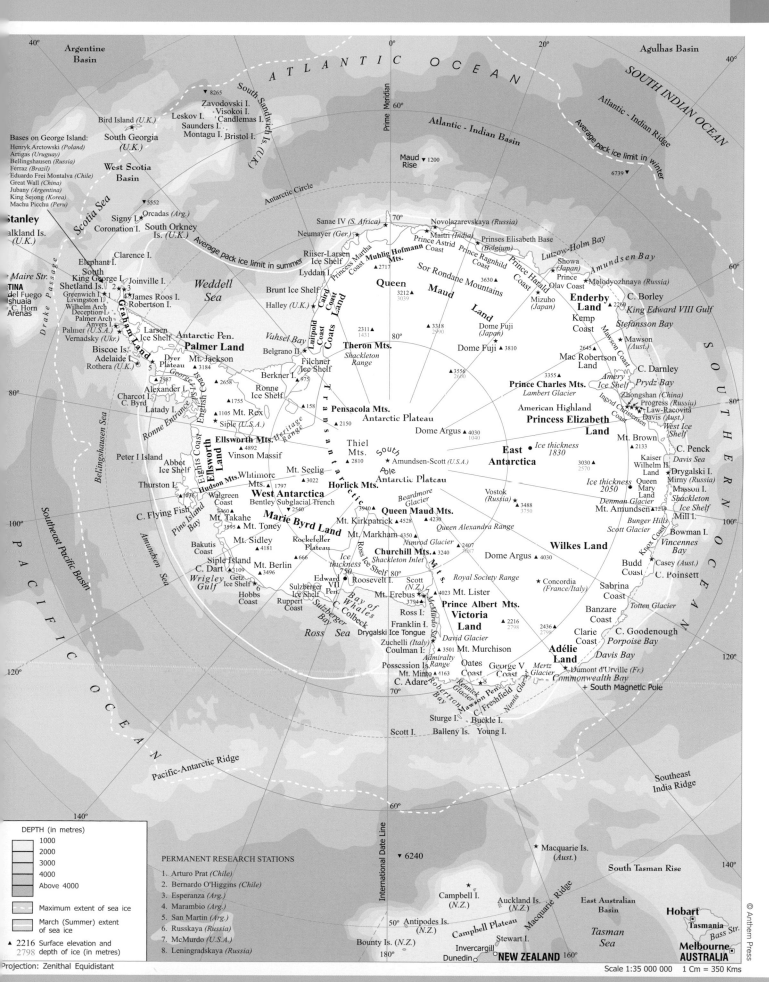

DEPTH (in metres)
1000
2000
3000
4000
Above 4000

Maximum extent of sea ice

March (Summer) extent of sea ice

▲ 2216 Surface elevation and
2798 depth of ice (in metres)

PERMANENT RESEARCH STATIONS
1. Arturo Prat (Chile)
2. Bernardo O'Higgins (Chile)
3. Esperanza (Arg.)
4. Marambio (Arg.)
5. San Martin (Arg.)
6. Russkaya (Russia)
7. McMurdo (U.S.A.)
8. Leningradskaya (Russia)

Projection: Zenithal Equidistant

Scale 1:35 000 000   1 Cm = 350 Kms

Antarctica is the coldest, driest and windiest continent on Earth. Covered by ice at least a mile (1.6 km) thick on average, Antarctica is larger than Europe. In 1908–09 Ernest Shackleton's Nimrod Expedition climbed Mount Erebus, crossed the Trans-Antarctic mountains and set foot on the South Polar Plateau. In 1911 Roald Amundsen reached the South Pole, narrowly beating the tragic expedition of Robert Scott. The 1959 Antarctic Treaty protects the continent.

ALTITUDE
(in metres)

5000 4000 2000 400 200 0 200 1000 2000 4000

EUROPE'S HIGHEST MOUNTAINS

1. ELBRUS, RUS (5,642 m)	4. DOM, CHE (4,545 m)
2. MONT BLANC, FRA–ITA (4,808 m)	5. LISKAMM, CHE (4,527 m)
3. MONTE ROSA, CHE (4,634 m)	6. WEISSHORN, CHE (4,506 m)

EUROPE'S LONGEST RIVERS

1. VOLGA (3,700 km)	4. DNIEPER (2,285 km)
2. DANUBE (2,850 km)	5. DON (1,990 km)
3. URAL (2,535 km)	6. PECHORA (1,790 km)

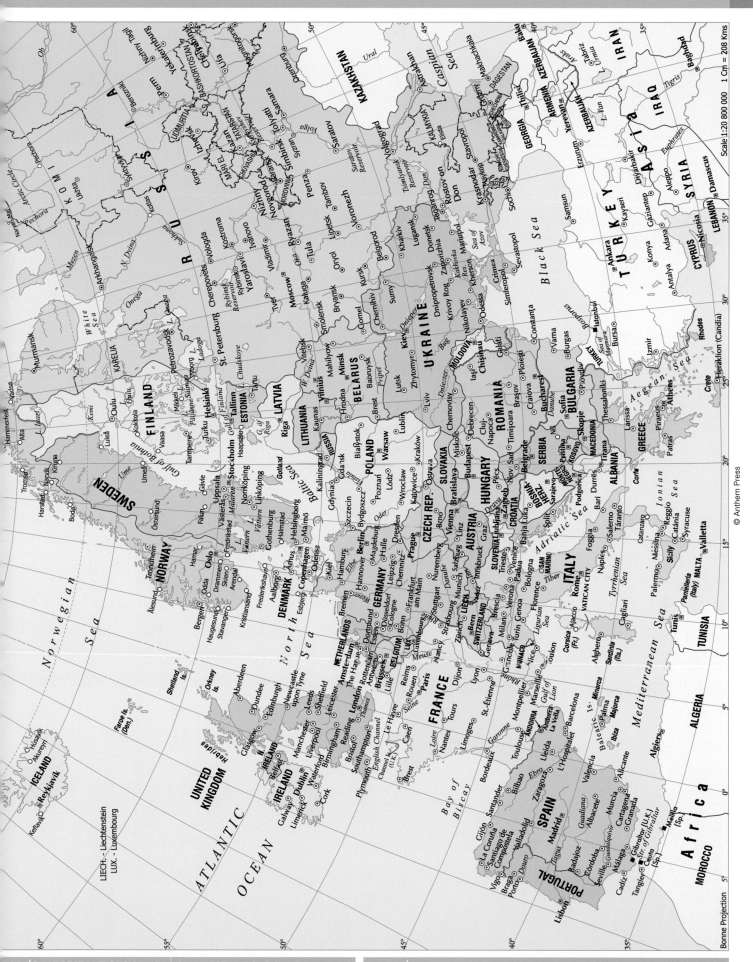

Scale 1:20 800 000   1 Cm = 208 Kms

Bonne Projection

ROPE'S LARGEST NATIONS (AREA)	SMALLEST NATIONS (AREA)	EUROPE'S LARGEST CITIES (POP.)	
RUSSIA (3.96 million sq km)	1. VATICAN CITY (0.44 sq km)	1. MOSCOW, RUS (13.5 million)	4. MADRID, ESP (5.95 million)
UKRAINE (603,700 sq km)	2. MONACO (1.95 sq km)	2. LONDON, GBR (12 million)	5. ST PETERSBURG, RUS (4.8 million)
FRANCE (547,030 sq km)	3. SAN MARINO (61 sq km)	3. PARIS, FRA (10 million)	6. BARCELONA, ESP (4.2 million)

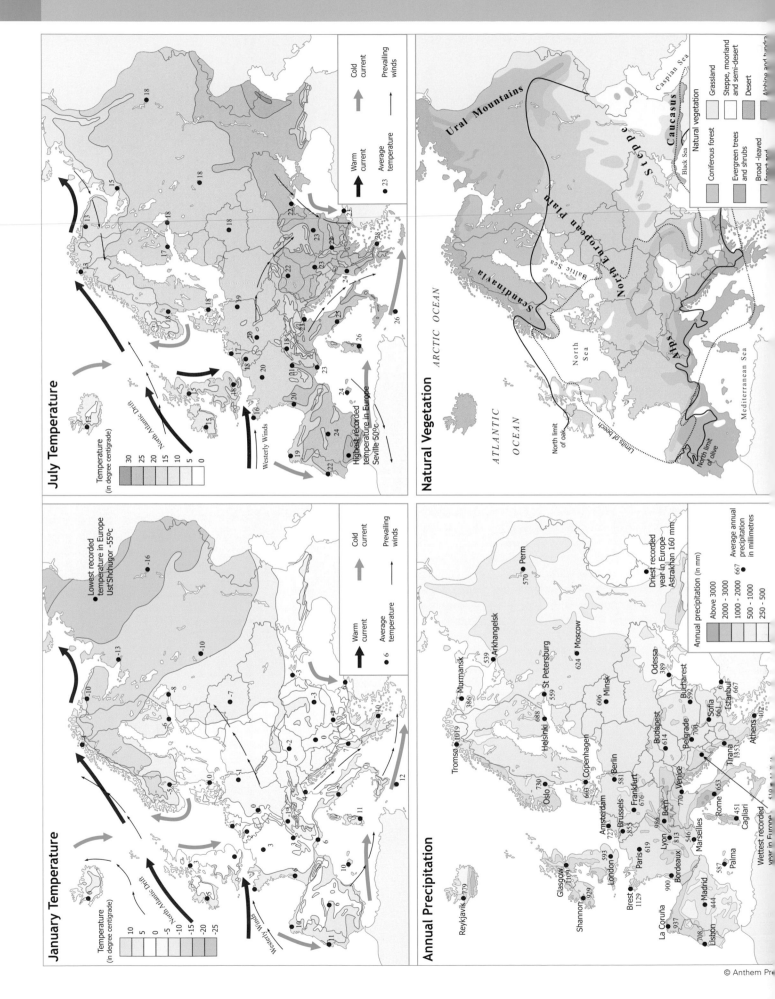

July Temperature

Temperature (in degree centigrade)
30
25
20
15
10
5
0

North Atlantic Drift

Westerly Winds

Highest recorded temperature in Europe Seville 50°c

Warm current
Cold current

Average temperature · 23
Prevailing winds

January Temperature

Temperature (in degree centigrade)
10
5
0
-5
-10
-15
-20
-25

Lowest recorded temperature in Europe Ust'Shchugor -55°c

North Atlantic Drift

Westerly Winds

Warm current
Cold current

Average temperature · 6
Prevailing winds

Natural Vegetation

Ural Mountains
Caucasus
Caspian Sea
Black Sea
Baltic Sea
North European Plain
Steppe
Scandinavia
Alps
North Sea
Mediterranean Sea
ARCTIC OCEAN
ATLANTIC OCEAN

North limit of oak
North limit of olive
(Limits of beech)

Natural vegetation
Coniferous forest
Evergreen trees and shrubs
Broad-leaved forest
Grassland
Steppe, moorland and semi-desert
Desert

Annual Precipitation

Annual precipitation (in mm)
Above 3000
2000 - 3000
1000 - 2000
500 - 1000
250 - 500

Driest recorded year in Europe Astrakhan 160 mm

Wettest recorded year in Europe

Average annual precipitation in millimetres · 667

Perm 570
Arkhangelsk 539
Murmansk 386
Moscow 624
St Petersburg 559
Odessa 389
Minsk 606
Helsinki 688
Tromsø 1019
Bucharest 592
Istanbul 661
Budapest 614
Sofia 661
Copenhagen 603
Berlin 581
Belgrade 706
Tirana 1353
Athens
Oslo 730
Frankfurt 676
Venice 770
Rome 653
Amsterdam 727
Brussels 855
Bern 986
Cagliari 451
Glasgow 1109
London 593
Paris 619
Lyon 813
Marseilles 546
Palma 587
Shannon 929
Brest 1129
Bordeaux 900
Reykjavík 779
La Coruña 937
Madrid 444
Lisbon 708

© Anthem Pre

Land Use and Agriculture

Land use
- Arable
- Arable and pasture
- Market gardening
- Pasture
- Woods and forests
- Rough grazing
- Non-productive

Agriculture
- Beef cattle
- Dairy cattle
- Pigs
- Sheep
- Reindeer
- Barley
- Maize
- Oats
- Rye
- Wheat
- Potatoes
- Citrus fruit
- Fruit & vegetables
- Olives
- Vines
- Sugarbeet
- Tobacco
- Main fishing areas

Scale 1:25 750 000

Structure and Minerals

Minerals

Iron-ferro-alloys
- Chrome
- Cobalt
- Iron Ore
- Manganese
- Nickel Ore

Non-ferrous metals
- Bauxite
- Copper
- Lead
- Tin
- Zinc
- Uranium
- Aluminium

Precious metals
- Silver

Fertilizers
- Phosphates
- Potash

Structure
- Pre-Cambrian shield
- Palaeozoic folding
- Cenozoic folding
- Igneous structures

... Projection

Scale 1:46 300 000   1 Cm = 463 Kms

Energy

Energy
- Oil
- Natural gas
- Coal and lignite
- Nuclear power
- Hydro-electric power

Energy production per capita million tonnes of oil equivalent
- Over 10
- 5 - 10
- 0.5 - 5
- Less than 0.5

Scale 1:46 300 000   1 Cm = 463 Kms

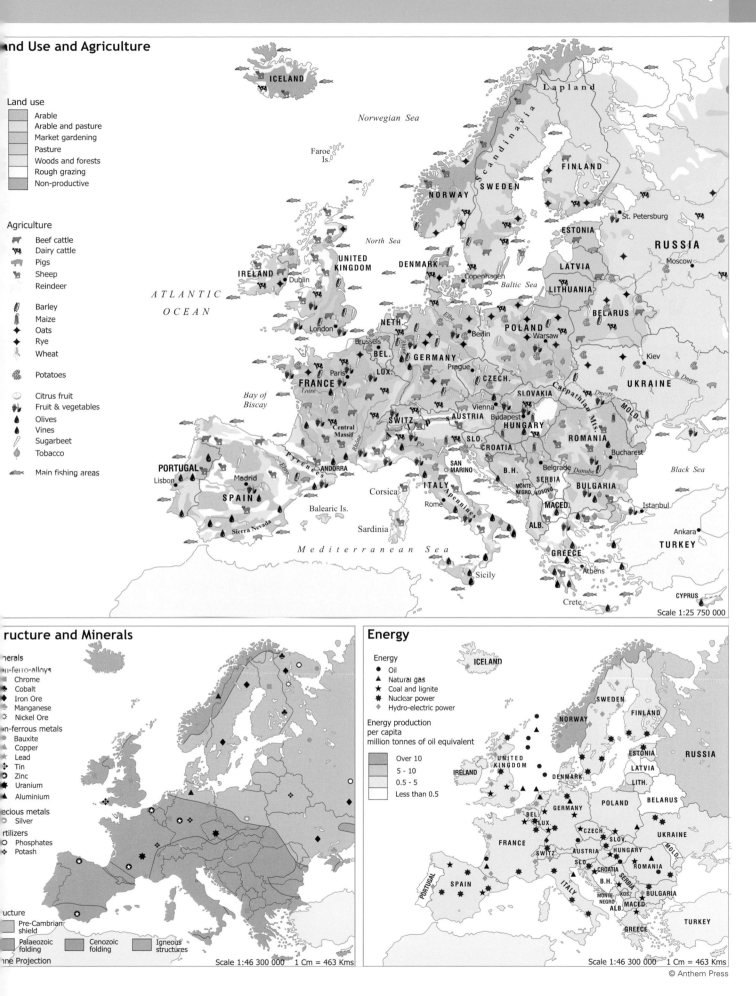

© Anthem Press

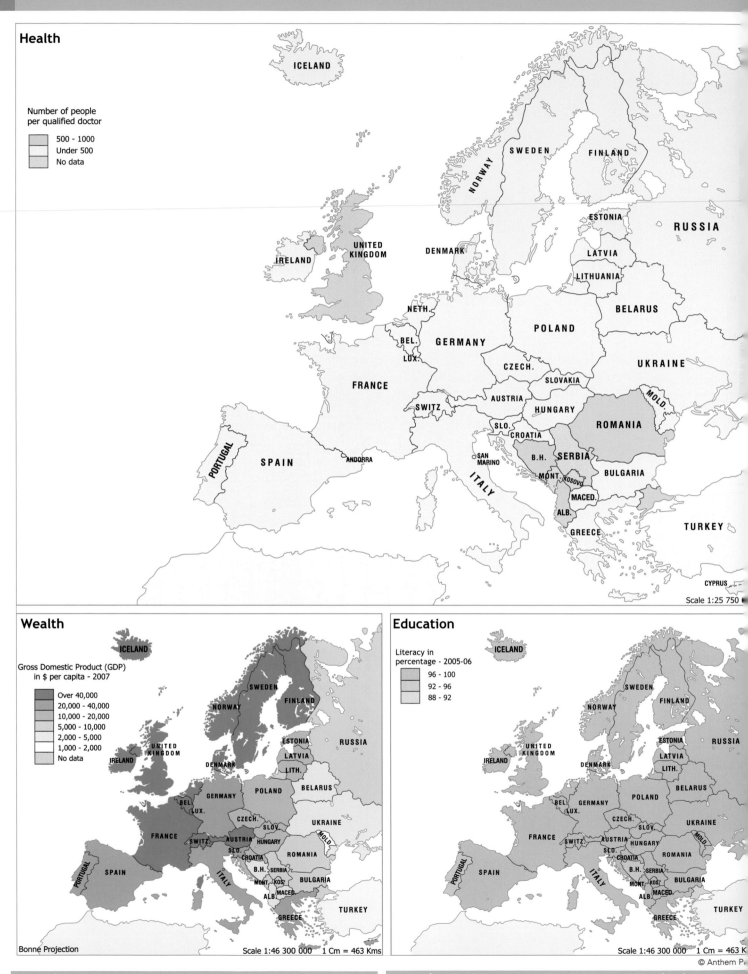

Health

Number of people
per qualified doctor

- 500 - 1000
- Under 500
- No data

ICELAND

NORWAY
SWEDEN
FINLAND

ESTONIA
RUSSIA

IRELAND
UNITED
KINGDOM
DENMARK
LATVIA
LITHUANIA

NETH.
BELARUS

BEL.
GERMANY
POLAND
LUX.

FRANCE
CZECH.
SLOVAKIA
UKRAINE

AUSTRIA
SWITZ
HUNGARY
MOLD

SLO.
ROMANIA
CROATIA

PORTUGAL
SPAIN
ANDORRA
SAN
MARINO
B.H. SERBIA
MONT.
KOSOVO
BULGARIA

ITALY
MACED.
ALB.
TURKEY

GREECE

CYPRUS

Scale 1:25 750

Wealth

Gross Domestic Product (GDP)
in $ per capita - 2007

- Over 40,000
- 20,000 - 40,000
- 10,000 - 20,000
- 5,000 - 10,000
- 2,000 - 5,000
- 1,000 - 2,000
- No data

ICELAND

SWEDEN
NORWAY
FINLAND

ESTONIA
RUSSIA

UNITED
KINGDOM
LATVIA
LITH.

IRELAND
DENMARK
BELARUS

GERMANY
POLAND
BEL.
LUX.
CZECH.
UKRAINE

SLOV.
FRANCE
AUSTRIA
MOLD
SWITZ
HUNGARY
SLO.
ROMANIA
CROATIA

PORTUGAL
SPAIN
B.H.
SERBIA
MONT.
KOS.
BULGARIA
ALB.
MACED.
ITALY
TURKEY
GREECE

Bonne Projection
Scale 1:46 300 000   1 Cm = 463 Kms

Education

Literacy in
percentage - 2005-06

- 96 - 100
- 92 - 96
- 88 - 92

ICELAND

SWEDEN
NORWAY
FINLAND

ESTONIA
RUSSIA

UNITED
KINGDOM
LATVIA
LITH.

IRELAND
DENMARK
BELARUS

GERMANY
POLAND
BEL.
LUX.
CZECH.
UKRAINE

SLOV.
FRANCE
AUSTRIA
MOLD
SWITZ
HUNGARY
SLO.
ROMANIA
CROATIA

PORTUGAL
SPAIN
B.H.
SERBIA
MONT.
KOS.
BULGARIA
ALB.
MACED.
ITALY
TURKEY
GREECE

Scale 1:46 300 000   1 Cm = 463 K

© Anthem P

EUROPE'S WEALTHIEST NATIONS	GDP PER CAPITA (PPP) US $
1. LUXEMBOURG ($89,571)	3. ICELAND ($53,023)
2. NORWAY ($66,960)	4. IRELAND ($52,899)

EUROPE'S POOREST NATIONS	GDP PER CAPITA (PPP) US $
1. MOLDOVA ($845)	3. BOSNIA-HERZOGVINA ($2,890)
2. UKRAINE ($2,278)	4. ALBANIA ($2,911)

Population Density

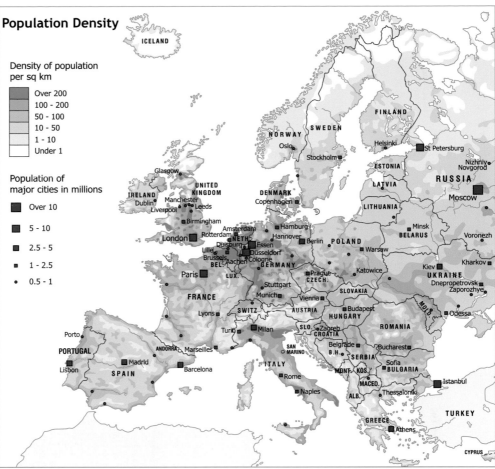

Density of population per sq km

- Over 200
- 100 - 200
- 50 - 100
- 10 - 50
- 1 - 10
- Under 1

Population of major cities in millions

- ■ Over 10
- ■ 5 - 10
- ■ 2.5 - 5
- ■ 1 - 2.5
- • 0.5 - 1

Population of major cities in millions - 2007

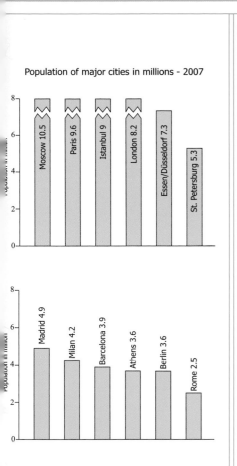

Moscow 10.5
Paris 9.6
Istanbul 9
London 8.2
Essen/Düsseldorf 7.3
St. Petersburg 5.3

Madrid 4.9
Milan 4.2
Barcelona 3.9
Athens 3.6
Berlin 3.6
Rome 2.5

Country	Population (in 000') (2004)
Albania	3,129
Andorra	67
Austria	8,189
Belarus	9,755
Belgium	10,419
Bosnia-Herzegovina	3,907
Bulgaria	7,725
Croatia	4,551
Czech Republic	10,219
Denmark	5,471
Estonia	1,329
Finland	5,302
France	60,495
Germany	82,689
Greece	11,119
Hungary	10,097
Iceland	309
Ireland	4,147
Italy	58,092
Latvia	2,306
Liechtenstein	34
Lithuania	3,369
Luxembourg	464
Macedonia	2,034
Malta	401
Moldova	4,205
Monaco	35
Montenegro	630
Netherlands	16,299
Norway	4,742
Poland	38,529
Portugal	10,494
Romania	21,711
San Marino	28
Serbia	7,800
Slovakia	5,400
Slovenia	2,066
Spain	45,061
Sweden	9,041
Switzerland	7,252
Ukraine	46,480
United Kingdom	60,776
Vatican City	0.8

Population Change

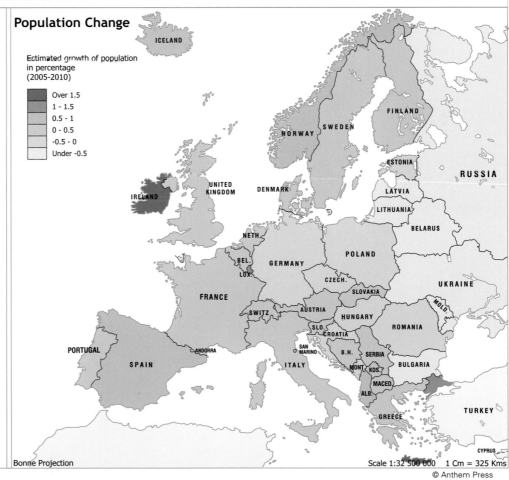

Estimated growth of population in percentage (2005-2010)

- Over 1.5
- 1 - 1.5
- 0.5 - 1
- 0 - 0.5
- -0.5 - 0
- Under -0.5

Bonne Projection

Scale 1:32 500 000   1 Cm = 325 Kms

© Anthem Press

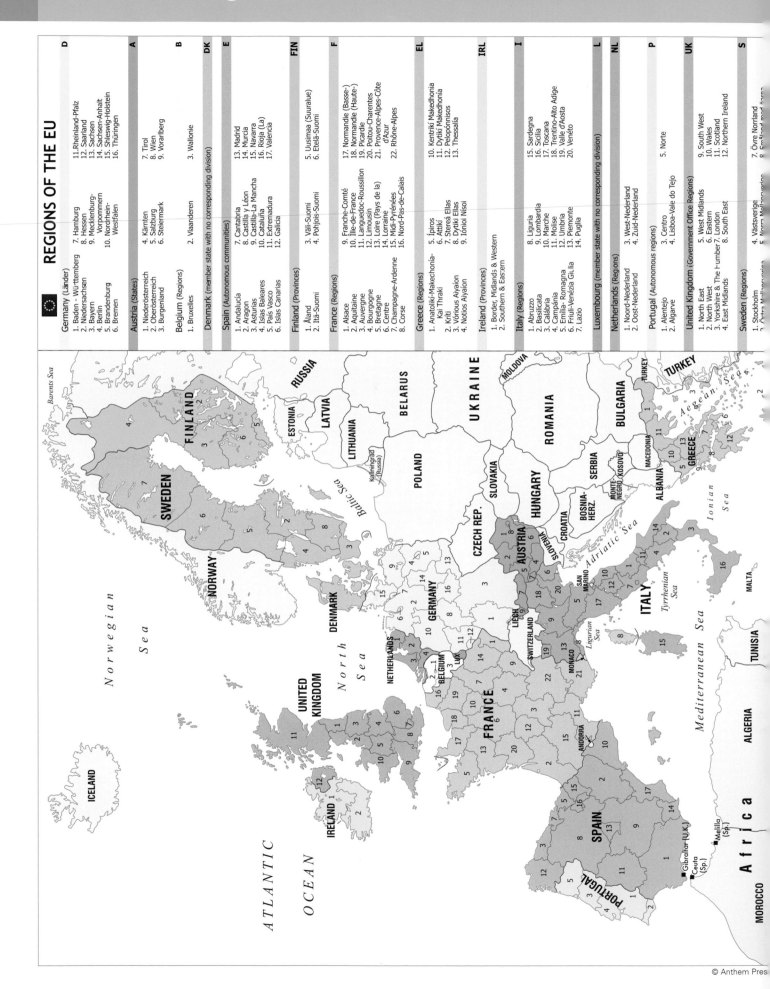

REGIONS OF THE EU

Germany (Länder)
1. Baden - Württemberg
2. Bayern
3. Berlin
4. Brandenburg
5. Bremen
6. Niedersachsen
7. Hamburg
8. Hessen
9. Mecklenburg-Vorpommern
10. Nordrhein-Westfalen
11. Rheinland-Pfalz
12. Saarland
13. Sachsen
14. Sachsen-Anhalt
15. Shleswig-Holstein
16. Thüringen

Austria (States)
1. Niederösterreich
2. Oberösterreich
3. Burgenland
4. Kärnten
5. Salzburg
6. Steiermark
7. Tirol
8. Wien
9. Vorarlberg

Belgium (Regions)
1. Bruxelles
2. Vlaanderen
3. Wallonie

Denmark (member state with no corresponding division)

Spain (Autonomous communities)
1. Andalucía
2. Aragon
3. Asturias
4. Islas Baleares
5. País Vasco
6. Islas Canarias
7. Cantabria
8. Castilla y Léon
9. Castilla-La Mancha
10. Cataluña
11. Extremadura
12. Galicia
13. Madrid
14. Murcia
15. Navarra
16. Rioja (La)
17. Valencia

Finland (Provinces)
1. Åland
2. Itä-Suomi
3. Väli-Suomi
4. Pohjois-Suomi
5. Uusimaa (Suuralue)
6. Etelä-Suomi

France (Regions)
1. Alsace
2. Aquitaine
3. Auvergne
4. Bourgogne
5. Bretagne
6. Centre
7. Champagne-Ardenne
8. Corse
9. Franche-Comté
10. Île-de-France
11. Languedoc-Roussillon
12. Limousin
13. Loire (Pays de la)
14. Lorraine
15. Midi-Pyrénées
16. Nord-Pas-de-Calais
17. Normandie (Basse-)
18. Normandie (Haute-)
19. Picardie
20. Poitou-Charentes
21. Provence-Alpes-Côte d'Azur
22. Rhône-Alpes

Greece (Regions)
1. Anatoliki-Makechonia-Kai Thraki
2. Kriti
3. Vórious Aiyaíon
4. Nótios Aiyaíon
5. Ípiros
6. Attikí
7. Stereá Ellas
8. Dytikí Ellas
9. Iónioi Nisoi
10. Kentrikí Makedhonia
11. Dytikí Makedhonia
12. Pelopónnisos
13. Thessalía

Ireland (Provinces)
1. Border, Midlands & Western
2. Southern & Eastern

Italy (Regions)
1. Abruzzo
2. Basilicata
3. Calábria
4. Campánia
5. Emilia- Romagna
6. Friuli-Venézia Giúlia
7. Lazio
8. Liguria
9. Lombardia
10. Marche
11. Molise
12. Umbria
13. Piemonte
14. Puglia
15. Sardegna
16. Sicilia
17. Toscana
18. Trentino-Alto Adige
19. Valle d'Aosta
20. Venéto

Luxembourg (member state with no corresponding division)

Netherlands (Regions)
1. Noord-Nederland
2. Oost-Nederland
3. West-Nederland
4. Zuid-Nederland

Portugal (Autonomous regions)
1. Alentejo
2. Algarve
3. Centro
4. Lisboa-Vale do Tejo
5. Norte

United Kingdom (Government Office Regions)
1. North East
2. North West
3. Yorkshire & The Humber
4. East Midlands
5. West Midlands
6. Eastern
7. London
8. South East
9. South West
10. Wales
11. Scotland
12. Northern Ireland

Sweden (Regions)
1. Stockholm
4. Västsverige
5. Norra Mellansverige
7. Övre Norrland

© Anthem Pres

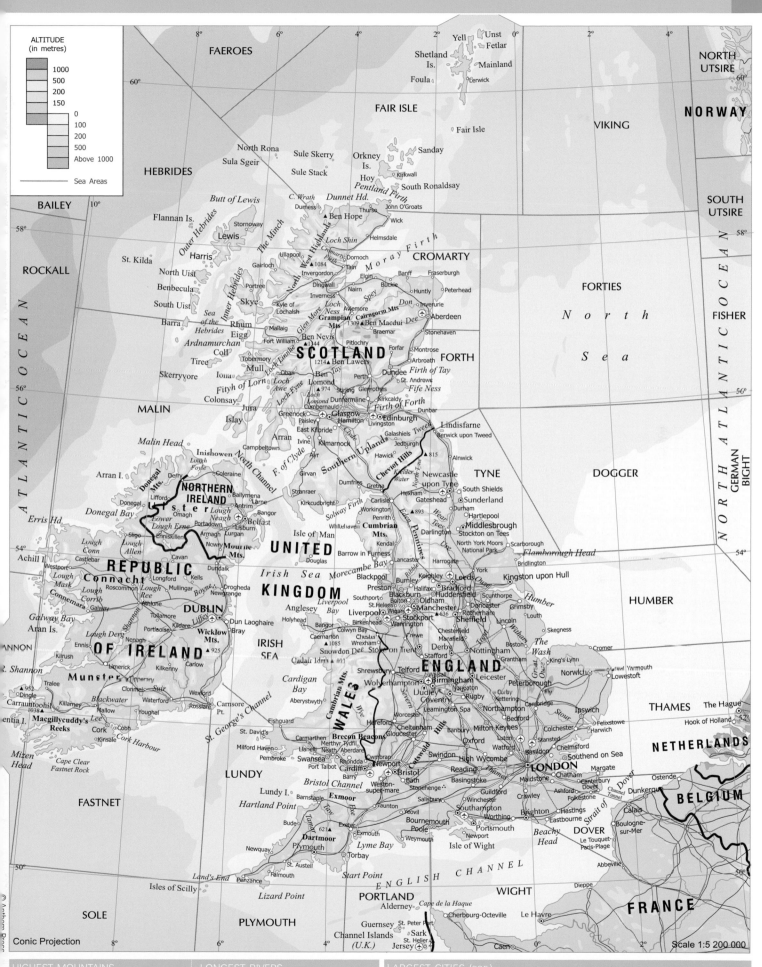

ALTITUDE
(in metres)

| 1000 |
| 500 |
| 200 |
| 150 |
| 0 |
| 100 |
| 200 |
| 500 |
| Above 1000 |

Sea Areas

Conic Projection

Scale 1:5 200 000

© Andrew Ross

HIGHEST MOUNTAINS	LONGEST RIVERS	LARGEST CITIES (POP.)	
1. BEN NEVIS, SCOTLAND (1,344 m)	1. SHANNON, IRELAND (386 km)	1. LONDON, ENGLAND (12 million)	4. GLASGOW, SCOTLAND (1,520,000)
2. BEN MACDHUI, SCOTLAND (1,309 m)	2. SEVERN, ENGLAND (354 km)	2. BIRMINGHAM, ENGLAND (2,550,000)	5. LIVERPOOL, ENGLAND (1,340,000)
3. BRAIERIACH, SCOTLAND (1,296 m)	3. THAMES, ENGLAND (346 km)	3. MANCHESTER, ENGLAND (2,475,000)	6. DUBLIN, IRELAND (1,060,000)

HIGHEST MOUNTAINS
1. SIGNAL DE BOTRANGE, BEL (694 m)
2. KNEIFF, LUX (560 m)

LONGEST RIVERS (TOTAL LENGTH)
1. RHINE (1,320 km)
2. MEUSE (925 km)

LARGEST CITIES (POP.)
1. BRUSSELS, BEL (1,910,000)
2. AMSTERDAM, NLD (745,000)
3. ROTTERDAM, NLD (1,480,000)
4. ANTWERP, BEL (1,110,000)

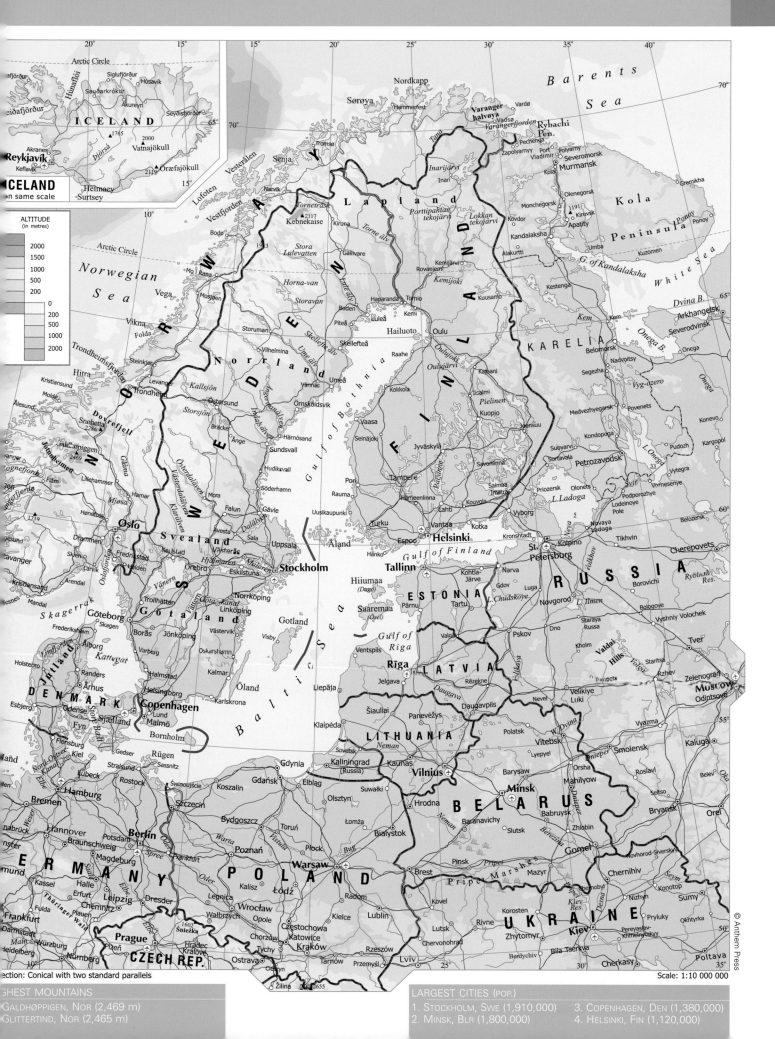

Projection: Conical with two standard parallels

Scale: 1:10 000 000

HIGHEST MOUNTAINS
GALDHØPPIGEN, NOR (2,469 m)
GLITTERTIND, NOR (2,465 m)

LARGEST CITIES (POP.)
1. STOCKHOLM, SWE (1,910,000)   3. COPENHAGEN, DEN (1,380,000)
2. MINSK, BLR (1,800,000)   4. HELSINKI, FIN (1,120,000)

ALTITUDE
(in metres)

3000
2000
1500
1000
500
200
0
50
100
200
500
1000

Conical with two standard parallels projection

HIGHEST MOUNTAINS
1. Mont Blanc, Fra–Ita (4,808 m)
2. Monte Rosa, Ita–Che (4,634 m)
3. Dom, Che (4,545 m)
4. Liskamm, Che (4,527 m)

LONGEST RIVERS
1. Danube (2,850 km)
2. Dniester (1,400 km)
3. Rhine (1,320 km)
4. Elbe (1,145 km)

ARGEST CITIES (POP.)

PARIS, FRA (10 million)   3. MILAN, ITA (3,475,000)   5. WARSAW, POL (2,375,000)   7. MUNICH, DEU (1,960,000)
BERLIN, DEU (4,250,000)   4. HAMBURG, DEU (2,575,000)   6. BUDAPEST, HUN (2,275,000)   8. FRANKFURT, DEU (1,920,000)

ALTITUDE
(in metres)

| 3000 | 2000 | 1500 | 1000 | 500 | 200 | 0 | 150 | 300 | 600 | 1500 | 3000 | 6000 | 9000 |

Projection: Conical with two standard parallels

© Anthem Press

Scale:1:4 950 000

HIGHEST MOUNTAINS	LONGEST RIVERS (TOTAL LENGTH)	LARGEST CITIES (POP.)	
1. MONT BLANC (4,808 m)	1. LOIRE (1,020 km)	1. PARIS (10 million)	3. LYON (1,430,000)
2. MONT MAUDIT (4,465 m)	2. SEINE (776 km)	2. MARSEILLE (1,480,000)	4. LILLE (1,143,000)

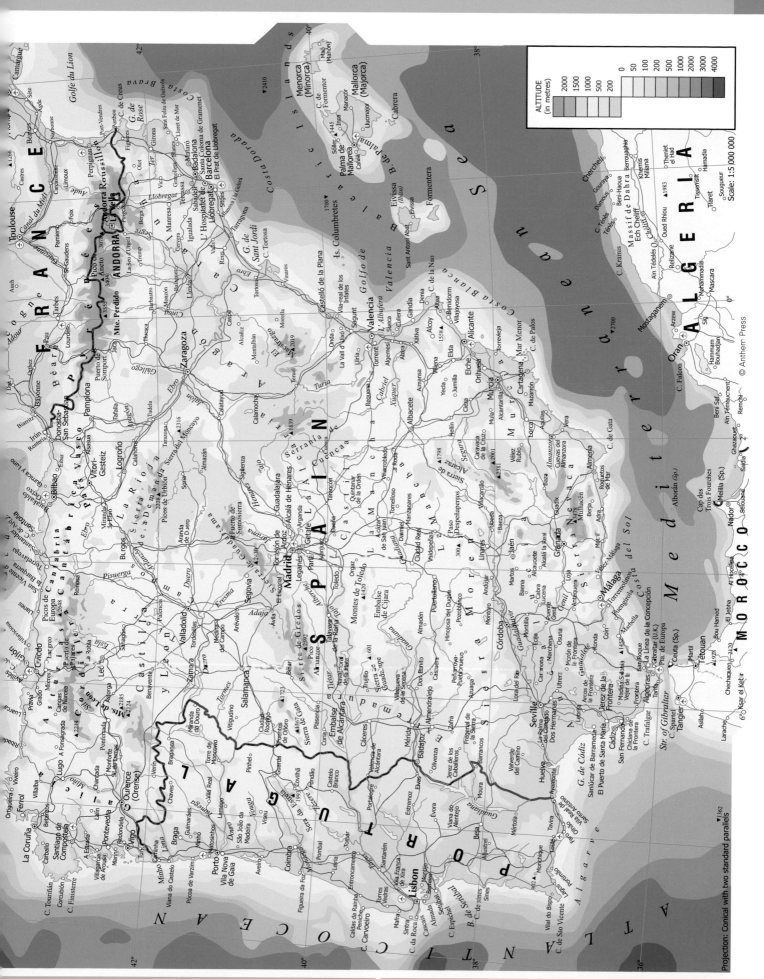

HIGHEST MOUNTAIN
Mulhacén, Granada, Esp (3,479 m)

LONGEST RIVER
Tagus (1,038 km)

LARGEST CITIES (POP.)
1. Madrid, Esp (5,950,000)　　2. Barcelona, Esp (4,175,000)

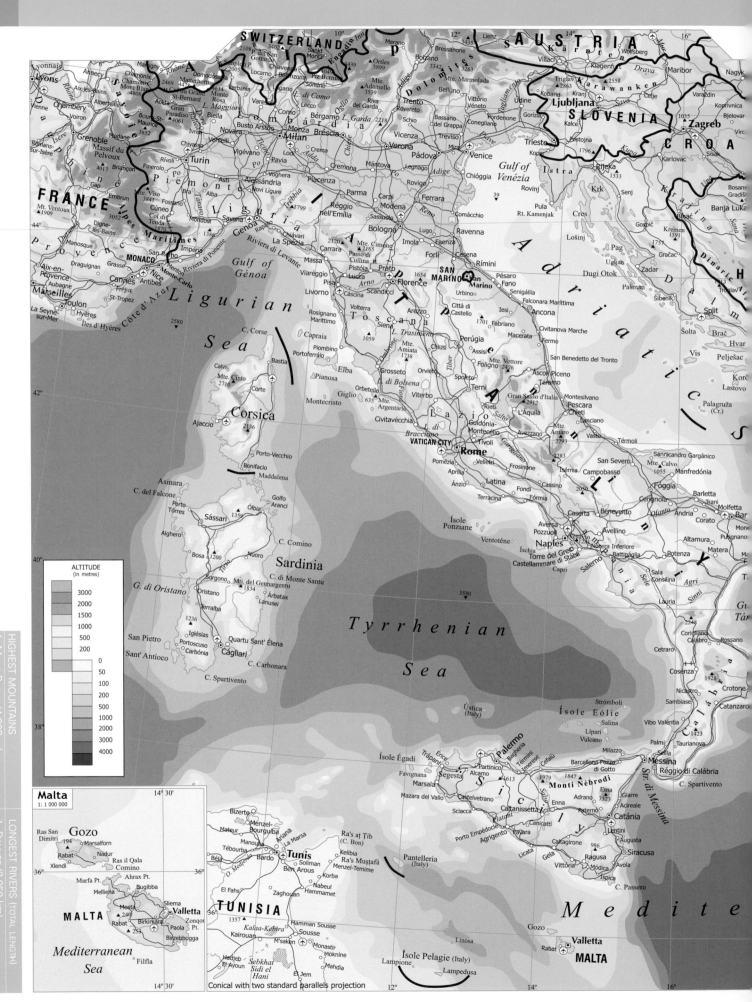

HIGHEST MOUNTAINS
1. Mont Blanc (4,808 m)
2. Monte Rosa (4,634 m)
3. Matterhorn (4,478 m)
4. Mont Maudit (4,465 m)

LONGEST RIVERS (TOTAL LENGTH)
1. Danube (2,850 km)
2. Sava (930 km)
3. Prut (850 km)
4. Po (652 km)

ALTITUDE
(in metres)

3000
2000
1500
1000
500
200
0
50
100
200
500
1000
2000
3000
4000

Malta
1 : 1 000 000

LARGEST CITIES (POP.)

1. ATHENS, GRC (3,725,000)
2. MILAN, ITA (3,525,000)
3. ROME, ITA (3,300,000)
4. NAPLES, ITA (1,260,000)
5. BUCHAREST, ROU (2,025,000)
6. TURIN, ITA (1,610,000)
7. BELGRADE, SER (1,510,000)
8. SOFIA, BGR (1,100,000)

Scale 1:5 000 000   1 Cm = 50 Kms

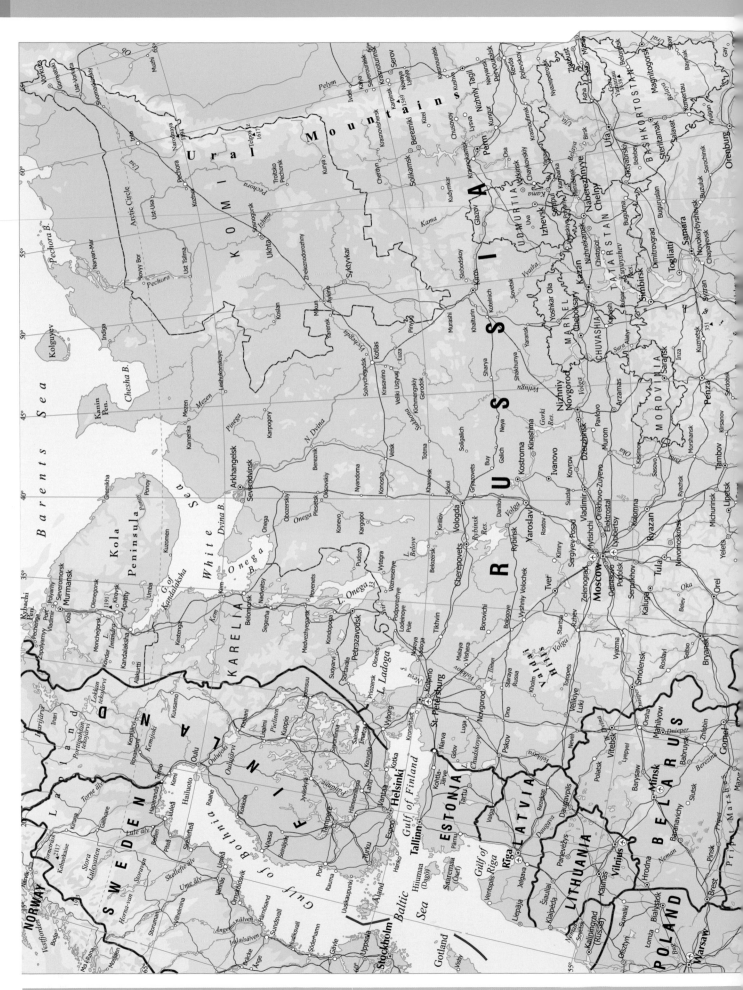

HIGHEST MOUNTAINS

1. ELBRUS, RUS (5,642 m) 2. ARARAT, TUR (5,165 m)

LONGEST RIVERS (TOTAL LENGTH)

1. VOLGA (3,700 km) 2. URAL (2,535 km)

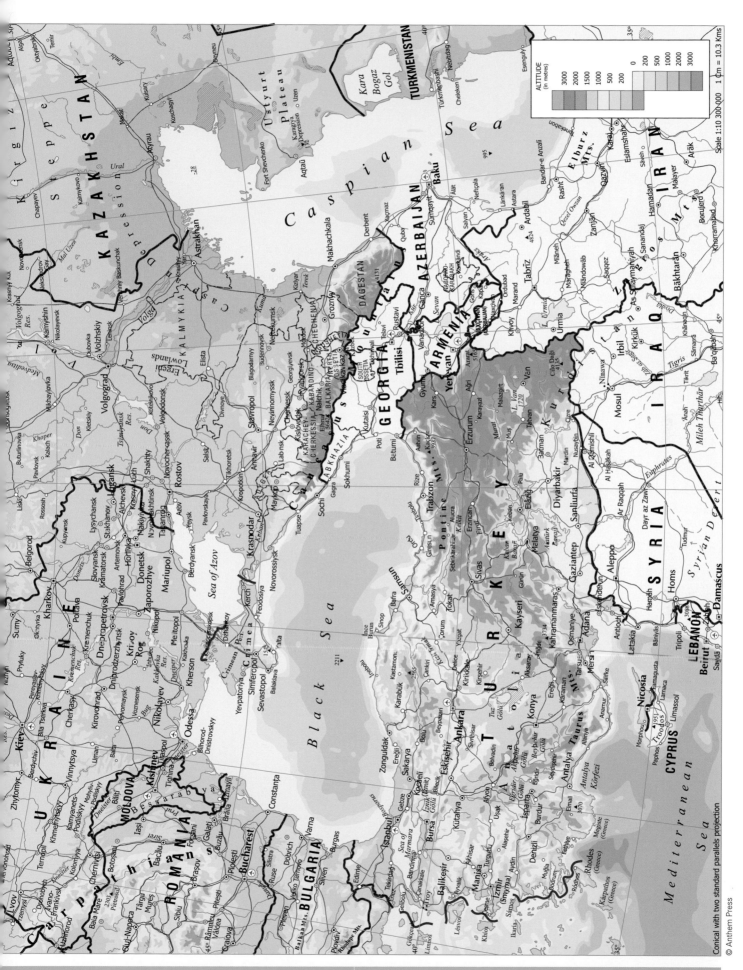

Scale 1:10 300 000   1 cm = 10.3 Kms

Conical with two standard parallels projection

ALTITUDE (in metres)

3000 2000 1500 1000 500 200   0   200 500 1000 2000 3000

LARGEST CITIES (POP.)

1. MOSCOW, RUS (13.5 million)   2. ISTANBUL. TUR (11.8 million)   3. ST PETERSBURG, RUS (4.8 million)   4. ANKARA, TUR (3.9 million)

ARCTIC OCEAN

PACIFIC OCEAN

INDIAN OCEAN

ATLANTIC OCEAN

ASIA'S HIGHEST MOUNTAINS

1. EVEREST, CHN–NPL (8,848 m)
2. K2, CHN–KASHMIR (8,611 m)
3. KANCHENJUNGA, IND–NPL (8,598 m)
4. LHOTSE, CHN–NPL (8,516 m)
5. MAKALU, CHN–NPL (8,481 m)
6. CHO OYU, CHN–NPL (8,201 m)

ASIA'S LONGEST RIVERS

1. Yangtze (6,380 km)
2. Yenisey–Angara (5,550 km)
3. Huang He (5,464 km)
4. Ob–Irtysh (5,410 km)
5. Mekong (4,500 km)
6. Amur (4,400 km)

ALTITUDE
(in metres)
4000 3000 2000 1000 500 200 0 200 1000 2000 4000 6000 8000

Scale 1: 50 000 000

Projection: Bonne

© Anthem Press

ASIA'S LARGEST NATIONS (AREA)	SMALLEST NATIONS (AREA)	ASIA'S LARGEST CITIES (POP.)	
1. RUSSIA (13.1 million sq km)	1. MALDIVES (300 sq km)	1. TOKYO, JPN (33.6 million)	4. DELHI, IND (21.5 million)
2. CHINA (9.6 million sq km)	2. BAHRAIN (665 sq km)	2. SEOUL, KOR (23.4 million)	5. SHANGHAI, CHN (17.5 million)
3. INDIA (3.2 million sq km)	3. SINGAPORE (704 sq km)	3. MUMBAI, IND (21.6 million)	6. OSAKA, JPN (16.7 million)

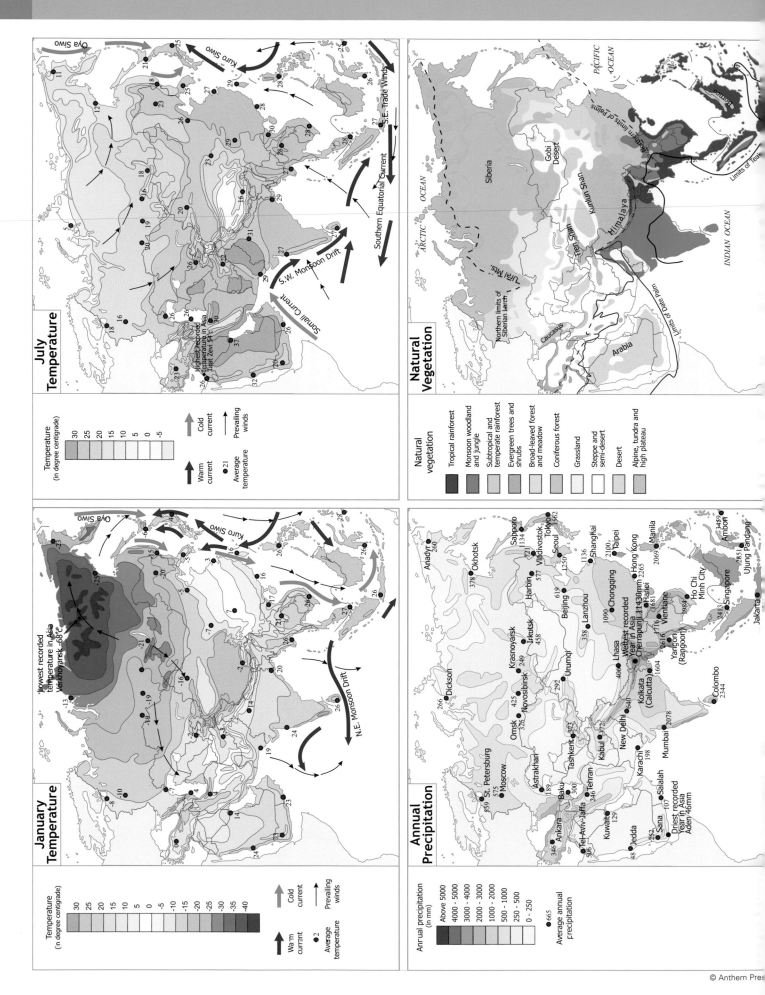

July Temperature

Oya Siwo
Kuro Siwo
S.E. Trade Winds
Southern Equatorial Current
S.W. Monsoon Drift
Somali Current

Highest recorded temperature in Asia Tirat Zevi 54°C

Temperature (in degree centigrade)
30 25 20 15 10 5 0 -5

Cold current
Prevailing winds
Warm current
Average temperature 21

Natural Vegetation

PACIFIC OCEAN
ARCTIC OCEAN
INDIAN OCEAN

Siberia
Gobi Desert
Kunlun Shan
Tien Shan
Himalaya
Caucasus
Arabia
Ural Mts.

Northern limits of Siberian Larch
Northern limits of Palms
Limits of Teak
Limits of Date Palm

Natural vegetation
Tropical rainforest
Monsoon woodland and jungle
Subtropical and temperate rainforest
Evergreen trees and shrubs
Broad-leaved forest and meadow
Coniferous forest
Grassland
Steppe and semi-desert
Desert
Alpine, tundra and high plateau

January Temperature

Oya Siwo
Kuro Siwo
N.E. Monsoon Drift

Lowest recorded temperature in Asia Verkhoyansk -68°C

Temperature (in degree centigrade)
30 25 20 15 10 5 0 -5 -10 -15 -20 -25 -30 -35 -40

Cold current
Prevailing winds
Warm current
Average temperature 2

Annual Precipitation

Anadyr 260
Okhotsk 378
Sapporo 1134
Vladivostok 721
Tokyo 1562
Seoul 577
Shanghai 1136
Taipei 2100
Manila 2069
Ambon 3459
Harbin 619
Beijing 1250
Chongqing 1090
Hong Kong 2265
Hanoi 1681
Yangon (Rangoon) 2616
Vientiane 1934
Ho Chi Minh City 2018
Singapore 2415
Ujung Pandang 2631
Jakarta 1755
Lanzhou 358
Urumqi 292
Lhasa 404
Kolkata (Calcutta) 1604
Colombo 2344
Mumbai 2078
Wettest recorded Year in Asia Cherrapunji 11430mm
Irkutsk 458
Krasnoyarsk 249
Novosibirsk 425
Omsk 325
Dickson 266
Ahadyr 260
St. Petersburg 575
Moscow 550
Astrakhan 189
Tashkent 372
Kabul 292
New Delhi 640
Baku 306
Tehran 246
Karachi 198
Sana 252
Salalah 107
Driest recorded Year in Asia Aden 46mm
Ankara 346
Tel-Aviv-Jaffa 506
Kuwait 129
Jedda 48
665 Average annual precipitation

Annual precipitation (in mm)
Above 5000
4000 - 5000
3000 - 4000
2000 - 3000
1000 - 2000
500 - 1000
250 - 500
0 - 250

© Anthem Press

Land Use and Agriculture

Land use
- Arable
- Arable and pasture
- Market gardening and plantations
- Pasture
- Woods and forests
- Rough grazing
- Non-productive

Agriculture
- Barley
- Maize
- Millet
- Oats
- Rice
- Wheat
- Groundnuts
- Potatoes
- Soya beans
- Cotton
- Rubber
- Sugarbeet
- Sugarcane
- Tobacco
- Coffee
- Tea
- Main fishing areas
- Beef cattle
- Dairy cattle
- Pigs
- Sheep
- Bananas
- Citrus fruit
- Date palms
- Fruits
- Vines

Projection: Bonne Scale: 1:53 900 000

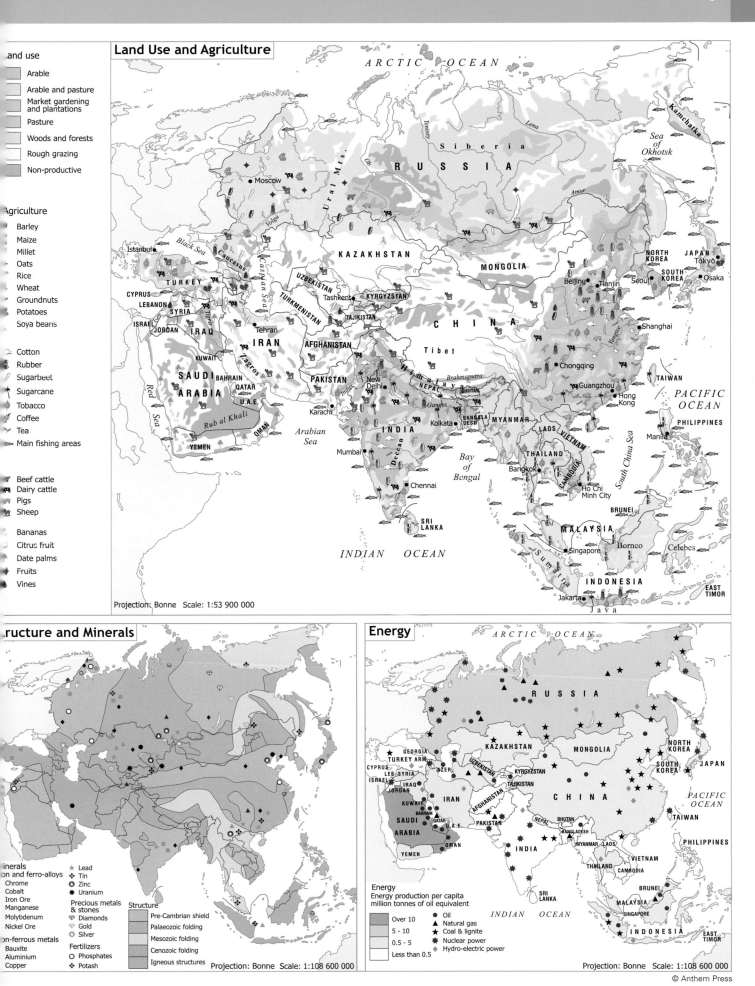

ARCTIC OCEAN
RUSSIA
Siberia
Moscow
Ural Mts.
Yenisey
Ob
Lena
Amur
Sea of Okhotsk
Kamchatka
KAZAKHSTAN
MONGOLIA
Black Sea
Istanbul
Caucasus
Caspian Sea
Volga
TURKEY
CYPRUS
LEBANON
SYRIA
ISRAEL
JORDAN
IRAQ
Tigris
IRAN
Tehran
Zagros
UZBEKISTAN
TURKMENISTAN
Tashkent
KYRGYZSTAN
TAJIKISTAN
AFGHANISTAN
PAKISTAN
CHINA
Tibet
Himalaya
Indus
Brahmaputra
Yangtze
Beijing
Tianjin
Chongqing
Guangzhou
Shanghai
NORTH KOREA
SOUTH KOREA
Seoul
JAPAN
Tōkyō
Osaka
TAIWAN
Hong Kong
PACIFIC OCEAN
KUWAIT
BAHRAIN
QATAR
U.A.E.
SAUDI ARABIA
Red Sea
Rub al Khali
OMAN
YEMEN
Arabian Sea
Karachi
New Delhi
NEPAL
BHUTAN
Ganges
INDIA
Deccan
Mumbai
Chennai
Kolkata
BANGLADESH
MYANMAR
LAOS
VIETNAM
THAILAND
Bangkok
CAMBODIA
Ho Chi Minh City
Bay of Bengal
SRI LANKA
INDIAN OCEAN
South China Sea
PHILIPPINES
Manila
BRUNEI
MALAYSIA
Singapore
Borneo
Celebes
Sumatra
INDONESIA
Jakarta
Java
EAST TIMOR

Structure and Minerals

Minerals

Iron and ferro-alloys
- Chrome
- Cobalt
- Iron Ore
- Manganese
- Molybdenum
- Nickel Ore

Non-ferrous metals
- Bauxite
- Aluminium
- Copper

- ★ Lead
- ✛ Tin
- ⊘ Zinc
- ✱ Uranium

Precious metals & stones
- ▽ Diamonds
- ⊕ Gold
- ▽ Silver

Fertilizers
- ○ Phosphates
- ✣ Potash

Structure
- Pre-Cambrian shield
- Palaeozoic folding
- Mesozoic folding
- Cenozoic folding
- Igneous structures

Projection: Bonne Scale: 1:108 600 000

Energy

Energy production per capita million tonnes of oil equivalent
- Over 10
- 5 - 10
- 0.5 - 5
- Less than 0.5

- ● Oil
- ▲ Natural gas
- ★ Coal & lignite
- ✱ Nuclear power
- ◆ Hydro-electric power

ARCTIC OCEAN
RUSSIA
KAZAKHSTAN
MONGOLIA
CHINA
GEORGIA
TURKEY
ARM
CYPRUS
LEB
SYRIA
ISRAEL
JORDAN
IRAQ
AZER
UZBEKISTAN
KYRGYZSTAN
TAJIKISTAN
IRAN
AFGHANISTAN
PAKISTAN
KUWAIT
BAHRAIN
QATAR
U.A.E.
SAUDI ARABIA
YEMEN
OMAN
NEPAL
BHUTAN
BANGLADESH
INDIA
MYANMAR
LAOS
VIETNAM
THAILAND
CAMBODIA
SRI LANKA
INDIAN OCEAN
NORTH KOREA
SOUTH KOREA
JAPAN
PACIFIC OCEAN
TAIWAN
PHILIPPINES
BRUNEI
MALAYSIA
SINGAPORE
INDONESIA
EAST TIMOR

Projection: Bonne Scale: 1:108 600 000

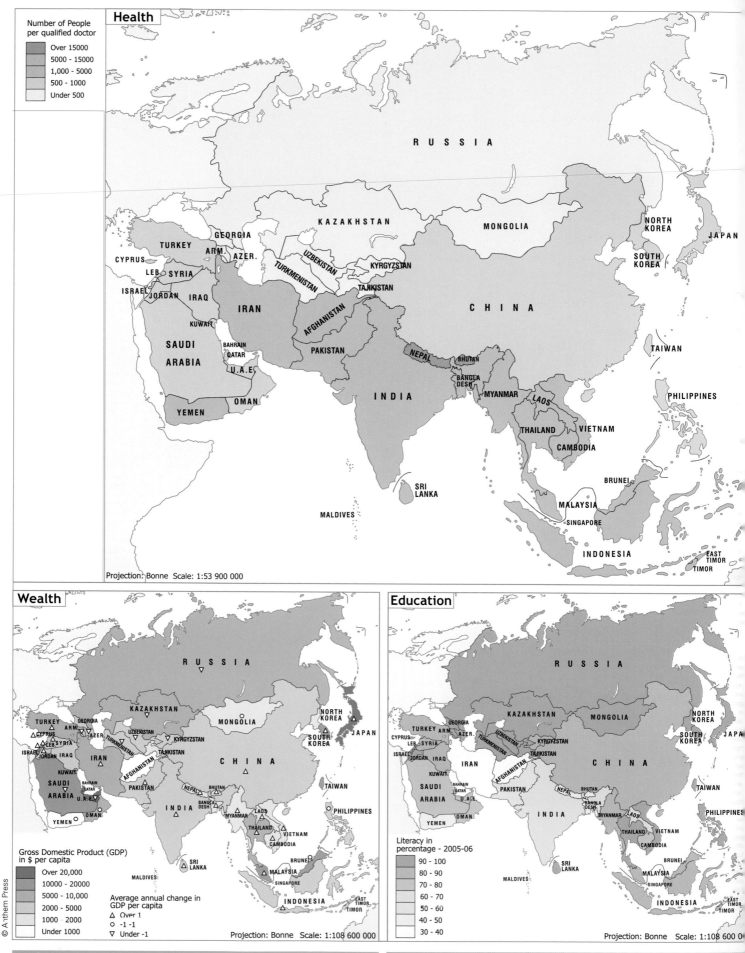

Health

Number of People per qualified doctor
- Over 15000
- 5000 - 15000
- 1,000 - 5000
- 500 - 1000
- Under 500

RUSSIA

KAZAKHSTAN

MONGOLIA

NORTH KOREA

JAPAN

GEORGIA

TURKEY

ARM.

AZER.

UZBEKISTAN

KYRGYZSTAN

SOUTH KOREA

CYPRUS

LEB.

SYRIA

TURKMENISTAN

TAJIKISTAN

ISRAEL

JORDAN

IRAQ

IRAN

AFGHANISTAN

CHINA

TAIWAN

KUWAIT

SAUDI ARABIA

BAHRAIN

QATAR

U.A.E.

PAKISTAN

NEPAL

BHUTAN

BANGLA DESH

MYANMAR

LAOS

PHILIPPINES

OMAN

INDIA

THAILAND

VIETNAM

CAMBODIA

YEMEN

SRI LANKA

BRUNEI

MALDIVES

MALAYSIA

SINGAPORE

INDONESIA

EAST TIMOR

Projection: Bonne Scale: 1:53 900 000

Wealth

RUSSIA

KAZAKHSTAN

MONGOLIA

NORTH KOREA

JAPAN

TURKEY

GEORGIA

ARM.

CYPRUS

AZER.

UZBEKISTAN

KYRGYZSTAN

SOUTH KOREA

LEB.

SYRIA

TURKMENISTAN

TAJIKISTAN

ISRAEL

JORDAN

IRAQ

IRAN

AFGHANISTAN

CHINA

TAIWAN

KUWAIT

SAUDI ARABIA

BAHRAIN

QATAR

U.A.E.

PAKISTAN

NEPAL

BHUTAN

PHILIPPINES

YEMEN

OMAN

INDIA

BANGLA DESH

MYANMAR

LAOS

THAILAND

VIETNAM

CAMBODIA

SRI LANKA

BRUNEI

MALDIVES

MALAYSIA

SINGAPORE

INDONESIA

EAST TIMOR

Gross Domestic Product (GDP) in $ per capita
- Over 20,000
- 10000 - 20,000
- 5000 - 10,000
- 2000 - 5000
- 1000 - 2000
- Under 1000

Average annual change in GDP per capita
- △ Over 1
- ○ -1 -1
- ▽ Under -1

© Anthem Press

Projection: Bonne Scale: 1:108 600 000

Education

RUSSIA

KAZAKHSTAN

MONGOLIA

NORTH KOREA

JAPAN

TURKEY

GEORGIA

ARM.

AZER.

UZBEKISTAN

KYRGYZSTAN

SOUTH KOREA

CYPRUS

LEB.

SYRIA

TURKMENISTAN

TAJIKISTAN

ISRAEL

JORDAN

IRAQ

IRAN

AFGHANISTAN

CHINA

TAIWAN

KUWAIT

SAUDI ARABIA

BAHRAIN

QATAR

U.A.E.

PAKISTAN

NEPAL

BHUTAN

PHILIPPINES

YEMEN

OMAN

INDIA

BANGLA DESH

MYANMAR

LAOS

THAILAND

VIETNAM

CAMBODIA

SRI LANKA

BRUNEI

MALDIVES

MALAYSIA

SINGAPORE

INDONESIA

EAST TIMOR

Literacy in percentage - 2005-06
- 90 - 100
- 80 - 90
- 70 - 80
- 60 - 70
- 50 - 60
- 40 - 50
- 30 - 40

Projection: Bonne Scale: 1:108 600 000

ASIA'S WEALTHIEST NATIONS	GDP PER CAPITA (PPP) US $	ASIA'S POOREST NATIONS	GDP PER CAPITA (PPP) US $
1. QATAR ($33,411)	3. UNITED ARAB EMIRATES ($30,615)	1. EAST TIMOR ($400)	3. AFGHANISTAN ($800)
2. KUWAIT ($30,897)	4. SINGAPORE ($29,605)	2. YEMEN ($745)	4. TUVALU ($1,100)

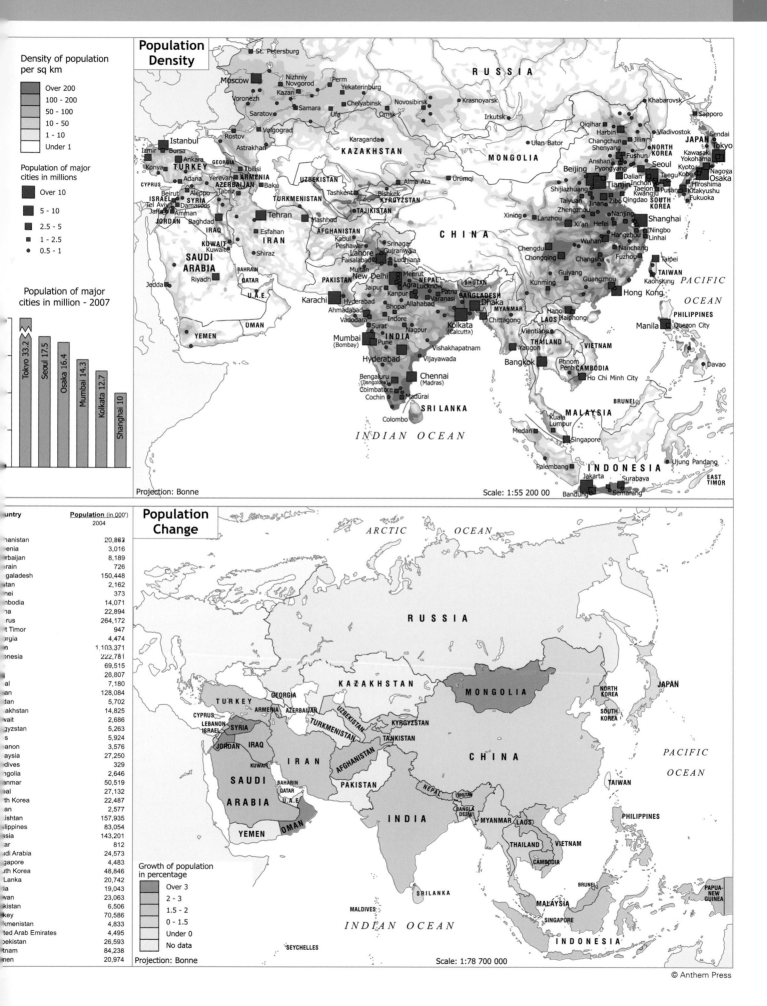

Population Density

Density of population per sq km

- Over 200
- 100 - 200
- 50 - 100
- 10 - 50
- 1 - 10
- Under 1

Population of major cities in millions

- Over 10
- 5 - 10
- 2.5 - 5
- 1 - 2.5
- 0.5 - 1

Population of major cities in million - 2007

- Tokyo 33.2
- Seoul 17.5
- Osaka 16.4
- Mumbai 14.3
- Kolkata 12.7
- Shanghai 10

Projection: Bonne

Scale: 1:55 200 00

Population Change

Growth of population in percentage

- Over 3
- 2 - 3
- 1.5 - 2
- 0 - 1.5
- Under 0
- No data

Projection: Bonne

Scale: 1:78 700 000

Country	Population (in 000') 2004
Afghanistan	20,862
Armenia	3,016
Azerbaijan	8,189
Bahrain	726
Bangladesh	150,448
Bhutan	2,162
Brunei	373
Cambodia	14,071
China	22,894
Cyprus	264,172
East Timor	947
Georgia	4,474
Iran	1,103,371
Indonesia	222,781
	69,515
	28,807
Israel	7,180
Japan	128,084
Jordan	5,702
Kazakhstan	14,825
Kuwait	2,686
Kyrgyzstan	5,263
Laos	5,924
Lebanon	3,576
Malaysia	27,250
Maldives	329
Mongolia	2,646
Myanmar	50,519
Nepal	27,132
North Korea	22,487
Oman	2,577
Pakistan	157,935
Philippines	83,054
Russia	143,201
Qatar	812
Saudi Arabia	24,573
Singapore	4,483
South Korea	48,846
Sri Lanka	20,742
Syria	19,043
Taiwan	23,063
Tajikistan	6,506
Turkey	70,586
Turkmenistan	4,833
United Arab Emirates	4,495
Uzbekistan	26,593
Vietnam	84,238
Yemen	20,974

Projection: Lambert's Conical Orthomorphic

ALTITUDE
(in metres)

4000
2000
1000
400
200
0
600

PACIFIC OCEAN

Bering Sea

Sea of Okhotsk

East Siberian Sea

Laptev Sea

Kolyma Range

Verkhoyansk Range

Cherski Range

Stanovoy Range

Dzhugdzur Range

Sredinny Range

Kamchatka Peninsula

Kuril Islands (Russia)

Sakhalin

Sikhote Alin Range

Yablonovyy Range

Great Khingan Mts.

Manchuria

MONGOLIA

Inner Mongolia

Gobi

Ala Shan

Qilian Shan

CHINA

UlanBator

Beijing

Seoul

SOUTH KOREA

NORTH KOREA

P'yongyang

JAPAN

Tokyo

Hokkaido

Sapporo

Honshū

Shikoku

Kyūshū

Sea of Japan

Yellow Sea

East China Sea

Scale 1:24 000 000

© Anthem Press

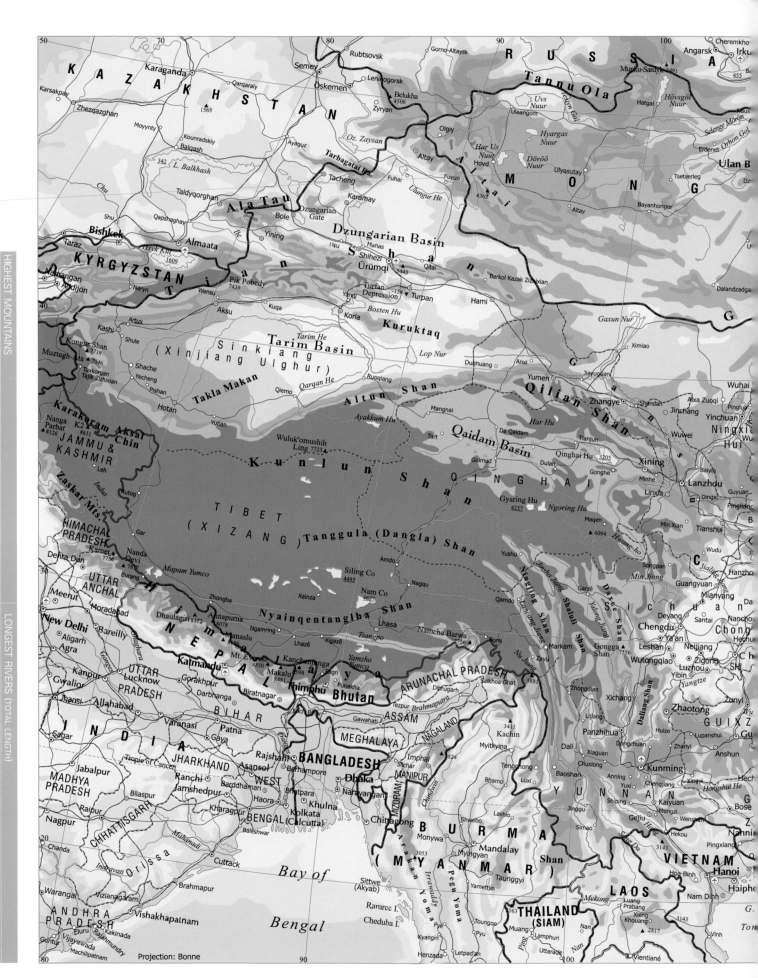

Projection: Bonne

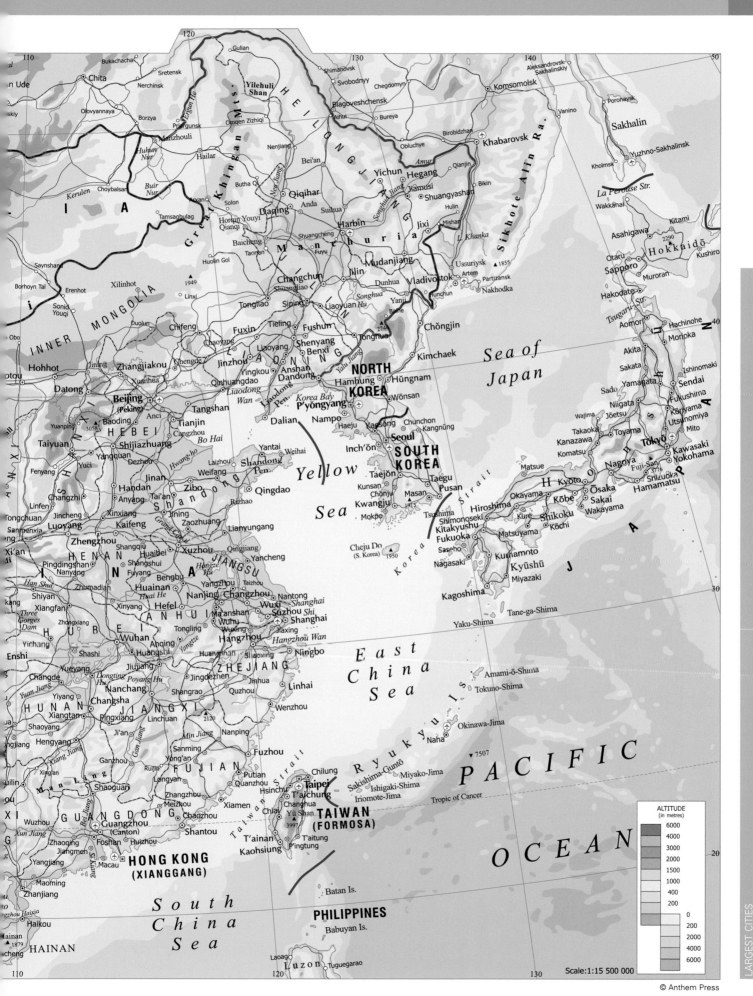

Map labels

120 · 110 · 130 · 140 · 50

Ulan Ude · Chita · Bukachacha · Sretensk · Shimanovsk · Svobodnyy · Chegdomyn · Komsomolsk · Aleksandrovsk-Sakhalinskiy · Poronaysk · Vanino

Olovyannaya · Nerchinsk · Gulian · Blagoveshchensk · Bureya · Birobidzhan · Khabarovsk · Yuzhno-Sakhalinsk

Borzya · Priargunsk · Ergun He · Yilehuli Shan · Aihui · Bikin · Kholmsk · Sakhalin

Manzhouli · Hailar · Oroqen Zizhiqi · Nenjiang · Yichun · Hegang · Qianjin · Hulin · Wakkanai · Kitami

Huhun Nur · Choybalsan · Buir Nur · Butha Qi · Bei'an · Jiamusi · Shuangyashan · La Pérouse Str. · Asahigawa · 2290 · Hokkaidō · Kushiro

Saynshand · Tamsagbulag · Solon · Aoxan · Daqing · Anda · Suihua · Songhua Jiang · Mishan · Otaru · Sapporo · Muroran

Horqin Youyi Qianqi · Baicheng · Taonan · Harbin · Shuangcheng · Fuyu · Jixi · L. Khanka · Hakodate · Tsugaru Str. · Aomori · Hachinohe

Borhoyn Tal · 1949 · Xilinhot · Linxi · Huolin Gol · Changchun · Jilin · Dunhua · Vladivostok · Ussuriysk · Artem · Partizansk · 40 N · Akita · Morioka

Erenhot · Duolun · Tongliao · Shuangliao · Siping · Liaoyuan · Hu · Songhua · Yanji · Hunchun · Nakhodka · Sakata · Ishinomaki

INNER MONGOLIA · Sonid Youqi · Chifeng · Fuxin · Tieling · Fushun · Tonghua · Chŏngjin · Sado · Yamagata · Sendai

Obo · Hohhot · Zhangjiakou · Chengde · Jinzhou · Liaoyang · Shenyang · Benxi · 274 · Yalu Jiang · Kimchaek · Sea of Japan · Wajima · Niigata · Kōriyama · Utsunomiya

Datong · Xuanhua · Qinhuangdao · Yingkou · Dandong · Hamhung · Hŭngnam · Takaoka · Jōetsu · Mito

Yuanping · Beijing (Peking) · Baoding · 3058 · Anci · Tianjin · Liaodong Wan · Liaodong Pen. · Korea Bay · P'yŏngyang · Wŏnsan · NORTH KOREA · Matsue · Kanazawa · Toyama · Tōkyō · Kawasaki · Yokohama

Taiyuan · HEBEI · Cangzhou · Bo Hai · Dalian · Nampo · Haeju · Kaesŏng · Chunchon · Kangnŭng · H · Kyōto · Ōsaka · Fuji-San · Shizuoka · Hamamatsu

Fenyang · Yuci · Shijiazhuang · Yangquan · Dezhou · Yantai · Weihai · Inch'ŏn · Seoul · SOUTH KOREA · Okayama · Kōbe · Sakai · Wakayama

Linfen · Jinan · Weifang · Shandong Pen. · Yellow Sea · Taejŏn · Taegu · Strait · Hiroshima · Kure · Shikoku · Kōchi · A

Tongchuan · Jincheng · Xinxiang · Anyang · Tai'an · Zibo · Qingdao · Kunsan · Chŏnju · Masan · Pusan · Tsushima · Shimonoseki · Kitakyushu · Matsuyama

Xi'an · Luoyang · Zhengzhou · Kaifeng · Jining · Zaozhuang · Rizhao · Kwangju · Fukuoka · Saseko · Nagasaki · Kumamoto · Kyūshū · J

Pingdingshan · Shangqiu · Huaibei · Xuzhou · Qingjiang · Lianyungang · Mokpo · Cheju Do (S. Korea) · 1950 · Korea · Miyazaki

Sanmenxia · HENAN · Nanyang · Fuyang · JIANGSU · Yancheng · Kagoshima

Han Shui · Zhumadian · Yingcheng · Shiyan · Xiangfan · Xinyang · Hefei · ANHUI · Huainan · Bengbu · Yangzhou · Changzhou · Nantong · Hongze Hu · Taizhou · Hangzhou Wan · Tane-ga-Shima

Three Gorges Dam · Zhongxiang · Huai He · Nanjing · Wuxi · Suzhou · Shanghai · Yaku-Shima

Yichang · HUBEI · Ma'anshan · Wuhu · Shanghai Shi · Jiaxing

Enshi · Wuhan · Anqing · Tongling · Huangshan · Huangshi · Hangzhou · East China Sea

Yueyang · Dongting Hu · Jingdezhen · Shaoxing · Ningbo · Amami-ō-Shima · Tokuno-Shima

Changde · Yuan Jiang · Nanchang · Shangrao · ZHEJIANG · 7507 · Okinawa-Jima

Yiyang · Poyang Hu · Jinhua · Quzhou · Linhai · Naha

HUNAN · Changsha · JIANGXI · Wenzhou · PACIFIC · Ryukyu Is.

Xiangtan · Pingxiang · Ji'an · Gan Jiang · Nanping · Sakishima-Guntō · Miyako-Jima

Shaoyang · Linchuan · Sanming · Yong'an · Fuzhou · Chilung · Ishigaki-Shima

Hengyang · Xiang Jiang · Nan Ling · Ruijin · FUJIAN · Putian · Quanzhou · Hsinchu · Taipei · Iriomote-Jima · Tropic of Cancer

Xing'an · Ganzhou · Shaoguan · Zhangzhou · Changhua · T'aichung · 3997 · Yü Shan

Wuzhou · Zhaoqing · GUANGDONG · Meizhou · Chaozhou · Xiamen · Chiai · TAIWAN (FORMOSA)

Foshan · Guangzhou (Canton) · Shantou · T'ainan · T'aitung

HONG KONG (XIANGGANG) · Huizhou · P'ingtung · Batan Is.

Yangjiang · Macau · Kaohsiung

Maoming · Zhanjiang · South China Sea · PHILIPPINES · Babuyan Is.

HAINAN · Haikou · 1879 · Tropic of Cancer · OCEAN · Luzon · Tuguegarao · Laoag

Scale: 1:15 500 000

ALTITUDE (in metres)
6000 · 4000 · 3000 · 2000 · 1500 · 1000 · 400 · 200 · 0 · 200 · 2000 · 4000 · 6000

© Anthem Press

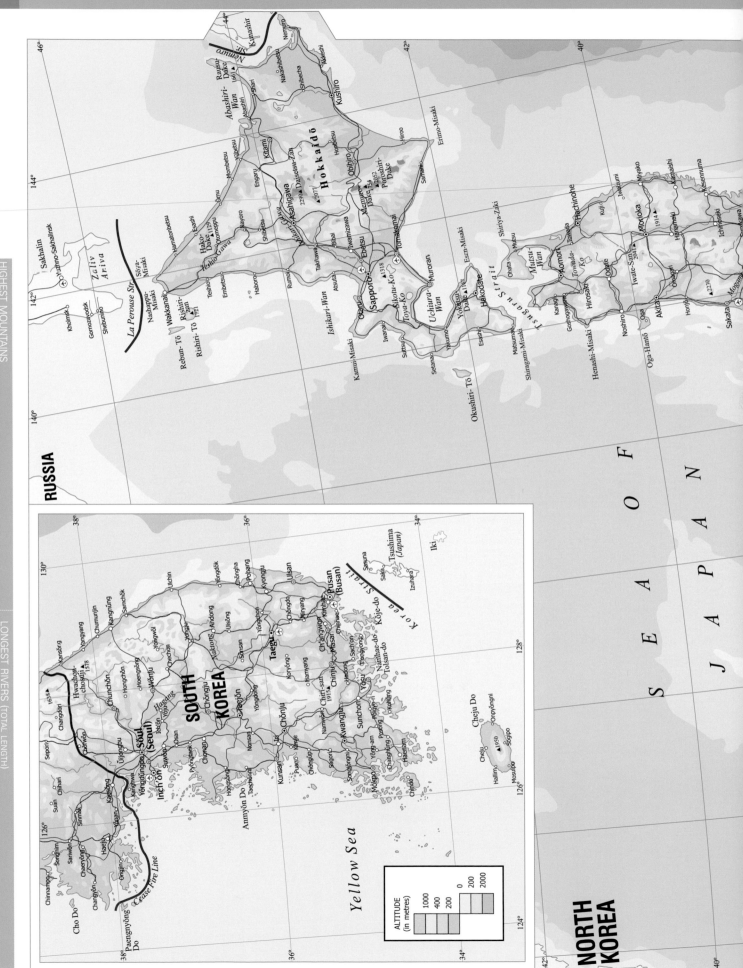

HIGHEST MOUNTAINS
1. Fuji-san, Jpn (3,776 m)
2. Kitdake, Jpn (3,193 m)
3. Hotakadake, Jpn (3,190 m)
4. Ainodake, Jpn (3,189 m)
5. Mount Yari, Jpn (3,180 m)
6. Mount Warusawa, Jpn (3,141 m)

LONGEST RIVERS (total length)
1. Nakdong, Kor (521 km)
2. Han, Kor (514 km)
3. Geum, Kor (401 km)
4. Shjano, Jpn (367 km)
5. Tone, Jpn (322 km)
6. Imjin, Kor (255 km)

ALTITUDE (in metres)
1000
400
200
2000
200
0

ALTITUDE
(in metres)

| 3000 | 2000 | 1500 | 1000 | 400 | 200 | | 0 | 200 | 2000 | 4000 | 6000 | 8000 |

Scale: 1:4 900 000

J A P A N

Honshū

Tokyo

Shikoku

Kyūshū

SOUTH KOREA

P A C I F I C   O C E A N

Nampō-Shotō

Projection: Conical with two standard parallels

© Anthem Press

LARGEST CITIES

1. Tokyo, Jpn (33.6 million)
2. Seoul, Kor (23.4 million)
3. Osaka, Jpn (16.7 million)
4. Nagoya, Jpn (8.25 million)
5. Busan, Kor (3.575 million)
6. Daegu, Kor (2.675 million)
7. Sapporo, Jpn (2.5 million)
8. Fukuoka, Jpn (2.4 million)
9. Hiroshima, Jpn (1.83 million)
10. Kitakyushu, Jpn (1.6 million)
11. Taejon, Kor (1.55 million)
12. Sendai, Jpn (1.54 million)

Ramree I.
Cheduba I.
MYANMAR
Prome
Bassein
Rangoon
Ma-ubin
Thaton
Moulmein
Ye
G. of Martaban
Chiang Mai
Luang Prabang
Hanoi
Haiphong
G. of Tonkin
CHINA
HaiKou
Hainan
Nam Dim
Vientiane
Ha Tinh
Tak
Phitsanulok
Uttaradit
Savannakhet
Dong Hoi
Hue
Da Nang
THAILAND
Nakhon Sawan
Khon Kaen
Ubon Ratchathani
Nakhon Ratchasima
VIETNAM
▲2598 Quang Ngai
Paracel Is.
Tavoy
Phra Nakhon Si Ayutthaya
Saraburi
Bangkok
Chon Buri
CAMBODIA
Batdambang
Srepok
Qui Nhon
S o
C h
Middle Andaman
Andaman Islands *(India)*
Little Andaman
Mergui
Mergui Arch.
Rayong
Tonle Sap
Buon Me Thuot
Kampong Cham
Mekong
Nha Trang
Da Lat
Cam Ranh
Phan Rang
Phnom Penh
Bien Hoa
Phan Thiet
S
Car Nicobar
10°
Andaman Sea
Isthmus of Kra
Gulf of Thailand
Kampong Saom
Long Xuyen
Rach Gia
Can Tho
My Tho
Ho Chi Minh City
Vung Tau
Soc Trang
Nicobar Islands *(India)*
Nakhon Si Thammarat
Ca Mau
Bac Lieu
Con Son
Spratly Is.
Amboyn
Trang
Phuket
Mui Ca Mau
Songkhla
Hat Yai
Yala
M A L A Y S
We
Banda Aceh
Strait of Malacca
Alor Setar
Kota Baharu
Kuala Terengganu
George Town
Butterworth
Taiping
Peninsular Malaysia
Laut
Kuala Bela
Langsa
Ipoh
Gunong Tahan ▲2190
Kuantan
Kepulauan Natuna Besar
Mi
S
Belawan
Teluk Intan
Kepulauan Anambas
Kepulauan Natuna Selatan
Sar
Binjai
Medan
Pematangsiantar
Kelang
Kuala Lumpur
Seremban Melaka
Sibu
u
Simeulue
Tanjungbalai
Rupat
Singkawang
Kuching
Kepulauan Banyak
Danau Toba
Sibolga
Muar
Keluang
Batu Pahat
Johor Baharu
Singapore
m
Nias
Padangsidempuan
Kepulauan Riau
Str. of Karimata
Kapuas
0° Equator
Pekanbaru
Kepulauan Lingga
G. Saran ▲1758
B O R
Kepulauan Batu
Bukittinggi
Payakumbuh
Pontianak
ALTITUDE
(in metres)
4000
2000
1000
400
200
0
200
6000
Siberut
Padang
Hari
Kerinci 3805▲
Sungaipenuh
Selat Berhala
Selat Bangka
Jambi
Kepulauan Karimata
K
Kuala
a
INDIAN OCEAN
Sipura
Kepulauan Mentawai
Musi
Pangkalpinang
Bangka
Tanjungpandan
I N D O
Banjarma
Enggano
Bengkulu
Pekanbaru
Palembang
Perabumulih
Lahat
Belitung
G r e a t e r *S u n d a*
Kotabumi
Bandar Lampung
J a v a
Krakatau
813▲
Serang
Karawang
Jakarta
Kandanghaur
Kepulauan Karimunjawa
Bawean
Madura
Selat Sunda
Bogor
Sukabumi
Bandung
Cirebon
Tegal
Pekalongan
Semarang
Tasikmalaya
Magelang
Madiun
Surakarta
Surabaya
Probolin
Kebumen
Yogyakarta
Kediri
Blitar
Malang
Banyu
Java Trench
▼6650
Christmas I. *(Australia)*
110°
100° Projection: Bonne

Singapore

103°45′ Johor Bahru
103°50′
103°55′
104°
MALAYSIA
103°45′
Pulau Bulan
Pasir Gudang
Sembawang
Woodlands
Pulau Seletar
Pulau Ubin
Pulau Tekong
Sungai Johor
Sarimbun Reservoir
Kranji Reservoir
Yishun
Jalan Kayu
Mandai
Punggol
Sungei Seletar
Serangoon Harbour
Pulau Serangoon
Chek Jawa
Murai Reservoir
Tanjong
Lim Chu Kang
Sungei Seletar
Lower Peirce Reservoir
Ang Mo
Hougang
Serangoon
Changi
1°25′
Tengeh Reservoir
Poyan Reservoir
Choa Chu Kang
Bukit Panjang
Upper Peirce Reservoir
Bukit Timah
Toa Payoh
Paya Lebar
Tampines
Bedok Reservoir
Jurong
Bukit Batok
Clementi
Tanglin
Siglap Katong
Bedok
1°20′
Jurong Island
Pandan
SINGAPORE
Bedok Jetty
1°20′
Pulau Sakra
Pulau Bukum
Pulau Brani
Mount Emban
Sentosa
Buran Darat
Strait of Singapore
1°15′
Projection: Mercator
103°45′
103°50′
103°55′
Scale: 1:500 000

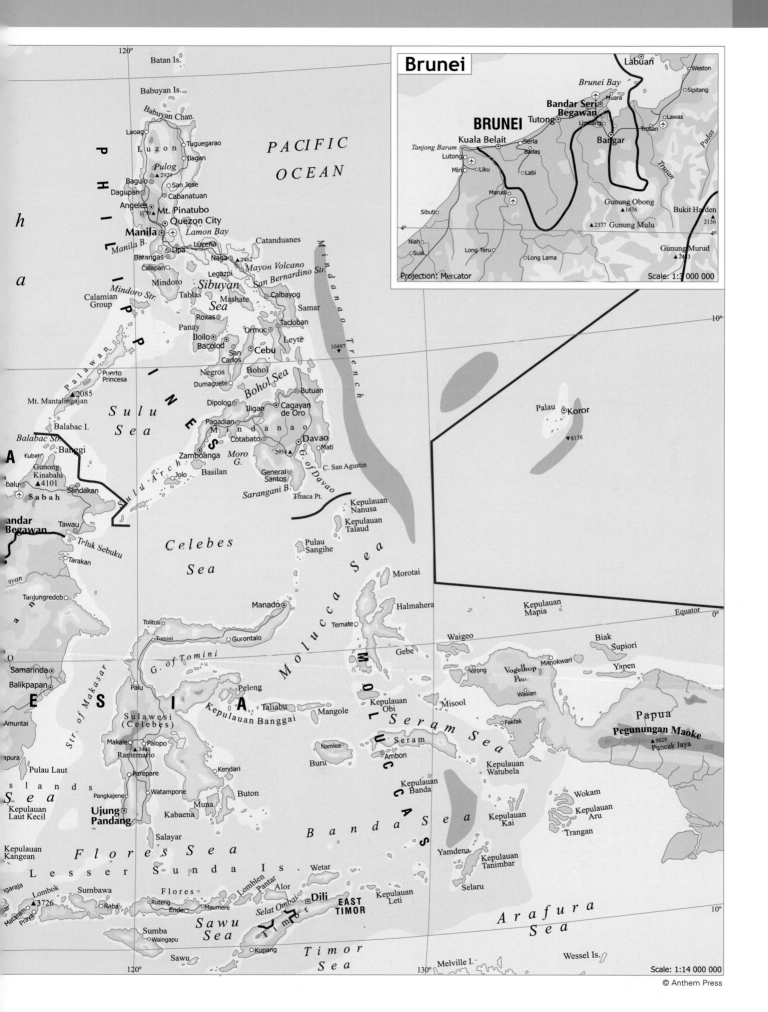

Brunei

Labuan
Weston
Brunei Bay
Sipitang
Muara
Bandar Seri
Begawan
BRUNEI
Tutong
Limbang
Lawas
Kuala Belait
Seria
Trusan
Tanjong Baram
Badas
Bangar
Lutong
Padas
Miri
Liku
Labi
Tresan
Marudi
Gunung Obong
Bukit Harden
▲1676
2136
Sibuti
▲2377 Gunung Mulu
4°
4°
Niah
Long Teru
Gunung Murud
Suai
Long Lama
▲2423

Projection: Mercator
Scale: 1:3 000 000

120°
Batan Is.
PACIFIC
OCEAN

Babuyan Is.
Babuyan Chan.
Laoag
Tuguegarao
Ilagan
P
Luzon
Pulog
H
▲2929
Baguio
San Jose
I
Dagupan
Cabanatuan
L
Angeles
Mt. Pinatubo
I
1759▲
Quezon City
P
Lamon Bay
Manila
P
Manila B.
Lipa
Lucena
Catanduanes
I
Batangas
Naga
N
Calapan
Mayon Volcano
San Bernardino Str.
E
Mindoro
Legazpi
Sibuyan
S
Mindoro Str.
Tablas
Sea
Calbayog
Calamian
Mashate
Samar
Group
Roxas
Panay
Tacloban
Ormoc
Iloilo
Leyte
Bacolod
Cebu
San
Carlos
10497▼
Puerto
Negros
Bohol
Princesa
Dumaguete
Bohol Sea
Butuan
▲2085
Dipolog
Iligan
Cagayan
Mt. Mantalingajan
Pagadian
de Oro
S u l u
Mindanao
Davao
Balabac I.
Cotabato
Mati
Sea
2954▲
Balabac Str.
Zamboanga
Moro
G. of Davao
Kubati
Banggi
Jolo
G.
C. San Agustin
Sulu Arch.
Basilan
General
Gunong
Santos
Kinabalu
Sarangani B.
Tinaca Pt.
balu
▲4101
Kepulauan
Sandakan
Nanusa
Sabah
Kepulauan
andar
Tawau
Talaud
Begawan
Teluk Sebuku
C e l e b e s
Tarakan
Sea
Pulau
ayan
Sangihe
Tanjungredeb
Manado
Tolitoli
Tomini
G. of Tomini
Samarinda
Palu
Balikpapan
Peleng
E
S
Sulawesi
A
Taliabu
(Celebes)
Kepulauan Banggai
Mangole
Amuntai
Makale
Palopo
Rantemario
▲3440
Parepare
Kendari
Pulau Laut
Pangkajene
Watampone
Muna
Buton
l s l a n d s
S e a
Ujung
Kabaena
Kepulauan
Pandang
Laut Kecil
Salayar
Kepulauan
F l o r e s *S e a*
Kangean
L e s s e r *S u n d a* *I s .*
Wetar
ngaraja
Lombok
Sumbawa
Flores
Pantar
Lomblen
Dili
ataram
▲3726
Raba
Ruteng
Ende
Alor
Timor
EAST
Praya
Maumere
Selat Ombai
TIMOR
Sawu
Timor
Sumba
Waingapu
Sea
Sawu
Kupang
T i m o r
S e a

10°
Palau
Koror
▼8138

Morotai
Halmahera
Kepulauan
Mapia
Equator
0°
Ternate
Waigeo
Biak
Supiori
Gebe
Sorong
Vogelkop
Manokwari
Yapen
M
Misool
Pen.
Wasian
O
Kepulauan
L
Obi
Papua
U
Pegunungan Maoke
C
S e r a m *S e a*
▲5029
Namlea
C
Seram
Puncak Jaya
Buru
Ambon
A
Kepulauan
S
Watubela
Wokam
Kepulauan
Kepulauan
Kai
Banda
Kepulauan
B a n d a *S e a*
Aru
Trangan
Yamdena
Kepulauan
Tanimbar
Selaru
A r a f u r a
S e a
10°

120°
130°
Melville I.
Wessel Is.
Scale: 1:14 000 000

© Anthem Press

Countries and regions: TURKMENISTAN, AFGHANISTAN, PAKISTAN, INDIA, SRI LANKA

Afghanistan provinces: FARYAB, BADGHIS, SAMANGAN, TAKHAR, BAGHLAN, BADAKHSHAN, PARVAN, GHOWR, ORUZGAN, BAMIAN, VARDAK, KAPISA, NURISTAN, KONARHA, NANGARHAR, LOWGAR, PAKTIA, KHOWST, GHAZNI, PAKTIKA, ZABOL, QANDAHAR, HELMAND, NIMRUZ, FARAH, HERAT

Pakistan regions: NORTH WEST FRONTIER, Tribal Areas, PUNJAB, BALUCHISTAN, SIND, Northern Areas

India states: JAMMU & KASHMIR, HIMACHAL PRADESH, PUNJAB, UTTARAKHAND, HARYANA, RAJASTHAN, GUJARAT, MADHYA PRADESH, MAHARASHTRA, KARNATAKA, GOA, TAMIL NADU, ANDHRA PRADESH, DADRA AND NAGAR HAVELI

Major cities: Kabul, Kandahar, Herat, Quetta, Islamabad, Rawalpindi, Lahore, Faisalabad, Multan, Karachi, Hyderabad, Srinagar, Amritsar, Ludhiana, Chandigarh, Dehra Dun, Delhi, Jaipur, Jodhpur, Udaipur, Kota, Gwalior, Ahmadabad, Vadodara, Surat, Mumbai, Pune, Nagpur, Bhopal, Indore, Nasik, Aurangabad, Hyderabad, Bangalore, Chennai, Mysuru, Coimbatore, Madurai, Cochin, Colombo, Kandy

Physical features: Hindu Kush, Karakoram, Himalaya, Aksai Chin, K2 8611, Nanga Parbat 8126, Arabian Sea, Mouths of the Indus, Gulf of Kachchh, Gulf of Khambhat, Rann of Kachchh, Little Rann, Thar Desert, Western Ghats, Eastern Ghats, Coromandal Coast, Malabar Coast, Palk Strait, Gulf of Mannar, Adam's Bridge, Adam's Peak 2243, Central Makran Range, Makran Coast Range, Chah Gay Hills, Sulaiman Range, Vindhya Range, Satpura Range

Rivers: Indus, Ganges, Brahmaputra, Sutlej, Chenab, Ravi, Jhelum, Beas, Luni, Chambal, Narmada, Tapti, Godavari, Krishna, Cauvery, Bhima, Tungabhadra, Penner, Helmand, Harirud

ALTITUDE (in metres)

| 6000 |
| 3000 |
| 2000 |
| 1500 |
| 1000 |
| 400 |
| 200 |
| 0 |
| 600 |

6° Projection : Conical with two standard parallels

South India & Sri Lanka

INKIANG
Kiunlun Shan
CHINA
QINGHAI
TIBET
Tanggula (Dangla) Shan
Tanggula Shankou
SICHUAN
Siling Co
Nyainqentanglha Shan
Nam Co
Tsangpo (Brahmaputra)
Lhasa
NEPAL
Katmandu
Bhaktapur
Thimphu
BHUTAN
SIKKIM
ARUNACHAL PRADESH
KACHIN
YUNNAN
Mt. Everest
Kanchenjunga
BIHAR
ASSAM
Guwahati
NAGALAND
Patna
Varanasi
MEGHALAYA
Shillong
SYLHET
MANIPUR
SAGAING
JHARKHAND
BANGLADESH
Dhaka
TRIPURA
Agartala
MIZORAM
CHIN Hills
Dhanbad
Asansol
WEST
BENGAL
Khulna
BARISAL
Chittagong
Mandalay
SHAN
Kolkata
MYANMAR
MAGWE
ORISSA
Bay of Bengal
The Sundarbans
Mouths of the Ganges
ARAKAN
KAYAH
THAILAND
PEGU YOMA
CHHATTISGARH
Raipur
Minicoy
Eight Degree Channel
Kelai
Thiladhunmathi
Atoll
Miladhunmadulu
Atoll
Faadhippolhu
Atoll
Maalhosmadulu
Atoll
MALDIVES
Male
Male
Atoll
Ari
Atoll
Felidhu Atoll
KAYIN
Dawna Range
Vishakhapatnam
Nilandhoo Atoll
Mulaku Atoll
Kolhumadulu
Atoll
Hadhdhunmathi
Atoll
One and a Half Degree Channel
Huvadhu Atoll
IRRAWADDY
Yangon
Bassein
MON
Moulmein
G. of Martaban
Mouths of the Irrawaddy
Addu
Atoll
MALDIVES
Scale 1:14 800 000
Preparis North Channel
Pariparit Kyun
(Myanmar)
Koko Kyunzu
(Myanmar)
Moscos Is.
INDIAN OCEAN
Scale 1:10 400 000

© Anthem Press

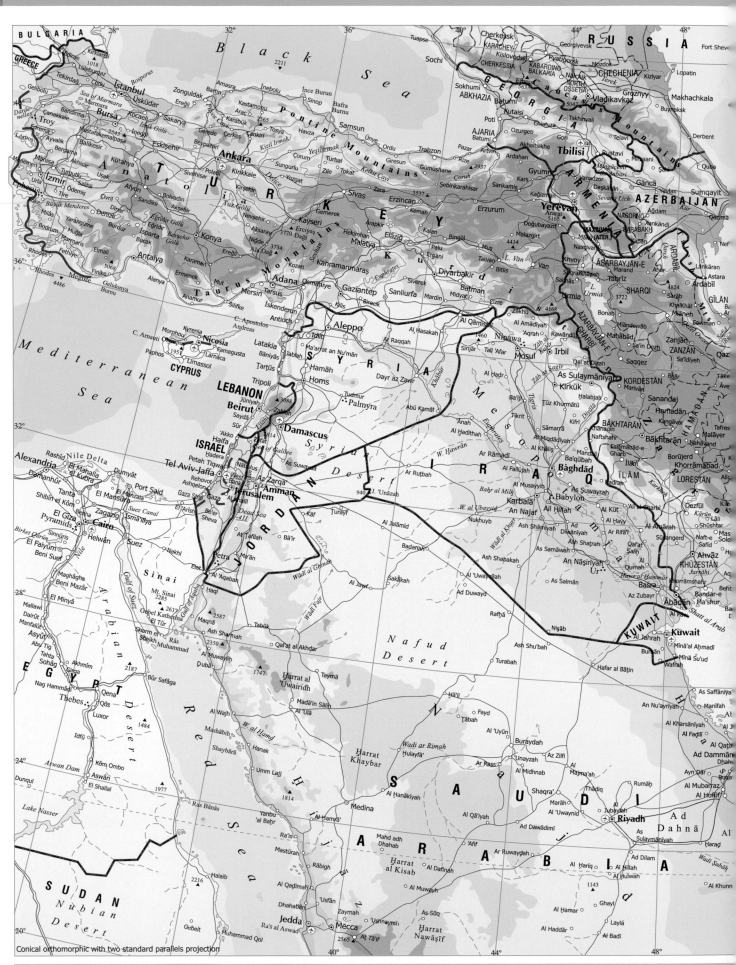

Conical orthomorphic with two standard parallels projection

HIGHEST MOUNTAINS	(EXCLUDING KASHMIR)	LONGEST RIVERS (TOTAL LENGTH)	
1. TRIVOR, PAK (7,720 m)	3. NOSHAQ, AFG (7,492 m)	1. INDUS (3,100 km)	3. AMUDARYA (2,540 km)
2. TIRICH MIR, PAK (7,690 m)	4. ISTOR-O-NAL, PAK (7,403 m)	2. EUPHRATES (2,700 km)	4. TIGRIS (1,900 km)

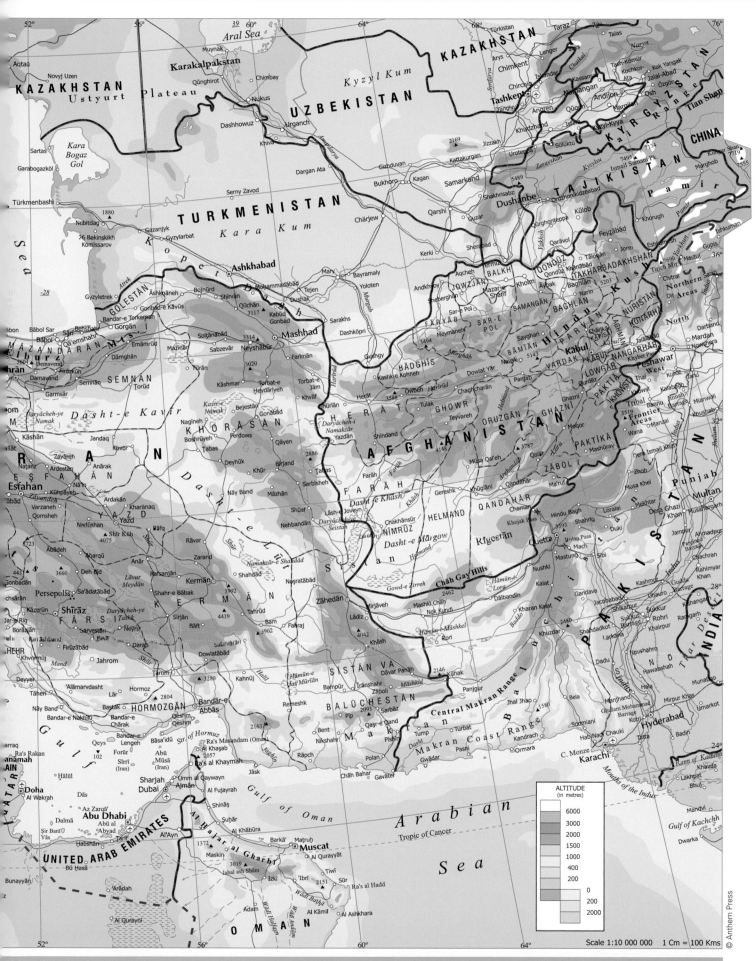

GEST CITIES (POP.)

ARACHI, PAK (15.1 million)   3. ISTANBUL, TUR (11.8 million)   5. BAGHDAD, IRQ (6.25 million)   7. ANKARA, TUR (3.875 million)

EHRAN, IRN (12.1 million)   4. LAHORE, PAK (7.95 million)   6. RIYADH, SAU (4.775 million)   8. JEDDA, SAU (3.175 million)

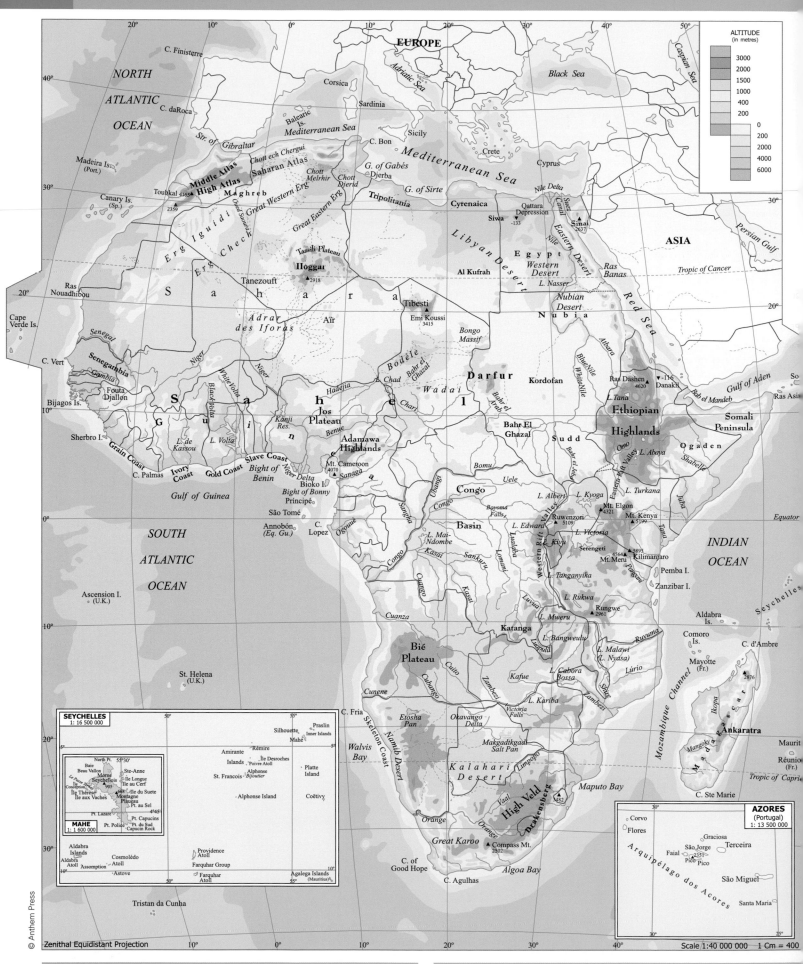

EUROPE

NORTH ATLANTIC OCEAN

C. Finisterre
C. daRoca

Madeira Is. (Port.)

Canary Is. (Sp.)

Ras Nouadhibou

Cape Verde Is.

C. Vert

Sherbro I.

C. Palmas

SOUTH ATLANTIC OCEAN

Ascension I. (U.K.)

St. Helena (U.K.)

Tristan da Cunha

Corsica
Sardinia
Balearic Is.
Mediterranean Sea
Str. of Gibraltar
Middle Atlas
High Atlas
Saharan Atlas
Toubkal 4165
2359
Maghreb
Chott ech Chergui
Chott Melrhir
Chott Djerid
Great Western Erg
Great Eastern Erg

Sicily
C. Bon
Crete
Cyprus
Mediterranean Sea
G. of Gabès
Djerba
G. of Sirte
Tripolitania
Cyrenaica

Persian Gulf

ASIA

Tropic of Cancer

Erg Iguidi
Erg Chech
Oued Saoura
Tanezrouft
Tassili Plateau
Hoggar 2918
S a h a r a

Libyan Desert
Egypt
Western Desert
Al Kufrah
L. Nasser
Nubian Desert
Nubia

Nile Delta
Suez Canal
Qattara Depression -133
Siwa
Sinai 2637
Eastern Desert
Ras Banas

Red Sea
Gulf of Aden
Bab el Mandeb
Ras Asir
So

Adrar des Iforas
Aïr
Tibesti
Emi Koussi 3415
Bongo Massif
Bodélé
Bahr el Ghazal
Chad
Wadai
Darfur
Kordofan
Atbara
Blue Nile
White Nile
Ras Dashen 4620
L. Tana
Ethiopian Highlands
Danakil -116
Somali Peninsula
Ogaden
Shabelle

Senegal
Senegambia
Gambia
Fouta Djallon
Bijagos Is.
Niger
Black Volta
White Volta
S u d a n
G u i n e a
Jos Plateau
Kanji Res.
Benue
L. de Kassou
L. Volta
Grain Coast
Ivory Coast
Gold Coast
Slave Coast
Bight of Benin
Niger Delta
Bioko I.
Adamawa Highlands
Mt. Cameroon 4070
Sanaga
Hadejia
Chari
Bahr el Arab
Bahr El Ghazal
Sudd
Bahr el Jebel
Omo
L. Abaya
Bomu
Uele
Juba

Gulf of Guinea
São Tomé
Príncipe
Bight of Bonny
Annobón (Eq. Gu.)
C. Lopez
Ogooué
Congo
Congo Basin
Sangha
Ubangi
Boyoma Falls
L. Albert
L. Edward
L. Kyoga
L. Victoria
L. Turkana
Mt. Elgon 4321
Ruwenzori 5109
Mt. Kenya 5199
Serengeti
Mt. Meru 4564
Kilimanjaro 5895
Tana
Pemba I.
Zanzibar I.
Pangani
L. Kivu
Western Rift Valley
Eastern Rift Valley
Equator

INDIAN OCEAN

Seychelles

L. Mai-Ndombe
Kasai
Sankuru
Lomami
Lualaba
L. Tanganyika
L. Rukwa
Rungwe 2961
Luvua
Cuango
Cuanza
Katanga
L. Mweru
L. Bangweulu
Luangwa
L. Malawi (L. Nyasa)
Lúrio
Ruvuma
Comoro Is.
C. d'Ambre
Mayotte (Fr.)
2876
Ankaratra
Madagascar
Ikopa
Mangoky
Maurit
Réunio (Fr.)
Aldabra Is.

Bié Plateau
Cuito
Cubango
Cunene
Kafue
Cabora Bossa
Zambezi
Sabi
L. Kariba
Victoria Falls
Makgadikgadi Salt Pan
Okavango Delta
Etosha Pan
Namib Desert
Skeleton Coast
Walvis Bay
C. Fria
Kalahari Desert
Limpopo
High Veld
Drakensberg 3482
Maputo Bay
Tropic of Capricorn
C. Ste Marie
Mozambique Channel

Cunene
Orange
Vaal
Great Karoo
Compass Mt. 2502
C. of Good Hope
C. Agulhas
Algoa Bay

© Anthem Press

Zenithal Equidistant Projection

Scale 1:40 000 000   1 Cm = 400

ALTITUDE (in metres)
3000
2000
1500
1000
400
200
0
200
2000
4000
6000

SEYCHELLES 1: 16 500 000
Praslin
Inner Islands
Silhouette
Mahé
North Pt.
Baie Beau Vallon
Morne Seychellois 905
Le Pouce
Île Conception
Île Thérèse
Île aux Vaches
Montagne Plateau 668
Île Longue
Île au Cerf
Île au Suete
Pt. au Sel
Pt. Lazare
Pt. du Sud
Pt. Police
Capucin Rock
Pt. Capucins
MAHE 1: 1 600 000
Ste-Anne
Amirante Islands
Poivre Atoll
Rémire
St. Francois
Bijoutier
Alphonse
Alphonse Island
Desroches
Platte Island
Coëtivy
Aldabra Islands
Aldabra Atoll
Assomption
Cosmolédo Atoll
Astove
Providence Atoll
Farquhar Group
Farquhar Atoll
Agalega Islands (Mauritius)

AZORES (Portugal) 1: 13 500 000
Corvo
Flores
Graciosa
Terceira
São Jorge
Faial
Pico 2351
São Miguel
Santa Maria
Arquipélago dos Açores

AFRICA'S HIGHEST MOUNTAINS
1. Mount Kilimanjaro, Tza (5,895 m)
2. Mount Kenya, Ken (5,199 m)
3. Mount Stanley, Drc–Uga (5,109 m)
4. Mount Speke, Uga (4,890 m)
5. Mount Baker, Uga (4,844 m)
6. Mount Emin, Drc (4,798 m)

AFRICA'S LONGEST RIVERS
1. Nile (6,670 km)
2. Congo (4,670 km)
3. Niger (4,180 km)
4. Zambezi (3,540 km)
5. Oubangi (2,250 km)
6. Kasai (1,950 km)

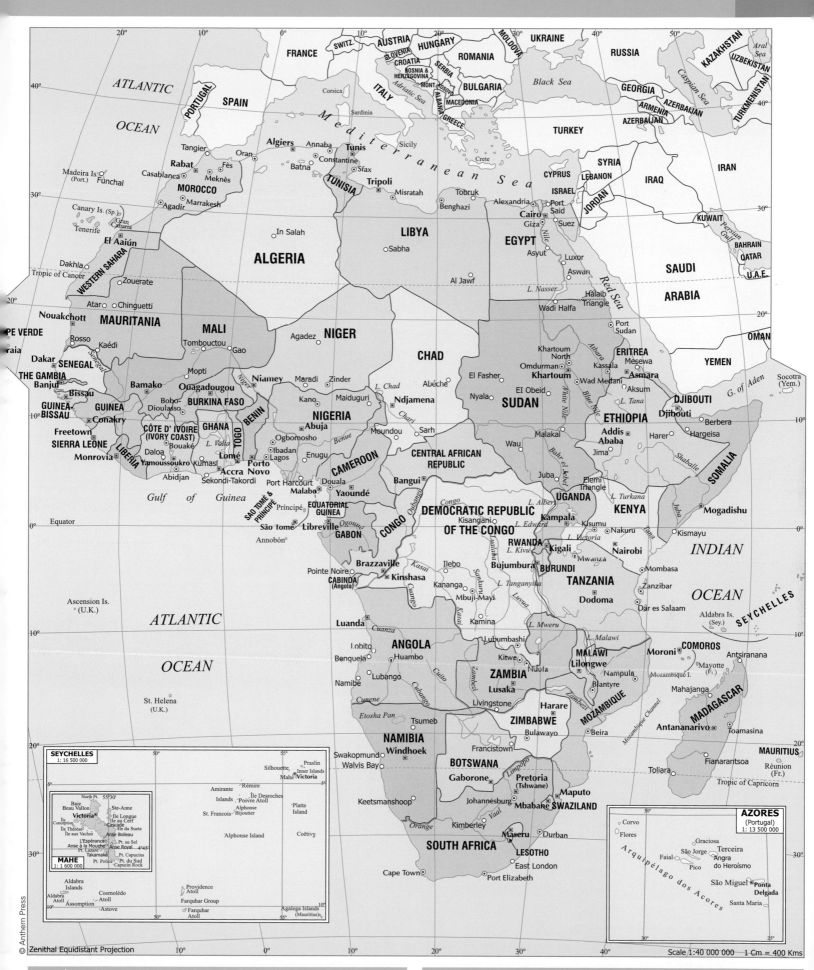

Scale 1:40 000 000   1 Cm = 400 Kms

© Anthem Press

AFRICA'S LARGEST NATIONS (AREA)	SMALLEST NATIONS (MAINLAND)	AFRICA'S LARGEST CITIES (POP.)	
1. SUDAN (2.51 million sq km)	1. THE GAMBIA (11,295 sq km)	1. CAIRO, EGY (16.1 million)	4. JOHANNESBURG, ZAF (7.8 million)
2. ALGERIA (2.38 million sq km)	2. SWAZILAND (17,364 sq km)	2. LAGOS, NGA (10.1 million)	5. KHARTOUM, SDN (5.45 million)
3. CONGO, DRC (2.34 million sq km)	3. DJIBOUTI (23,200 sq km)	3. KINSHASA, DRC (8.2 million)	6. ALEXANDRIA, EGY (5.1 million)

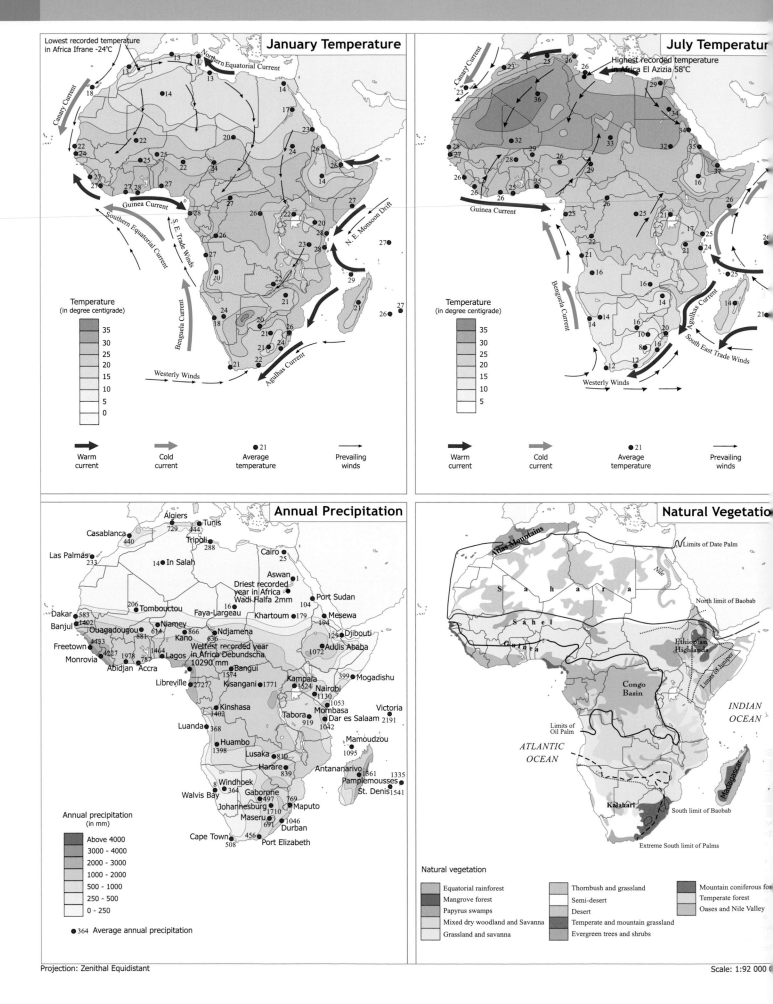

January Temperature

Lowest recorded temperature in Africa Ifrane -24°C

Northern Equatorial Current

Canary Current

Guinea Current

Southern Equatorial Current

S. E. Trade Winds

Benguela Current

N. E. Monsoon Drift

Temperature
(in degree centigrade)

35
30
25
20
15
10
5
0

Warm current

Cold current

•21 Average temperature

Prevailing winds

Westerly Winds

Agulhas Current

July Temperature

Highest recorded temperature in Africa El Azizia 58°C

Canary Current

Guinea Current

Benguela Current

Agulhas Current

South East Trade Winds

Temperature
(in degree centigrade)

35
30
25
20
15
10
5

Warm current

Cold current

•21 Average temperature

Prevailing winds

Westerly Winds

Annual Precipitation

Algiers
Tunis 444
729
Casablanca
440
Tripoli
288
Las Palmás
233
Cairo
25
14 In Salah
Aswan 1
Driest recorded year in Africa Wadi Halfa 2mm
Port Sudan
206 Tombouctou
104
16
Faya-Largeau
Khartoum 179 Mesewa
Dakar 583
194
Banjul 1402
Niamey 866 Ndjamena 129 Djibouti
Ouagadougou 614
Kano 636
Freetown 881
4433
Addis Ababa
1464
Wettest recorded year in Africa Debundscha 10290 mm 1072
Monrovia 4227 1978 787
Abidjan Accra Lagos
Bangui 1574
Libreville 27727 Kisangani 1771 Kampala 1624
399 Mogadishu
Nairobi 1130
Kinshasa 1402 1053
Victoria
Tabora Mombasa
919 Dar es Salaam 2191
Luanda 368 1042
Mamoudzou 1095
Huambo 1398
Lusaka 810
Harare 839
Antananarivo
1561 1335
Pamplemousses
St. Denis 1541
Windhoek 364
Gaborone 497
Walvis Bay 769 Maputo
Johannesburg 1710
Maseru 1046
Durban
Cape Town 456 Port Elizabeth
508

Annual precipitation
(in mm)

Above 4000
3000 - 4000
2000 - 3000
1000 - 2000
500 - 1000
250 - 500
0 - 250

•364 Average annual precipitation

Natural Vegetation

Atlas Mountains
Limits of Date Palm
Nile
Sahara
North limit of Baobab
Sahel
Guinea
Ethiopian Highlands
Limits of Juniper
Congo Basin
INDIAN OCEAN
Limits of Oil Palm
ATLANTIC OCEAN
Kalahari
South limit of Baobab
Madagascar
Extreme South limit of Palms

Natural vegetation

Equatorial rainforest
Mangrove forest
Papyrus swamps
Mixed dry woodland and Savanna
Grassland and savanna

Thornbush and grassland
Semi-desert
Desert
Temperate and mountain grassland
Evergreen trees and shrubs

Mountain coniferous forest
Temperate forest
Oases and Nile Valley

Projection: Zenithal Equidistant

Scale: 1:92 000 000

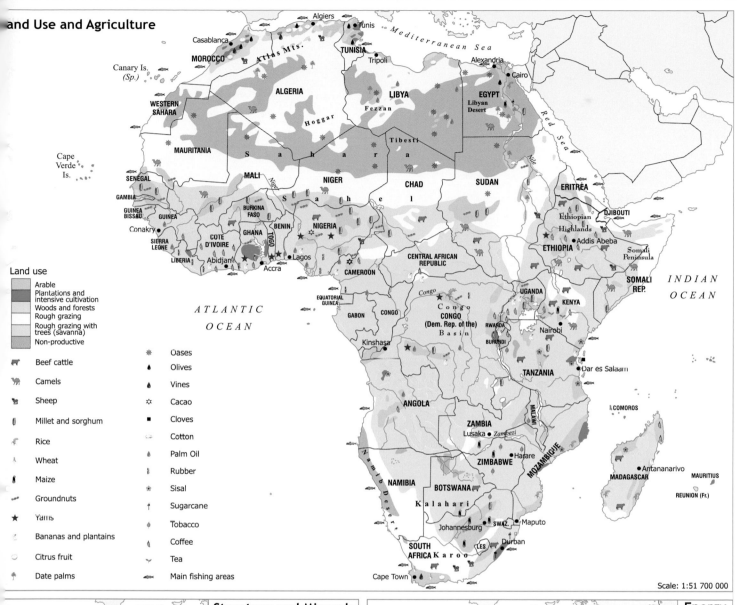

Land Use and Agriculture

Land use

- Arable
- Plantations and intensive cultivation
- Woods and forests
- Rough grazing
- Rough grazing with trees (savanna)
- Non-productive

🐂	Beef cattle
🐫	Camels
🐑	Sheep
	Millet and sorghum
	Rice
	Wheat
	Maize
	Groundnuts
★	Yams
	Bananas and plantains
	Citrus fruit
	Date palms

✳	Oases
	Olives
	Vines
✿	Cacao
■	Cloves
	Cotton
	Palm Oil
	Rubber
	Sisal
†	Sugarcane
	Tobacco
	Coffee
	Tea
🐟	Main fishing areas

Scale: 1:51 700 000

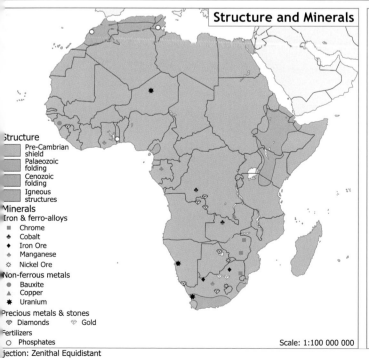

Structure and Minerals

Structure
- Pre-Cambrian shield
- Palaeozoic folding
- Cenozoic folding
- Igneous structures

Minerals

Iron & ferro-alloys
- Chrome
- Cobalt
- Iron Ore
- Manganese
- Nickel Ore

Non-ferrous metals
- Bauxite
- Copper
- Uranium

Precious metals & stones
- Diamonds
- Gold

Fertilizers
- Phosphates

Scale: 1:100 000 000

Projection: Zenithal Equidistant

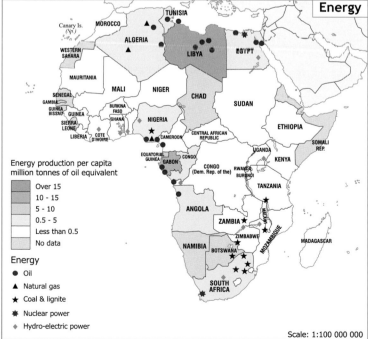

Energy

Energy production per capita million tonnes of oil equivalent
- Over 15
- 10 - 15
- 5 - 10
- 0.5 - 5
- Less than 0.5
- No data

Energy
- ● Oil
- ▲ Natural gas
- ★ Coal & lignite
- ✳ Nuclear power
- ◆ Hydro-electric power

Scale: 1:100 000 000

© Anthem Press

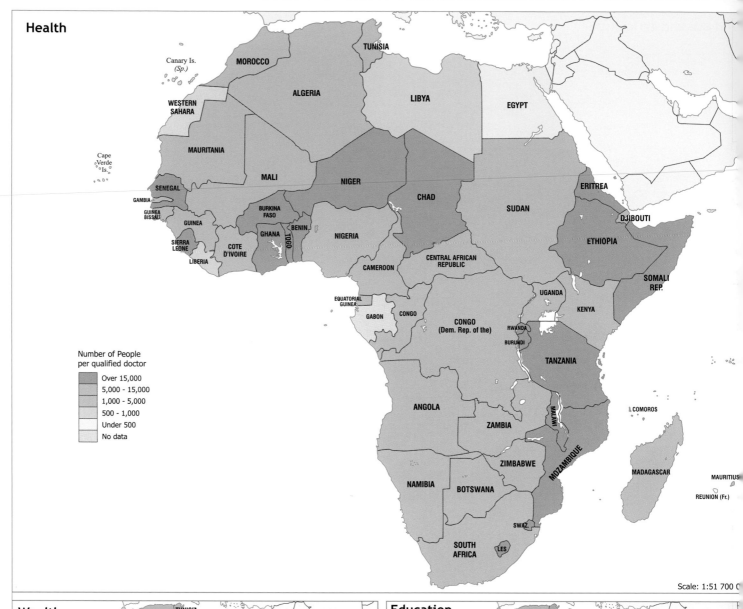

Health

Number of People
per qualified doctor

- Over 15,000
- 5,000 - 15,000
- 1,000 - 5,000
- 500 - 1,000
- Under 500
- No data

Scale: 1:51 700 0

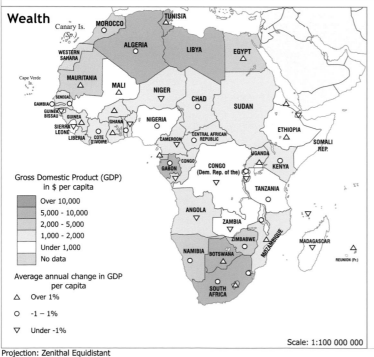

Wealth

Gross Domestic Product (GDP)
in $ per capita

- Over 10,000
- 5,000 - 10,000
- 2,000 - 5,000
- 1,000 - 2,000
- Under 1,000
- No data

Average annual change in GDP
per capita

- △ Over 1%
- ○ -1 – 1%
- ▽ Under -1%

Scale: 1:100 000 000

© Anthem Press

Projection: Zenithal Equidistant

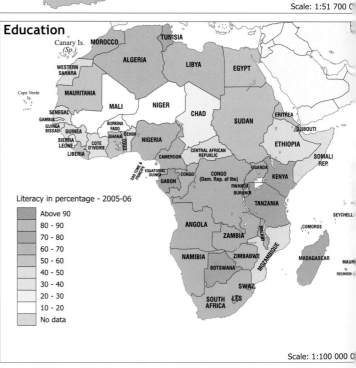

Education

Literacy in percentage - 2005-06

- Above 90
- 80 - 90
- 70 - 80
- 60 - 70
- 50 - 60
- 40 - 50
- 30 - 40
- 20 - 30
- 10 - 20
- No data

Scale: 1:100 000 000

AFRICA'S WEALTHIEST NATIONS	GDP PER CAPITA (PPP) US $
1. Equatorial Guinea ($16,507)	3. Seychelles ($12,135)
2. Kuwait ($13,029)	4. South Africa ($11,035)

AFRICA'S POOREST NATIONS	GDP PER CAPITA (PPP) US $
1. Malawi ($596)	3. D.R. Congo ($675)
2. Somalia ($600)	4. Tanzania ($720)

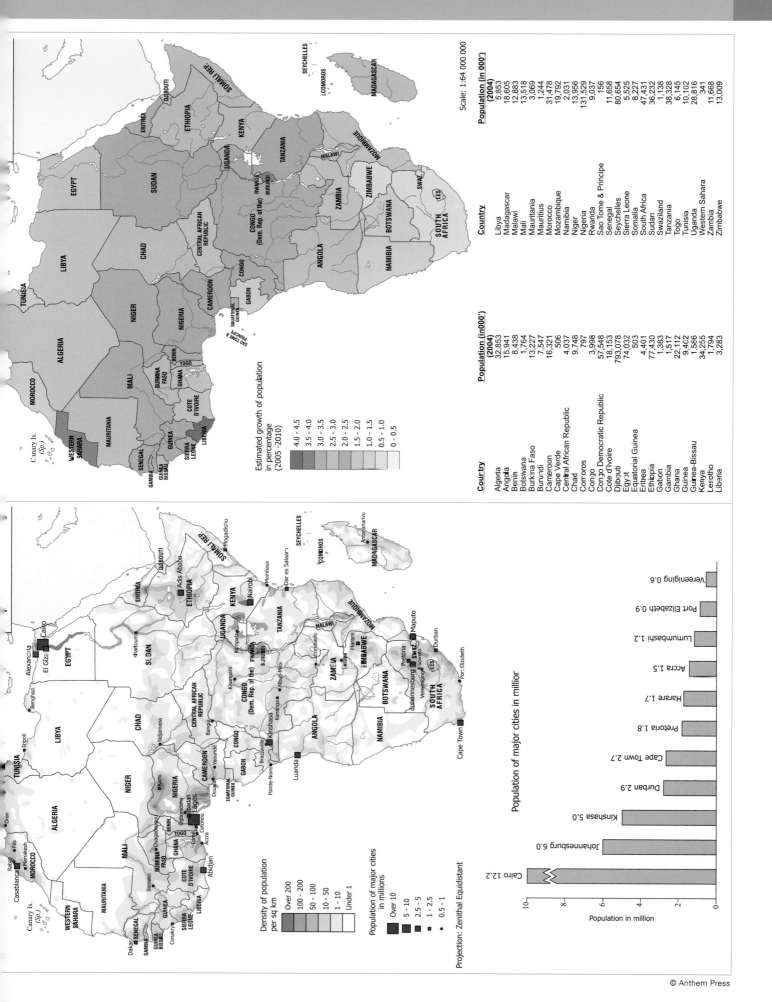

Scale: 1:64 000 000

Country	Population (in000') (2004)		Country	Population (in 000') (2004)
Algeria	32,853		Libya	5,853
Angola	15,941		Madagascar	18,605
Benin	8,438		Malawi	12,883
Botswana	1,764		Mali	13,518
Burkina Faso	13,227		Mauritania	3,069
Burundi	7,547		Mauritius	1,244
Cameroon	16,321		Morocco	31,478
Cape Verde	506		Mozambique	19,792
Central African Republic	4,037		Namibia	2,031
Chad	9,748		Niger	13,956
Comoros	797		Nigeria	131,529
Congo	3,998		Rwanda	9,037
Congo Democratic Republic	57,548		Sao Tome & Principe	156
Cote d'Ivoire	18,153		Senegal	11,658
Djibouti	793,078		Seychelles	80,654
Egypt	74,032		Sierra Leone	5,525
Equatorial Guinea	503		Somalia	8,227
Eritrea	4,401		South Africa	47,431
Ethiopia	77,430		Sudan	36,232
Gabon	1,383		Swaziland	1,138
Gambia	1,517		Tanzania	38,328
Ghana	22,112		Togo	6,145
Guinea	9,402		Tunisia	10,102
Guinea-Bissau	1,586		Uganda	28,816
Kenya	34,255		Western Sahara	341
Lesotho	1,794		Zambia	11,668
Liberia	3,283		Zimbabwe	13,009

Estimated growth of population in percentage (2005-2010)

- 4.0 - 4.5
- 3.5 - 4.0
- 3.0 - 3.5
- 2.5 - 3.0
- 2.0 - 2.5
- 1.5 - 2.0
- 1.0 - 1.5
- 0.5 - 1.0
- 0 - 0.5

Density of population per sq km

- Over 200
- 100 - 200
- 50 - 100
- 1 - 10
- Under 1

Population of major cities in millions

- Over 10
- 5 - 10
- 2.5 - 5
- 1 - 2.5
- 0.5 - 1

Projection: Zenithal Equidistant

Population of major cities in million

- Cairo 12.2
- Johannesburg 6.0
- Kinshasa 5.0
- Durban 2.9
- Cape Town 2.7
- Pretoria 1.8
- Harare 1.7
- Accra 1.5
- Lumumbashi 1.2
- Port Elizabeth 0.9
- Vereeniging 0.6

Population in million

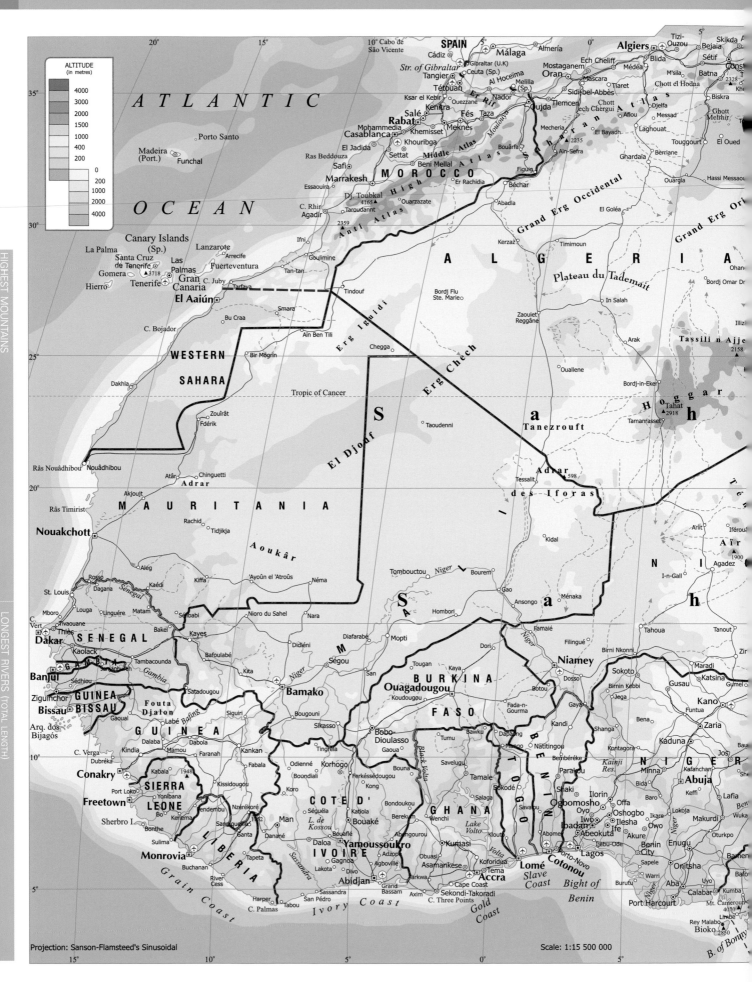

ATLANTIC

OCEAN

ALTITUDE
(in metres)

4000
3000
2000
1500
1000
400
200
0
200
1000
2000
4000

SPAIN

Cabo de São Vicente
Málaga Almería
Algiers Tizi-Ouzou
Cádiz Gibraltar (U.K.) Bejaia Skikda
Str. of Gibraltar Ceuta (Sp.) Mostaganem Ech Cheliff Blida Sétif Const
Tangier Al Hoceima Oran Médéa Batna 2328
Tétouan Melilla (Sp.) Mascara Tiaret M'sila Chott el Hodna Biskra
Ksar el Kebir Nador Oujda Tlemcen Djelfa Ghott Melrhir
Salé Ouezzane Fés Taza Ech Chergui Aflou Messad El Oued
Rabat Kenitra Mecheria El Bayadh Touggourt
Mohammedia Meknès Bouârfa 2235 Ain-Sefra Laghouat
Casablanca Khemisset Figuig Ghardaïa Bèrriane
El Jadida Khouribga Middle Atlas Abadla Béchar El Goléa Hassi Messaou
Settat Béni Mellal High Atlas Er Rachidia Ouargla
Safi Marrakesh MOROCCO Saharan Atlas Grand Erg Occidental Grand Erg Ori
Ras Beddouza Essaouira 2359 Kerzaz Timimoun
C. Rhir Dj. Toubkal Ouarzazate Plateau du Tademait Ohan
Agadir 4165 High Atlas ALGERIA In Salah Bordj Omar Dr
Ifni Taroudannt Anti Atlas Bordj Flu Ste. Marie Zaouiet Reggane
Goulimine Tan-tan Ste. Marie Arak Illizi
Madeira (Port.) Porto Santo Tindouf Erg Iguidi Chegga Tassili n Ajje 2158
Funchal

Canary Islands (Sp.)
La Palma Lanzarote
Santa Cruz de Tenerife Arrecife
Gomera 3718 Fuerteventura
Hierro Tenerife Gran Canaria C. Juby Tarfaya
Las Palmas El Aaiún Smara Bu Craa
WESTERN Bir Mogrin Erg Chech
SAHARA Tropic of Cancer Taoudenni
Dakhla Zouïrat Fdérik El Djouf Tanezrouft Hoggar Tahat 2918
Ras Nouâdhibou Nouâdhibou S a h Tamanrasset
Atâr Chinguetti Adrar des Iforas 598 Adrar Tessalit
Adrar Akjoujt El Djouf Arlit Iférouâ
Ras Timirist MAURITANIA Kidal Aïr
Nouakchott Rachid Tidjikja Aoukâr 1900 Agadez
Rosso Aleg Kiffa 'Ayoûn el 'Atroûs Néma I-n-Gall NI
Dagana Kaédi Tombouctou Niger Bourem Tahoua h
St. Louis Linguère Matam Sélibabi Nara Gao Ménaka Tanout
Louga Nioro du Sahel Ansongo Birni Nkonni Zi
Mboro Bakel Kayes Diaférabé Mopti Dori Dosso Maradi Katsina
Thiaroye Kidira Didiéni Ségou Tougan Filingué Sokoto Gusau
Thiès SENEGAL Bafoulabé Kita San Kaya Niamey Birnin Kebbi Kano
Dakar Kaolack Tambacounda M Bamako BURKINA Jega Funtua Zaria
GAMBIA Satadougou Gambia Bougouni Ouagadougou Fada-n-Gourma Kandi Shanga Kaduna
Banjul Sédhiou Sikasso FASO Gayéri Bemberéké Kontagora NIGER
GUINEA Ziguinchor Siguiri Koudougou Bawku Dapaong Parakou Kainji Res. Jos
BISSAU Labé Tingréla Bobo-Dioulasso Tumu Mango Natitingou Minna Abuja
Bissau Fouta Djalon Bafing Gaoua Savelugu Baro Keffi Lafia
Gaoual Dalaba Dabola Odienné Korhogo Bouna Tamale Shaki Ilorin Lokoja Makurdi
GUINEA Dalaba Kankan Ferkéssédougou Salaga Sokodé Ogbomosho Offa Ilesha Owo Wuka
C. Verga Kindia Mamou Fabala Kong Savalou Iwo Oshogbo Ife Ikare Oturkpo
Conakry Dubréka Faranah Boundiali Bondoukou GHANA Oyo Abeokuta Akure Enugu
SIERRA Kabala 1948 Kissidougou Koro Berekum Wenchi Lake Volta TOGO BENIN Ibadan Benin City Onitsha
LEONE Port Loko Faranah COTE D' Katiola Abengourou Kloutó Porto-Novo Ijebu-Ode Sapele
Freetown Yonibana Kenema Séguéla Bouaké IVOIRE Aného Lomé Cotonou Warri Aba
Sherbro I. Bo Nzérékoré 1752 L. de Kossou Bouaflé Obuasi Asamankese Koforidua Slave Coast Port Harcourt Calabar
Bonthe Man Daloa Yamoussoukro Kumasi Tema Accra Benin City Uyo
Monrovia LIBERIA Danané Gagnoa Divo Grand Bassam Cape Coast Bight of Mt. Cameroon Kumba 4070
Buchanan Sassandra Lakota Abidjan Axim Sekondi-Takoradi Gold Coast Benin Rey Malabo Limbe
River Cess Sassandra Agboville C. Three Points Bioko 2850
Grain Coast Tabou San Pédro Ivory Coast
Harper C. Palmas

SAHARA

S a h a r a

Sahel

S a h e l

Niger

Tropic of Cancer

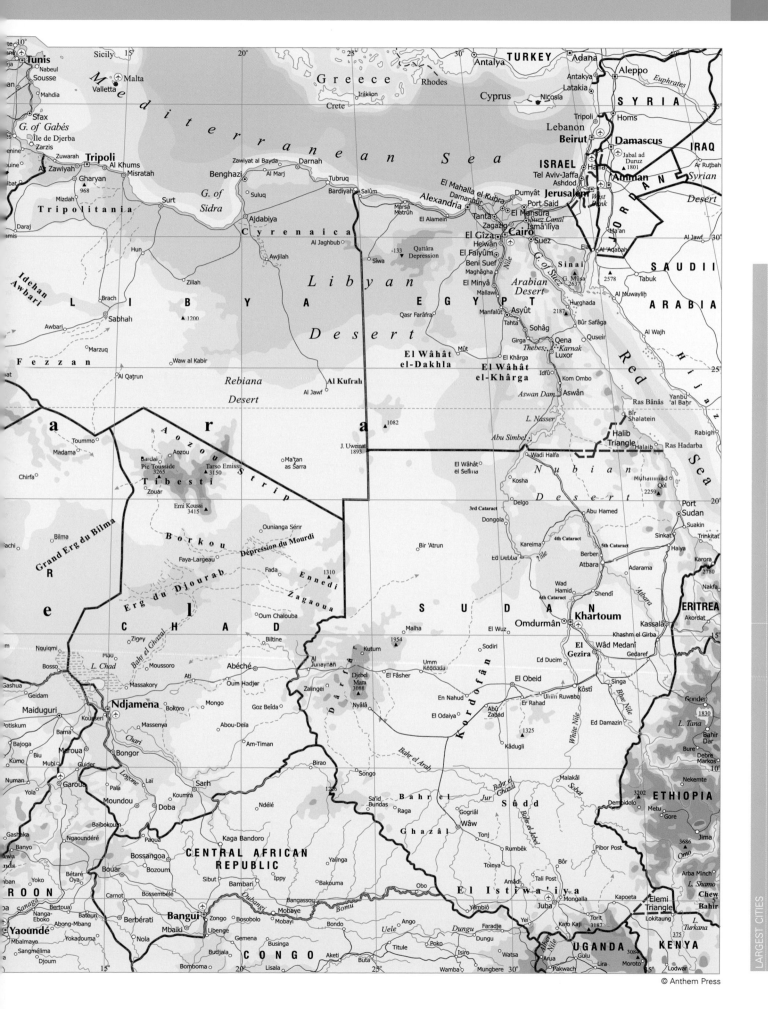

LARGEST CITIES

1. Cairo, Egy (16.1 million)
2. Lagos, Nga (10.1 million)
3. Khartoum, Sdn (5.45 million)
4. Alexandria, Egy (5.1 million)
5. Abidjan, Civ (4.2 million)
6. Casablanca, Mor (3.9 million)
7. Kano, Ngo (3.6 million)
8. Accra, Gha (3.35 million)
9. Ibadan, Nga (3.2 million)
10. Addis Ababa, Eth (3.1 million)
11. Dakar, Sen (2.55 million)
12. Tunis, Tun (2.55 million)

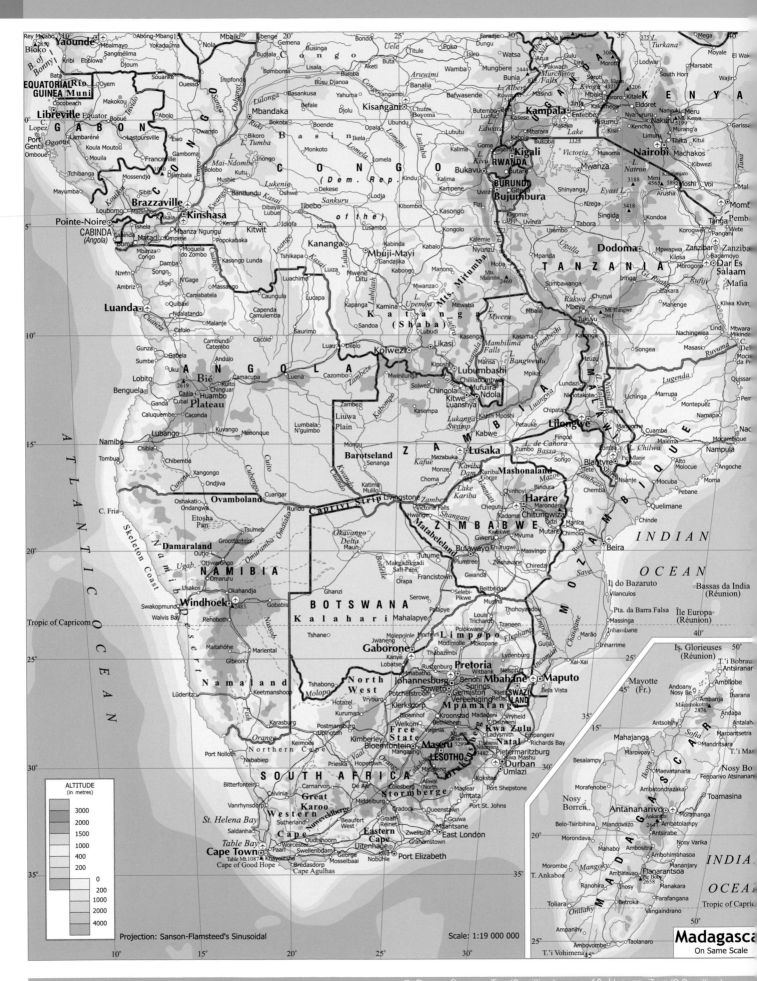

ALTITUDE
(in metres)

3000
2000
1500
1000
400
200
0
200
1000
2000
4000

Projection: Sanson-Flamsteed's Sinusoidal

Scale: 1:19 000 000

Madagascar
On Same Scale

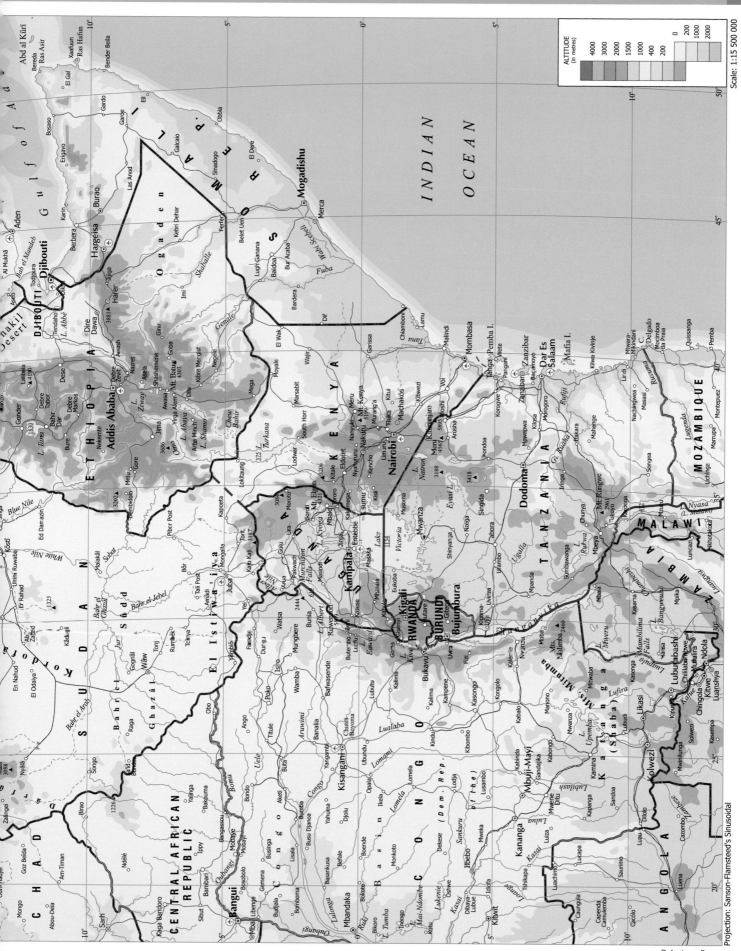

Scale: 1:15 500 000

Projection: Sanson-Flamsteed's Sinusoidal

© Anthem Press

HIGHEST MOUNTAINS	LONGEST RIVERS	LARGEST CITIES (POP.)	
KILIMANJARO, TZA (5,895 m)	1. NILE (6,670 km)	1. KINSHASA, DRC (8.2 million)	3. NAIROBI, KEN (3.2 million)
MOUNT KENYA, KEN (5,199 m)	2. CONGO (4,670 km)	2. KHARTOUM, SDN (5.45 million)	4. ADDIS ABABA, ETH (3.1 million)

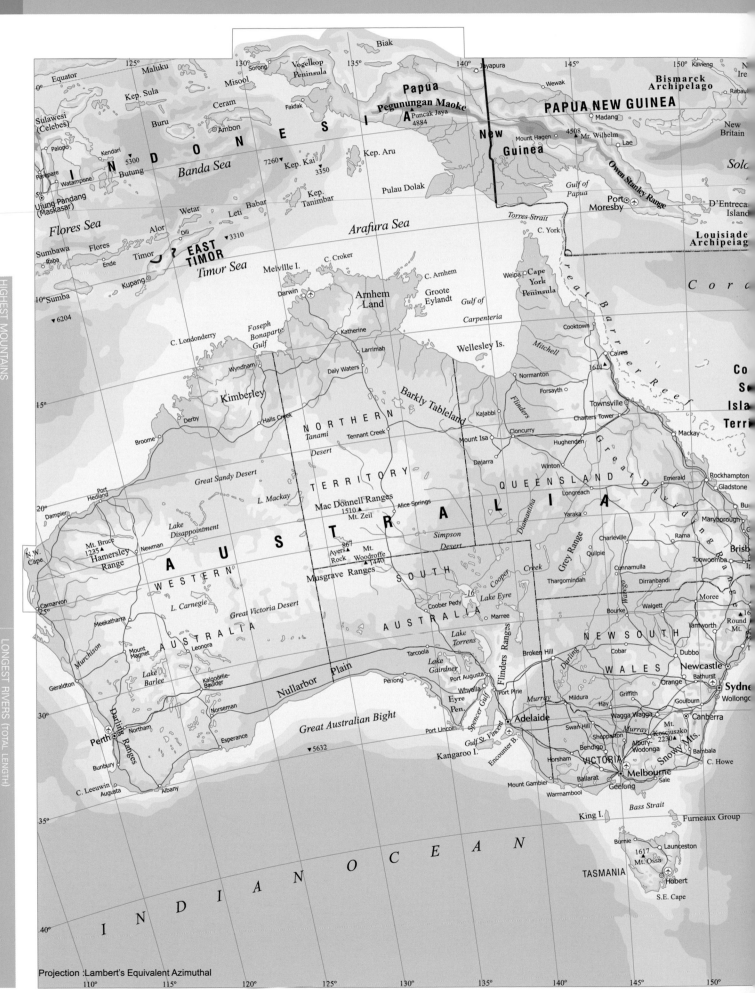

Projection : Lambert's Equivalent Azimuthal

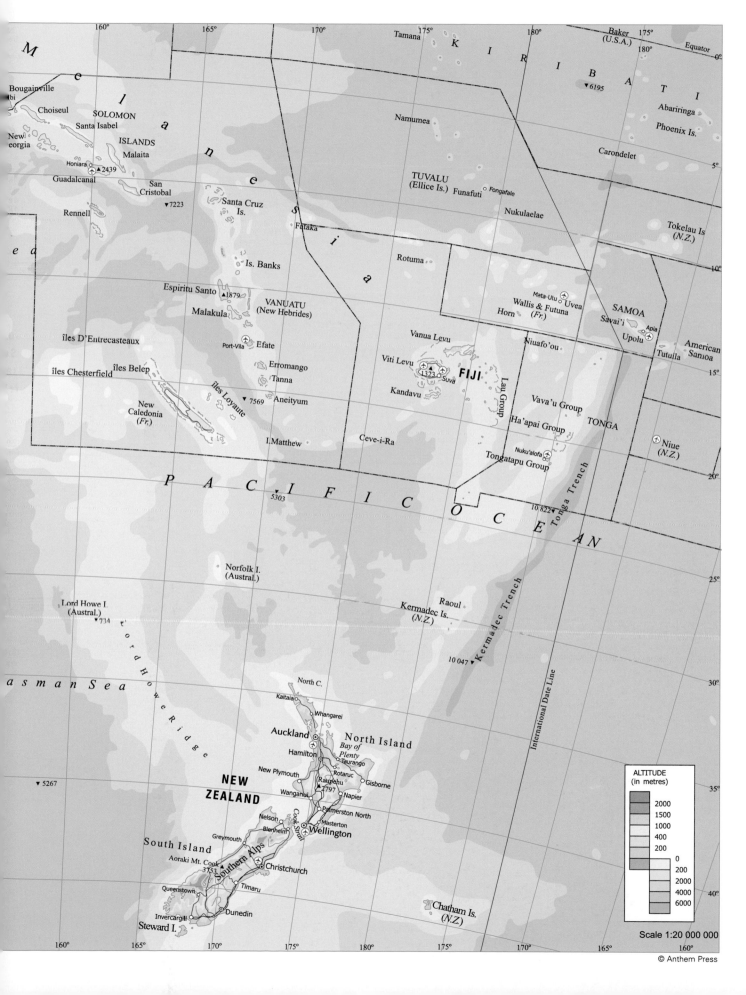

Scale 1:20 000 000

ALTITUDE
(in metres)

| 2000 |
| 1500 |
| 1000 |
| 400 |
| 200 |
| 0 |
| 200 |
| 2000 |
| 4000 |
| 6000 |

LARGEST CITIES

1. Sydney, Aus (4.3 million)
2. Melbourne, Aus (3.75 million)
3. Brisbane, Aus (1.86 million)
4. Perth, Aus (1.51 million)
5. Auckland, Nzl (1.26 million)
6. Adelaide, Aus (1.15 million)
7. Gold Coast, Aus (422,000)
8. Wellington, Nzl (398,000)
9. Christchurch, Nzl (361,000)
10. Canberra, Aus (340,000)
11. Newcastle, Aus (280,000)
12. Port Moresby, Png (255,000)

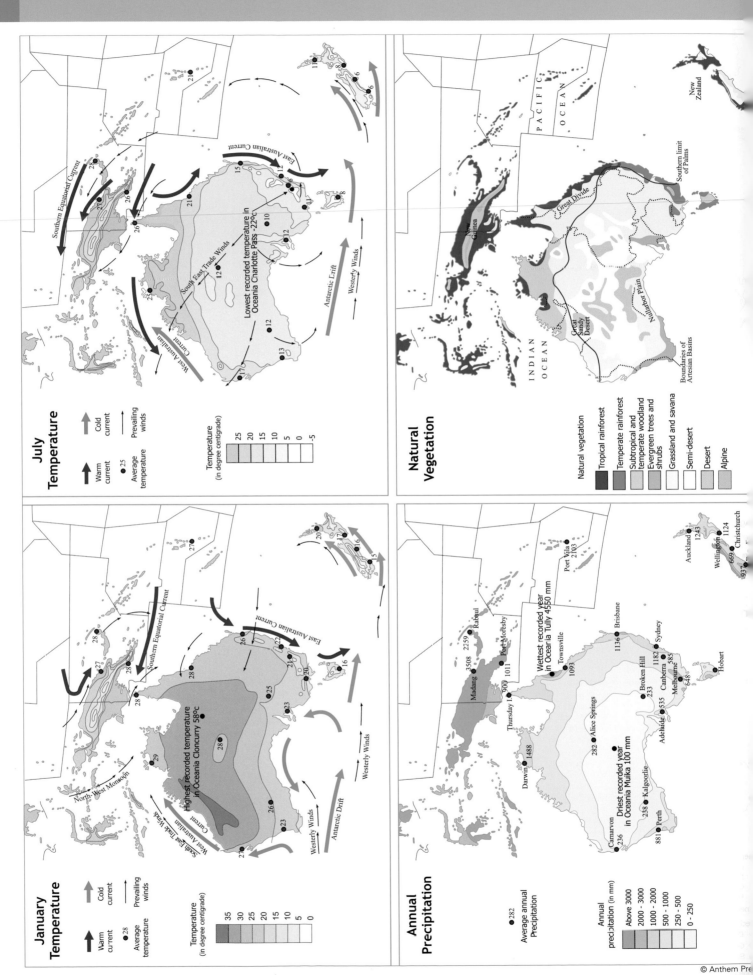

Lowest recorded temperature in Oceania Charlotte Pass -22°c

July Temperature

Cold current
Prevailing winds
Warm current
25 Average temperature

Temperature (in degree centigrade)
25 20 15 10 5 0 -5

Natural Vegetation

PACIFIC OCEAN

New Zealand

Great Divide

Southern limit of Palms

New Guinea

Nullarbor Plain

Great Sandy Desert

INDIAN OCEAN

Boundaries of Artesian Basins

Natural vegetation
Tropical rainforest
Temperate rainforest
Subtropical and temperate woodland
Evergreen trees and shrubs
Grassland and savana
Semi-desert
Desert
Alpine

Highest recorded temperature in Oceania Cloncurry 58°c

January Temperature

Cold current
Prevailing winds
Warm current
28 Average temperature

Temperature (in degree centigrade)
35 30 25 20 15 10 5 0

Southern Equatorial Current
East Australian Current
West Australian Current
South East Trade Winds
North-West Monsoon
Westerly Winds
Antarctic Drift

Annual Precipitation

Wettest recorded year in Oceania Tully 4550 mm

Driest recorded year in Oceania Muika 100 mm

Auckland 1243
Wellington 669
Christchurch 1124
937

Port Vila 2103
Rabaul 2259
Madang 3508
Port Moresby 1011
900
Thursday 1488
Darwin
Townsville 1093
Brisbane 1136
Broken Hill 233
Sydney 1182
Canberra 585
Melbourne 648
Hobart
Adelaide 535
282 Alice Springs
Kalgoorlie 238
Perth 881
Carnarvon 236

282 Average annual Precipitation

Annual precipitation (in mm)
Above 3000
2000 - 3000
1000 - 2000
500 - 1000
250 - 500
0 - 250

© Anthem Pre

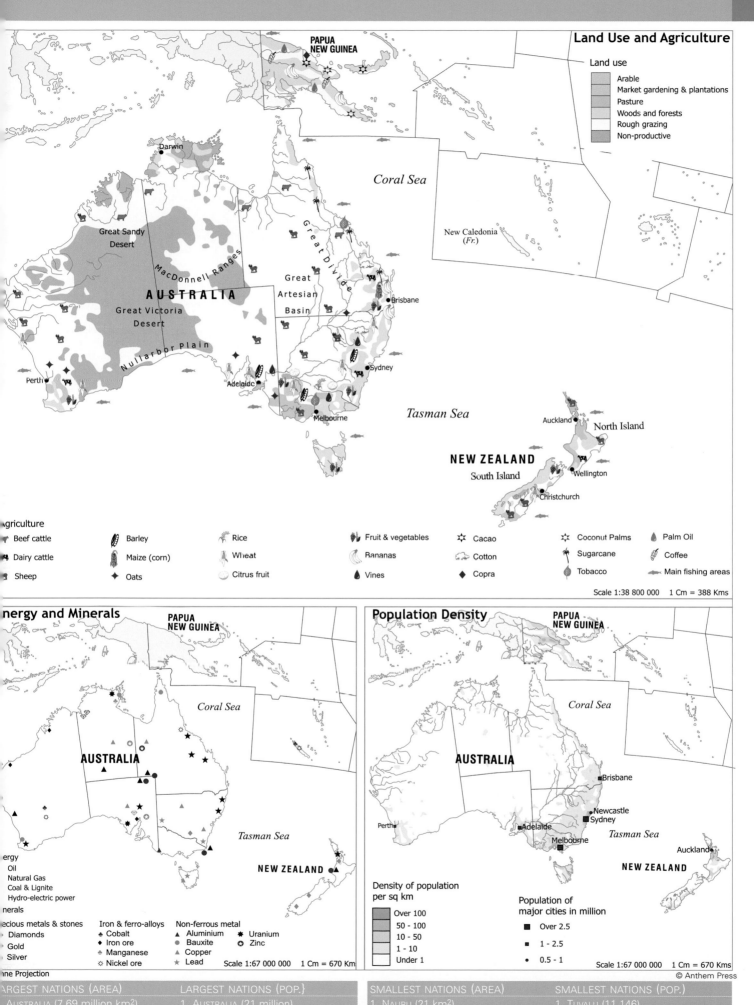

Land Use and Agriculture

Land use
- Arable
- Market gardening & plantations
- Pasture
- Woods and forests
- Rough grazing
- Non-productive

PAPUA NEW GUINEA

Coral Sea

New Caledonia (*Fr.*)

Darwin

Great Sandy Desert

MacDonnell Ranges

AUSTRALIA

Great Victoria Desert

Great Divide

Great Artesian Basin

Nullarbor Plain

Perth

Adelaide

•Brisbane

•Sydney

Melbourne

Tasman Sea

Auckland

North Island

NEW ZEALAND

South Island

Wellington

Christchurch

Agriculture

Beef cattle	Barley	Rice	Fruit & vegetables	Cacao	Coconut Palms	Palm Oil
Dairy cattle	Maize (corn)	Wheat	Bananas	Cotton	Sugarcane	Coffee
Sheep	Oats	Citrus fruit	Vines	Copra	Tobacco	Main fishing areas

Scale 1:38 800 000   1 Cm = 388 Kms

Energy and Minerals

PAPUA NEW GUINEA

Coral Sea

AUSTRALIA

Tasman Sea

NEW ZEALAND

Energy
- Oil
- Natural Gas
- Coal & Lignite
- Hydro-electric power

Minerals

Precious metals & stones
- Diamonds
- Gold
- Silver

Iron & ferro-alloys
- Cobalt
- Iron ore
- Manganese
- Nickel ore

Non-ferrous metal
- Aluminium
- Bauxite
- Copper
- Lead

- Uranium
- Zinc

Sine Projection

Scale 1:67 000 000   1 Cm = 670 Km

Population Density

PAPUA NEW GUINEA

Coral Sea

AUSTRALIA

Perth

Adelaide

Melbourne

Brisbane

Newcastle
Sydney

Tasman Sea

Auckland

NEW ZEALAND

Density of population per sq km
- Over 100
- 50 - 100
- 10 - 50
- 1 - 10
- Under 1

Population of major cities in million
- Over 2.5
- 1 - 2.5
- 0.5 - 1

Scale 1:67 000 000   1 Cm = 670 Kms

© Anthem Press

LARGEST NATIONS (AREA)	LARGEST NATIONS (POP.)	SMALLEST NATIONS (AREA)	SMALLEST NATIONS (POP.)
AUSTRALIA (7.69 million km²)	1. AUSTRALIA (21 million)	1. NAURU (21 km²)	1. TUVALU (11,146)
INDONESIA [OCEANIA] (500,000 km²)	2. PAPUA NEW GUINEA (5.1 million)	2. TUVALU (26 km²)	2. NAURU (12,329)

C. Maria
Van Diemen
C.Reinga
North C.
Parengarenga
Harb.
Rangaunu B.
Doubtless B.
Houhora
C. Karl Kari
Whangaruru Harb.
Cavalli I.
Kaeo
C. Brett
Ahipara B.
Awanui
Kaitaia
Herekino
Kohukohu
Okaihau
Bay of Islands
Hokianga
Harb.
Donnelly's
Crossing
Opua
Whangaruru Harb.
Poor Knights
Island
Hen. & Chickens
Islands
Dargaville
Whangarei
Bream
Bay
Needles Pt.
Lit.Barrier
I.
Great
Barrier I.
C. Rodney
C. Barrier
Kawau I.
Cuvier I.
Hauraki
Gulf
Mercury Is.
Takapuna
Waiheke
I.
Mercury B.
Birkenhead
Auckland
Howick
Coromandel
Peninsula
Papatoetoe
Manukau
Whangamata
Manukau Harb.
Mayor I.
Waikato
Waikato L.
Matakana I.
White I.
C. Runaway
Hicks Bay
Huntly
Te
Puke
Bay of
Plenty
Le Kaha
Te Araroa
East C.
Raglan Harb.
Cambridge
Rotoehu
Edgecumbe
Whakatane
Aotea Harb.
Hamilton
Te Awamutu
Rotorua
Opotiki
Moutohora
Waipiro
Tokomaru Bay

North
Island

Albatross Pt.
Kihikihi
Tirua Pt.
Arapuni
Taumarunui
Ngatapa
Gisborne
Tuaheni Pt.
Poverty Bay

Mokau
Waikato
Itī
North Taranaki Bight
Pukearuhe
Ohura
Mahia
Peninsula
New Plymouth
Waitara
Tahora
Okato
Taumarunui
Portland
I.
C. Egmont
Egmont
Rahotu
Eltham
Napier
Opunake
Hawke Bay
Hawera
Manaia
C. Kidnappers
South Taranaki Bight
Patea
Hastings
Havelock North
Wanganui
Waitotara
Mangaweka

Tasman
sea

Feilding
Danevirke
Palmerston North
Porangahau
Longburn
Pahiatua
Weber
Turnagain
Foxton
Eketahuna
Levin
Kapiti
Otaki
Alfredton
Castlepoint
Stephens
I.
Tararua
Masterton
C.
Farewell
Farewell
Spit
Stephens
D'Urville
Island
Carterton
Greytown
Golden
Bay
Flat Pt.
Kahurangi Pt.
Devil
River Pk.
Up Hutt
Martinborough
Tasman
Mts.
Tasman
Bay
Petone
Aorangi
Mts.
Nelson
Wellington
Karamea
Richmond Ra.
Blenheim
C. Palliser
Karamea
Bight
Seddon
Palliser
Bay
Westport
L. Rotoiti
Ward
Mt. Owen
Campbell
C. Foulwind
Rotoroa
Mt.
Franklyn
Tapuaenuku

PACIFIC

OCEAN

Reefton
Manakau
Greymouth
Kaikoura
Brunner
Amur
Pass
Kaikoura
Pen.
Brunner
L.
Harper
Pass
Hanmer
Waiau
Pripaua
Arthur's
Hope Pass
Parnassus
Pass
Sumner
Hurunui
Domett
Crossley
Scargill
Waipara
Pegasus
Bay
Wanganui
Amberley
Whataroa
Coleridge
Ashley
Riccarton
New Brighton
Rakaia
Christchurch
Lyttelton
Banks
Leeston
Peninsula
Springburn
Akaroa Harb.
Tasman
Mt.Cook
Tekapo
L.Ellesmere
Haast
Geraldine
Ashburton
Open Bay Is.
Winchester
South
Jackson Bay
Temuka
Island
Cascade Pt.
Pukaki
Timaru
Canterbury Bight
Awarua Pt.
St. Andrews
Yates Pt.
Waitaki
Milford Sd.
Wanaka
Waihao
Hawea
Mt. Earnslaw
Tokarahi
Sutherland Sd.
Oamaru
George Sd.
Fiordland
Maheno
Caswell Sd.
Hampden
Thompson Sd.
Wakatipu
Shag Pt.
Secretary I.
Murchison Mts.
Coal
Waikouaiti
Doubtful Sd.
Mt.Lyall
Creek Flat
Downs
Daggs Sd.
Kepler Mts.
Roxburgh
Breaksea Sd.
Beaumont
Resolution
I.
SOUTHLAND
C West C.
Waimea
Providence
Dunedin
Chalky
Gore
Inlet
L. Hauroa
Dipton
Milton
Puysegur Pt.
Tuatapere
Winton
Kaitangata
Clinton
Invercargill
Nugget Pt.
Solander
Mt.Anglem
I.
Codfish I.
Long Pt.
Mason B.
Oban
Waipapa Pt.
Doughboy B.
Stewart
Long I.
Island
Port Pegasus
Southwest C.

Projection: Conical with two standard parallels

© Anthem Press

Scale: 1:6 200

ALTITUDE (in metres)	
	3000
	2000
	1500
	1000
	400
	200
	0
	200

HIGHEST MOUNTAINS	LONGEST RIVERS	LARGEST CITIES (POP.)	
1. AORAKI (MOUNT COOK) [S.I.] (3,754 m)	1. WAIKATO [N.I.] (425 km)	1. AUCKLAND [N.I.] (1.21 million)	4. HAMILTON [N.I.] (185,000)
2. MOUNT TASMAN [S.I.] (3,497 m)	2. CLUTHA [S.I.] (322 km)	2. WELLINGTON [N.I.] (398,000)	5. NAPIER [N.I.] (118,000)
3. MOUNT DAMPIER [S.I.] (3,440 m)	3. WHANGANUI [N.I.] (290 km)	3. CHRISTCHURCH [S.I.] (361,000)	6. DUNEDIN [S.I.] (111,000)

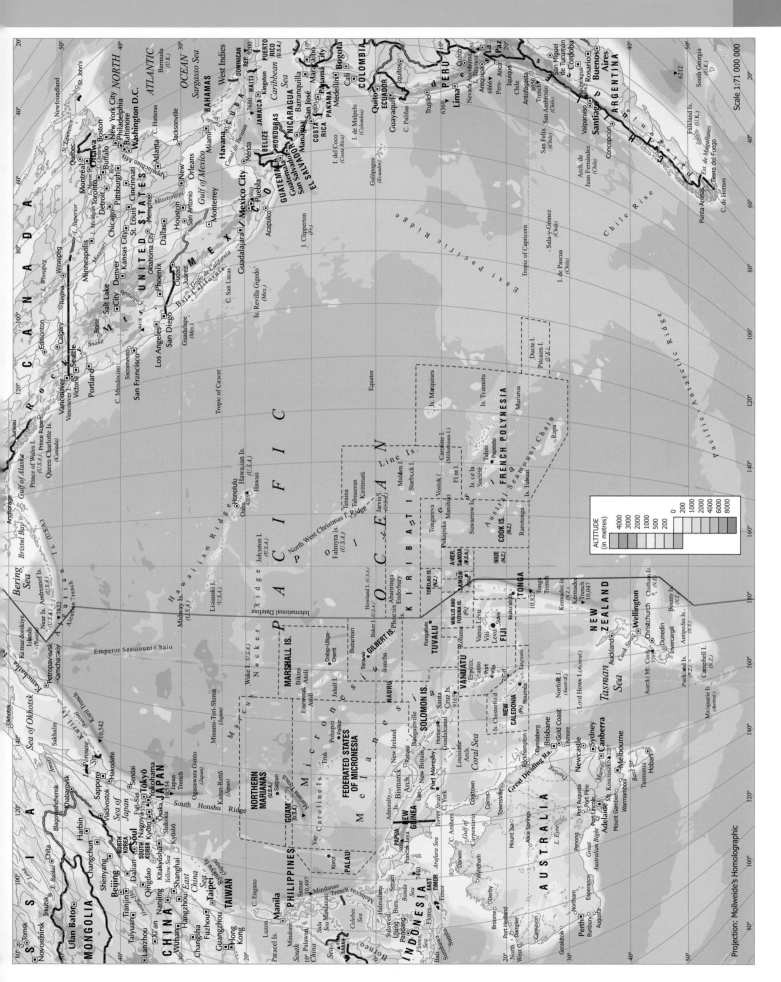

Scale 1:71 000 000

Projection: Mollweide's Homolographic

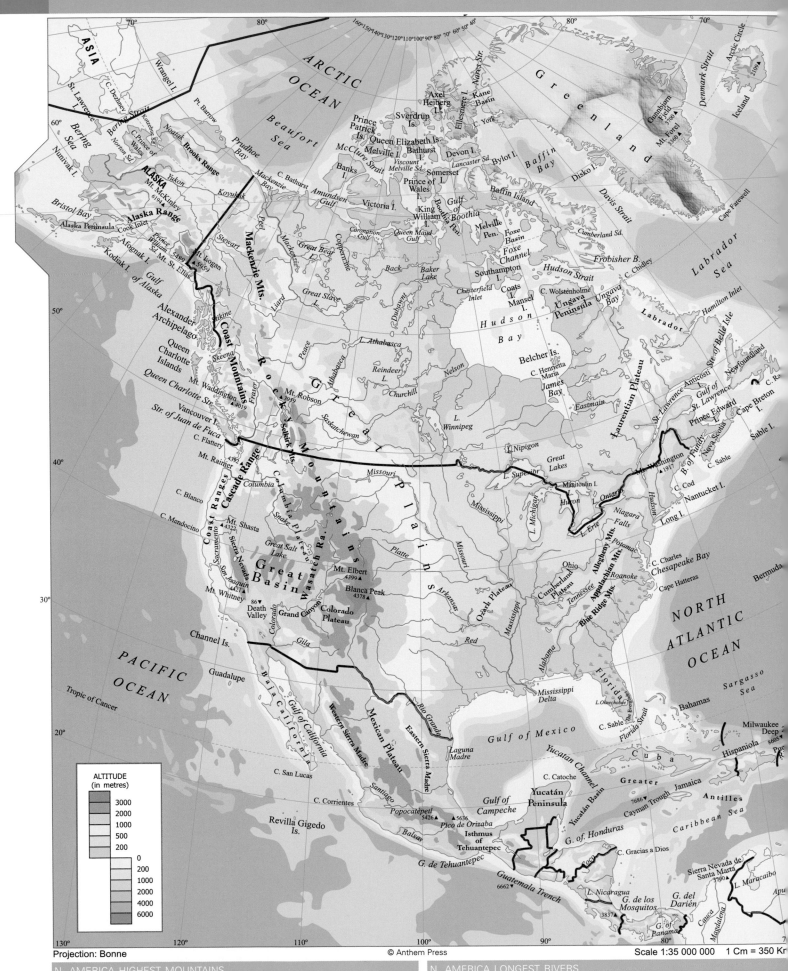

ALTITUDE
(in metres)

3000
2000
1000
500
200
0
200
1000
2000
4000
6000

Projection: Bonne

© Anthem Press

Scale 1:35 000 000   1 Cm = 350 Km

N. AMERICA HIGHEST MOUNTAINS

1. MT MCKINLEY, USA [AK] (6,194 m)
2. MT LOGAN, CAN (5,959 m)
3. PICO DE ORIZABA, MEX (5,700 m)
4. MT ST ELIAS, USA–CAN (5,489 m)
5. POPOCATÉPETL, MEX (5,452 m)
6. MT FORAKER, USA [AK] (5,304 m)

N. AMERICA LONGEST RIVERS

1. MISSISSIPPI–MISSOURI (6,020 km)
2. MACKENZIE (4,240 km)
3. MISSOURI (3,767 km)
4. MISSISSIPPI (3,766 km)
5. YUKON (3,185 km)
6. RIO GRANDE (3,030 km)

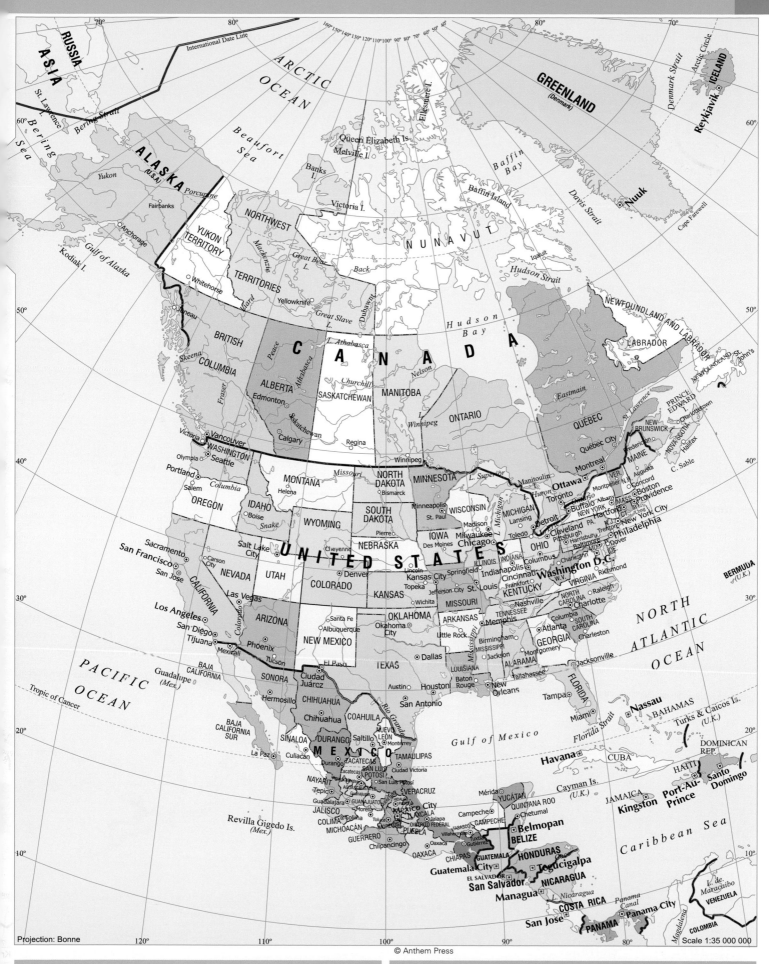

Projection: Bonne

© Anthem Press

Scale 1:35 000 000

N. AMERICA LARGEST NATIONS (AREA)	SMALLEST NATIONS (AREA)	N. AMERICA LARGEST CITIES (POP.)	
1. CANADA (9.98 million km²)	1. ST KITTS & NEVIS (261 km²)	1. MEXICO CITY, MEX (22.4 million)	4. CHICAGO, USA (9.8 million)
2. UNITED STATES (9.83 million km²)	2. GRENADA (344 km²)	2. NEW YORK CITY, USA (21.9 million)	5. WASHINGTON, USA (8.2 million)
3. MEXICO (1.97 million km²)	3. ST VINCENT & GRENADINES (389 km²)	3. LOS ANGELES, USA (18 million)	6. DALLAS, USA (6.15 million)

January Temperature

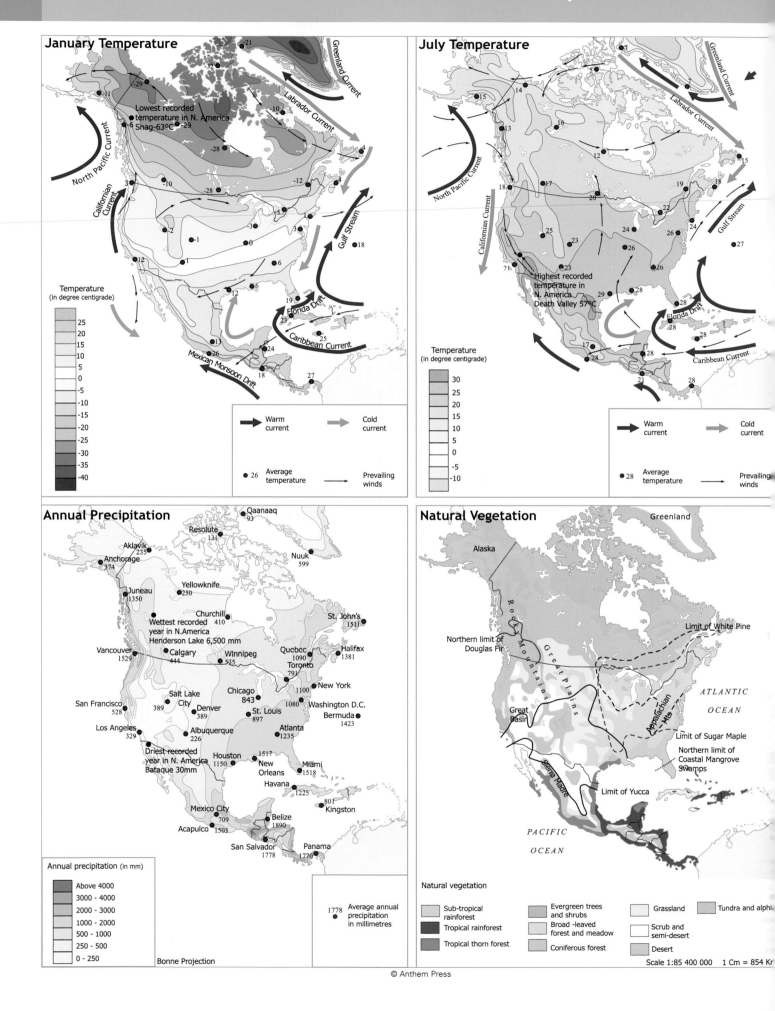

Greenland Current

Labrador Current

North Pacific Current

Californian Current

-21
-32
-29
Lowest recorded
temperature in N. America
-6 Snag-63ºC -29
-28
-10
-3
4
-10
-28
3
-2
-1
0
-3
3
-12
18
-1
1
6
12
6
6
Florida Drift
19
23
Caribbean Current
25
13
26
24
Mexican Monsoon Drift
18
27
Gulf Stream

Temperature
(in degree centigrade)

| 25 |
| 20 |
| 15 |
| 10 |
| 5 |
| 0 |
| -5 |
| -10 |
| -15 |
| -20 |
| -25 |
| -30 |
| -35 |
| -40 |

→ Warm current   → Cold current

• 26 Average temperature   → Prevailing winds

July Temperature

Greenland Current

Labrador Current

North Pacific Current

Californian Current

7
14
5
15
13
16
12
18
17
20
25
23
26
24
26
24
27
19
22
23
21
Highest recorded
temperature in
N. America
Death Valley 57ºC
29
28
28
28
Florida Drift
28
28
28
17
28
28
21
28
15
Gulf Stream
Caribbean Current

Temperature
(in degree centigrade)

| 30 |
| 25 |
| 20 |
| 15 |
| 10 |
| 5 |
| 0 |
| -5 |
| -10 |

→ Warm current   → Cold current

• 28 Average temperature   → Prevailing winds

Annual Precipitation

Qaanaaq 93
Resolute 131
Aklavik 235
Anchorage 374
Juneau 1350
Nuuk 599
Yellowknife 250
Churchill 410
Wettest recorded
year in N.America
Henderson Lake 6,500 mm
St. John's 1511
Vancouver 1529
Calgary 444
Winnipeg 535
Quebec 1090
Halifax 1381
Toronto 791
San Francisco 528
Salt Lake City 389
Chicago 843
New York 1100
Denver 389
St. Louis 897
Washington D.C. 1080
Bermuda 1423
Los Angeles 329
Albuquerque 226
Atlanta 1235
Driest recorded
year in N. America
Bataque 30mm
Houston 1150
New Orleans 1517
Miami 1518
Havana 1225
Kingston 801
Mexico City 709
Belize 1890
Acapulco 1503
San Salvador 1778
Panama 1770

Annual precipitation (in mm)

	Above 4000
	3000 - 4000
	2000 - 3000
	1000 - 2000
	500 - 1000
	250 - 500
	0 - 250

• 1778 Average annual precipitation in millimetres

Bonne Projection

Natural Vegetation

Greenland
Alaska
Rocky Mountains
Great Plains
Great Basin
Appalachian Mts
Sierra Madre
Northern limit of Douglas Fir
Limit of White Pine
Limit of Sugar Maple
Northern limit of Coastal Mangrove Swamps
Limit of Yucca
ATLANTIC OCEAN
PACIFIC OCEAN

Natural vegetation

	Sub-tropical rainforest		Evergreen trees and shrubs		Grassland		Tundra and alphia
	Tropical rainforest		Broad-leaved forest and meadow		Scrub and semi-desert	
	Tropical thorn forest		Coniferous forest		Desert	

Scale 1:85 400 000   1 Cm = 854 Km

© Anthem Press

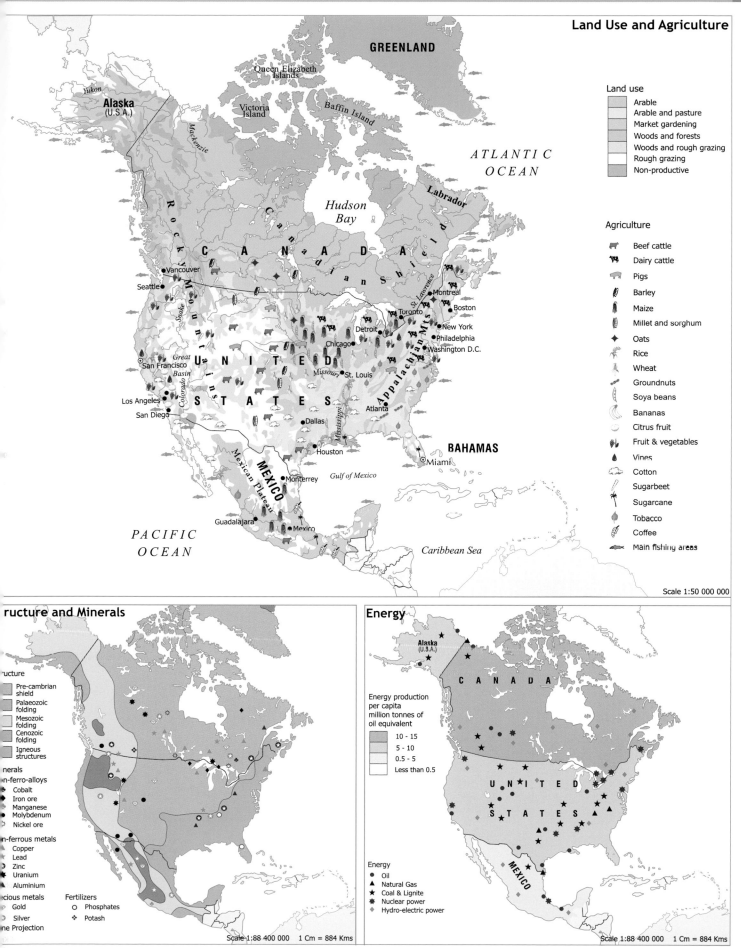

Land Use and Agriculture

Land use
- Arable
- Arable and pasture
- Market gardening
- Woods and forests
- Woods and rough grazing
- Rough grazing
- Non-productive

Agriculture
- Beef cattle
- Dairy cattle
- Pigs
- Barley
- Maize
- Millet and sorghum
- Oats
- Rice
- Wheat
- Groundnuts
- Soya beans
- Bananas
- Citrus fruit
- Fruit & vegetables
- Vines
- Cotton
- Sugarbeet
- Sugarcane
- Tobacco
- Coffee
- Main fishing areas

GREENLAND

Queen Elizabeth Islands

Alaska (U.S.A.)

Yukon

Victoria Island

Baffin Island

ATLANTIC OCEAN

Mackenzie

Hudson Bay

Labrador

C A N A D A

Canadian Shield

Rocky Mountains

Vancouver

Seattle

St. Lawrence

Montreal

Boston

Toronto

Detroit

New York

Philadelphia

Washington D.C.

Chicago

Snake

Great Basin

San Francisco

U N I T E D

Missouri

St. Louis

Appalachian Mts.

Colorado

Los Angeles

San Diego

S T A T E S

Atlanta

Dallas

Mississippi

Houston

BAHAMAS

Miami

Gulf of Mexico

M E X I C O

Mexican Plateau

Monterrey

PACIFIC OCEAN

Guadalajara

Mexico

Caribbean Sea

Scale 1:50 000 000

Structure and Minerals

Structure
- Pre-cambrian shield
- Palaeozoic folding
- Mesozoic folding
- Cenozoic folding
- Igneous structures

Minerals

Ferro-alloys
- Cobalt
- Iron ore
- Manganese
- Molybdenum
- Nickel ore

Non-ferrous metals
- Copper
- Lead
- Zinc
- Uranium
- Aluminium

Precious metals
- Gold
- Silver

Fertilizers
- Phosphates
- Potash

ne Projection

Scale 1:88 400 000   1 Cm = 884 Kms

Energy

Alaska (U.S.A.)

C A N A D A

Energy production per capita million tonnes of oil equivalent
- 10 - 15
- 5 - 10
- 0.5 - 5
- Less than 0.5

U N I T E D

S T A T E S

M E X I C O

Energy
- Oil
- Natural Gas
- Coal & Lignite
- Nuclear power
- Hydro-electric power

Scale 1:88 400 000   1 Cm = 884 Kms

© Anthem Press

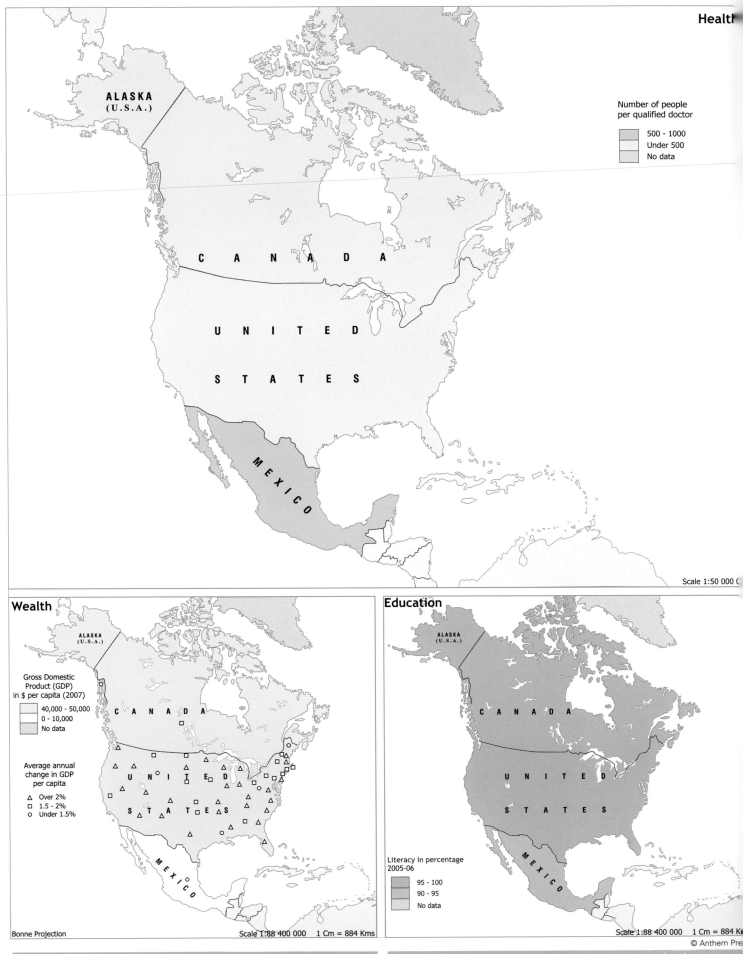

Health

Number of people
per qualified doctor

- 500 - 1000
- Under 500
- No data

Scale 1:50 000 0

Wealth

Gross Domestic
Product (GDP)
in $ per capita (2007)

- 40,000 - 50,000
- 0 - 10,000
- No data

Average annual
change in GDP
per capita

- △ Over 2%
- □ 1.5 - 2%
- ○ Under 1.5%

Bonne Projection   Scale 1:88 400 000   1 Cm = 884 Kms

Education

Literacy in percentage
2005-06

- 95 - 100
- 90 - 95
- No data

Scale 1:88 400 000   1 Cm = 884 Km

N.AMERICA'S WEALTHIEST NATIONS	GDP PER CAPITA (PPP) US $
1. UNITED STATES ($41,557)	3. BAHAMAS ($19,139)
2. CANADA ($34,444)	4. BARBADOS ($17,170)

N.AMERICA'S POOREST NATIONS	GDP PER CAPITA (PPP) US $
1. HAITI ($1,614)	3. HONDURAS ($2,793)
2. NICARAGUA ($2,779)	4. CUBA ($3,000)

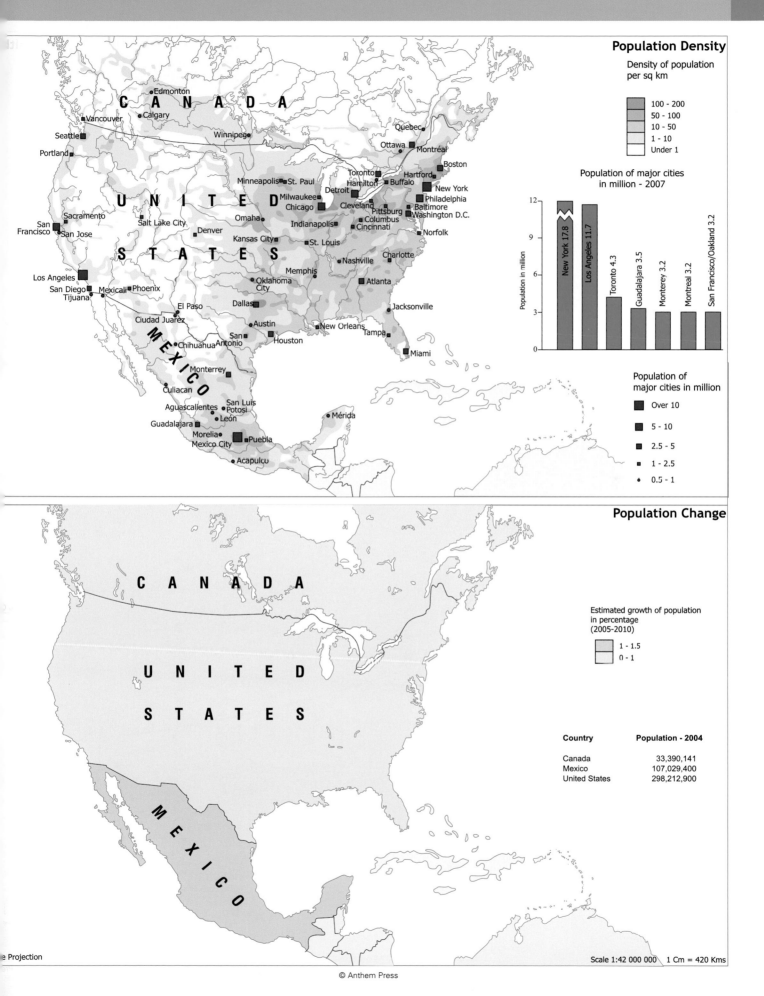

Population Density

Density of population per sq km

	100 - 200
	50 - 100
	10 - 50
	1 - 10
	Under 1

Population of major cities in million - 2007

New York 17.8
Los Angeles 11.7
Toronto 4.3
Guadalajara 3.5
Monterey 3.2
Montreal 3.2
San Francisco/Oakland 3.2

Population in million

Population of major cities in million

■	Over 10
■	5 - 10
■	2.5 - 5
■	1 - 2.5
•	0.5 - 1

Population Change

Estimated growth of population in percentage (2005-2010)

	1 - 1.5
	0 - 1

Country	Population - 2004
Canada	33,390,141
Mexico	107,029,400
United States	298,212,900

Projection

Scale 1:42 000 000 1 Cm = 420 Kms

NORTHWEST TERRITORIES, NUNAVUT
Scale 1:40 000 000

Bonne Projection

HIGHEST MOUNTAINS		LONGEST RIVERS	
1. MOUNT LOGAN, YT (5,959 m)	3. MOUNT LUCANIA, YT (5,227 m)	1. MACKENZIE (4,240 km)	3. ST LAWRENCE (3,058 km)
2. MT SAINT ELIAS, YT–AK (5,489 m)	4. MOUNT STEELE, YT (5,073 m)	2. YUKON (3,185 km)	4. NELSON (2,575 km)

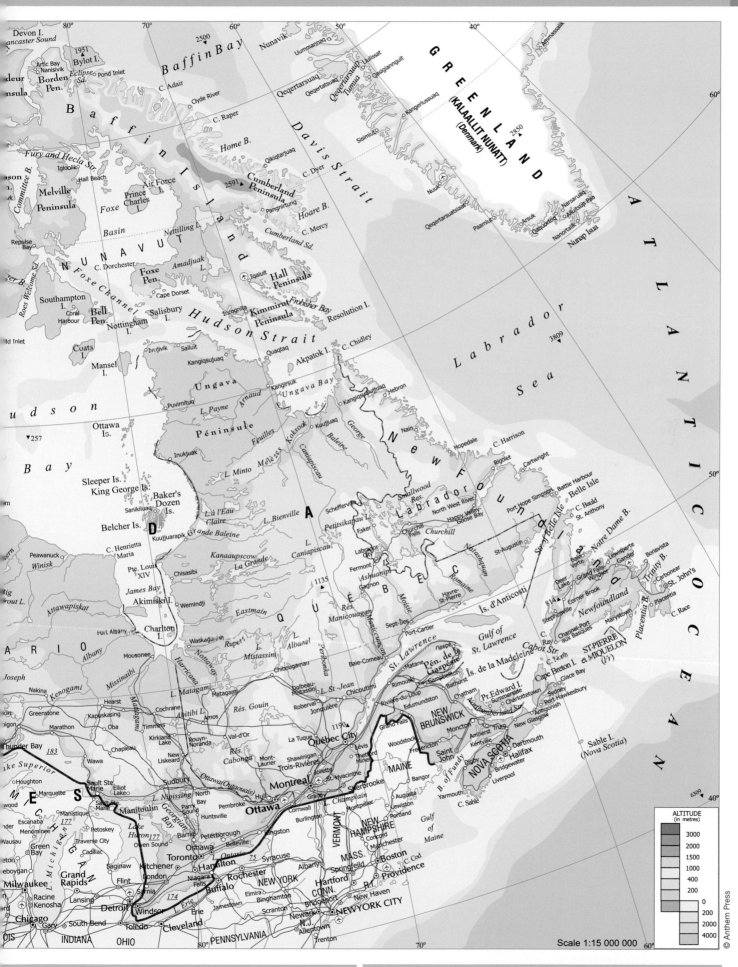

ALTITUDE
(in metres)

3000
2000
1500
1000
400
200
0
200
2000
4000

Scale 1:15 000 000

© Anthem Press

LARGEST PROVIN./TERRIT. (AREA)
QUÉBEC (1,356,128 km²)
BRITISH COLUMBIA (925,186 km²)

SMALLEST PROVIN./TERRIT. (AREA)
1. PRINCE EDWARD I. (5,660 km²)
2. NOVA SCOTIA (53,338 km²)

LARGEST CITIES (POP.)
1. TORONTO, ON (5.35 million)
2. MONTRÉAL, QC (3.75 million)
3. VANCOUVER, BC (2.2 million)
4. OTTAWA, ON (1.17 million)

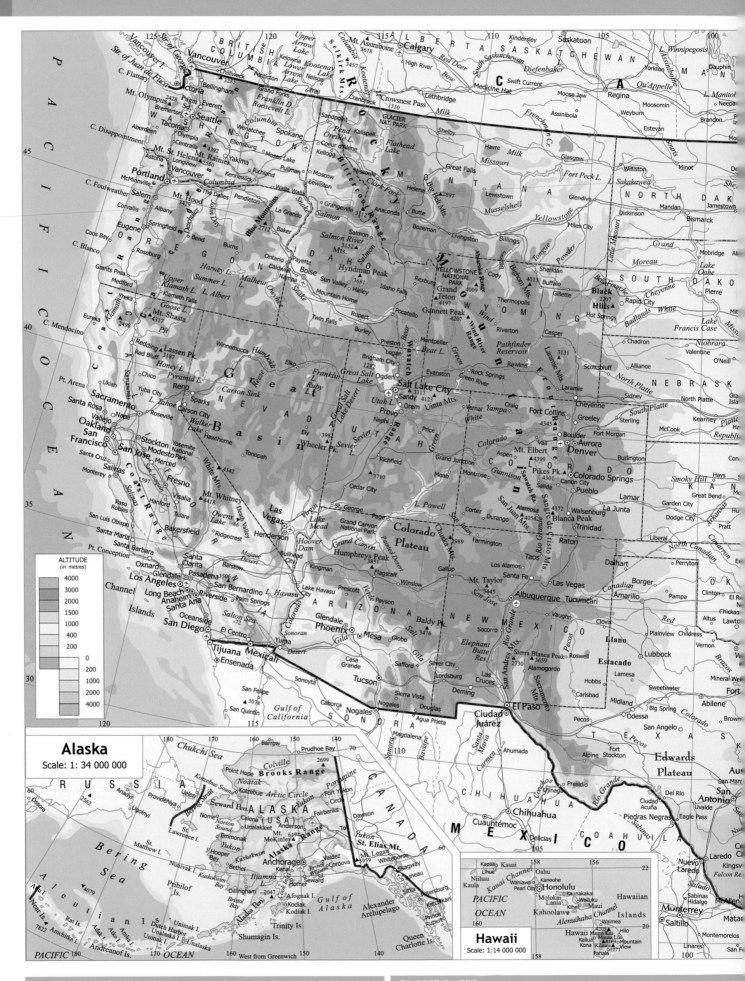

HIGHEST MOUNTAINS
1. MOUNT MCKINLEY, AK (6,194 m)
2. MT SAINT ELIAS, AK–CAN (5,489 m)
3. MOUNT FORAKER, AK (5,300 m)
4. MOUNT BONA, AK (5,005 m)

LONGEST RIVERS
1. MISSOURI (3,767 km)
2. MISSISSIPPI (3,766 km)
3. YUKON (3,185 km)
4. RIO GRANDE (3,030 km)

© Anthem Press

Projection: Albers' Equal Area with two standard parallels

Scale:1:12 400 000

LARGEST STATES (AREA)		SMALLEST STATES (AREA)	
1. ALASKA (1,717,854 km²)	3. CALIFORNIA (423,970 km²)	1. RHODE ISLAND (2,706 km²)	3. CONNECTICUT (12,548 km²)
2. TEXAS (695,621 km²)	4. MONTANA (380,838 km²)	2. DELAWARE (2,706 km²)	4. HAWAII (16,635 km²)

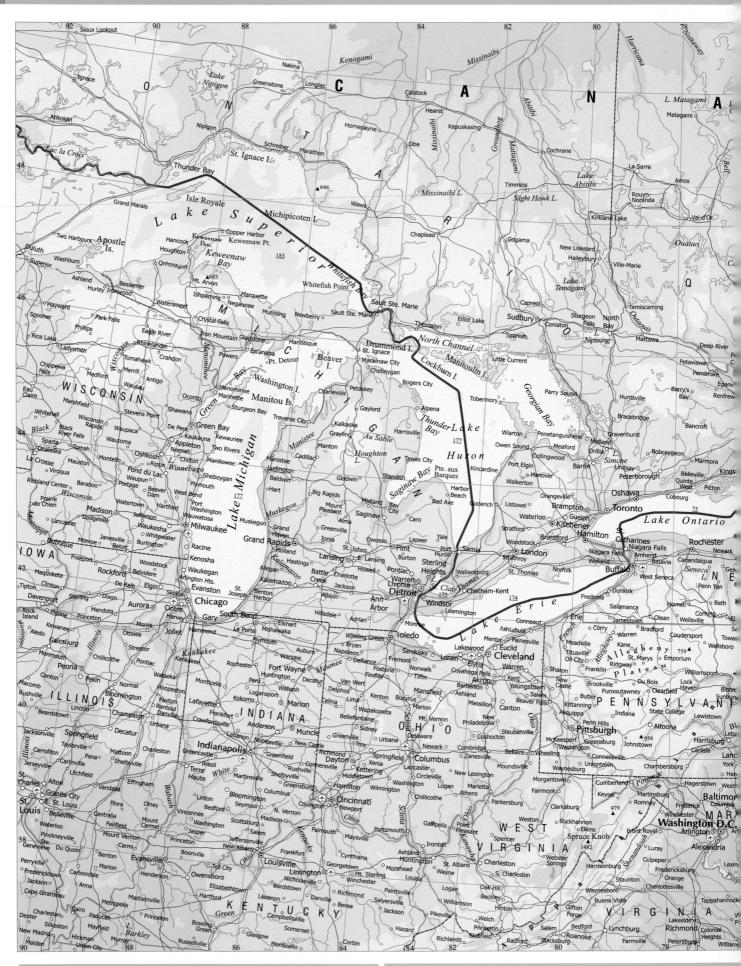

LARGEST STATES (POP.)
1. CALIFORNIA (36.5 million)   3. NEW YORK (19.3 million)
2. TEXAS (23.9 million)   4. FLORIDA (18.3 million)

SMALLEST STATES (POP.)
1. VERMONT (621,254)   3. ALASKA (683,478)
2. NORTH DAKOTA (639,254)   4. SOUTH DAKOTA (796,214)

Jamaica
Scale 1:3 000 000

JAMAICA

Guadeloupe
Scale 1:2 000 000

GUADELOUPE *(Fr.)*

BASSE-TERRE
Îles des Saintes

Martinique
Scale 1:2 000 000

MARTINIQUE *(Fr.)*

ALTITUDE
(in metres)

3000	
2000	
1500	
1000	
400	
200	
0	
200	
2000	
4000	
6000	

Bonne Projection

HIGHEST MOUNTAINS
1. Pico de Orizaba, Mex (5,640 m)
2. Popocatépetl, Mex (5,465 m)
3. Iztaccíhuatl, Mex (5,230 m)
4. Nevado de Toluca, Mex (4,680 m)
5. Sierra Negra, Mex (4,640 m)
6. Matlalcueitl, Mex (4,461 m)

LARGEST COUNTRIES (AREA)
1. Mexico (1,972,550 sq km)
2. Nicaragua (129,494 sq km)
3. Honduras (112,090 sq km)
4. Cuba (110,860 sq km)
5. Guatemala (108,890 sq km)
6. Panama (52,853 sq km)

GEST COUNTRIES (POP.)
MEXICO (106.2 million) — 4. DOMINICAN REPUBLIC (8.95 million)
UATEMALA (14.7 million) — 5. HONDURAS (6.98 million)
UBA (11.3 million) — 6. EL SALVADOR (6.7 million)

LARGEST CITIES (POP.)
1. MEXICO CITY, MEX (22.4 million) — 4. HAVANA, CUB (2.33 million)
2. GUADALAJARA, MEX (4.45 million) — 5. PUEBLA, MEX (1.89 million)
3. MONTERREY, MEX (4 million) — 6. TOLUCA, MEX (1.71 million)

© Anthem Press

PACIFIC

COEAN

ATLANTIC

COEAN

SOUTH

ATLANTIC

COEAN

Caribbean Sea

Lesser Windward Islands

ALTITUDE (in metres)

4000
3000
2000
1000
500
200
0
200
600

Projection: Lambert's Equivalent Azimuthal

© Anthem Press

Scale 1:32 000 000

S. AMERICA HIGHEST MOUNTAINS		
1. Aconcagua, Arg (6,960 m)	4. Pissis, Arg (6,779 m)	
2. Bonete, Arg (6,872 m)	5. Mercedario, Arg-Chi (6,770 m)	
3. Ojos del Salado, Arg-Chi (6,863 m)	6. Huascarán, Per (6,768 m)	

S. AMERICA LONGEST RIVERS		
1. Amazon (6,450 km)	4. Madeira (3,200 km)	
2. Paraná-Plate (4,500 km)	5. São Francisco (2,900 km)	
3. Purus (3,350 km)	6. Paraná (2,800 km)	

C. Gracias a Dios
NICARAGUA
Managua
COSTA RICA
San José
Limón
C. Blanco
Laguna de Perla
I. de San Andres (Colombia)
Pta. Gallinas
Pen. de la Guajira
Aruba (Neth.)
Curaçao (Neth.)
Bonaire (Neth.)
Los Roques (Ven.)
La Tortuga (Ven.)
I. de Margarita (Ven.)
Willemstad
Lesser Windward Islands
Martinique (Fr.)
ST. LUCIA
ST. VINCENT
BARBADOS
Bridgetown
GRENADA
Tobago
TRINIDAD & TOBAGO
Port of Spain

Santa Marta
Barranquilla
Valledupar
Maracaibo
Puerto Cabello
Barcelona
Valencia
Caracas
Puerto La Cruz
Tucupita
El Tigre
Ciudad Guayana
Ciudad Bolívar

Panamá City
G. del Darién
Colón
Sincelejo
Montería
Cúcuta
Mérida
Barinas
San Cristóbal
Bucaramanga
VENEZUELA
Apure
Arauca
San Fernando de Apure
Orinoco
Caroni
Angel Falls
Kaieteur Falls
Guyuni
Essequibo
New Amsterdam
Georgetown
GUYANA
Paramaribo
SURINAME
Cayenne
FRENCH GUIANA
C. Orange

G. de Panamá
I. de Coiba
C. Corrientes
Quibdó
Medellín
Tunja
Pereira
Ibagué
BOGOTÁ
Buenaventura
Cali
Palmira
Neiva
Popayán
Pasto
Tumaco
Florencia
Mocoa
COLOMBIA
Meta
Vichada
Guaviare
Vaupés
Mitú
Vaupés
Guainía
Casiquiare
RORAIMA
Boa Vista
Branco
AMAPÁ
Macapá
Amapá
I. Caviana
I. Mexiana
I. de Marajó
B. de São Marcos
São Luís
Bragança
Belém
Abaetetuba

Equator

Santo Domingo de los Colorados
Manta
Quito
Latacunga
Ambato
ECUADOR
Salinas
Guayaquil
G. de Guayaquil
Cuenca
Machala
Ibarra
Tulcán
Ipiales
Napo
Iquitos
Leticia
Putumayo
Içá
Caquetá
Japurá
Negro
Manaus
Itacoatiara
Parintins
Óbidos
Santarém
Altamira
Itaituba
Tapajós
AMAZONAS
Solimões (Amazon)
Amazonas (Amazon)
Cametá
Tucuruí
Pinheiro
Parnaíba
Bacabal
Camocim
Sobral
MARANHÃO
Imperatriz
Marabá
Caxias
Teresina
Barra do Corda
PIAUÍ
CEARÁ
Fortaleza
Acaraú
Mossoró
C. de São Roque
Aracati
Natal
Cabedelo

Talara
Paita
Piura
Sullana
Chiclayo
Trujillo
Salaverry
Chimbote
Cajamarca
Chachapoyas
Marañón
Huallaga
Ucayali
Yavarí
Benjamin Constant
Cruzeiro do Sul
Pucallpa
Sena Madureira
ACRE
Rio Branco
Abunã
Purus
Fapurá
Juruá
Madeira
Manicoré
Humaitá
Tapauá
PARÁ
Xingu
Tocantins
Araguaia
Estreito
Picos
PERNAMBUCO
Petrolina
Represa de Sobradinho
Juazeiro do Norte
João Pessoa
Jaboatão
Recife
Garanhuns
Maceió
ALAGOAS
SERGIPE
Aracaju

Huaraz
Cerro de Pasco
Huánuco
PERU
Huancayo
Callao
Lima
Chincha Alta
Pisco
Ica
Nazca
Coracora
Abancay
Cuzco
Juliaca
L. Titicaca
Puno
La Paz
RONDÔNIA
Pôrto Velho
Guajará Mirim
Madre de Dios
Beni
Puerto Maldonado
Trinidad
San Ignacio de Velasco
BOLIVIA
Santa Cruz
Puerto Suárez
Corumbá
MATO GROSSO
Cuiabá
Rondonópolis
Cáceres
Diamantino
BRAZIL
MATO GROSSO
Aruanã
Goiânia
GOIÁS
DIST. FED.
Taguatinga
Brasília
Anápolis
TOCANTINS
Xique-Xique
BAHIA
Januária
Montes Claros
Feira de Santana
Cachoeira
Salvador
B. de Todos os Santos
Jequié
Itabuna
Vitória da Conquista
Pedra Azul
Pôrto Seguro
Teófilo Otoni
São Mateus
Linhares
MINAS GERAIS
Uberlândia
Uberaba
Patos de Minas
Belo Horizonte
Pôço de Caldas
Franca
Juiz de Fora
Cariacica
Vila Velha
Campos
RIO DE JANEIRO
Nova Iguaçu
Rio De Janeiro

Arequipa
Tacna
Arica
Pisagua
Iquique
Calama
Chuquicamata
Mejillones
Tocopilla
Antofagasta
Oruro
L. de Poopó
Sucre
Potosí
Pulacayo
Tarija
Salar de Uyuni
Puerto Suárez
Campo Grande
Dourados
Presidente Prudente
MATO GROSSO DO SUL
PARAGUAY
Concepción
Asunción
Formosa
Foz do Iguaçu
Encarnación
Paraná
Londrina
Maringá
Ponta Grossa
São Paulo
São Bernardo do Campo
Guarulhos
Campinas
Sorocaba
Piracicaba
Rio Claro
Bauru
Três Lagoas
SÃO PAULO

Tropic of Capricorn

Salta
San Salvador de Jujuy
Orán
Andalgalá
San Miguel de Tucumán
Catamarca
La Rioja
Pilcomayo
Bermejo
Teuco
Salado Grande
Resistencia
Añatuya
Reconquista
Corrientes
Santo Ángel
Santa María
Uruguaiana
Artigas
Rivera
Bagé
Caxias do Sul
Criciúma
Florianópolis
SANTA CATARINA
Itajaí
São Francisco do Sul
Curitiba
PARANÁ
Guarapuava

PACIFIC OCEAN

Caldera
Copiapó
Huasco
La Serena
Ovalle
Illapel
Vallenar
San José de Jáchal
San Juan
Mendoza
Córdoba
Rafaela
Santa Fe
Paraná
Concordia
Paysandú
Salado
L. Mar Chiquita
Rosario
San Nicolás
Zárate
URUGUAY
Montevideo
Minas
Maldonado
Rocha
Treinta y Tres
Melo
Pelotas
Rio Grande
Pôrto Alegre
L. dos Patos
L. Mirim
RIO GRANDE DO SUL
Santa Maria
Mercedes

Viña del Mar
Valparaíso
San Bernardo
Santiago
San Fernando
Talca
Constitución
Linares
Talcahuano
Concepción
Chillán
Los Ángeles
Temuco
Valdivia
Osorno
San Luis
Junín
Buenos Aires
Avellaneda
La Plata
General Pico
Santa Rosa
Olavarría
Azul
Dolores
Tandil
Balcarce
Mar del Plata
Necochea
Tres Arroyos
Punta Alta
Bahía Blanca
Colorado
Neuquén
Negro
Maquinchao
Puerto Madryn
Pen. Valdés
Golfo San Matías
Rawson

L. Llanquihue
Puerto Montt
I. de Chiloé
Aneud
C. Quilán
ARGENTINA
Boca del Guafo
Puerto Aisén
Sarmiento
Chubut
Golfo San Jorge
Deseado
C. Dos Bahías
C. Tres Puntas
Puerto Deseado
Pen. de Taitao
I. Campana
G. de Penas
I. Wellington
I. Madre de Dios
Santa Cruz
Río Gallegos
L. Viedma
L. Argentino
Bahía Grande
C. Vírgenes

PACIFIC OCEAN

Falkland Islands (Islas Malvinas) (U.K.)
West Falkland
East Falkland
Stanley

SOUTH ATLANTIC OCEAN

ATLANTIC OCEAN

Estrecho de Concepción
I. Hanover
El Turbio
Punta Arenas
Estrecho de Magallanes (Magellan's Str.)
I. Desolación
I. Santa Inés
Isla Grande de Tierra del Fuego
Ushuaia
I. de Los Estados (Staten I.)
Canal Beagle
I. Hoste
I. Navarino
C. de Hornos (C.Horn)
Canal Cockburn

S. AMERICA LARGEST NATIONS (AREA)	SMALLEST NATIONS (AREA)	S. AMERICA LARGEST CITIES (POP.)	
BRAZIL (8.51 million km²)	1. SURINAME (163,270 km²)	1. SÃO PAULO, BRA (20.6 million)	4. BOGOTÁ, COL (8.55 million)
ARGENTINA (2.77 million km²)	2. GUYANA (214,970 km²)	2. BUENOS AIRES, ARG (13.6 million)	5. LIMA, PER (8.25 million)
PERU (1.285 million km²)	3. ECUADOR (283,560 km²)	3. RIO DE JANEIRO, BRA (12.3 million)	6. SANTAIGO, CHI (5.85 million)

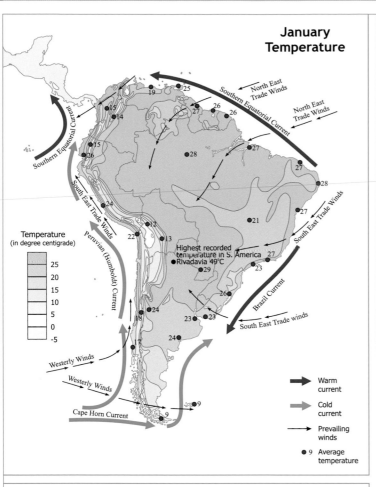

January Temperature

Temperature
(in degree centigrade)

25
20
15
10
5
0
-5

Highest recorded temperature in S. America
Rivadavia 49°C

North East Trade Winds

Southern Equatorial Current

North East Trade Winds

Southern Equatorial Current

South East Trade Winds

South East Trade Winds

Brazil Current

South East Trade winds

Peruvian (Humboldt) Current

Westerly Winds

Westerly Winds

Cape Horn Current

Warm current

Cold current

Prevailing winds

● 9 Average temperature

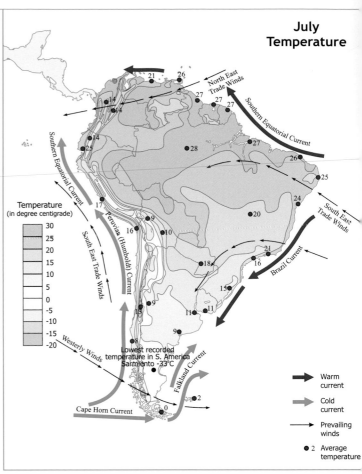

July Temperature

Temperature
(in degree centigrade)

30
25
20
15
10
5
0
-5
-10
-15
-20

North East Trade Winds

Southern Equatorial Current

South East Trade Winds

Brazil Current

Southern Equatorial Current

Peruvian (Humboldt) Current

South East Trade Winds

Westerly Winds

Lowest recorded temperature in S. America
Sarmiento -33°C

Falkland Current

Cape Horn Current

Warm current

Cold current

Prevailing winds

● 2 Average temperature

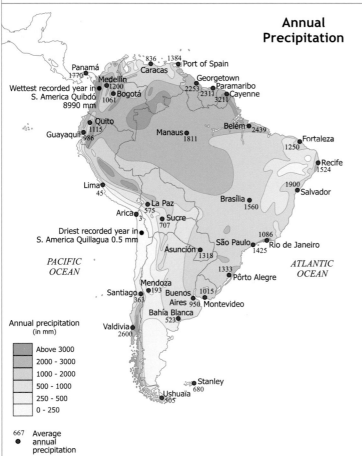

Annual Precipitation

Panamá 1770
Port of Spain 1384
836
Caracas
Medellin 1200
Wettest recorded year in S. America Quibdó 8990 mm
Bogotá 1061
2253
Georgetown
2311 Paramaribo
3211 Cayenne
Quito 1115
Guayaquil 986
Manaus 1811
Belém 2439
Fortaleza 1250
Recife 1524
Lima 45
La Paz
Arica 3
575
Sucre 707
Brasília 1560
1900 Salvador
Driest recorded year in S. America Quillagua 0.5 mm
São Paulo 1318
1086
Rio de Janeiro 1425
Asunción
1333 Pôrto Alegre
Mendoza 193
Santiago 363
Buenos Aires 950
1015
Montevideo
Bahía Blanca 523
Valdivia 2600
Stanley 680
Ushuaïa 505

PACIFIC OCEAN

ATLANTIC OCEAN

Annual precipitation
(in mm)

Above 3000
2000 - 3000
1000 - 2000
500 - 1000
250 - 500
0 - 250

667 Average annual precipitation
●

Natural Vegetation

Guiana Highlands

Amazon Basin

South limit of wild rubber

Atacama Desert

Andes

South limit of Quebracho

Brazilian Highlands

Pampas

Patagonia

PACIFIC OCEAN

ATLANTIC OCEAN

Natural Vegetation

Tropical rainforest
Tropical thorn forest
Temperate rainforest
Evergreen trees and shrubs
Grassland and savanna
Semi-desert
Desert
Alpine and high plateau

© Artthem Press

Projection: Lambert's Equivalent Azimuthal

Scale: 1:79 800 0

Land use and Agriculture

Land Use

- Arable
- Market gardening and plantations
- Pasture
- Woods and forests
- Rough grazing
- Non-productive

Agriculture

- Beef cattle
- Dairy cattle
- Pigs
- Sheep
- Maize
- Millet and sorghum
- Rice
- Wheat
- Groundnuts
- Potatoes
- Soya beans
- Bananas
- Citrus fruit
- Fruit & vegetables
- Vines
- Cacao
- Coconut palms
- Cotton
- Sugarcane
- Tobacco
- Coffee
- Tea
- Main fishing areas

Scale: 1:56 600 000

Structure and Minerals

Structure

- Pre-Cambrian shield
- Palaeozoic folding
- Mesozoic folding
- Cenozoic folding
- Igneous structures

Minerals

Iron and ferro-alloys
- Chrome
- Cobalt
- Iron ore
- Manganese
- Molybdenum
- Nickel ore

Non-ferrous metals
- Aluminium
- Bauxite
- Copper
- Tin

Precious metals & stones
- Diamonds
- Gold
- Silver

Fertilizers
- Phosphates

Scale: 1:100 500 000

Projection: Lambert's Equivalent Azimuthal

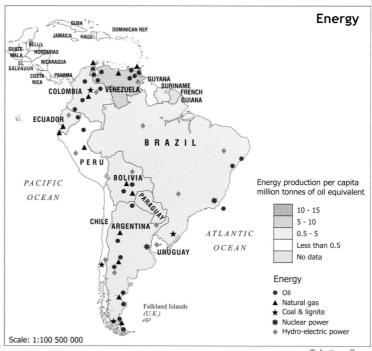

Energy

Energy production per capita
million tonnes of oil equivalent

- 10 - 15
- 5 - 10
- 0.5 - 5
- Less than 0.5
- No data

Energy

- Oil
- Natural gas
- Coal & lignite
- Nuclear power
- Hydro-electric power

Scale: 1:100 500 000

Health

CUBA
JAMAICA
HAITI
DOMINICAN REP.
GUATE-MALA
BELIZE
HONDURAS
NICARAGUA
EL SALVADOR
COSTA RICA
PANAMA

Caribbean Sea

VENEZUELA
GUYANA
SURINAME
FRENCH GUIANA
COLOMBIA

Galapagos Is. (U.K.)

ECUADOR

B R A Z I L

P E R U

BOLIVIA

PACIFIC OCEAN

PARAGUAY

CHILE

ATLANTIC OCEAN

ARGENTINA

URUGUAY

Falkland Islands (U.K.)

Number of people per qualified doctor

	5,000 - 15,000
	1,000 - 5,000
	500 - 1,000
	Under 500
	No data

Scale: 1:56 600 000

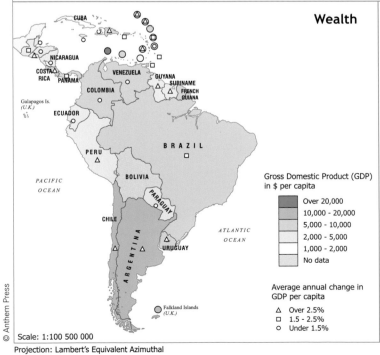

Wealth

CUBA
NICARAGUA
COSTA RICA
PANAMA
VENEZUELA
GUYANA
SURINAME
FRENCH GUIANA
COLOMBIA
Galapagos Is. (U.K.)
ECUADOR
B R A Z I L
PERU
BOLIVIA
PACIFIC OCEAN
PARAGUAY
CHILE
ATLANTIC OCEAN
ARGENTINA
URUGUAY
Falkland Islands (U.K.)

Gross Domestic Product (GDP) in $ per capita

	Over 20,000
	10,000 - 20,000
	5,000 - 10,000
	2,000 - 5,000
	1,000 - 2,000
	No data

Average annual change in GDP per capita

△	Over 2.5%
☐	1.5 - 2.5%
○	Under 1.5%

© Anthem Press

Scale: 1:100 500 000

Projection: Lambert's Equivalent Azimuthal

Education

CUBA
JAMAICA
HAITI
DOMINICAN REP.
GUATE-MALA
BELIZE
HONDURAS
NICARAGUA
EL SALVADOR
COSTA RICA
PANAMA
Puerto Rico (U.S.)
VENEZUELA
GUYANA
SURINAME
FRENCH GUIANA
COLOMBIA
Galapagos Is. (U.K.)
ECUADOR
B R A Z I L
PERU
BOLIVIA
PACIFIC OCEAN
PARAGUAY
CHILE
ATLANTIC OCEAN
ARGENTINA
URUGUAY
Falkland Islands (U.K.)

Literacy in percentage - 2005-06

	90 - 100
	80 - 90
	70 - 80
	60 - 70
	50 - 60
	No Data

Scale: 1:100 500 000

S. AMERICA WEALTHIEST NATIONS	GDP PER CAPITA (PPP) US $
1. ARGENTINA ($15,000)	3. URUGUAY ($9,619)
2. CHILE ($11,537)	4. BRAZIL ($8,745)

S. AMERICA'S POOREST NATIONS	GDP PER CAPITA (PPP) US $
1. BOLIVIA ($3,049)	3. PARAGUAY ($4,663)
2. ECUADOR ($4,010)	4. GUAYANA ($4,685)

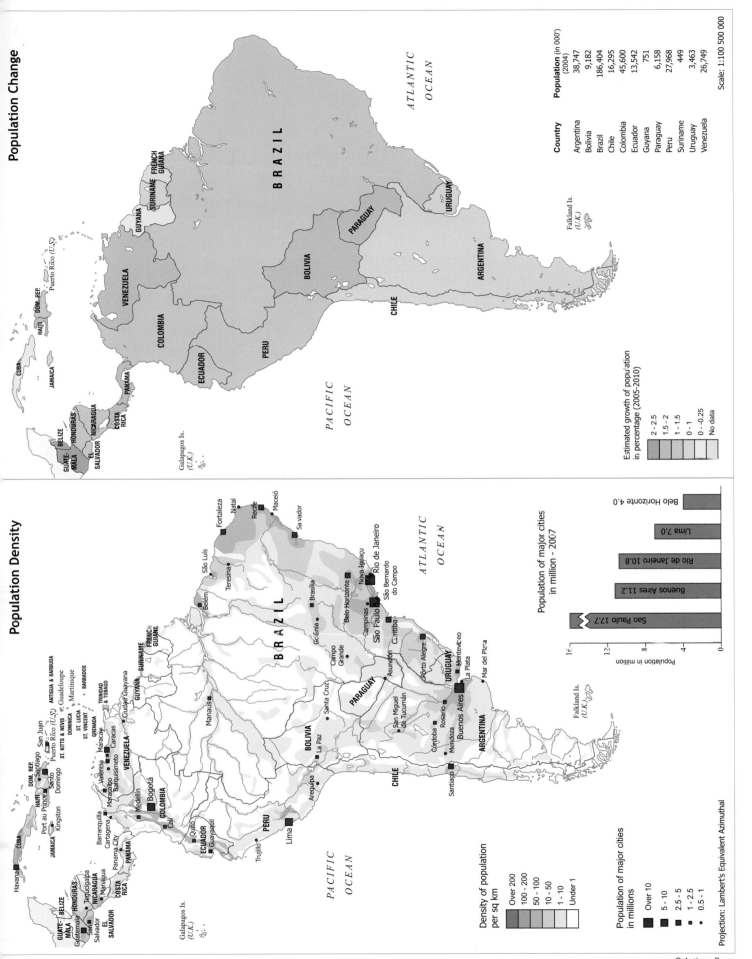

Population Change

Country	Population (in 000') (2004)
Argentina	38,747
Bolivia	9,182
Brazil	186,404
Chile	16,295
Colombia	45,600
Ecuador	13,542
Guyana	751
Paraguay	6,158
Peru	27,968
Suriname	449
Uruguay	3,463
Venezuela	26,749

Scale: 1:100 500 000

Estimated growth of population in percentage (2005-2010)

- 2 - 2.5
- 1.5 - 2
- 1 - 1.5
- 0 - 1
- 0 - 0.25
- No data

Population Density

Density of population per sq km

- Over 200
- 100 - 200
- 50 - 100
- 1 - 10
- Under 1

Population of major cities in millions

- Over 10
- 5 - 10
- 2.5 - 5
- 1 - 2.5
- 0.5 - 1

Population of major cities in million - 2007

- Belo Horizonte 4.0
- Lima 7.0
- Rio de Janeiro 10.8
- Buenos Aires 11.2
- Sao Paulo 17.7

Population in million

Projection: Lambert's Equivalent Azimuthal

© Anthem Press

COUNTRY	POPULATION							LAND & AGRICULTURE				TRADE, TOURISM & ENERGY					
	Total pop. (millions) 2006	Pop. density (people per km² 2006	Life expectancy at birth (years) 2005	Annual pop. growth rate (%) 2006	Fertility rate (births per woman) 2005	Infant mortality rate (per 000s births) 2005	Urban pop. (% of total) 2005	Land area (000s km²)	Arable & permanent crops (% of land area) 2006	Permanent pasture (% of land area) 2006	Forest (% of land area) 2000	Exports (US$ million) 2006	Imports (US$ million) 2006	Tourist arrivals (000s) 2004	Energy produced (million tonnes oil equiv.) 2004	Energy consumed per capita (kg oil equiv.) 2004	CO_2 emissions per capita (tonnes) 2004
Afghanistan	31.1	48	46	4.6	7.5	149	23	652	12	46	2	365	2,218	4	0.08	12	0.0
Albania	3.1	109	74	0.4	2.3	25	45	29	24	19	36	662	2,634	42	0.9	551	1.0
Algeria	33.4	14	71	1.5	2.5	37	63	2,382	3	13	1	32,082	18,308	866	188.4	1,240	5.1
Andorra	0.07	150		0.4		4	91	0.5	25			123	1,766	2,791			
Angola	16.4	13	41	2.8	6.8	139	53	1,247	3	43				194	50.3	238	0.6
Antigua & Barbuda	0.08	175		1.3			39	0.4	23		21	121	526	245		2,024	5.0
Argentina	39.1	14	75	1.0	2.4	15	90	2,780	10	52	13	40,106	28,689	3,354	86.0	1,568	3.4
Armenia	3.0	101	72	-0.4	1.3	30	64	30	19	30	12	937	1,692	263	0.4	598	1.1
Australia	20.3	3	81	1.1	1.8	5	88	7,741	6	52	20	105,752	118,922	4,774	247	5,169	18.8
Austria	8.2	98	79	0.2	1.4	5	66	84	17	23	47	114,390	116,627	19,373	6.4	3,487	9.4
Azerbaijan	8.5	98	67	0.6	1.9	76	0.6	87	23	31	13	4,347	4,211	1,349	20.5	1,593	3.5
Bahamas	0.3	24	70	1.4	2.3	14	90	14	1	0.2	84	376	1,927	1,561		2,217	6.0
Bahrain	0.7	1,064	75	1.6	2.5	14	97	0.7	8	6	-	9,733	7,540	3,514	16.3	10,736	31.0
Bangladesh	144.4	1,003	63	1.9	3.3	59	25	144	55	5	10	8,268	11,373	271	11.4	108	0.3
Barbados	0.2	628	75	0.3	1.5	11	53	0.4	40	5	5	361	1,672	552	0.1	1,383	4.4
Belarus	9.7	47	68	-0.6	1.2	15	72	208	27	15	45	15,979	16,708	67	2.5	2,487	5.3
Belgium	10.4	342	79	0.2	1.7	4	97	31	28	21	22	334,106	320,130	6,710	4.2	4,340	12.2
Belize	0.3	12	72	2.1	3.2	31	48	23	4	2	59	208	439	231	0.009	1,018	3.0
Benin	8.7	77	54	3.2	5.9	105	40	113	26	5	24	288	899	174	0.02	100	0.3
Bhutan	2.2	47	63	2.2	4.4	56	11	47	3	9	64			9	0.2	65	0.2
Bolivia	9.4	9	64	2.0	4.0	56	64	1,099	3	31	49	2,797	2,343	319	4.7	350	0.9
Bosnia-Herzogovina	3.9	76	74	0.3	1.3	14	46	51	21	20	45	2,388	7,054	190	3.2	1,170	4.9
Botswana	1.8	3	37	0.1	3.2	51	57	582	1	45	22	3,802	3,964	975			2.3
Brazil	188.9	22	70	1.4	2.4	27	84	8,514	8	25	64	116,129	76,436	4,794	129.4	817	1.6
Brunei	0.3	66	77	2.3	2.5	6	74	6	3	1	84	4,144	1,244	984	22.4	8,962	12.7
Bulgaria	7.7	69	73	-0.7	1.2	13	70	111	32	16	33	11,725	18,180	4,630	6.4	1,872	6.8
Burkina-Faso	13.6	50	48	3.2	6.7	121	18	274	18	22	26	397	1,267	222	0.009	28	0.1
Burma (Myanmar)	51.0	75	60	1.1	2.5	75	31	677	16	1	52			242	9.4	74	0.2
Burundi	7.8	281	43	3.0	6.8	106	10	28	49	38	4	83	173	36	0.01	12	0.0
Cambodia	14.4	79	56	2.0	4.1	95	20	181	21	8	53	2,798	2,063	1,055	0.004	13	0.0
Cameroon	16.6	35	46	1.9	4.7	94	55	475	15	4	51	2,447	2,737	190	7.0	80	0.2
Canada	32.6	3	80	1.0	1.5	5	80	9,971	5	3	27	360,136	314,436	19,095	393.5	8,535	18.0
Cape Verde	0.5	129	70	2.4	3.8	30	57	4	12	1	21	15	429	157	0.001	219	0.3
Central African Rep.	4.1	7	40	1.3	5.0	98	38	623	3	5	37	470	187	6	0.007	22	0.1
Chad	10.0	8	44	3.4	6.7	116	25	1,284	3	36	10			21		4	0.0
Chile	16.5	22	78	1.1	2.0	8	88	757	3	17	21	38,596	29,857	1,785	4.1	1,511	3.7
China	1,323.6	138	72	0.6	1.7	35	40	9,597	16	43	18	761,953	659,953	41,761	1,242.4	970	3.2
Colombia	46.3	41	72	1.6	2.6	26	73	1,139	3	40	48	21,190	21,204	791	71.6	467	1.3
Comoros	0.8	366	63	2.6	4.9	58	37	2	48	8	4	7	72	18		46	0.1
Congo	4.1	12	52	3.0	6.3	72	60	342	2	29	65	1,722	682	22	11.4	137	0.4
Congo, Dem. Rep.	59.3	25	43	2.8	6.7	119	32	2,345	3	7	60			35	1.7	19	0.0
Costa Rica	4.4	86	79	1.9	2.3	10	62	51	10	46	39	7,151	9,173	1,453	0.7	535	1.5
Croatia	4.6	81	74	0.2	1.4	7	56	57	28	28	32	8,773	18,560	7,912	3.9	2,013	5.1
Cuba	11.3	102	77	0.3	1.6	6	76	111	34	26	21	2,332	5,610	2,017	3.9	743	2.3
Cyprus	0.8	91	79	1.2	1.6	6	69	9	15	0.4	19	1,546	6,382	2,349		2,822	8.9
Czech Republic	10.2	129	75	-0.1	1.2	6	74	79	42	13	34	78,209	76,527	6,061	26.6	3,575	12.4
Denmark	5.4	126	77	0.3	1.8	5	86	43	53	9	11	82,415	74,265	3,358	29.2	3,303	11.3
Djibouti	0.8	35	53	2.1	5.1	93	86	23	0	57	<			26		158	0.5
Dominica	0.08	93		0.3		20	73	0.8	28		61	42	165	79	0.003	558	1.8
Dominican Republic	9.0	186	69	1.5	2.7	35	67	49	33	44	28			2,978	0.2	669	2.5
East Timor	1.0	68	55	5.4	7.8	94	26	15	13	-					7.3	57	0.2
Ecuador	13.4	47	74	1.4	2.8	25	63	284	11	18	38	9,869	9,608	819	28.6	558	1.8
Egypt	75.4	75	70	1.9	3.3	37	43	1,001	3	0	<	7,913	13,332	7,795	71.5	842	2.0
El Salvador	7.0	333	71	1.8	2.9	26	60	21	43	38	6	1,658	5,380	966	0.2	315	1.0
Equatorial Guinea	0.5	18	44	2.3	5.9	102	39	28	8	4	63				7.9	957	0.3
Eritrea	4.6	39	54	4.3	5.5	65	19	118	5	58	14	7	433	87		57	0.2
Estonia	1.3	29	71	-0.6	1.4	10	69	45	12	2	49	7,710	10,164	1,750	3.2	3,843	14.2
Ethiopia	79.3	72	48	2.4	5.9	100	16	1,104	11	18	4	513	2,686	210	0.2	27	0.1
Fiji	0.9	47	68	0.9	2.9	22	51	18	15	10	45	702	1,607	499	0.04	426	1.3
Finland	5.3	16	79	0.3	1.7	4	61	338	7	0	72	65,238	58,472	2,840	4.1	5,280	14.0
France	60.7	110	80	0.4	1.9	4	77	552	35	18	28	434,425	475,999	75,121	47.5	2,811	6.8
Gabon	1.4	5	55	1.7	4.0	58	84	268	2	18	85	2,780	965	222	10.9	450	0.9
Gambia	1.6	138	56	2.8	4.8	77	54	11	28	46	48	5	260	90		62	0.2
Georgia	4.4	64	71	-1.1	1.5	40	52	70	15	28	44	866	2,491	368	0.6	417	0.8

WEALTH						SOCIAL INDICATORS										COUNTRY
GDP (million current US$) 2005	GDP per capita current US$ 2005	Average annual growth GDP per capita (%) 1990-2006	Employed in industry (%) 2005	Employed in agriculture (%) 2005	Unemployed (% of labour force) 2005	Human Develop. Index (HDI value) 2007	Pop. with access to safe drinking water (%) 2006	Doctors. per 10,000 pop. 2006	Estimated adult HIV prevalence rate (age 15-49) 2000	Gender Develop. Index (GDI value) 2007	Total adult literacy rate 2005	Televisions per 1,000 people 2006	Internet users per 100 people 2004	Aid donated (-)/received (US$ per capita) 2002	Military spending (% of GDP) 2005	
6,504	218	-				-	22	2	<0.1	-	28	67	1	63	9.9	Afghanistan
8,538	3,709	5.2	13.5	58.4	14.4	0.801	97	12	-	0.797	99	7	6	90	1.4	Albania
102,257	3,112	1.3	26.0	20.7	17.7	0.733	85	11	0.1	0.720	70	189	6	6	2.9	Algeria
3,091	46,029	-				-	100	36	-	-	-	462	33		-	Andorra
28,853	1,810	21				0.446	51	<1	3.7	0.439	67	21	1	35	5.7	Angola
856	10,507	1.8	18.6	4.0		0.815	91	2	-	-	-	465	36		-	Antigua & Barbuda
183,310	4,731	1.3	23.5	1.1	10.6	0.869	96	30	0.6	0.865	97	326	18	256	1	Argentina
4,868	1,614	5.2	16.5	46.0	8.1	0.775	98	37	0.1	0.772	99	293	5	57	2.7	Armenia
709,446	35,199	2.5	21.1	3.6	5.1	0.962	100	25	0.1	0.960	-	665	70	-45	1.8	Australia
306,065	37,373	1.9	27.5	5.5	4.9	0.948	100	37	0.3	0.934	-	657	49	-63	0.9	Austria
12,561	1,493	1.5	12.1	39.3	1.4	0.746	78	36	0.1	0.743	99	331	8	18	2.5	Azerbaijan
5,870	18,168	0.4	17.8	3.5	10.2	0.845	97	-	3.3	0.841	-	248	32	33	0.7	Bahamas
13,348	18,370	2.3				0.866	-	27	-	0.857	87	414	21		3.6	Bahrain
64,058	452	3	13.7	51.7	4.3	0.547	80	3	<0.1	0.539	48	83	0	11	1	Bangladesh
2,996	9,616	1.5	17.3	3.3	9.8	0.892	100	12	1.5	0.887	-	289	59	30	0.8	Barbados
29,566	3,031	2.8	34.9	21.2	1.5	0.804	100	48	0.3	0.803	100	386	35	19	1.2	Belarus
370,815	35,590	1.8	24.9	2.0	8.4	0.946	-	42	0.3	0.940	-	555	46	-104	1.1	Belgium
1,105	4,097	2.3	17.0	27.5	10.0	0.778	91	11	2.5	-	70	200	14	230	-	Belize
4,378	519	1.4				0.437	65	<1	1.8	0.422	35	59	6	47	-	Benin
917	424	4.8				0.579	81	<1	<0.1	-	-	32	3	33		Bhutan
9,728	1,059	1.3	28.2	4.9	5.5	0.695	86	12	0.1	0.691	87	134	5	68	1.6	Bolivia
9,132	2,337	11.6				0.803	99	14	<0.1	-	97	249	21	163	1.9	Bosnia-Herzogovina
8,850	5,014	4.8	22.0	22.6	23.8	0.654	96	4	24.1	0.639	81	44	3	46	3	Botswana
799,413	4,289	1.1	21.0	21.0	8.9	0.800	91	12	0.5	0.798	89	358	21	163	1.6	Brazil
6,280	12,944	-0.8	21.4	1.4		0.894	-	11	<0.1	0.886	93	644	36	11	3.9	Brunei
26,419	12,600	2	34.2	8.9	10.7	0.824	99	3	<0.1	0.823	98	453	21	40	2.4	Bulgaria
5,397	408	1.5				0.370	72	<1	2	0.364	24	12	0	36	1.3	Burkina-Faso
10,938	217	6.6	12.2	62.7		0.583	80	4	1.3	-	90	7	0	3	-	Burma (Myanmar)
845	112	-2.5			14.0	0.413	71	<1	3.3	0.409	59	40	1	15	6.2	Burundi
5,397	384	5.8	10.5	70.2	2.5	0.598	65	2	1.6	0.594	74	8	0	41	1.8	Cambodia
16,823	1,031	9.7	9.1	60.6	7.5	0.532	70	2	5.4	0.524	68	45	2	78	1.3	Cameroon
1,131,760	35,073	2.2	22.0	2.7	6.8	0.961	100	19	0.3	0.956	-	706	68	-4	1.1	Canada
1,038	2,048	3.3				0.736	80	5	-	0.723	81	105	6	340	0.7	Cape Verde
1,325	328	-0.6				0.384	66	<1	10.7	0.368	49	6	0	20	-	Central African Rep.
4,942	507	2.4				0.388	48	<1	3.5	0.370	26	6	0	25	1	Chad
111,339	6,833	3.7	23.0	13.2	6.9	0.867	95	11	0.3	0.859	96	321	29	3	3.8	Chile
1,981,648	1,533	8.8	17.7	44.1	4.2	0.777	88	14	0.1	0.776	91	382	8	2	2	China
121,878	2,673	0.8	18.8	22.4	11.8	0.791	93	14	0.6	0.789	93	251	10	7	3.7	Colombia
380	477	-0.4				0.561	85	2	<0.1	0.544	-	27	3	14		Comoros
5,528	1,382	-0.8				0.548	71	2	5.3	0.540	85	13	1	53	1.4	Congo
7,212	125	-4.7				0.411	46	1	3.2	0.398	67	4	0	3	2.4	Congo, Dem. Rep.
19,818	4,580	2.4	21.6	15.2	6.6	0.846	98	13	0.3	0.842	95	251	21	3	-	Costa Rica
36,947	8,118	2.8	28.6	17.3	12.7	0.850	99	25	<0.1	0.848	98	320	32	15	1.6	Croatia
46,932	4,165	3.5	19.1	21.2	1.9	0.838	91	59	0.1	0.839	100	267	2	6	-	Cuba
16,723	22,432	2.3	24.0	4.8	5.3	0.903	100	333	-	0.899	97	384	39	62	1.4	Cyprus
122,345	11,972	2.1	39.5	4.0	7.9	0.891	100	36	0.1	0.887	-	603	29	11	1.8	Czech Republic
258,718	47,641	1.9	26.1	2.9	5.0	0.949	100	36	0.2	0.944	-	975	53	-302	1.8	Denmark
705	889	-2.4	7.9			0.516	92	2	3.1	0.507	-	78	1	72	-	Djibouti
283	3,580	1.4	18.2	23.7	11.0	0.798	97	5	-	-	-	252	-		-	Dominica
29,101	2,392	3.7	21.1	15.9	17.9	0.779	95	19	1.1	0.773	87	225	17	27	0.5	Dominican Republic
354	438	-				0.514	62	1	-	-	-		-	2,200	-	East Timor
33,062	2,499	1	21.2	8.3	7.9	0.772	95	15	0.3	-	91	250	7	9	2.6	Ecuador
101,406	1,370	2.4	19.8	29.9	11.0	0.708	98	24	<0.1	-	71	250	7	16	2.8	Egypt
16,980	2,468	1.6	23.7	19.1	6.8	0.735	84	12	0.9	0.726	81	236	9	38	0.6	El Salvador
5,651	11,222	21.6				0.642	43	3	3.2	0.631	87		1	68	-	Equatorial Guinea
1,077	245	0	18.7			0.483	60	<1	2.4	0.469	-	59	2	18	24.1	Eritrea
12,762	9,598	4.9	34.0	5.3	7.9	0.860	100	33	1.3	0.858	100	507	52	83	1.5	Estonia
9,297	120	1.9	2.6	93.0	5.0	0.406	42	<1	-	0.393	36	8	0	5	2.6	Ethiopia
2,998	3,536	1.4			5.4	0.762	47	5	0.1	0.757	-	117	8	45	1.2	Fiji
193,155	36,978	2.6	25.6	4.8	8.3	0.952	100	33	0.1	0.947	-	679	53	-73	1.4	Finland
2,126,579	34,128	1.6	24.6	4.0	9.9	0.952	100	34	0.4	0.950	-	633	43	-89	2.5	France
7,919	5,273	-1			18.0	0.677	87	3	7.9	0.670	84	163	5	236	1.5	Gabon
480	316	0.3				0.502	86	1	2.4	0.496	-	15	4	30	0.5	Gambia
6,490	1,450	1	9.3	54.3	13.8	0.754	99	47	0.2	-	-	386	6	32	3.5	Georgia

COUNTRY	POPULATION							LAND & AGRICULTURE				TRADE, TOURISM & ENERGY					
	Total pop. (millions) 2006	Pop. density (people per km²) 2006	Life expectancy at birth (years) 2005	Annual pop. growth rate (%) 2006	Fertility rate (births per woman) 2005	Infant mortality rate (per 000s births) 2005	Urban pop. (% of total) 2005	Land area (000s km²)	Arable & permanent crops (% of land area) 2006	Permanent pasture (% of land area) 2006	Forest (% of land area) 2000	Exports (US$ million) 2006	Imports (US$ million) 2006	Tourist arrivals (000s) 2004	Energy produced (million tonnes oil equiv.) 2004	Energy consumed (kg oil equiv.) 2004	CO₂ emissions per capita (tonnes) 2004
Germany	82.7	232	79	0.1	1.3	4	75	357	34	14	31	977,028	776,843	20,137	95.8	3,571	10.5
Ghana	22.6	95	57	2.1	4.4	62	48	239	27	37	28	1,779	4,074	584	0.5	112	0.4
Greece	11.1	84	79	0.3	1.3	6	59	132	29	36	28	17,434	54,893	13,969	9.1	2,823	9.9
Grenada	0.1	298		0.3		17	31	344	35		15	32	251	134		925	2.2
Guatemala	12.9	119	67	2.4	4.6	39	47	109	15	24	26	5,381	10,500	1,182	1.2	290	0.9
Guinea	9.6	39	54	2.2	5.9	106	33	246	7	43	28	526	667	45	0.04	46	0.1
Guinea-Bissau	1.6	45	45	3.0	7.1	120	30	36	15	39	61		8			65	0.2
Guyana	0.8	3	63	0.2	2.3	49	28	215	2	6	79	539	778	122		626	2.2
Haiti	8.7	312	52	1.4	4.0	62	39	28	40	18	3			96	0.02	62	0.3
Honduras	7.4	66	68	2.3	3.7	32	46	112	13	13	48	1,883	4,565	672	0.2	337	0.9
Hungary	10.1	108	73	-0.3	1.3	8	66	93	52	12	20	63,241	66,741	3,270	8.0	2,374	6.0
Iceland	0.3	3	81	0.9	2.0	3	93	103	0	23	<	3,091	4,979	836	0.7	4,918	7.5
India	1,119.5	341	64	1.6	3.1	68	29	3,287	52	4	22	103,404	149,750	3,457	300.2	338	1.2
Indonesia	225.5	118	67	1.3	2.4	43	48	1,905	18	6	58	85,660	57,701	5,321	234.7	467	1.4
Iran	70.3	43	71	0.9	2.1	34	67	1,648	11	27	5	60,012	38,675	1,659	283.2	2,323	5.6
Iraq	29.5	67	59	2.8	4.8	94	67	438	14	9	2			127	129.9	988	2.7
Ireland	4.2	60	78	1.7	1.9	5	60	70	17	48	10	109,994	70,292	6,982	1.9	3,618	11.1
Israel	6.8	309	80	2.0	2.9	5	92	21	19	7	6	42,771	45,032	1,506	0.1	3,050	10.6
Italy	58.1	193	80	0.1	1.3	5	68	301	36	15	34	367,867	380,561	37,071	22.2	3,108	8.4
Ivory Coast	18.4	57	46	1.6	5.1	118	45	322	21	41	22	5,493	3,536	301	2.3	101	0.3
Jamaica	2.7	242	71	0.5	2.4	15	53	11	26	21	30	1,412	3,817	1,415	0.01	1,252	4.1
Japan	128.2	339	82	0.2	1.3	3	66	378	13	1	64	594,491	515,866	6,138	39.0	3,460	9.9
Jordan	5.8	65	72	2.7	3.5	23	82	89	5	8	1	4,279	10,455	2,853	0.3	857	3.2
Kazakhstan	14.8	5	64	-0.3	2.0	61	57	2,725	8	69	5	19,939	12,636	3,073	121.0	3,621	10.7
Kenya	35.1	60	47	2.2	5.0	68	21	580	9	37	30	2,683	4,564	1,199	0.2	95	0.3
Kiribati	0.08	116	63	2.1	4.3	43	47	0.8	51		38	4	74	3		92	0.3
Korea, North (DPRK)	22.6	187	63	0.6	2.0	46	62	121	24	0.4	68			128	20.1	937	3.5
Korea, South (RoK)	48.0	482	77	0.4	1.2	4	81	99	19	1	63	284,418	261,236	5,818	13.2	3,225	9.6
Kuwait	2.8	155	77	3.7	2.4	10	98	18	1	8	<	16,165	7,869	91	135.1	10,559	31.1
Kyrgyzstan	5.3	27	67	0.2	2.7	55	36	200	7	49	5	672	1,108	398	1.4	547	1.0
Lao PDR	6.1	26	55	2.3	4.8	88	21	237	4	4	54			236	0.3	65	0.2
Latvia	2.3	36	72	-0.6	1.3	10	68	65	29	10	47	5,303	8,771	1,079	0.3	1,402	3.2
Lebanon	3.6	348	72	1.0	2.3	22	87	10	30	2	4	1,746	9,397	1,278	0.1	1,286	5.4
Lesotho	1.8	59	37	0.1	3.7	67	19	30	11	67	1	358	800	304			0.4
Liberia	3.4	30	43	1.4	6.8	43	58	111	5	21	31				0.02	53	0.1
Libya	6.0	3	74	2.0	3.0	19	85	1,760	1	8	<	10,195	6,318	149	83.9	2,616	8.9
Liechtenstein	0.04	208		1.0	1.4		15	160	25	47				49			7.1
Lithuania	3.4	52	72	-0.4	1.3	9	67	65	46	8	32	12,070	15,704	1,800	1.7	1,714	3.6
Luxembourg	0.4	182	78	1.3	1.7	5	83	3	28	-		12,715	17,586	852	0.08	9,711	23.6
Macedonia, TFYR	2.0	79	74	0.2	1.5	16	69	26	24	25	28	2,041	3,228	165	2.1	1,558	5.2
Madagascar	19.1	33	56	2.8	5.4	79	27	587	6	41	20	427	1,204	229	0.06	38	0.1
Malawi	13.1	111	40	2.3	6.1	111	17	118	22	20	27	496	1,165	471	0.2	34	0.1
Malaysia	25.8	78	73	1.9	2.9	10	67	330	23	1	59	140,963	114,584	15,703	90.4	2,531	6.4
Mali	13.9	11	48	3.0	6.9	133	30	1,240	4	25	11	983	1,360		0.02	19	0.0
Malta	0.4	1,277	79	0.5	1.5	7	95	0.3	34	0	-	2,275	3,661	1,158		2,004	6.2
Marshall Islands	0.06	281	74	3.5	5.7	37	67	0.1	56				68	9			
Mauritania	3.2	3	53	3.0	5.8	97	40	1,026	0	38	<	175	1,343	30	0.003	269	0.9
Mauritius	1.3	616	73	1.0	2.0	15	42	2	52	4	8	2,004	3,160	719	0.01	835	2.6
Mexico	108.3	55	75	1.3	2.4	21	76	1,958	14	42	29	214,207	221,819	20,618	237.9	1,365	4.0
Micronesia	0.1	158	68	0.6	4.4	38	22	0.7	51	16				19			1.3
Moldova, Rep. of	4.2	124	68	-0.3	1.2	26	47	34	63	12	10	1,091	2,293	24	0.005	836	1.7
Monaco	0.03	21,477		1.1			100	0.001	0					250			3.8
Mongolia	2.7	2	64	1.2	2.5	58	57	1,567	1	83	7	1,064	1,182	301	1.5	853	3.1
Montenegro	0.6	45	75	-0.1	1.7			14	15			3,801	11,366	239	10.6	1,451	4.8
Morocco	31.9	72	70	1.5	1.5	38	59	447	21	47	7	10,632	20,342	5,477	0.2	360	1.2
Mozambique	20.2	25	42	2.0	5.5	101	35	802	6	56	39	1,783	2,408	470	0.8	80	0.1
Namibia	2.1	2	49	1.4	4.0	44	35	824	1	46	10	1,304	1,428	695			1.2
Nauru	0.01	479	58	2.2	4.0		100	0.02	0							3,590	10.8
Nepal	27.7	188	62	2.1	3.7	64	16	147	17	12	27	652	1,801	464	0.2	42	0.1
Netherlands	16.4	394	79	0.5	1.7	5	80	42	23	29	11	320,065	283,172	10,003	71.9	5,586	11.0
New Zealand	4.1	15	79	1.1	2.0	5	86	241	12	52	30	21,730	26,219	1,787	10.0	3,448	8.8
Nicaragua	5.6	43	70	2.0	3.3	30	59	130	16	40	27	866	2,520	615	0.05	253	0.7
Niger	14.4	11	44	3.4	7.9	153	17	1,267	11	9	1	209	558	55	0.1	32	0.1
Nigeria	134.3	145	44	2.2	5.9	114	48	924	36	4	15	24,078	14,892	962	150.2	155	0.4

WEALTH						SOCIAL INDICATORS										COUNTRY
GDP (million current US$) 2005	GDP per capita current US$ 2005	Average annual growth GDP per capita (%) 1990-2006	Employed in industry (%) 2005	Employed in agriculture (%) 2005	Unemployed (% of labour force) 2005	Human Develop. Index (HDI value) 2005	Pop. with access to safe drinking water (%) 2006	Doctors per 10,000 pop. 2006	Estimated adult HIV prevalence rate (age 15-49) 2000	Gender Develop. Index (GDI value) 2006	Total adult literacy rate 2005	Televisions per 1,000 people 2006	Internet users per 100 people 2004	Aid donated (-) /received (US$ per capita) 2002	Military spending (% of GDP) 2005	
2,794,857	33,800	1.4	29.7	2.4	11.1	0.935	100	34	0.1	0.931	-	675	43	-68	1.4	Germany
10,393	470	2.1	14.0	55.0		0.553	80	2	2.3	0.549	58	52	2	332	0.7	Ghana
225,201	20,252	2.7	22.4	12.4	9.6	0.926	100	50	0.2	0.922	96	537	18	509	4.1	Greece
454	4,415	2.3	23.9	13.8		0.777	94	10	-	-	-	383	19		-	Grenada
31,923	2,534	1.2	20.0	38.7	1.4	0.689	96	9	0.9	0.675	69	158	8	17	0.3	Guatemala
3,058	372	1.3				0.456	70	1	1.5	0.446	30	18	1	39	2	Guinea
298	188	-2.5				0.374	57	1	3.5	0.355	-	45	2	82	4	Guinea-Bissau
786	1,046	3	22.6	27.8		0.750	93	5	2.4	0.742	-	167	21	361	-	Guyana
3,884	455	-2	10.7	50.6	23.9	0.529	58	3	3.8		-	63	7	16	-	Haiti
8,374	1,162	0.6	20.9	22.0	4.1	0.700	84	6	1.5	0.694	80	143	4	82	0.6	Honduras
109,239	10,818	3.2	32.4	33.7	7.2	0.874	100	30	0.9	0.872	-	530	30	25	1.5	Hungary
15,814	53,687	2.3	23.1	7.2	2.3	0.968	100	38	0.2	0.962	-	345	62	-	-	Iceland
800,783	726	4.4	12.9	66.7	4.3	0.619	89	6	0.9	0.600	61	84	5	3	2.8	India
281,276	1,263	2.4	18.0	44.0	9.1	0.728	80	1	0.9	0.721	90	152	7	12	1.2	Indonesia
216,713	3,117	2.5	30.4	24.9	11.5	0.759	94	9	0.2	0.750	82	174	11	6	5.8	Iran
33,379	1,159	-			26.8	-	77	7	-	-	74	83	0	32	-	Iraq
201,763	48,642	6	27.8	5.9	4.2	0.959	-	29	0.2	0.940	-	694	34	-71	0.6	Ireland
129,648	19,280	1.5	21.7	2.0	9.0	0.932	100	37	0.2	0.927	-	354	24	107	9.7	Israel
1,762,475	30,339	1.3	30.7	4.2	10.5	0.941	-	37	0.5	0.936	98	494	48	-17	1.9	Italy
16,785	925	-0.5				0.432	81	1	7.1	0.413	49	52	1	58	-	Ivory Coast
10,063	3,796	0.7	17.7	18.0	10.9	0.736	93	9	1.5	0.732	80	380	46	6	0.6	Jamaica
4,558,950	35,593	0.9	27.9	4.4	4.4	0.953	100	21	>0.1	0.942	-	843	67	-55	1	Japan
12,535	2,198	1.8	21.8	3.6		0.773	98	24	-	0.760	91	190	13	99	5.3	Jordan
56,088	3,783	2.8	17.4	33.5	8.4	0.794	96	39	0.1	0.792	100	497	4	40	1.1	Kazakhstan
19,184	560	0	19.5	18.6		0.521	57	1	6.1	0.521	74	48	3	14	1.7	Kenya
72	721	1.9				-	65	2	-	-	-	44	2	-	-	Kiribati
12,260	517	-				-	100	33	-	-	-	172	-	-	-	Korea, North (DPRK)
787,627	16,472	4.5	26.8	7.9	4.4	0.921	92	16	>0.1	0.910	-	477	68	-4	2.6	Korea, South (RoK)
74,214	27,621	0.6			0.8	0.891	-	18	-	0.884	93	407	26	-4	4.8	Kuwait
2,441	464	-0.9	10.3	52.7	8.5	0.696	89	24	0.1	0.692	99	188	5	10	3.1	Kyrgyzstan
2,872	485	4.1	3.5	85.4		0.601	60	4	0.1	0.593	69	57	0	40	-	Lao PDR
15,244	6,608	4.2	25.8	12.1	8.7	0.855	99	31	0.8	0.853	100	859	45	42	1.7	Latvia
21,184	5,923	2.5				0.772	100	24	0.1	0.759	-	357	20	230	4.5	Lebanon
1,335	859	2.3	15.2	56.5	39.3	0.549	78	<1	23.2	0.541	82	44	3	22	2.3	Lesotho
561	171	2.2				-	64	<1			52	25	-	28	-	Liberia
37,173	6,457	-				0.818	71	13	-	0.797	84	149	4	3	2	Libya
3,482	100,860	-				-	-	-	-	-	-	535	63	-	-	Liechtenstein
24,864	7,247	2.5	29.1	14.0	8.3	0.862	-	40	0.2	0.861	100	518	26	63	1.2	Lithuania
36,468	78,442	3.3	20.9	1.2	4.7	0.944	100	27	0.2	0.924	-	598	68	-294	0.8	Luxembourg
176,602	2,778	0.2	32.3	19.5	37.3	0.801	100	26	>0.1	0.795	96	250	8	119	2.2	Macedonia, TFYR
4,950	266	-0.5	6.7	78.0	4.5	0.533	47	3	0.5	0.530	59	18	1	20	1.1	Madagascar
2,140	166	1.1				0.437	76	<1	14.1	0.432	64	6	0	45	0.7	Malawi
130,770	5,159	3.2	30.1	14.8	3.6	0.811	99	7	0.5	0.802	89	219	42	7	2.4	Malaysia
5,181	383	2.2			8.8	0.380	60	<1	1.7	0.380	24	36	1	50	2.3	Mali
5,573	13,877	2.7	29.4	2.1	7.5	0.878	100	39	0.1	0.873	88	554	32	63	0.7	Malta
111	1,791	-2.2			25.4	-	88	5	-	-	-	-	-	-	-	Marshall Islands
1,672	545	0.5				0.550	60	1	0.7	0.543	51	41	1	73	3.6	Mauritania
6,288	5,052	3.7	32.4	10.0	9.6	0.804	100	11	0.6	0.796	84	370	24	35	0.2	Mauritius
768,438	7,180	1.5	25.7	15.1	3.5	0.829	95	20	0.3	0.820	92	276	17	11	0.4	Mexico
239	2,168	-0.2				-	94	6	-	-	-	25	13	-	-	Micronesia
2,917	694	-2	16.0	40.6	7.3	0.708	90	27	1.1	0.704	99	307	13	23	0.3	Moldova, Rep. of
1,203	34,128	-				-	-	58	-	-	-	762	51	-	-	Monaco
1,867	706	3.3	16.1	40.2	4.6	0.700	72	26	>0.1	0.695	98	81	10	119	1.6	Mongolia
2,042	3,310	2.6			15.2	-	98	20	-	-	96	282	-	-	-	Montenegro
51,461	1,617	1.6	20.2	43.9	10.8	0.646	83	5	0.1	0.621	52	168	15	18	4.5	Morocco
6,682	338	4.4				0.384	42	<1	16.1	0.373	39	21	1	34	0.9	Mozambique
6,130	3,018	1.5	12.2	31.1	33.8	0.650	93	3	19.6	0.645	85	81	4	80	3.2	Namibia
55	4,068	-				-	-	8	-	-	-	44	-	-	-	Nauru
7,412	273	1.9	5.5	78.5		0.534	89	2	0.5	0.520	49	11	1	16	2.1	Nepal
624,187	38,296	1.8	20.2	20.8	5.2	0.953	100	37	0.2	0.951	-	761	74	-202	1.5	Netherlands
109,607	27,209	2.1	22.0	7.1	3.7	0.943	97	21	0.1	0.935	-	586	68	-25	1	New Zealand
4,910	895	1.9	18.0	30.5	9.8	0.710	79	4	0.2	0.696	77	121	2	138	0.7	Nicaragua
3,245	232	-0.5				0.374	42	<1	1.1	0.355	29	12	0	30	1.2	Niger
113,461	863	0.7	22.0	2.9		0.470	47	3	3.9	0.456	69	68	4	2	0.7	Nigeria

COUNTRY	POPULATION							LAND & AGRICULTURE				TRADE, TOURISM & ENERGY					
	Total pop. (millions) 2006	Pop. density (people per km² 2006	Life expectancy at birth (years) 2005	Annual pop. growth rate (%) 2006	Fertility rate (births per woman) 2005	Infant mortality rate (per 000s births) 2005	Urban pop. (% of total) 2005	Land area (000s km²) 2006	Arable & permanent crops (% of land area) 2006	Permanent pasture (% of land area) 2006	Forest (% of land area) 2000	Exports (US$ million) 2006	Imports (US$ million) 2006	Tourist arrivals (000s) 2004	Energy produced (million tonnes oil equiv.) 2004	Energy consumed per capita (kg oil equiv.) 2004	CO₂ emissions per capita (tonnes) 2004
Niue	0.001	7	71	-2.2	3.0		37	0.3	27					3		507	2.0
Norway	4.6	12	80	0.5	1.8	4	77	324	3	1	29	103,759	55,488	3,104	234.2	7,406	9.4
Oman	2.6	8	75	1.0	3.8	16	71	310	0	5		20,327	8,827	630	56.1	4,784	12.9
Pakistan	161.2	202	63	2.0	4.3	79	35	796	25	6	3	16,050	25,096	648	34.7	319	0.8
Palau	0.02	42	70	0.7	3.0	18	70	0.4	13					123	95	0.002	4,106	12.3
Palestine (OPT)																	
Panama	3.2	44	75	1.8	2.7	21	71	76	9	21	39	964	4,155	621	0.3	650	1.9
Papua New Guinea	6.0	13	56	2.1	4.1	71	13	463	2	0.2	68	2,260	1,302	59	2.4	163	0.4
Paraguay	6.3	15	71	2.4	3.9	37	58	407	8	55	59	1,626	3,097	309	4.4	310	0.7
Peru	28.3	22	70	1.5	2.9	33	73	1,285	3	21	51	17,114	12,501	1,208	8.1	410	1.0
Philippines	84.5	282	70	1.8	3.2	28	63	300	36	5	19	41,221	46,953	2,291	5.1	0.3	1.0
Poland	38.5	119	74	-0.1	1.3	9	62	323	41	14	30	89,378	101,539	14,290	75.8	2,329	8.0
Portugal	10.5	115	78	0.5	1.5	6	58	89	25	16	40	38,086	61,167	11,617	1.0	2,018	6.2
Qatar	0.8	76	74	5.9	3.0	12	95	11	2	5	<	25,736	10,061	732	81.6	33,324	63.1
Romania	21.6	91	72	-0.4	1.3	18	54	238	41	21	28	27,730	40,463	6,600	24.7	1,553	5.1
Russia	142.5	8	73	-0.5	1.3	17	73	17,075	7	5	50	241,244	98,577	19,892	1,160.6	4,232	10.3
Rwanda	9.2	350	44	2.4	5.7	116	19	26	56	19	12	50	261	113	0.02	22	0.1
St Kitts and Nevis	0.04	176	70	1.1	2.6		32	0.2	22		11	34	210	118		1,080	3.0
St Lucia	0.1	301	73	0.8	2.2	15	28	0.5	29	3	15	64	475	298		749	2.1
St Vincent & Gren.	0.1	308	71	0.5	2.3	26	46	0.4	35		15	40	240	87	0.003	595	1.6
Samoa	0.2	66	71	0.8	4.4	26	22	2.8	45		37	87	239	98	0.003	304	0.8
San Marino	0.03	475	84	0.9	1.3		97	0.06	17					42			
São Tomé & P.									57								
Saudi Arabia	25.2	12	72	2.7	4.1	23	81	2,150	2	79	1	180,737	59,511	8,599	554.5	6,020	13.0
Senegal	11.9	61	56	2.4	5.1	83	42	197	13	29	32	1,471	3,498	363	0.04	120	0.4
Serbia	7.4	84	75	-0.1	1.7			102		18		3,801	11,366	580	10.7	1,451	4.8
Sierra Leone	5.7	79	41	4.1	6.5	165	41	72	9	31	15	41	352	44		44	0.1
Singapore	4.4	6,412	79	1.5	1.4	3	100	0.7	3	0	3	229,652	200,050	5,705		3,482	11.3
Slovakia	5.4	110	74	<	1.2	8	56	49	32	18	45	31,997	34,446	1,401	2.9	2,784	8.0
Slovenia	2.0	97	77	-	1.2	5	51	20	10	15	55	17,896	19,626	1,499	1.9	2,745	8.2
Solomon Islands	0.5	17	63	2.6	4.3	34	17	29	3	1	89			21		111	0.4
Somalia	8.5	13	46	3.2	6.4	126	35	638	2	69	12			10			0.0
South Africa	47.6	39	49	0.8	2.8	43	59	1,221	13	69	7	46,995	55,033	6,678	137.3	2,328	7.8
Spain	43.4	86	80	1.1	1.3	5	77	498	37	23	29	192,798	289,611	52,430	17.1	2,730	7.9
Sri Lanka	20.9	319	74	0.9	2.0	17	15	66	29	7	30	6,160	8,207	566	0.3	203	0.5
Sudan	37.0	15	57	1.9	4.5	72	41	2,506	7	49	26	4,355	6,976	61	15.1	95	0.3
Suriname	0.5	3	70	0.7	2.6	26	74	163	0	0	91	306	743	58	0.7	1,631	5.1
Swaziland	1.0	59	33	0.2	4.0	73	24	17	11	71	30	974	891	459			0.9
Sweden	9.0	20	80	0.4	1.6	3	84	450	6	1	66	130,264	111,351	7,627	12.3	3,093	6.2
Switzerland	7.3	176	81	0.2	1.4	4	75	41	10	27	30	125,927	121,216	6,530	5.4	2,589	6.2
Syria	19.5	105	73	2.5	3.5	18	51	185	29	45	3	5,383	7,049	3,032	30.2	1,001	2.7
Taiwan								36	25	-							
Tajikistan	6.6	46	64	1.1	3.8	89	25	143	7	23	3	692	644	4	1.5	520	0.7
Tanzania, United Rep.	39.0	41	45	2.0	5.0	104	24	945	5	40	44	1,415	2,757	566	0.4	39	0.1
Thailand	64.8	126	70	0.9	1.9	20	32	513	34	2	29	110,110	118,164	11,737	36.4	1,268	3.9
Togo	6.3	111	54	2.7	5.4	93	40	57	46	19	9	360	593	83	0.01	113	0.4
Tonga	0.1	158	72	0.4	3.5	21	24	0.6	35		6	9	69	41		355	1.1
Trinidad & Tobago	1.3	255	70	0.3	1.6	14	12	5	24	2	51	9,612	5,694	443	30.8	9,929	22.1
Tunisia	10.2	62	73	1.1	2.0	22	65	164	30	31	3	10,494	13,174	5,998	5.7	770	2.1
Turkey	74.1	95	69	1.4	2.5	42	67	775	33	17	13	73,476	116,774	16,826	19.8	1,031	3.1
Turkmenistan	4.9	10	63	1.4	2.8	78	46	488	5	65	8	2,506	1,786	300	63.5	3,536	9.2
Tuvalu	0.01	368	65	0.5	3.7		48	0.03	67					1			0.5
Uganda	29.9	124	47	3.4	7.1	81	13	241	30	26	21	813	2,054	512	0.2	24	0.1
Ukraine	46.0	76	66	-1.1	1.1	16	68	604	55	13	17	34,228	36,122	15,629	61.4	2,698	6.6
United Arab Emirates	4.7	56	79	6.5	2.5	9	77	84	3	4	4	82,750	61,588	5,871	179.5	13,438	33.6
United Kingdom	59.8	246	79	0.3	1.7	5	90	242	23	46	12	384,365	515,782	27,755	217.9	3,711	9.4
USA	301.0	31	78	1.0	2.0	7	81	9,629	18	26	25	904,340	1,732,320	46,085	1,424.9	6,980	20.0
Uruguay	3.5	20	76	0.7	2.3	13	92	175	8	77	7	3,405	3,879	1,756	0.4	663	1.3
Uzbekistan	27.0	60	67	1.5	2.7	58	37	447	11	54	5			262	62.2	2,332	4.8
Vanuatu	0.2	18	69	2.0	4.2	34	23	12	9		37	23	87	61		139	0.4
Venezuela	27.2	30	73	1.8	2.7	18	93	912	4	21	56	55,487	21,848	492	197.4	2,329	5.6
Viet Nam	85.3	257	70	1.4	2.3	30	26	332	27	2	30	26,316	31,079	2,928	27.3	352	0.9
Yemen	21.6	41	61	3.1	6.2	69	27	528	3	30	1	5,609	4,863	274	20.0	261	0.9
Zambia	11.9	16	38	1.7	5.7	95	35	753	7	40	42	1,852	2,575	515	0.8	117	0.2
Zimbabwe	13.1	33	38	0.6	3.6	62	36	394	9	44	49	1,926	2,204	1,854	2.9	272	0.9

WEALTH						SOCIAL INDICATORS										COUNTRY
GDP (million current US$) 2005	GDP per capita current US$ 2005	Average annual growth GDP per capita (%) 1990-2006	Employed in industry (%) 2005	Employed in agriculture (%) 2005	Unemployed (% of labour force) 2005	Human Develop. Index (HDI value) 2005	Pop. with access to safe drinking water (%) 2006	Doctors per 10,000 pop. 2006	Estimated adult HIV prevalence rate (age 15-49) 2000	Gender Develop. Index (GDI value) 2006	Total adult literacy rate 2005	Televisions per 1,000 people 2006	Internet users per 100 people 2004	Aid donated (-)/received (US$ per capita) 2004	Military spending (% of GDP) 2006	
		-					100	20	-		-	277	-			Niue
295,513	63,960	2.6	20.8	3.3	4.6	0.968	100	38	0.1	0.957	-	1,554	58	-304	1.7	Norway
30,269	19,868	1.8	11.2	6.4		0.814	82	17	-	0.788	81	620	11	26	11.9	Oman
110,017	697	1.4	20.8	42.1	7.7	0.551	90	8	0.1	0.525	50	82	7	5	3.5	Pakistan
123	6,150	-					89	16	-	-	-		-	-	-	Palau
		-2.8				0.731	-	-	-	-	92		7		-	Palestine (OPT)
15,241	4,716	2.3	17.2	15.7	10.3	0.812	92	15	0.9	0.810	92	195	6	66	-	Panama
5,330	905	0.2	3.6	72.3	2.8	0.530	40	<1	1.8	0.529	57	24	2	74	0.6	Papua New Guinea
7,684	1,248	-0.5	15.8	31.5	8.1	0.755	77	11	0.4	0.744	94	216	3	14	0.7	Paraguay
76,607	2,739	2.3	23.8	0.7	11.4	0.773	84	12	0.6	0.769	88	199	16	33	1.4	Peru
97,653	1,176	1.7	14.9	37.0	7.4	0.771	93	12	>0.1	0.768	93	192	5	14	0.9	Philippines
290,006	7,527	4.9	29.2	17.4	17.7	0.870	-	20	0.1	0.867	-	229	26	26	1.9	Poland
183,300	17,466	1.9	32.2	12.5	7.6	0.897	99	34	0.4	0.895	94	421	27	-26	2.3	Portugal
42,113	51,809	-	41.0	2.7	3.9	0.875	100	26	-	0.863	89	423	28	8	-	Qatar
98,566	4,540	2	30.3	32.1	7.2	0.813	88	19	>0.1	0.812	97	893	22	17	2	Romania
765,968	5,349	0.6	29.8	10.2	7.8	0.802	97	43	1.1	0.801	99	350	15	7	4.1	Russia
2,118	234	0.3	2.9	90.1	0.6	0.452	65	<1	3.1	0.450	65	8	1	47	2.9	Rwanda
453	10,612	2.8				0.821	99	11	-	-	-	312	-		-	St Kitts and Nevis
851	5,292	1.8	17.7	11.4	16.4	0.795	98	52	-	-	-	341	34	259	-	St Lucia
428	3,596	1.7	19.7	15.4		0.761	-	8	-	-	-	234	8		-	St Vincent & Gren.
406	2,196	2.5				0.785	88	3	-	0.776	99	148	3		-	Samoa
1,315	28,708	-	40.9	0.4	2.8	-	-	474	-	-	-	904	-		-	San Marino
73	464	0.5				0.654	86	5	-	0.637	85	127	15		-	São Tomé & P.
314,021	12,779	0.1	21.0	4.7	5.2	0.812	89	14	-	0.783	83	275	12	-64	8.2	Saudi Arabia
8,274	710	1.2				0.499	77	<1	0.9	0.492	39	45	5	33	1.5	Senegal
24,207	3,244	-			15.2	-	99	20	-	-	96	282	-	185	2.6	Serbia
1,162	210	-0.8				0.336	53	<1	1.6	0.320	35	13	0	17	1	Sierra Leone
116,775	26,997	3.7	34.2	0.3	5.3	0.922	-	15	0.3	-	89	307	40	0.3	4.7	Singapore
46,417	8,594	2.9	38.8	4.7	16.2	0.863	100	31	>0.1	0.860	-	424	35	21	1.7	Slovakia
34,030	17,302	3.3	37.2	8.8	5.0	0.917	-	24	>0.1	0.914	100	366	55	31	1.5	Slovenia
299	626	-2.3				0.602	70	1	-	-	-	11	1	56	-	Solomon Islands
2,182	265	-				-	29	<1	0.9	-	-	26	1	7	-	Somalia
238,825	5,035	0.8	24.5	10.3	26.6	0.674	93	8	18.8	0.667	82	195	11	11	1.5	South Africa
1,124,612	26,115	2.5	29.7	5.3	9.2	0.949	100	33	0.6	0.944	97	549	40	-33	1.1	Spain
23,927	1,154	3.8	23.4	34.3	7.7	0.743	82	6	>0.1	0.735	91	125	2	29	2.6	Sri Lanka
24,667	681	3.7				0.526	70	3	1.6	0.502	61	387	8	4	-	Sudan
1,503	3,346	1.4	14.5	6.1	14.0	0.774	92	5	1.9	0.767	90	266	7	108	-	Suriname
2,588	2,507	0.4				0.547	60	2	33.4	0.529	80	36	4	87	1.8	Swaziland
357,683	39,561	2.2	22.0	2.0	6.0	0.956	100	33	0.2	0.955	-	965	76	-189	1.5	Sweden
365,887	50,451	0.7	22.6	3.9	4.4	0.955	100	40	0.4	0.946	-	580	51	-147	1	Switzerland
25,812	1,355	1.4	26.9	30.3	11.7	0.724	89	5	-	0.710	81	192	6	11	5.1	Syria
						-								-	2.2	Taiwan
2,342	360	-3.1			2.7	0.673	67	20	0.1	0.669	100	375	0	9	-	Tajikistan
12,586	337	1.6	2.6	82.1	5.1	0.467	55	<1	6.5	0.464	69	41	1	33	1.1	Tanzania, United Rep.
5,651	2,749	2.8	20.2	42.6	1.4	0.781	98	4	1.4	0.779	93	285	11	2	1.1	Thailand
2,187	356	-0.1				0.512	59	<1	3.2	0.494	53	130	6	14	1.5	Togo
214	2,089	1.9				0.819	100	3	-	0.814	99	70	3		1	Tonga
14,763	11,311	4.7	28.4	6.9	10.4	0.814	94	8	2.6	0.808	98	354	12	22	-	Trinidad & Tobago
29,049	2,875	3.7			14.2	0.766	94	13	0.1	0.750	74	218	9	38	1.6	Tunisia
362,614	4,954	1.9	24.7	29.5	10.3	0.775	97	16	-	0.763	87	537	15	4	2.8	Turkey
5,826	1,205	-6.8				0.713	-	25	>0.1	-	99	183	1	3	-	Turkmenistan
26	2,516	-				-	93	9	-	-	-		-		-	Tuvalu
9,115	316	3.1	7.6	69.1	3.2	0.505	64	<1	6.7	0.501	67	17	2	53	2.3	Uganda
81,669	1,757	-1.5	24.2	19.4	7.2	0.788	97	31	1.4	0.785	99	357	10	13	2.4	Ukraine
133,757	29,751	-0.9	33.4	7.9	2.3	0.868	100	17	-	0.855	89	197	29	2	2	United Arab Emirates
1,442,777	36,851	2.3	22.0	1.4	5.0	0.946	100	23	0.2	0.944	-	1,101	54	-75	2.7	United Kingdom
11,713,000	39,650	2.1	20.6	1.6	5.1	0.951	99	26	0.6	0.937	-	882	66	-24	4.1	USA
13,215	3,842	1.2	21.9	4.6	12.2	0.852	100	37	0.5	0.849	97	259	21	7	1.3	Uruguay
11,788	450	0.7	19.4	38.5	0.4	0.702	88	27	0.2	0.699	-	290	3	3	0.5	Uzbekistan
291	1,405	-0.3				0.674	59	1	-	-	74	13	3		-	Vanuatu
111,958	4,260	-0.6	19.8	10.7	15.8	0.792	89	19	0.7	0.787	93	191	13	3	1.2	Venezuela
45,819	551	6	17.4	57.9	2.1	0.733	92	6	0.5	0.732	90	208	13	34	-	Viet Nam
13,080	643	1.5	11.1	54.1	11.5	0.508	66	3	-	0.472	54	337	1	23	7	Yemen
5,315	463	0			12.0	0.434	58	1	17	0.425	68	64	3	62	2.3	Zambia
4,546	351	-2.4		70.0	6.0	0.513	81	2	20.1	0.505	89	61	8	14	2.3	Zimbabwe

This detailed index contains the names of all the main places – cities, towns, states, countries, etc. – and important physical features (rivers, mountains, islands, etc.) shown on the maps. After the name, we have specified (in *italics*) the country or region in which the place or feature is located. For instance:

Aachen *Germany*

Names in the index

All names are listed in alphabetic order, except that "Mc" is treated as if it were spelled out "Mac", and concatenation as if spelled out in full; thus "St" is treated as "Saint". When a name has two or more words, the names are treated as one, thus retaining strict alphabetic order. For instance:

Eastbourne *UK*
East Cape *N. Zealand*
East China Sea *Asia*
Eastern Ghats *India*

Names of countries and continents appear in capitals. For instance:

ANGOLA *Africa*

Physical features also appear alphabetically by their proper name and a description. The description often is abbreviated. Names of ocean, sea, river, lake and human-built water features (canals, reservoirs) appear in italics. For instance:

Elephant Butte Res. *USA*
Elephant I. *Antarctica*
Elephants, R. *Africa*

But if a description forms part of the proper name, it usually appears in full and in alphabetic order. For instance:

Mountain View *USA*
Mount Carmel *USA*

If there is more than one place with the same name, places are listed by alphabetic order of country. If there is more than one place with the same name in the same country, places are listed in alphabetic order of sub-division (state, county, etc.) or in order of size. For instance:

Ashland *KY, USA*
Ashland *OH, USA*
Ashland *WI, USA*

Page number

After each name and location, we have given (in **bold**) the page number of the map where that place or feature can be found. If the place or feature appears on more than one map, we have listed its clearest representation. For instance:

Loire, R. *France* **94**

Latitude and longitude

Every map has grid lines of latitude and longitude. The index has the latitude and longitude of every main place or feature on the maps. Both latitude and longitude are measured in degrees and minutes (there are 60 minutes in a degree). The first co-ordinate indicates latitude – the distance north or south of the Equator. The second co-ordinate indicates longitude – the distance east or west of the Greenwich Meridian. Latitude is followed by N (north) or S (south) and longitude by E (east) or W (west). For instance:

Loire, R. *France* **94** 47 16N 2 10W
Lomblen *Indonesia* **113** 8 30S 123 32 E

Abbreviations used in the Index

Afghan. = Afghanistan
AL = Alabama
AK = Alaska
Arch. = Archipelago
AZ = Arizona
AR = Arkansas
B. = Bay, Baie, Bahia, Bucht, Bugt
C. = Cape, Cabo, Cap
CAR = Central African Republic
CA = California
Ch. = Channel
CO = Colorado
CT = Connecticut
DE = Delaware
DRC = Democratic Republic of Congo
E. = East
FL = Florida
G. = Gulf, Golfe, Golfo
GA = Georgia
Hd. = Head
I./Is. = Island(s), Ile, Ilha, Insel, Isla, Isle(s)
IL = Illinois
IN = Indiana
KA = Kansas
KY = Kentucky
L. = Lake, Lac, Lacul, Lago, Lagoa, Limni, Loch, Lough
LA = Louisiana
Lux. = Luxembourg
ME = Maine
MD = Maryland
MA = Massachusetts
MI = Michigan
MN = Minnesota
MS = Mississippi
MO = Missouri
MT = Montana
Mt./Mts. = Mountain(s), Mont, Monte, Monti, Montaña
N. = North, Nord, Norte, Norghern
NC = North Carolina
ND = North Dakota
NE = Nebraska
NH = New Hampshire
NJ = New Jersey
NM = New Mexico
NY = New York
Neths. = Netherlands
NV = Nevada
OH = Ohio
OK = Oklahoma
OR = Oregon
PNG = Papua New Guinea
PA = Pennsylvania
Pen. = Peninsula, Peninsule
Pk. = Peak
Plat. = Plateau
Pt. = Point
Pta. = Ponta, Punta
Pte. = Pointe
R. = River, Rio
RI = Rhode Island
Ra./Ras. = Range(s)
Rep. = Republic
Res. = Reserve
Res. = Reservoir
S. = San, South
Saudi = Saudi Arabia
SC = South Carolina
SD = South Dakota
Sa. = Serra, Sierra
Sd. = Sound
St. = Saint, Sankt, Sint
Str. = Strait, Stretto
TN = Tennessee
TE = Texas
UAE = United Arab Emirates
UK = United Kingdom
USA = United States of America
UT = Utah
VA = Virginia
VT = Vermont
W. = West
WV = West Virgina
WA = Washington
WI = Wisconsin
WY = Wyoming

A

Aachen *Germany* **92** 50 45N 6 6 E
Aalst *Belgium* **90** 50 56N 4 2 E
Aarau *Switzerland* **92** 47 23N 8 4 E
Aare, R. *Switzerland* **92** 47 33N 8 14 E
Aba *Nigeria* **124** 5 10N 7 19 E
Abadan *Iran* **116** 30 22N 48 20 E
Abancay *Peru* **149** 13 35S 72 55W
Abariringa *Kiribati* **129** 2 50S 171 40W
Abaya, L. *Ethiopia* **118** 6 30N 37 50 E
Abbeville *France* **94** 50 6N 1 49 E
Abéché *Chad* **125** 13 50N 20 35 E
Abeokuta *Nigeria* **124** 7 3N 3 19 E
Aberdare *UK* **89** 51 43N 3 27W
Aberdeen *UK* **89** 57 9N 2 5W
Aberdeen *SD, USA* **142** 45 28N 98 29W
Aberdeen *WA, USA* **142** 46 59N 123 50W
Aberystwyth *UK* **89** 52 25N 4 5W
Abidjan *Ivory Coast* **124** 5 26N 3 58W
Abilene *USA* **142** 32 28N 99 43W
Abitibi, L. *Canada* **141** 48 40N 79 40W
Abkhazia *Georgia* **116** 43 12N 41 5 E
Abomey *Benin* **124** 7 10N 2 5 E
Absaroka Ra. *USA* **142** 44 45N 109 50W
Abu Dhabi *UAE* **117** 24 28N 54 22 E
Abu Hamed *Sudan* **125** 19 32N 33 13 E
Abuja *Nigeria* **124** 9 5N 7 32 E
Abuna *Brazil* **149** 9 40S 65 20W
Abuna R. *Brazil* **148** 9 41S 65 20W

Ac

Acaponeta *Mexico* **146** 22 30N 105 20W
Acapulco *Mexico* **146** 16 51N 99 56W
Acarai Serra *Brazil* **148** 1 50N 57 50W
Accomac *USA* **145** 37 43N 75 40W
Accra *Ghana* **124** 5 35N 0 6W
Acheron, R. *N. Zealand* **132** 42 16S 173 4 E
Achill I. *Ireland* **89** 53 58N 10 1W
Acklins I. *Bahamas* **147** 22 30N 74 0W
Acre *Brazil* **149** 9 1S 71 0W
Acre, R. *Brazil* **148** 8 45S 67 22W

Ad

Ad Dammam *Saudi* **116** 26 20N 50 5 E
Ad Diwaniyah *Iraq* **116** 32 0N 45 0 E
Adair, C. *Canada* **141** 71 30N 71 34W
Adak I. *USA* **142** 51 45N 176 45W
Adamawa H. *Cameroon* **125** 7 20N 12 20 E
Adana *Turkey* **99** 37 0N 35 16 E
Adelaide *Australia* **128** 34 52S 138 30 E
Adelaide I. *Antarctica* **81** 67 15S 68 30W
Adelaide Pen. *Canada* **140** 68 15N 97 30W
Adélie Land *Antarctica* **81** 68 0S 140 0 E
Aden *Yemen* **101** 12 45N 45 0 E
Aden, G. of *Asia* **100** 12 30N 47 30 E
Adilabad *India* **114** 19 37N 78 30 E
Adirondack Mts. *USA* **145** 44 0N 74 0W
Adjuntas *Puerto Rico* **147** 18 10N 66 43W
Adoni *India* **114** 15 38N 77 19 E
Adour, R. *France* **94** 43 32N 1 32W
Adrar *Mauritania* **124** 20 30N 7 30W
Adrar d. Iforas *Algeria* **124** 27 51N 0 11 E
Adrian *USA* **144** 41 54N 84 2W
Adriatic Sea *Medit. Sea* **96** 43 0N 16 0 E
Adygea *Russia* **99** 45 0N 40 0 E
Aegean Sea *Medit. Sea* **97** 38 30N 25 0 E
AFGHANISTAN *Asia* **114** 33 0N 65 0 E
AFRICA *continent* **82** 10 0N 20 0 E
Afyon *Turkey* **99** 38 45N 30 33 E

Ag

Agadez *Niger* **124** 16 58N 7 59 E
Agadir *Morocco* **124** 30 28N 9 55W
Agartala *Bangladesh* **115** 23 50N 91 23 E
Agen *France* **94** 44 12N 0 38 E
Agra *India* **114** 27 17N 77 58 E
Agri *Turkey* **99** 39 44N 43 3 E
Agua Prieta *Mexico* **146** 31 20N 109 32W
Aguadilla *Puerto Rico* **147** 18 26N 67 10W
Aguascalientes *Mexico* **146** 21 53N 102 12W
Agulhas, C. *South Africa* **118** 34 52S 20 0 E

Ah

Ahaura, R. *New Zealand* **132** 42 21S 171 34 E
Ahipara Bay *New Zealand* **132** 35 5S 173 5 E
Ahmadabad *India* **114** 23 0N 72 40 E
Ahmadnagar *India* **114** 19 7N 74 46 E
Ahmadpur *Pakistan* **114** 29 12N 71 10 E
Ahvaz *Iran* **116** 31 20N 48 40 E
Aihui *China* **109** 50 10N 127 30 E
Aïr *Niger* **124** 18 30N 8 0 E
Air Force I. *Canada* **141** 67 58N 74 5W
Airdrie *Canada* **140** 51 18N 114 2W
Aisne R. *France* **94** 49 26N 2 50 E
Aix-en-Provence *France* **94** 43 32N 5 27 E
Aix-les-Bains *France* **94** 45 41N 5 53 E
Aizawl *India* **115** 23 40N 92 44 E
Ajaccio *France* **94** 41 55N 8 40 E
Ajaria *Georgia* **116** 41 30N 42 0 E
Ajdabiya *Libya* **125** 30 54N 20 4 E
Ajman *UAE* **117** 25 25N 55 30 E
Ajmer *India* **114** 26 27N 74 42 E
Akhisar *Turkey* **99** 38 56N 27 48 E

Ak

Akimiski I. *Canada* **141** 52 50N 81 30W
Akita *Japan* **110** 39 45N 140 7 E
'Akko *Israel* **116** 32 55N 35 4 E
Aklavik *Canada* **140** 68 12N 135 0W
Akpatok I. *Canada* **141** 60 25N 68 8W
Akranes *Iceland* **91** 64 19N 22 5W
Akron *USA* **144** 41 5N 81 31W
Aksaray *Turkey* **99** 38 25N 34 2 E
Aksehir Gölü *Turkey* **99** 38 30N 31 25 E
Aksu *China* **108** 41 5N 80 10 E
Akure *Nigeria* **124** 7 15N 5 5 E
Akureyri *Iceland* **91** 65 40N 18 6W

Al

Al 'Aqabah *Jordan* **116** 29 31N 35 0 E
Al 'Ayn *UAE* **117** 24 15N 55 45 E
Al Qamishli *Syria* **116** 37 2N 41 14 E
Al Qatif *Saudi* **116** 26 35N 50 0 E
Alabama *USA* **143** 33 0N 87 0W
Alabama R. *USA* **143** 31 8N 87 57W
Alagoinhas *Brazil* **149** 12 7S 38 20W
Alai Range *Asia* **117** 39 45N 72 0 E
Alamogordo *USA* **142** 32 54N 105 57W
Alamosa *USA* **142** 37 28N 105 52W
Åland Is. *Finland* **91** 60 15N 20 0 E
Alanya *Turkey* **99** 36 38N 32 0 E
Alasehir *Turkey* **99** 38 23N 28 30 E
Alaska *USA* **142** 64 0N 154 0W
Alaska, G. of *Pacific* **142** 58 0N 145 0W
Alaska Pen. *USA* **142** 56 0N 159 0W
Alaska Ra. *USA* **142** 62 50N 151 0W
Albacete *Spain* **95** 39 0N 1 50W
Albanel, L. *Canada* **141** 50 55N 73 12W
Albania *Europe* **97** 41 0N 20 0 E
Albany *Australia* **128** 35 1S 117 58 E
Albany, R. *Canada* **141** 52 17N 81 31W
Albany *GA, USA* **143** 31 35N 84 10W
Albany, *NY, USA* **145** 42 39N 73 45W
Albany, *OR, USA* **142** 44 38N 123 6W
Albatross Pt. *N. Zealand* **132** 38 7S 174 44 E
Albemarle Sound *USA* **143** 36 5N 76 0W
Albert, L. *Africa* **118** 1 30N 31 0 E
Albert Lea *USA* **143** 43 39N 93 22W
Albert Nile, R. *Uganda* **126** 3 36N 32 2 E
Alberta *Canada* **140** 54 0N 115 0W
Albertville *France* **94** 45 40N 6 22 E
Albi *France* **94** 43 56N 2 9 E
Albion *USA* **144** 42 15N 84 45W
Ålborg *Denmark* **91** 57 2N 9 54
Albuquerque *USA* **142** 35 5N 106 39
Albury Wodonga *Australia* **128** 36 3S 146 56
Alcalá de Henares *Spain* **95** 40 28N 3 22
Alchevsk *Ukraine* **99** 48 30N 38 45
Aldabra Is. *Seychelles* **118** 9 22S 46 28
Aldan, R. *Russia* **107** 63 28N 129 35
Alderney I. *UK* **89** 49 42N 2 11
Alençon *France* **94** 48 27N 0 4
Alenuihaha Ch. *Pacific* **142** 20 30N 156 0
Aleppo *Syria* **116** 36 10N 37 15
Alès *France* **94** 44 9N 4 5
Alessándria *Italy* **92** 44 54N 8 37
Ålesund *Norway* **91** 62 28N 6 12
Aleutian Trench *Pacific* **100** 48 0N 180 0
Alexander Arch. *USA* **142** 56 0N 136 0
Alexander I. *Antarctica* **81** 69 0S 70 0
Alexandria *LA, USA* **143** 31 18N 92 27
Alexandria, *VA, USA* **144** 38 48N 77 3
Al Faw *Iraq* **116** 30 0N 48 30
Alfredton *New Zealand* **132** 40 41S 175 54
Algarve *Portugal* **95** 36 58N 8 20
Algeciras *Spain* **95** 36 9N 5 28
ALGERIA *Africa* **119** 28 30N 2 0
Algiers *Algeria* **125** 36 42N 3 8
Algoa Bay *South Africa* **118** 33 50S 25 45
Al Hillah *Iraq* **116** 32 30N 44 25
Al Hoceïma *Morocco* **124** 35 8N 3 58
Al Hufuf *Saudi* **116** 25 25N 49 45
Alicante *Spain* **95** 38 23N 0 30
Alice Springs *Australia* **128** 23 40S 133 50
Aligarh *India* **114** 27 55N 78 10
Alipur Duar *India* **115** 26 30N 89 35
Aliquippa *USA* **144** 40 37N 80 15
Al Jawf *Libya* **125** 24 10N 23 24

161

AL KAHLIL–BELLINGHAM

:halil *West Bank* 116 31 32N 35 6 E
.humms *Libya* 125 32 40N 14 17 E
.naar *Neths.* 90 52 37N 4 45 E
.ufrah *Algeria* 118 24 17N 23 15 E
.ut *Iraq* 116 32 30N 46 0 E
.habad *India* 115 25 25N 81 58 E
.gan *USA* 144 42 32N 85 51W
.gheny Mts. *USA* 143 38 15N 80 10W
.gheny *R. USA* 144 40 27N 80 1W
.ntown *USA* 145 40 37N 75 29W
.ppey *India* 114 9 30N 76 28 E
.nes Bay *Barbados* 147 13 13N 59 39W
.ance *USA* 142 42 6N 102 52W
.r, R. *France* 94 46 57N 3 4 E
.gator Pond *Jamaica* 146 17 52N 77 43W
.tsup Paa *Greenland* 141 60 30N 45 35W
.a *USA* 144 43 23N 84 39W
.a Ata *Kazakhstan* 106 43 15N 76 57 E
.Manamah *Bahrain* 117 26 10N 50 30 E
.elo *Neths.* 90 52 22N 6 42 E
.ería *Spain* 95 36 52N 2 27W
.ora *India* 114 29 37N 79 40 E
.Mubarraz *Saudi* 116 25 30N 49 40 E
.Musayyib *Iraq* 116 32 49N 44 20 E
.wick *UK* 89 55 24N 1 42W
. *Indonesia* 128 8 15S 124 30 E
. Setar *Malaysia* 112 6 7N 100 22 E
.ena *USA* 144 45 4N 83 27W
.s Maritimes *Europe* 92 44 10B 7 10 E
.ne *USA* 142 30 22N 103 40W
.s *Europe* 92 46 30N 9 30 E
.ace *France* 94 48 15N 7 25 E
.nbulag *Mongolia* 108 50 16N 106 30 E
.y *China* 108 47 48N 88 10 E
.n *USA* 143 38 53N 90 11W
.ona *USA* 144 40 31N 78 24W
.n Shan *China* 108 38 30N 88 0 E
.s *USA* 142 34 38N 99 20W
.ra *Turkey* 99 40 22N 38 47 E
.ar *India* 114 27 38N 76 34 E
.a Zuoqi *China* 108 38 50N 105 40 E
.adjuak, *L. Canada* 141 65 0N 71 8W
.agasaki *Japan* 111 34 42N 135 20 E
.apá *Brazil* 149 2 5N 50 50W
.arillo *USA* 142 35 13N 101 50W
.asya *Turkey* 99 40 40N 35 50 E
.azon, *R. S. America* 148 0 5S 50 0W
.azonas *Brazil* 149 5 0S 65 0W
.bala *India* 114 30 23N 76 56 E
.bato *Ecuador* 149 1 5S 78 42W
.bergris Cay *Belize* 146 18 0N 88 0W
.berley *New Zealand* 133 43 9S 172 44 E
.bikapur *India* 115 23 15N 83 15 E
.bllobe *Madagascar* 126 13 10S 49 3 E
.bon *Indonesia* 113 3 43S 128 12 E
.chitka I. *USA* 142 51 32N 179 0 E
.eca *Mexico* 146 20 30N 104 0W
.erican Highland *Antarctica*
81 73 0S 75 0 E
.erican Samoa *Pacific Ocean*
129 14 20S 170 40W
.ersfoort *Neths.* 90 52 9N 5 23 E
.es *USA* 143 42 2N 93 37W
.herst *Canada* 141 45 48N 64 8W
.iens *France* 94 49 54N 2 16 E
.irante Is. *Seychelles* 100 6 0S 53 0 E
.lia I. *USA* 142 52 4N 173 30W
.aman *Jordan* 116 31 57N 35 52 E
.os *Canada* 141 48 35N 78 5W
.ravati *India* 114 20 55N 77 45 E
.ritsar *India* 114 31 37N 74 55 E
.roha *India* 114 28 54N 78 31 E
.sterdam *Neths.* 90 52 23N 4 54 E
.udarya, *R. Uzbekistan*
100 43 58N 59 34 E
.undsen G. *Canada* 140 71 0N 124 0W
.undsen Sea *Antarctica*
81 72 0S 115 0W
.u, R. *Russia* 109 52 56N 141 10 E
.ur Pass *N. Zealand* 132 42 31S 172 11 E
Najaf *Iraq* 116 32 3N 44 15 E
Nasiriyah *Iraq* 116 31 0N 46 15 E
.aconda *USA* 142 46 8N 112 57W
.adyr, *G. of Russia* 107 64 0N 180 0 E
.aheim *USA* 142 33 50N 117 55W
.ambas Kepulauan *Indonesia*
112 3 20N 106 30 E
.amur *Turkey* 99 36 8N 32 58 E
.antapur *India* 114 14 39N 77 42 E
.antnag *India* 114 33 43N 75 17 E
.ápolis *Brazil* 149 16 15S 48 50W
.ar *Iran* 117 30 55N 55 13 E
.atolia *Turkey* 99 39 0N 30 0 E
.atuya *Argentina* 149 28 20S 62 50W
.chorage *USA* 142 61 13N 149 54W
.cohuma *Bolivia* 148 16 0S 68 50W
.cona *Italy* 96 43 38N 13 30 E
.cud, *G. de Chile* 148 42 0S 73 0W
.dalgala *Argentina* 149 27 40S 66 30W
.dalucía *Spain* 95 37 35N 5 0W
.dalusia *USA* 143 31 18N 86 29W
.daman Is. *Indian O.* 100 12 30N 92 45 E
.derson *R. Canada* 140 69 42N 129 0W
.derson *AK, USA* 142 64 25N 149 15W
.derson *IN, USA* 144 40 10N 85 41W
.derson *SC, USA* 143 34 31N 82 39W
.dhra Pradesh *India* 114 18 0N 79 0 E
.dong *South Korea* 110 36 40N 128 43 E
.DORRA *Europe* 83 42 30N 1 30 E
.dreanof Is. *USA* 142 51 30N 176 0W
.dria *Italy* 96 41 13N 16 17 E
.dros I. *Bahamas* 147 24 30N 78 0W
.egada I. *Br. Virgin Is.* 147 18 45N 64 20W
.eityum I. *Vanuatu* 129 20 12S 169 45 E
.gara, *R. Russia* 107 58 5N 94 20 E
.garsk *Russia* 107 52 30N 104 0 E
.ge *Sweden* 91 62 31N 15 35 E
.gel Falls *Venezuela* 148 5 57N 62 30W
.geles *Philippines* 113 15 9N 120 33 E
.germanälven *Sweden* 98 62 40N 18 0 E
.gers *France* 94 47 30N 0 35W
.glem, Mt. *N. Zealand* 132 46 45S 167 53 E
.goche *Mozambique* 126 16 8S 39 55 E
.GOLA *Africa* 119 12 0S 18 0 E
.goulême *France* 94 45 39N 0 10 E

Angoumois *France* 94 45 50N 0 25 E
Angren *Uzbekistan* 117 41 1N 70 12 E
Anguilla *W. Indies* 147 18 14N 63 5W
Anhui *China* 109 32 0N 117 0 E
Anjou *France* 94 47 20N 0 15W
Ankang *China* 109 32 40N 109 1 E
Ankara *Turkey* 99 39 57N 32 54 E
Anmyon Do *S. Korea* 110 36 25N 126 25 E
Ann, C. *USA* 145 42 38N 70 35W
Annaba *Algeria* 125 36 50N 7 46 E
Annapolis *USA* 144 38 59N 76 30W
Annapurna *Nepal* 115 28 34N 83 50 E
Ann Arbor *USA* 144 42 17N 83 45W
Annecy *France* 94 45 55N 6 8 E
Anning *China* 108 24 55N 102 26 E
Anniston *USA* 143 33 39N 85 50W
Annobón *Atlantic Ocean* 118 1 25S 5 36 E
Annotto Bay *Jamaica* 146 18 17N 76 45W
Anqing *China* 109 30 30N 117 3 E
Anshan *China* 109 41 5N 122 58 E
Anshun *China* 108 26 18N 105 57 E
Antalya *Turkey* 99 36 52N 30 45 E
Antananarivo *Madag.* 126 18 55S 47 31 E
Antarctic Pen. *Antarc.* 81 67 0S 60 0W
Anti Atlas *Morocco* 124 30 0N 8 30W
Antibes *France* 94 43 34N 7 6 E
Anticosti, Île. d' *Canada* 141 49 30N 63 0W
Antigonish *Canada* 141 45 38N 61 58W
Antioch *Turkey* 99 36 14N 36 10 E
Antofagasta *Chile* 149 23 50S 70 30W
Antrim *UK* 89 54 43N 6 14W
Antsirabe *Madagascar* 126 19 55S 47 2 E
Antsiranana *Madagascar*
126 12 25S 49 20 E
Antwerp *Belgium* 90 51 13N 4 25 E
Anuradhapura *Sri Lanka*
114 8 22N 80 28 E
Anxi *China* 108 40 30N 95 43 E
Anyang *China* 109 36 5N 114 21 E
Ao
Aomori *Japan* 110 40 45N 140 45 E
Aoraki *New Zealand* 129 43 36S 170 9 E
Aorangi Mts. *New Zealand*
132 41 49S 175 22 E
Aozou *Chad* 125 22 0N 19 0 E
Apalachee Bay USA 143 30 0N 84 0W
Apaporis, R. Colombia 148 1 23S 69 25W
Apatity *Russia* 98 67 34N 33 22 E
Apeldoorn *Neths.* 90 52 13N 5 57 E
Apia *Samoa* 129 13 50S 171 50W
Apostle Is. *USA* 143 47 0N 90 40W
Appalachian Mts. *USA* 144 38 0N 80 0W
Appennini *Italy* 96 44 0N 10 0 E
Appleton *USA* 144 44 16N 88 25W
Apure, R. Venezuela 148 7 37N 66 25W
Ar
Aqtöbe *Kazakhstan* 99 50 17N 57 10 E
Ara *India* 115 25 35N 84 32 E
Arabian Desert *Egypt* 125 27 30N 32 30 E
Arabian Sea Indian O. 100 16 0N 65 0 E
Aracaju *Brazil* 149 10 55S 37 4W
Aracati *Brazil* 149 4 30S 37 44W
Arafura Sea East Indies 113 9 0S 135 0 E
Aragón *Spain* 95 41 25N 0 40W
Araguacema *Brazil* 149 8 50S 49 20W
Araguaia, R. Brazil 148 5 21S 48 41W
Arak *Iran* 116 34 0N 49 40 E
Arakan Coast *Myanmar* 115 19 0N 94 0 E
Arakan Yoma *Myanmar* 115 20 0N 94 40 E
Araks, R. Asia 116 40 5N 48 29 E
Aral *Kazakhstan* 106 46 41N 61 45 E
Aral Sea Asia 106 44 30N 60 0 E
Aran Is. *Ireland* 89 53 6N 9 38W
Arapiraca *Brazil* 149 9 45S 36 39W
Arapun *New Zealand* 132 38 3S 175 37 E
Ararat, Mt. *Turkey* 99 39 50N 44 15 E
Arauca, R. Venezuela 148 7 24N 66 35W
Arbroath *UK* 89 56 34N 2 35W
Arcachon *France* 94 44 40N 1 10W
Arctic Ocean 80 78 0N 160 0W
Ardabil *Iran* 116 38 15N 48 18 E
Ardennes *Belgium* 90 49 50N 5 5 E
Ardmore *USA* 143 34 10N 97 8W
Ardnamurchan Pt. *UK* 89 56 43N 6 14W
Arecibo *Puerto Rico* 147 18 29N 66 43W
Arena Pt. *USA* 142 38 57N 123 44W
Arendal *Norway* 91 58 28N 8 46 E
ARGENTINA *South America*
149 35 0S 66 0W
Århus *Denmark* 91 56 8N 10 11 E
Arica *Chile* 149 18 32S 70 20W
Arípuana, R. Brazil 148 5 7S 60 25W
Arizona *USA* 142 34 0N 112 0W
Arkansas *USA* 143 35 0N 92 30W
Arkansas City *USA* 143 37 4N 97 27W
Arkansas R. USA 143 33 47N 91 4W
Arkhangelsk *Russia* 98 64 38N 40 36 E
Arles *France* 94 43 41N 4 40 E
Arlington *USA* 144 38 53N 77 7W
Arlon *Belgium* 90 49 42N 5 49 E
Armagh *UK* 89 54 21N 6 39W
Armavir *Russia* 99 45 2N 41 7 E
ARMENIA *Asia* 116 40 20N 45 0 E
Arnaud R. Canada 141 59 59N 69 46W
Arnhem *Neths.* 90 51 58N 5 55 E
Arnhem, C. *Australia* 128 12 20S 137 30 E
Arnhem Land *Australia* 128 13 10S 134 30 E
Arois *France* 94 50 20N 2 30 E
Ar Ramadi *Iraq* 116 33 25N 43 20 E
Arran *UK* 89 55 34N 5 12W
Arras *France* 94 50 17N 2 46 E
Arrecife *Canary Is.* 124 28 57N 13 37W
Artemovsk *Ukraine* 99 48 35N 38 0 E
Arthur's Pass *New Zealand*
132 42 54S 171 35 E
Artigas *Uruguay* 149 30 20S 56 30W
Artvin *Turkey* 116 41 14N 41 44 E
Aru Kepulauan *Indon.* 113 6 0S 134 30 E
Arua *Uganda* 126 3 1N 30 58 E
Aruana *Brazil* 149 14 54S 51 10W
Aruba *W. Indies* 147 12 30N 70 0W
Arusha *Tanzania* 126 3 20S 36 40 E
Arviat *Canada* 140 61 6N 94 3W
Arxan *China* 109 47 11N 119 57 E
Arzamas *Russia* 98 55 27N 43 55 E
As
Asahigawa *Japan* 110 43 46N 142 22 E
Asamankese *Ghana* 124 5 50N 0 40W

Asansol *India* 115 23 40N 87 1 E
Asbury Park *USA* 145 40 13N 74 1W
Ashburton *N. Zealand* 132 43 53S 171 48 E
Asheville *USA* 143 35 36N 82 33W
Ashford *UK* 89 51 8N 0 53 E
Ashkhabad *Turkmen.* 106 38 0N 57 50 E
Ashland *KY, USA* 144 38 28N 82 38W
Ashland *OH, USA* 144 40 52N 82 19W
Ashland *WI, USA* 144 46 35N 90 53W
Ashqelon *Israel* 116 31 42N 34 35 E
Ashtabula *USA* 144 41 52N 80 47W
Ashuanipi, L. Canada 141 52 45N 66 15W
ASIA *continent* 100 45 0N 75 0 E
Aspen *USA* 142 39 11N 106 49W
Aspiring, Mt. *New Zealand*
132 44 23S 168 46 E
Assen *Neths.* 90 53 0N 6 35 E
Assiniboia *Canada* 140 49 40N 105 59W
Assiniboine, R. Canada 140 49 53N 97 8W
Assisi *Italy* 96 43 4N 12 37 E
As Sulaymaniyah *Iraq* 116 35 35N 45 29 E
As Suwayrah *Iraq* 116 32 55N 45 0 E
Astana *Kazakhstan* 106 51 10N 71 30 E
Asti *Italy* 92 44 54N 8 12 E
Astoria *USA* 142 46 11N 123 50W
Astrakhan *Russia* 99 46 25N 48 5 E
Asturias *Spain* 95 43 15N 6 0W
Asunción *Paraguay* 149 25 10S 57 30W
Aswan *Egypt* 125 24 4N 32 57 E
Aswan Dam *Egypt* 125 23 54N 32 54 E
At
Asyût *Egypt* 125 27 11N 31 4 E
Atatürk Baraji, L. Turkey
99 37 28N 38 30 E
'Atbara *Sudan* 125 17 42N 35 59 E
Atbara, R. Sudan 125 17 40N 33 56 E
Atchafalaya Bay USA 143 29 25N 91 25W
Athabasca *Canada* 140 54 45N 113 20W
Athabasca, L. Canada 140 59 15N 109 15W
Athabasca R. Canada 140 58 40N 110 50W
Athens *GA, USA* 143 33 57N 83 23W
Athens *OH, USA* 144 39 20N 82 6W
Athlone *Ireland* 89 53 25N 7 56W
Athol *New Zealand* 132 45 30S 168 35 E
Atiamuri *New Zealand* 132 38 24S 176 5 E
Atka I. *USA* 142 52 7N 174 30W
Atlanta *USA* 143 33 45N 84 23W
Atlantic City *USA* 143 39 21N 74 27W
Atlantic Ocean 100 0 0 20 0W
Atlin *Canada* 140 59 31N 133 41W
At Ta'if *Saudi Arabia* 116 21 5N 40 27 E
Attawapiskat R. Canada 141 52 57N 82 18W
Attu I. *USA* 142 52 55N 172 55 E
Atyrau *Kazakhstan* 99 47 5N 52 0 E
Au
Aube, R. France 94 48 34N 3 43 E
Auburn *IN, USA* 144 41 22N 85 4W
Auburn *NY, USA* 144 42 56N 76 34W
Auch *France* 94 43 39N 0 36 E
Auckland *New Zealand* 129 36 52S 174 46 E
Aude, R. France 94 43 13N 3 14 E
Augsburg *Germany* 92 48 25N 10 52 E
Augusta *Australia* 128 34 19S 115 9 E
Augusta *GA, USA* 143 33 28N 81 58W
Augusta *ME, USA* 143 44 19N 69 47W
Aunis *France* 94 46 5N 0 50W
Aurangabad *India* 115 24 45N 84 18 E
Aurillac *France* 94 44 55N 2 26 E
Aurora *CO, USA* 142 39 44N 104 52W
Aurora *IL, USA* 144 41 45N 88 19W
Au Sable R. USA 144 44 25N 83 20W
Austin *USA* 142 30 17N 97 45W
Austral Seamount Chain *Pacific Ocean*
133 24 0S 150 0W
AUSTRALIA *Oceania* 128 23 0S 135 0W
AUSTRIA *Europe* 92 47 0N 14 0 E
Autun *France* 94 46 58N 4 17 E
Auvergne *France* 94 45 20N 3 15 E
Auxerre *France* 94 47 48N 3 32 E
Av
Avallon *France* 94 47 30N 3 53 E
Avellaneda *Argentina* 149 34 50S 58 10W
Aviemore *UK* 89 57 12N 3 50W
Avignon *France* 94 43 57N 4 50 E
Ávila *Spain* 95 40 39N 4 43W
Avranches *France* 94 48 40N 1 20W
Awanui *New Zealand* 132 35 4S 173 17 E
Awarua Pt. *N. Zealand* 132 44 15S 168 5 E
Awatere, R. N. Zealand 132 41 37S 174 10 E
Axel Heiberg I. *Canada* 80 80 0N 90 0W
Axiós, R. Greece 97 40 57N 22 35 E
Ayers Rock *Australia* 128 25 23S 131 5 E
Aylmer, L. Canada 140 64 0N 110 8W
Ayr *UK* 89 55 28N 4 38W
Ayvalik *Turkey* 99 39 20N 26 46 E
Az Zarqa' *Jordan* 116 32 5N 36 4 E
Az Zawiyah *Libya* 125 32 52N 12 56 E
Azamgarh *India* 115 26 5N 83 13 E
AZERBAIJAN *Asia* 116 40 20N 48 0 E
Azov *Russia* 99 47 3N 39 25 E
Azov, Sea of Europe 99 46 0N 36 30 E
Azuero, Pen. de *Panama* 147 7 30N 80 30W
Azul *Argentina* 149 36 42S 59 43W

B

Bab el Mandeb *Red Sea* 118 12 35N 43 25 E
Babine, L. Canada 140 54 48N 126 0W
Babol *Iran* 117 36 40N 52 50 E
Babruysk *Belarus* 93 53 10N 29 15 E
Babuyan Channel *Philippines*
113 18 40N 121 30 E
Babylon *Iraq* 116 32 34N 44 22 E
Bacau *Romania* 93 46 35N 26 55 E
Back, R. Canada 140 65 10N 104 0W
Bacolod *Philippines* 113 10 40N 122 57 E
Badagara *India* 114 11 35N 75 40 E
Badajoz *Spain* 95 38 50 N 6 59 W
Badakhshan *Afghan.* 117 36 30N 71 0 E
Badalona *Spain* 95 41 26N 2 15 E
Bad Axe *USA* 144 43 48N 83 0W
Baden *Austria* 92 48 20N 8 40 E
Badghis *Afghanistan* 117 35 0N 63 0 E
Badrinath *India* 114 30 44N 79 32 E
Badulla *Sri Lanka* 114 7 0N 81 1 E
Baffin Island *Canada* 141 68 0N 75 0W
Baffin Bay Canada 141 72 0N 64 0W

Bafoussam *Cameroon* 124 13 50N 10 55W
Bafra *Turkey* 99 41 34N 35 54 E
Bagé *Brazil* 149 31 20S 54 15W
Baghdad *Iraq* 116 33 20N 44 30 E
Baghlan *Afghanistan* 117 32 12N 68 46 E
Baguio *Philippines* 113 16 26N 120 34 E
BAHAMAS *Caribbean* 135 24 0N 75 0W
Bahawalpur *Pakistan* 114 29 24N 71 40 E
Bahdrampur *India* 115 24 2N 88 27 E
Bahía *Brazil* 149 12 0S 42 0W
Bahía Blanca *Argentina* 149 38 35S 62 13W
Bahr el Ghazal *Sudan* 118 7 0N 28 0 E
Bahraich *India* 115 27 38N 81 37 E
BAHRAIN *Asia* 101 26 0N 50 35 E
Baia Mare *Romania* 93 47 40N 23 35 E
Baidoa *Somalia* 127 3 8N 43 30 E
Ba'iji *Iraq* 116 35 0N 43 30 E
Baikal, L. Russia 107 53 0N 108 0 E
Baiyin *China* 108 36 45N 104 14 E
Baja California *Mexico* 146 31 10N 115 12W
Baja Pta. *Mexico* 146 29 50N 116 0W
Baker I. *Pacific Ocean* 129 0 10N 176 35W
Baker, L. Canada 140 64 0N 96 0W
Baker Lake *Canada* 140 64 20N 96 3W
Baker's Dozen Is. *Canada*
141 56 45N 78 45W
Bakersfield *USA* 142 35 23N 119 1W
Bakhtaran *Iran* 116 34 23N 47 0 E
Bakony *Hungary* 93 47 10N 17 30 E
Baku *Azerbaijan* 116 40 29N 49 56 E
Balabac Str. East Indies 113 7 53N 117 5 E
Balaghat *India* 114 21 48N 80 15 E
Balaklava *Ukraine* 99 44 30N 33 30 E
Balakovo *Russia* 98 52 4N 47 55 E
Balashov *Russia* 99 51 30N 43 10 E
Balaton *Hungary* 93 46 50N 17 40 E
Balcarce *Argentina* 149 38 0S 58 10W
Baldwin *USA* 144 43 54N 85 51W
Baldy Pk. *USA* 142 33 54N 109 34W
Balearic Islands *Spain* 95 39 30N 3 0 E
Baleshwar *India* 115 21 35N 87 3 E
Bale-St-Paul *Canada* 146 47 28N 70 32W
Bali *Indonesia* 113 8 20S 115 0 E
Balikesir *Turkey* 99 39 39N 27 53 E
Balikpapan *Indonesia* 113 1 10S 116 55 E
Balkan Mts. *Bulgaria* 99 43 15N 23 0 E
Balkhash, L. Kazakhstan 106 46 0N 74 50 E
Ballarat *Australia* 128 37 33S 143 50 E
Balleny Is. *Antarctica* 81 66 30S 163 0 E
Ballymena *UK* 89 54 52N 6 17W
Balrampur *India* 115 27 30N 82 20 E
Balsas, R. Mexico 146 17 55N 102 10W
Balti *Moldova* 93 47 48N 27 58 E
Baltic Sea Europe 91 57 0N 19 0 E
Baltimore *USA* 144 39 17N 76 37W
Baluchistan *Pakistan* 114 27 30N 65 0 E
Bamako *Mali* 124 12 34N 7 55W
Bamberg *Germany* 92 49 54N 10 54 E
Bamian *Afghanistan* 117 35 0N 67 0 E
Banaba *Kiribati* 133 0 45S 169 50 E
Banbury *UK* 89 52 4N 1 20W
Banda *India* 114 25 30N 80 26 E
Banda Aceh *Indonesia* 112 5 35N 95 20 E
Banda Kepulauan *Indonesia*
113 4 37S 129 50 E
Banda Sea Indonesia 113 6 0S 130 0 E
Bandar-e Abbas *Iran* 117 27 15N 56 15 E
Bandar-e Anzali *Iran* 116 37 30N 49 30 E
Bandar-e Ma'shur *Iran* 116 30 35N 49 10 E
Bandar-e Torkeman *Iran*
117 37 0N 54 10 E
Bandar Lampung *Indonesia*
112 5 20S 105 10 E
Bandar Seri Begawan *Brunei*
113 4 52N 115 0 E
Bandirma *Turkey* 99 40 20N 28 0 E
Bandundu *DRC* 126 3 15S 17 22 E
Bandung *Indonesia* 112 6 54S 107 36 E
Banes *Cuba* 147 21 0N 75 42W
Banff *Canada* 140 51 10N 115 34W
Banff *UK* 89 57 40N 2 33W
Bangalore *India* 114 12 59N 77 40 E
Bangka *Indonesia* 112 2 0S 105 50 E
Bangkok *Thailand* 112 13 45N 100 35 E
BANGLADESH *Asia* 101 24 0N 90 0 E
Bangor *USA* 143 44 48N 68 46W
Bangor *N. Ireland, UK* 89 54 40N 5 40W
Bangor *Wales, UK* 89 53 14N 4 8W
Bangweulu, L. Zambia 118 11 0S 30 0 E
Bani *Dominican Rep.* 147 18 16N 70 22W
Banjarmasin *Indonesia* 112 3 20S 114 35 E
Banjul *Gambia* 125 13 28N 16 40W
Banks I. *Canada* 140 73 15N 121 30W
Banks Is. *Vanuatu* 129 13 50S 167 30 E
Banks Pen. *N. Zealand* 132 43 45S 173 15 E
Bannu *Pakistan* 114 33 0N 70 18 E
Banská Bystrica *Slovakia*
93 48 46N 19 14 E
Banswara *India* 114 23 30N 74 24 E
Banyak Kepulauan *Indonesia*
112 2 10N 97 10 E
Banyuwangi *Indonesia* 112 8 13S 114 21 E
Baoding *China* 109 38 50N 115 28 E
Baoji *China* 108 34 20N 107 5 E
Baoshan *China* 108 25 10N 99 5 E
Baotou *China* 109 40 32N 110 2 E
Ba'qubah *Iraq* 116 33 45N 44 50 E
Bar Harbor *USA* 145 44 23N 68 13W
Baracoa *Cuba* 147 20 20N 74 30W
Barahona *Dominican R.* 147 18 13N 71 7W
Barakaldo *Spain* 95 43 18N 2 59W
Baramula *India* 114 34 10N 74 30 E
Baran *India* 114 25 5N 76 33 E
Baranavichy *Belarus* 93 53 10N 26 0 E
BARBADOS *Caribbean* 149 13 10N 59 30W
Barberton *USA* 144 41 0N 81 39W
Barcelona *Spain* 95 41 21N 2 10 E
Barcelona *Venezuela* 149 10 10N 64 40W
Barceloneta *Puerto Rico* 147 18 27N 66 32W
Barddhaman *India* 115 23 16N 87 54 E
Bardiyah *Libya* 125 34 45N 25 5 E
Bardstown *USA* 144 37 49N 85 28W
Bareilly *India* 114 28 22N 79 27 E
Barents Sea Arctic 80 73 0N 39 0 E
Barhi *India* 115 24 15N 85 25 E

Bari *Italy* 96 41 8N 16 51 E
Barisal *Bangladesh* 115 22 45N 90 20 E
Barkly Tableland *Australia*
128 17 50S 136 40 E
Bar-le-Duc *France* 94 48 47N 5 10 E
Barlee, L. Australia 128 29 15S 119 30 E
Barletta *Italy* 96 41 19N 16 17 E
Barmer *India* 114 25 45N 71 20 E
Barnaul *Russia* 106 53 20N 83 40 E
Barnstaple *UK* 89 51 5N 4 4W
Barquísimeto *Venezuela* 149 10 4N 69 19W
Barra *UK* 89 57 0N 7 29W
Barranquilla *Colombia* 149 11 0N 74 50W
Barre *USA* 145 44 12N 72 30W
Barrie *Canada* 141 44 24N 79 40W
Barrier, C. *N. Zealand* 132 36 25S 175 32 E
Barrow *USA* 142 71 18N 156 47W
Barrow in Furness *UK* 89 54 7N 3 14W
Barry *UK* 89 51 24N 3 16W
Barsi *India* 114 18 13N 75 44 E
Barstow *USA* 142 34 54N 117 1W
Bartlesville *USA* 143 36 45N 95 59W
Barysaw *Belarus* 93 54 17N 28 28 E
Basas da India *Indian Ocean*
126 22 0S 39 0 E
Bashkortostan *Russia* 98 54 0N 57 0 E
Basilan I. *Philippines* 113 6 35N 122 0 E
Basildon *UK* 89 51 34N 0 28 E
Basingstoke *UK* 89 51 15N 1 5W
Basra *Iraq* 116 30 30N 47 50 E
Bass Strait Australia 128 39 15S 146 30 E
Bassein *Myanmar* 115 16 45N 94 30 E
Basse-Pointe *Martinique* 146 14 52N 61 8W
Basseterre *St. Kitts* 147 17 17N 62 43W
Basse-Terre *Guadeloupe* 147 16 0N 61 44W
Basti *India* 115 26 48N 82 46 E
Bata *Equatorial Guinea* 126 1 57N 9 50 E
Batabanó, G. de Cuba 147 22 30N 82 30W
Batangas *Philippines* 113 13 35N 121 10 E
Batavia *USA* 144 43 0N 78 11W
Bath *UK* 89 51 23N 2 22W
Bath *ME, USA* 145 43 55N 69 49W
Bath *NY, USA* 144 42 20N 77 19W
Bathsheba *Barbados* 147 13 13N 59 31W
Bathurst *Australia* 128 33 25S 149 31 E
Bathurst *Canada* 141 47 37N 65 43W
Bathurst, C. *Canada* 140 70 34N 128 0W
Batman *Turkey* 99 37 55N 41 5 E
Batna *Algeria* 125 34 34N 6 15 E
Baton Rouge *USA* 143 30 27N 91 11W
Batticaloa *Sri Lanka* 114 7 43N 81 45 E
Battle Creek *USA* 144 42 19N 85 11W
Batu Kepulauan *Indon.* 112 0 30S 98 25 E
Batu Pahat *Malaysia* 112 1 50N 102 56 E
Batumi *Georgia* 116 41 39N 41 44 E
Bauld, C. *Canada* 141 51 38N 55 26W
Bauru *Brazil* 149 22 10S 49 0W
Bay City *USA* 144 43 36N 83 54W
Bayamo *Cuba* 147 20 20N 76 40W
Bayamón *Puerto Rico* 147 18 24N 66 10W
Bayanhongor *Mongolia* 108 46 8N 102 43 E
Bayern *Germany* 92 48 50N 12 0 E
Bayeux *France* 94 49 17N 0 42W
Bay of Bengal Indian O. 100 15 0N 90 0 E
Bay of Is. New Zealand 132 35 15S 174 6 E
Bayonne *France* 94 43 30N 1 28W
Be
Beachy Head *UK* 89 50 44N 0 15 E
Beacon *USA* 145 41 30N 73 58W
Bear, L. USA 142 41 59N 111 21W
Bear R. USA 142 41 30N 112 8W
Beardmore Glacier *Antarctica*
81 84 30S 170 0 E
Béarn *France* 94 43 20N 0 30W
Beatrice *USA* 143 40 16N 96 45W
Beaufort Sea Arctic 80 72 0N 140 0W
Beaufort West *S. Africa* 126 32 18S 22 36 E
Beauharnois *Canada* 146 45 20N 73 52W
Beaumont *USA* 143 30 5N 94 6W
Beaune *France* 94 47 2N 4 50 E
Beauvais *France* 94 49 25N 2 8 E
Beaver Creek *Canada* 140 63 0N 141 0W
Beaver Falls *USA* 144 40 46N 80 20W
Beaver I. *USA* 144 45 40N 85 33W
Beawar *India* 114 26 3N 74 18 E
Beckley *USA* 144 37 47N 81 11W
Bedford *UK* 89 52 8N 0 28W
Bedford *IN, USA* 144 38 52N 86 29W
Bedford *VT, USA* 144 37 20N 79 31W
Be'er Sheva *Israel* 116 31 15N 34 48 E
Bei'an *China* 109 48 10N 126 20 E
Beihai *China* 109 21 28N 109 6 E
Bei Jiang, R. China 109 23 2N 112 58 E
Beijing *China* 109 39 55N 116 20 E
Beira *Mozambique* 126 19 50S 34 52 E
Beirut *Lebanon* 116 33 53N 35 31 E
Beitbridge *Zimbabwe* 126 22 12S 30 0 E
Béja *Tunisia* 125 36 43N 9 12 E
Bejaia *Algeria* 125 36 42N 5 2 E
Bela *Pakistan* 114 26 12N 66 20 E
Bela *India* 115 25 56N 82 2 E
BELARUS *Europe* 93 53 30N 27 0 E
Belau *Pacific Ocean* 100 7 30N 134 30 E
Belcher Is. *Canada* 141 56 15N 78 45W
Belém *Brazil* 149 1 20S 48 30W
Belet Uen *Somalia* 127 4 30N 45 5 E
Belfast *UK* 89 54 37N 5 56W
Belfast *USA* 144 26N 69 1W
Belfort *France* 94 47 38N 6 50 E
Belgaum *India* 114 15 55N 74 35 E
BELGIUM *Europe* 90 50 30N 5 0 E
Belgorod *Russia* 99 50 35N 36 35 E
Belitung *Indonesia* 112 3 10S 107 50 E
BELIZE *Central America*
135 17 0N 88 30W
Belize City *Belize* 146 17 25N 88 0W
Bella Coola *Canada* 140 52 25N 126 40W
Bellaire *USA* 144 40 1N 80 45W
Bellary *India* 114 15 10N 76 56 E
Belle Fourche R. USA 142 44 26N 102 18W
Belle Isle I. *Canada* 141 51 57N 55 25W
Bellefontaine *USA* 144 40 22N 83 46W
Belle-Île *France* 94 47 20N 3 10W
Belleplaine *Barbados* 147 13 15N 59 34W
Belleville *Canada* 141 44 10N 77 23W
Bellingham *USA* 142 48 46N 122 29W

BELLINGSHAUSEN SEA–CAPE FEAR R.

165
FRANKLYN, MT.–HAWERA

ranklyn, Mt. New Zealand 132 42 4S 172 42 E
ranscois, L. Canada 140 54 0N 125 30W
ranz Josef Land I. Russia 106 82 0N 55 0 E
raser R. Canada 140 49 7N 123 11W
raserburgh UK 89 57 42N 2 1W
rederick USA 144 39 25N 77 25W
redericksburg USA 144 38 18N 77 28W
redericton Canada 141 45 57N 66 40W
rederikshavn Denmark 91 57 28N 10 31 E
redonia USA 144 42 26N 79 20W
redrikstad Norway 91 59 13N 10 57 E
reeport USA 143 28 57N 95 21W
ree State South Africa 126 28 30S 27 0 E
reetown Sierra Leone 124 8 30N 13 17W
reiburg Germany 92 47 59N 7 51 E
remont USA 144 41 21N 83 7W
rench Polynesia Pacific Ocean 133 20 0S 145 0W
RENCH GUIANA South America 149 4 0N 53 0W
resnillo Mexico 146 23 10N 103 0W
resno USA 142 36 44N 119 47W
ria, C. Namibia 118 18 0S 12 0 E
riesland Neths. 90 53 5 N 5 50 E
robisher Bay Canada 141 62 30N 66 0W
robisher, L. Canada 140 56 20N 108 15W
ront Ra. USA 142 40 25N 105 45W
ront Royal USA 144 38 55N 78 12W
rýdek-Místek Czech Rep. 93 49 40N 18 20 E
uerte R. Mexico 146 25 50N 109 25W
uerteventura Canary Is. 124 28 30N 14 0W
uhai China 108 47 2N 87 25 E
uji Japan 111 35 9N 138 39 E
ujian China 109 26 0N 118 0 E
uji-san Japan 100 35 22N 138 44 E
ukui Japan 111 36 5N 136 10 E
ukuoka Japan 111 33 39N 130 21 E
ukushima Japan 111 37 44N 140 28 E
ukuyama Japan 111 34 35N 133 20 E
ulda Germany 92 50 32N 9 40 E
ulda R. Germany 92 51 25N 9 39 E
ulton USA 144 43 19N 76 25W
unabashi Japan 111 35 45N 140 0 E
unchal Morocco 124 32 38N 16 54W
urneaux Group Australia 128 40 10S 147 50 E
ürth Germany 92 49 28N 10 59 E
ury and Hecla Strait Canada 141 69 56N 84 0W
ushun China 109 41 50N 123 56 E
ustic Barbados 147 13 16N 59 38W
uxin China 109 42 5N 121 48 E
uzhou China 109 26 5N 119 16 E
yn Denmark 91 55 20N 10 30 E

G

Gabès Tunisia 125 33 53N 10 2 E
Gabès, G. de Tunisia 125 34 0N 10 30 E
GABON Africa 119 0 10S 10 0 E
Gaborone Botswana 126 24 45S 25 57 E
Gabrovo Bulgaria 97 42 52N 25 19 E
Gachsaran Iran 117 30 15N 50 45 E
Gadag India 114 15 25N 75 42 E
Gadarwara India 114 22 50N 78 50 E
Gadsden USA 143 34 1N 86 1W
Gafsa Tunisia 125 34 24N 8 43 E
Gagnoa Ivory Coast 124 6 56N 5 16W
Gagnon Canada 141 51 50N 68 5W
Gainesville GA, USA 143 34 18N 83 50W
Gainesville FL, USA 143 29 40N 82 20W
Gairdner, L. Australia 128 31 30S 136 0 E
Gairloch UK 89 57 43N 5 41W
Galashiels UK 89 55 37N 2 49W
Galati Romania 93 45 27N 28 2 E
Galdhøpiggen Norway 82 61 38N 8 18 E
Galesburg USA 143 40 57N 90 22W
Galicia Spain 95 42 43N 7 45W
Galilee, Sea of Israel 116 32 45N 35 35 E
Galina Point Jamaica 146 18 24N 76 58W
Galle Sri Lanka 114 6 5N 80 10 E
Gallinas, Pta. Colombia 148 12 28N 71 40W
Gallipolis USA 144 38 49N 82 12W
Gällivare Sweden 91 67 9N 20 40 E
Gallup USA 142 35 32N 108 45W
Galoya Sri Lanka 114 8 5N 80 51 E
Galway Ireland 89 53 22N 9 1W
Galway Bay Ireland 89 53 13N 9 10W
GAMBIA Africa 119 13 25N 16 0W
Gambia, R. Africa 124 13 28N 16 34W
Gan Jiang, R. China 109 29 15N 116 0 E
Gananoque Canada 146 44 20N 76 10W
Gäncä Azerbaijan 116 40 45N 46 20 E
Gandak, R. India 115 25 39N 85 13 E
Gander Canada 141 48 58N 54 35W
Gandhi Sagar, L. India 114 24 40N 75 40 E
Ganganagar India 114 29 56N 73 56 E
Ganges, R. India 115 23 20N 90 30 E
Gangtok India 115 27 20N 88 37 E
Gannett Pk. USA 142 43 11N 109 39W
Gansu China 108 36 0N 104 0 E
Ganzhou China 109 25 51N 114 56 E
Gao Mali 124 16 15N 0 5W
Gap France 94 44 33N 6 5 E
Gar China 108 32 10N 79 58 E
Garanhuns Brazil 149 8 50S 36 30W
Garda, L. Italy 96 45 40N 10 41 E
Garden City USA 142 37 58N 100 53W
Gardez Afghanistan 114 33 37N 69 9 E
Garissa Kenya 126 0 25S 39 40 E
Garoe Somalia 127 8 25N 48 33 E
Garonne, R. France 94 45 2N 0 36W
Garoua Cameroon 125 9 19N 13 21 E
Garry, L. Canada 140 65 58N 100 18W
Gary USA 144 41 36N 87 20W
Garzê China 108 31 38N 100 1 E
Gascogne France 94 43 45N 0 20 E
Gascogne, G. de France 94 44 0N 2 0W
Gaspé Canada 141 48 52N 64 50W
Gaspésie, Pen. de la Canada 141 48 45N 65 40W
Gateshead UK 89 54 57N 1 35W
Gatineau, R. Canada 146 45 27N 75 42W
Gävle Sweden 91 60 40N 17 9 E
Gaxun Nur, L. China 108 42 22N 100 30 E
Gaya India 115 24 47N 85 4 E
Gaylord USA 144 45 2N 84 41W
Gaza Palestine 116 31 30N 34 28 E
Gaza Strip Asia 116 31 29N 34 25 E
Gaziantep Turkey 99 37 6N 37 23 E
Gdansk Poland 93 54 22N 18 40 E
Gdynia Poland 93 54 35N 18 33 E
Gebze Turkey 99 40 47N 29 25 E
Gedaref Sudan 125 14 2N 35 28 E
Gedser Denmark 91 54 35N 11 55 E
Geelong Australia 128 38 10S 144 22 E
Gejiu China 108 23 20N 103 10 E
Gelderland Neths. 90 52 5N 6 10 E
Gelibolu Turkey 99 40 28N 26 43 E
Gelsenkirchen Germany 92 51 32N 7 6 E
General Pico Argentina 149 35 45S 63 50W
General Santos Philippines 113 6 5N 125 14 E
Geneva Switzerland 92 46 12N 6 9 E
Geneva USA 144 42 52N 76 59W
Geneva, L. Europe 82 46 26N 6 30 E
Genk Belgium 90 50 58N 5 32 E
Gennargentu, Mt. del. Italy 96 40 1N 9 19 E
Gent Belgium 90 51 2N 3 42 E
George South Africa 126 33 58S 22 29 E
George, L. USA 143 29 17N 81 36W
George, R. Canada 141 58 49N 66 10W
George Sd. N. Zealand 132 44 52S 167 25 E
George Town Malaysia 112 5 25N 100 20 E
Georgetown Guyana 149 6 50N 58 12W
Georgetown SC, USA 143 33 23N 79 17W
Georgetown KY, USA 144 38 13N 84 33W
GEORGIA Asia 106 42 0N 43 0 E
Georgia USA 143 32 50N 83 15W
Georgian Bay Canada 141 45 15N 81 0W
Georgiyevsk Russia 99 44 12N 43 28 E
Gera Germany 92 50 53N 12 4 E
Geraldine New Zealand 132 44 5S 171 15 E
Geraldton Australia 128 28 48S 114 32 E
GERMANY Europe 92 51 0N 10 0 E
Germiston South Africa 126 26 15S 28 10 E
Getafe Spain 95 40 18N 3 44W
Ghaghara, R. India 115 24 45N 84 40 E
GHANA Africa 119 8 0N 1 0W
Ghardaïa Algeria 124 32 20N 3 37 E
Gharyan Libya 125 32 10N 13 0 E
Ghazal Bahr, el R. Chad 125 13 0N 15 47 E
Ghazâl Bahr, el R. Sudan 125 9 31N 30 25 E
Ghaziabad India 114 28 42N 77 26 E
Ghazipur India 115 25 34N 83 35 E
Ghazni Afghanistan 114 33 30N 68 28 E
Ghowr Afghan. 117 34 0N 64 20 E
Ghudamis Libya 125 30 11N 9 29 E
Gibraltar Europe 95 36 7N 5 22W
Gibraltar, Str. of Spain 95 35 55N 5 40W
Gila, R. USA 142 32 43N 114 33W
Gilan Iran 116 37 0N 50 0 E
Gilbert Is. Kiribati 133 1 0N 172 0 E
Gilgit India 114 35 50N 74 15 E
Gillam Canada 140 56 20N 94 40W
Gillespie Pt. N. Zealand 132 43 24S 169 49 E
Gillette USA 142 44 18N 105 30W
Gimie, Mt. St. Lucia 147 13 54N 61 0W
Giresun Turkey 99 40 55N 38 30 E
Giridih India 115 24 10N 86 21 E
Girona Spain 95 41 58N 2 46 E
Gironde, R. France 94 45 32N 1 7W
Girvan UK 89 55 14N 4 51W
Gisborne New Zealand 129 38 39S 178 5 E
Gitega Burundi 126 3 26S 29 56 E
Gizhiga Russia 107 62 3N 160 30 E
Gjoa Haven Canada 140 68 38N 95 53W
Glace Bay Canada 141 46 11N 59 58W
Glacier Nat. Park USA 142 48 30N 113 18W
Gladstone Australia 128 23 52S 151 16 E
Gladstone USA 144 45 51N 87 1W
Gladwin USA 144 43 59N 84 29W
Glasgow UK 89 55 51N 4 15W
Glasgow MT, USA 142 48 12N 106 38W
Glasgow KY, USA 144 37 0N 85 55W
Glazov Russia 98 58 9N 52 40 E
Glen More, R. UK 89 57 9N 4 37W
Glenavy New Zealand 132 44 54S 171 7 E
Glendale AZ, USA 142 33 32N 112 11W
Glendale CA, USA 142 34 9N 118 15W
Glendive USA 142 47 7N 104 43W
Glenmary, Mt. New Zealand 132 44 0S 169 55 E
Glenrothes UK 89 56 12N 3 10W
Glens Falls USA 145 43 19N 73 39W
Gliwice Poland 93 50 22N 18 41 E
Globe USA 142 33 24N 110 47W
Głogów Poland 92 51 37N 16 5 E
Gloucester UK 89 51 53N 2 15W
Gloversville USA 145 43 3N 74 21W
Gniezno Poland 93 52 30N 17 35 E
Goa India 114 15 33N 73 59 E
Goalpara India 115 26 11N 90 41 E
Gobi Desert Asia 100 44 0N 110 0 E
Godavari, R. India 115 16 25N 82 18 E
Godhra India 114 22 49N 73 40 E
Gods, L. Canada 140 54 40N 94 15W
Gods, R. Canada 140 56 22N 92 51W
Goiânia Brazil 149 16 43S 49 20W
Goiás Brazil 149 15 55S 50 10W
Gold Coast West Africa 124 4 0N 1 40W
Golden B. New Zealand 132 40 40S 172 50 E
Goldsboro USA 143 35 23N 77 59W
Goma DRC 126 1 37S 29 10 E
Gomel Belarus 93 52 28N 31 0 E
Gomera Canary Is. 124 28 7N 17 14W
Gómez Palacio Mexico 146 25 40N 104 0W
Gonabad Iran 117 34 15N 58 45 E
Gonaïves Haiti 147 19 20N 72 42W
Gonbad-e Kavus Iran 117 37 20N 55 25 E
Gonda India 115 27 28N 82 1 E
Gondia India 114 21 28N 80 29 E
Gonghe China 108 36 18N 100 32 E
Good Hope, Cape of South Africa 126 34 24S 18 30 E
Goose, L. USA 142 41 56N 120 26W
Gorakhpur India 115 26 47N 83 23 E
Gore New Zealand 132 46 5S 168 58 E
Gorgan Iran 117 36 55N 54 30 E
Görlitz Germany 92 51 9N 14 58 E
Gorontalo Indonesia 113 0 35N 125 5 E
Gorzów Wielkopolski Poland 92 52 43N 15 15 E
Göta Kanal Sweden 91 58 30N 15 58 E
Göteborg Sweden 91 57 43N 11 59 E
Gotha Germany 92 50 56N 10 42 E
Gotland Sweden 91 57 30N 18 33 E
Göttingen Germany 92 51 31N 9 55 E
Gouda Neths. 90 52 1N 4 42 E
Gouin Res. Canada 141 48 35N 74 40W
Goulburn Australia 128 34 44S 149 44 E
Goulimine Morocco 124 28 56N 10 0W
Gozo Malta 96 36 3N 14 15 E
Graaff-reinet S. Africa 126 32 13S 24 32 E
Gracias a Dios, C. Honduras 147 15 0N 83 10W
Grafton Australia 128 29 38S 152 58 E
Grafton USA 143 48 25N 97 25W
Grahamstown S. Africa 126 33 19S 26 31 E
Grain Coast Africa 124 4 20N 10 0W
Grampian Mts. UK 89 56 50N 4 0W
Granada Spain 95 37 10N 3 35W
Granby Canada 141 45 25N 72 45W
Gran Canaria Canary Is. 124 27 55N 15 35W
Grand Bahama Bahamas 147 26 40N 78 30W
Grand-Bourg Guadeloupe 146 15 53N 61 19W
Grand Canyon National Park USA 142 36 15N 112 30W
Grand Cayman Cayman Is. 147 19 20N 81 20W
Grande Baleine, R. Canada 141 55 16N 77 47W
Grande Prairie Canada 140 55 10N 118 50W
Grande, R. Bolivia 148 15 51S 64 39W
Grand Falls Canada 141 47 3N 67 44W
Grand Falls-Windsor Canada 141 48 56N 55 40W
Grand Forks USA 143 47 55N 97 3W
Grand Haven USA 144 43 4N 86 13W
Grand Island USA 142 40 55N 98 21W
Grand Junction USA 142 39 4N 108 33W
Grand L. Canada 146 45 57N 66 7W
Grand-mère Canada 146 46 36N 72 40W
Grand R. USA 142 45 40N 100 45W
Grand Rapids Canada 140 53 12N 99 19W
Grand Rapids USA 144 42 58N 85 40W
Gran Sasso d'Italia Italy 96 42 27N 13 42 E
Grand Teton USA 142 43 54N 111 50W
Grangeville USA 142 45 56N 116 7W
Grantham UK 89 52 55N 0 38W
Grants Pass USA 142 42 26N 123 19W
Granville USA 145 43 24N 73 16W
Grasse France 94 43 38N 6 56 E
Graulhet France 94 43 45N 1 59 E
Grayling USA 144 44 40N 84 43W
Graz Austria 92 47 4N 15 27 E
Great Abaco I. Bahamas 147 26 25N 77 10W
Great Australian Bight Australia 128 33 30S 130 0 E
Great Barrier I. New Zealand 132 36 11S 175 25 E
Great Barrier Reef Australia 128 18 0S 146 50 E
Great Bear L. Canada 140 65 30N 120 0W
Great Bear R. Canada 140 65 0N 124 0W
Great Bend USA 142 38 22N 98 46W
Great Britain Europe 82 54 0N 2 15W
Great Camanoe Br. Virgin Is. 147 18 30N 64 35W
Great Dividing Ra. Australia 128 23 0S 146 0 E
Great Exuma I. Bahamas 147 23 30N 75 50W
Great Falls USA 142 47 30N 111 17W
Great Inagua I. Bahamas 147 21 0N 73 20W
Great Karoo S. Africa 126 31 55S 21 0 E
Great Ouse, R. UK 89 52 48N 0 21 E
Great Pedro Bluff, C. Jamaica 146 17 51N 77 44W
Great Salt L. USA 142 41 15N 112 40W
Great Salt Lake Desert USA 142 40 50N 113 30W
Great Sandy Desert Australia 128 21 0S 124 0 E
Great Slave L. Canada 140 61 23N 115 38W
Great Snow Mt. Canada 140 57 26N 124 0W
Great Victoria Desert Australia 128 29 30S 126 30 E
Great Wall China 109 38 30N 109 30 E
Great Yarmouth UK 89 52 37N 1 44 E
Greater Antilles W. Indies 147 17 40N 74 0W
Greater Sunda Is. Indonesia 112 7 0S 112 0 E
GREECE Europe 97 40 0N 23 0 E
Green Bay USA 144 44 31N 88 0W
Green R. KY, USA 144 37 54N 87 30W
Green R. UT, USA 142 38 11N 109 53W
Green River USA 142 41 32N 109 28W
Greencastle USA 144 39 38N 86 52W
Greenfield IN, USA 144 39 47N 85 46W
Greenfield MA, USA 145 42 35N 72 36W
GREENLAND North America 135 66 0N 45 0W
Greenland Sea Arctic 80 73 0N 10 0W
Greenock UK 89 55 57N 4 46W
Greensboro USA 143 36 4N 79 48W
Greensburg IN, USA 144 39 20N 85 29W
Greensburg PA, USA 144 40 18N 79 33W
Greenville AL, USA 143 31 50N 86 38W
Greenville MN, USA 145 45 28N 69 35W
Greenville MI, USA 143 33 24N 91 4W
Greenville OH, USA 144 40 6N 84 38W
Greenville SC, USA 143 34 51N 82 24W
Greenwood USA 143 33 31N 90 11W
Gremikha Russia 98 67 59N 39 47 E
GRENADA West Indies 149 12 10N 61 40W
Grenoble France 94 45 12N 5 42 E
Gretna UK 89 55 0N 3 3W
Grey, R. New Zealand 132 42 27S 171 12 E
Grey Ra. Australia 128 27 0S 143 30 E
Greymouth N. Zealand 129 42 29S 171 13 E
Greytown N. Zealand 132 41 5S 175 29 E
Griffith Australia 128 34 18S 146 2 E
Grimsby UK 89 53 34N 0 5W
Gris-Nez, C. France 94 50 52N 1 35 E
Groningen Neths. 90 53 15N 6 35 E
Groote Eylandt Australia 128 14 0S 136 40 E
Gros Islet St Lucia 147 14 5N 60 58W
Gros Piton St Lucia 147 13 49N 61 5W
Gros Piton Pt. St Lucia 147 13 49N 61 5W
Grossglockner Austria 82 47 5N 12 40 E
Groznyy Russia 99 43 20N 45 45 E
Grudziadz Poland 93 53 30N 18 47 E
Guadalajara Mexico 146 20 40N 103 20W
Guadalajara Spain 95 40 37N 3 12W
Guadalcanal Solomon Islands 129 9 32S 160 12 E
Guadalete, R. Spain 95 36 35N 6 13W
Guadalquivir, R. Spain 95 36 47N 6 22W
Guadarrama, Sierra de Spain 95 41 0N 4 0W
Guadiana, R. Portugal 95 37 14N 7 22W
Guadix Spain 95 37 18N 3 11W
Guajará Mirim Brazil 149 10 50S 65 20W
Guajira, Pen. de la, Colombia 148 12 0N 72 0W
Guam Pacific Ocean 133 13 27N 144 45 E
Guamúchil Mexico 146 25 25N 108 3W
Guana I. Br. Virgin Is. 147 18 30N 64 30W
Guanajuato Mexico 146 21 0N 101 20W
Guane Cuba 147 22 10N 84 7W
Guangdong China 109 23 0N 113 0 E
Guangxi Zhuang China 109 24 0N 109 0 E
Guangzhou China 101 23 5N 113 10 E
Guanica Puerto Rico 147 17 59N 66 55W
Guantánamo Cuba 147 20 10N 75 14W
Guaporé, R. Brazil 148 11 55S 65 4W
Guarapuava Brazil 149 25 20S 51 30W
Guarulhos Brazil 149 23 29S 46 33W
GUATEMALA Central America 135 15 40N 90 30W
Guatemala City Guatemala 146 14 40N 90 22W
Guatemala Trench Pacific Ocean 146 14 40N 90 22W
Guaviare, R. Colombia 148 4 3N 67 44W
Guayama Puerto Rico 147 17 59N 66 7W
Guayaquil Ecuador 149 2 15S 79 52W
Guayaquil, G. de Ecuador 148 3 10S 81 0W
Guaymas Mexico 146 27 59N 110 54W
Gubkin Russia 99 51 17N 37 32 E
Guadalajara Spain 95 40 37N 3 12W
Gudur India 114 14 9N 79 54 E
Guéret France 94 46 11N 1 51 E
Guernsey UK 89 49 26N 2 35W
Guildford UK 89 51 14N 0 34W
Guilin China 109 25 18N 110 15 E
Guinea Africa 119 8 0N 8 0 E
GUINEA West Africa 118 10 20N 11 30W
Guinea, Gulf of Atlantic Ocean 118 3 0N 2 30 E
GUINEA-BISSAU Africa 119 12 0N 15 0W
Guingamp France 94 48 34N 3 10W
Guizhou China 108 27 0N 107 0 E
Guiyang China 108 26 32N 106 40 E
Gujarat India 114 23 20N 71 0 E
Gujranwala Pakistan 114 32 10N 74 12 E
Gujrat Pakistan 114 32 40N 74 2 E
Gulbarga India 114 17 20N 76 50 E
Gulf, The Asia 117 27 0N 50 0 E
Gulfport USA 143 30 22N 89 6W
Guna India 114 24 40N 77 19 E
Gunnison R. USA 142 39 4N 108 35W
Guntakal India 114 15 11N 77 25 E
Gurdespur India 114 32 3N 75 27 E
Gurguéa, R. Brazil 148 6 50S 43 24W
Gurkha Nepal 115 28 5N 84 40 E
Gürün Turkey 99 38 43N 37 15 E
Gurupi, R. Brazil 148 1 13S 46 6W
Gusau Nigeria 124 12 12N 6 40 E
Gushgy Turkmenistan 117 35 20N 62 18 E
Guwahati India 115 26 10N 91 45 E
GUYANA South America 149 5 0N 59 0W
Guyenne France 94 44 30N 0 40 E
Gwadar Pakistan 114 25 10N 62 18 E
Gwalior India 114 26 12N 78 10 E
Gwanda Zimbabwe 126 20 55S 29 0 E
Gweru Zimbabwe 126 19 28S 29 45 E
Gyaring Hu, L. China 115 34 50N 97 40 E
Gympie Australia 128 26 11S 152 38 E
Györ Hungary 93 47 41N 17 40 E
Gyzylarbat Turkmenistan 117 39 4N 56 23 E

H

Ha'apai Group Tonga 129 19 47S 174 27W
Haarlem Neths. 90 52 23N 4 39 E
Haast New Zealand 132 43 51S 169 1 E
Haast Pass New Zealand 132 44 6S 169 21 E
Haast, R. New Zealand 132 43 50S 169 2 E
Hachinohe Japan 110 40 30N 141 29 E
Hadong South Korea 110 35 5N 127 44 E
Haeju North Korea 109 38 3N 125 45 E
Haenam South Korea 110 34 34N 126 15 E
Hafizabad Pakistan 114 32 5N 73 40 E
Hagang, R. S. Korea 110 37 50N 126 30 E
Hagen Germany 92 51 21N 7 27 E
Hagerstown USA 145 39 39N 77 43W
Hague, C. de la France 94 49 44N 1 56W
Haifa Israel 116 32 46N 35 0 E
Haikou China 109 20 1N 110 16 E
Ha'il Saudi Arabia 116 27 28N 41 45 E
Hailar China 109 49 10N 119 38 E
Hailey USA 142 43 31N 114 19W
Hainan China 109 19 0N 109 30 E
Haines Junction Canada 140 60 45N 137 30W
Haiphong Vietnam 108 20 47N 106 41 E
HAITI West Indies 135 19 0N 72 30W
Hakodate Japan 110 41 45N 140 44 E
Halberstadt Germany 92 51 54N 11 3 E
Halden Norway 91 59 9N 11 23 E
Haldia India 115 22 5N 88 3 E
Haldwani India 114 29 31N 79 30 E
Halifax UK 89 53 43N 1 52W
Halifax Canada 141 44 38N 63 35W
Halle Germany 92 51 30N 11 56 E
Hallim South Korea 110 33 24N 126 15 E
Hall Pen. Canada 141 63 30N 66 0W
Halls Creek Australia 128 18 16S 127 38 E
Halmahera Indonesia 113 0 40N 128 0 E
Halmstad Sweden 91 56 41N 12 52 E
Hamadan Iran 116 34 52N 48 32 E
Hamah Syria 116 35 5N 36 40 E
Hamamatsu Japan 111 34 45N 137 45 E
Hamar Norway 91 60 48N 11 7 E
Hambantota Sri Lanka 114 6 10N 81 10 E
Hamburg Germany 91 53 33N 9 59 E
Hämeenlinna Finland 91 61 0N 24 28 E
Hameln Germany 92 52 6N 9 21 E
Hami China 108 42 55N 93 25 E
Hamilton New Zealand 129 37 47S 175 19 E
Hamilton UK 89 55 46N 4 2W
Hamilton USA 144 39 24N 84 34W
Hamirpur India 114 25 85N 80 12 E
Hamm Germany 92 51 40N 7 50 E
Hammerfest Norway 91 70 39N 23 41 E
Hammond USA 144 41 38N 87 30W
Hammonton USA 145 39 39N 74 48W
Hampden New Zealand 132 45 18S 170 50 E
Hamyang South Korea 110 35 32N 127 42 E
Hancock USA 144 47 8N 88 35W
Handan China 109 36 35N 114 28 E
Hanford USA 142 36 20N 119 39W
Hangzhou China 109 30 18N 120 11 E
Hangzhou Wan China 109 30 15N 120 45 E
Hanmer New Zealand 132 42 32S 172 50 E
Hanna Canada 140 51 40N 111 54W
Hannibal USA 143 39 42N 91 22W
Hannover Germany 92 52 22N 9 46 E
Hanoi Vietnam 108 21 5N 105 55 E
Hanover USA 144 39 48N 76 59W
Hanover I. Chile 148 51 0S 74 50W
Hanumangarh India 114 29 35N 74 21 E
Hanzhong China 108 33 10N 107 1 E
Haora India 115 22 37N 88 20 E
Haparanda Sweden 91 65 52N 24 8 E
Happy Valley-Goose Bay Canada 141 53 15N 60 20W
Haquenau France 94 48 49N 7 47 E
Har Hu, L. China 108 38 20N 97 38 E
Har Us Nuur, L. Mongolia 108 48 0N 92 0 E
Harad Saudi Arabia 116 24 22N 49 0 E
Harare Zimbabwe 126 17 43S 31 2 E
Harbin China 109 45 48N 126 40 E
Harbor Beach USA 144 43 51N 82 39W
Hardangerfjorden Norway 91 60 5N 6 0 E
Hardoi India 114 27 23N 80 10 E
Hardy Pt. St Lucia 147 14 6N 60 56W
Hargeisa Somalia 127 9 30N 44 2 E
Haridwar India 114 29 58N 78 9 E
Haringhata, R. India 115 22 0N 89 58 E
Harirud, R. Asia 117 37 24N 60 38 E
Harlingen USA 142 26 12N 97 42W
Harlingen Neths. 90 53 11N 5 25 E
Harney, L. USA 142 43 14N 119 8W
Härnösand Sweden 91 62 38N 17 55 E
Harricana, R. Canada 141 50 56N 79 32W
Harris Mts. N. Zealand 132 44 49S 168 49 E
Harrisburg USA 144 40 16N 76 53W
Harrison, C. Canada 141 54 55N 57 55W
Harrisonburg USA 144 38 27N 78 52W
Harrisville USA 144 44 39N 83 17W
Harrogate UK 89 54 0N 1 33W
Hart USA 144 43 42N 86 22W
Hartford CT, USA 145 41 46N 72 41W
Hartford KY, USA 144 37 27N 86 55W
Hartland Pt. UK 89 51 1N 4 32W
Hartlepool UK 89 54 42N 1 13W
Harvey USA 144 41 36N 87 50W
Harwich UK 89 51 56N 1 17 E
Haryana India 114 29 0N 76 10 E
Harz Germany 92 51 38N 10 44 E
Hasa Saudi Arabia 116 25 50N 49 0 E
Hassan India 114 13 1N 76 10 E
Hasselt Belgium 90 50 56N 5 21 E
Hastings UK 89 50 51N 0 35 E
Hastings New Zealand 132 39 39S 176 52 E
Hastings USA 142 40 35N 98 23W
Hatgal Mongolia 108 50 26N 100 9 E
Hathras India 114 27 36N 78 6 E
Hatia Bangladesh 115 22 30N 91 5 E
Hatteras, C. USA 143 35 14N 75 32W
Hattiesburg USA 143 31 20N 89 17W
Haugesund Norway 91 59 23N 5 13 E
Hauhungaroa Ra. New Zealand 132 38 42S 175 40 E
Hauraki Gulf N. Zealand 132 36 35S 175 5 E
Havana Cuba 147 23 8N 82 22W
Havasu, L. USA 142 34 18N 114 28W
Havel, R. Germany 92 52 50N 12 3 E
Havelock North New Zealand 132 41 17S 173 48 E
Havre USA 142 48 33N 109 41W
Havre-St-Pierre Canada 141 50 18N 63 33W
Hawaii USA 142 19 30N 156 30W
Hawaii I. Pacific Ocean 133 20 0N 155 0W
Hawaiian Ridge Pacific Ocean 133 24 0N 165 0W
Hawaiian Is. Pacific Ocean 132 20 30N 156 0W
Hawea Flat N. Zealand 132 44 40S 169 19 E
Hawea, L. New Zealand 132 44 28S 169 19 E
Hawera New Zealand 132 39 35S 174 19 E

166 INDEX
HAWICK–KANGIQSUALUJJUAQ

Hawick UK 89 55 26N 2 47W
Hawke B. New Zealand 132 39 25N 177 20 E
Hawke's Bay New Zealand 132 39 45S 176 35 E
Hawkesbury Canada 146 45 37N 74 37W
Hay, R. Canada 140 60 50N 116 26W
Hayes, R. Canada 140 57 3N 92 12W
Hays USA 142 38 53N 99 20W
Hazard USA 144 37 15N 83 12W
Hazaribag India 115 23 58N 85 26 E
Health, Pte. Canada 146 49 8N 61 40W
Hearst Canada 141 49 40N 83 41W
Heath Mts. N. Zealand 132 45 39S 167 9 E
Hebei China 109 39 0N 116 0 E
Hebrides UK 82 57 30N 7 0W
Hebrides, Sea of the UK 89 57 5N 7 0W
Hebron Canada 141 58 5N 62 30W
Hecate Strait Canada 140 53 10N 130 30W
Hechi China 108 24 40N 108 2 E
Hechuan China 108 30 2N 106 12 E
Heerlen Neths. 90 50 55N 5 58 E
Hefei China 109 31 52N 117 18 E
Hegang China 109 47 20N 130 19 E
Heidelberg Germany 92 49 24N 8 42 E
Heilbronn Germany 92 49 9N 9 13 E
Heilongjiang China 109 48 0N 126 0 E
Hekou China 108 22 30N 103 59 E
Helena USA 142 46 36N 112 2W
Helgoland Germany 92 54 10N 7 53 E
Helmand, R. Afghanistan 114 31 12N 61 34 E
Helmond Neths. 90 51 29N 5 41 E
Helmsdale UK 89 58 7N 3 39W
Helsingborg Sweden 91 56 3N 12 42 E
Helsinki Finland 91 60 15N 25 3 E
Hen & Chickens Is. New Zealand 132 35 58S 174 45 E
Henan China 109 34 0N 114 0 E
Henares, R. Spain 95 40 28N 3 22W
Henderson KY, USA 144 37 50N 87 35W
Henderson NV, USA 142 36 2N 114 59W
Hengelo Neths. 90 52 16N 6 48 E
Hengyang China 109 26 59N 112 22 E
Henlopen, C. USA 145 38 48N 75 6W
Henrietta Maria, C. Canada 141 55 9N 82 20W
Herat Afghanistan 114 34 20N 62 7 E
Hereford UK 89 52 4N 2 43W
Herekino New Zealand 132 35 18S 173 11 E
Herford Germany 92 52 7N 8 39 E
Hermosillo Mexico 146 29 10N 111 0W
Hernád, R. Hungary 93 47 56N 21 8 E
Herne Germany 90 51 32N 7 14 E
Hessen Germany 92 50 30N 9 0 E
Hexham UK 89 54 58N 2 4W
Hibbing USA 143 47 25N 92 56W
Hicks Bay New Zealand 132 37 34S 178 21 E
Hidalgo del Parral Mexico 146 26 58N 105 40W
Hierro Canary Is. 124 27 44N 18 0W
Higashiosaka Japan 111 34 40N 135 37 E
High Atlas South Africa 118 32 30N 5 0W
High Level Canada 140 58 31N 117 8W
High Prairie Canada 140 55 30N 116 30W
High River Canada 140 50 30N 113 50W
High Veld South Africa 118 27 0S 27 0 E
High Wycombe UK 89 51 37N 0 45W
Hiiumaa (Dagö) Estonia 98 58 50N 22 45 E
Hikurangi, Mt. New Zealand 132 37 55S 178 4 E
Hildesheim Germany 92 52 9N 9 56 E
Hillcrest Barbados 147 13 13N 59 32W
Hillsdale USA 144 41 56N 84 38W
Hilo USA 142 19 44N 155 5W
Hilversum Neths. 90 52 14N 5 10 E
Himachal Pradesh India 114 31 30N 77 0 E
Himalaya Asia 100 29 0N 84 0 E
Himatnagar India 114 23 42N 73 2 E
Himeji Japan 111 34 50N 134 40 E
Hindu Kush Asia 114 36 0N 71 0 E
Hinganghat India 114 20 34N 78 53 E
Hingoli India 114 19 41N 77 15 E
Hinton USA 144 37 40N 80 54W
Hirosaki Japan 110 40 34N 140 28 E
Hiroshima Japan 111 34 24N 132 30 E
Hisar India 114 29 12N 75 45 E
Hispaniola W. Indies 147 19 0N 71 0W
Hjälmaren Sweden 91 59 18N 15 40 E
Ho Chi Minh City Vietnam 101 10 58N 106 40 E
Hoare Bay Canada 141 65 17N 62 30W
Hobbs USA 142 32 42N 103 8W
Hobert Australia 128 42 50S 147 21 E
Hodgson Canada 140 51 13N 97 36W
Hódmezovásárhely Hungary 93 46 28N 20 22 E
Hoengsong S. Korea 110 37 29N 127 59 E
Hoggar Algeria 124 23 0N 6 30 E
Hohe Rhön Germany 92 50 24N 9 58 E
Hohhot China 109 40 52N 111 40 E
Hokianga Harbour New Zealand 132 35 31S 173 22 E
Hokkaido Japan 110 43 30N 143 0 E
Holetown Barbados 147 13 11N 59 38W
Holguín Cuba 147 20 50N 76 20W
Holland USA 144 42 47N 86 7W
Holyhead UK 89 53 18N 4 38W
Homer USA 142 59 39N 151 33W
Homs Syria 116 34 40N 36 45 E
HONDURAS Central America 135 14 40N 86 30W
Honduras, G. de Caribbean 146 16 50N 87 0W
Honey, L. USA 142 40 15N 120 19W
Hong Kong China 109 22 11N 114 14 E
Hongchon South Korea 110 37 44N 127 53 E
Hongjiang China 109 27 7N 109 59 E
Hongshui He, R. China 109 23 48N 109 30 E
Hongsong South Korea 110 36 37N 126 38 E
Hongze Hu, L. China 109 33 15N 118 35 E
Honiara Solomon Is. 129 9 27S 159 57 E
Honolulu USA 142 21 19N 157 52W
Honshu Japan 111 36 0N 138 0 E
Hood, Mt. USA 142 45 23N 121 42W
Hoogeveen Neths. 90 52 44N 6 28 E
Hooper Bay USA 142 61 32N 166 6W
Hoopeston USA 144 40 28N 87 40W
Hoorn Neths. 90 52 38N 5 4 E
Hoover Dam USA 142 36 1N 114 44W
Hope USA 143 33 40N 93 36W
Hopedale Canada 141 55 28N 60 13W
Hopetown South Africa 126 29 34S 24 3 E
Hopkinsville USA 143 36 52N 87 29W
Horlivka Ukraine 99 48 19N 38 5 E
Hormozgan Iran 117 27 30N 56 0 E
Hormuz, Str. of The Gulf 117 26 30N 56 30 E
Horn Is. Wallis & Futana 129 14 16S 178 6W
Horna-van, L. Sweden 91 66 15N 17 30 E
Hornell USA 144 42 20N 77 40W
Hornos, C. de Chile 148 55 50S 67 30W
Horqin Youyi Qianqi China 109 46 5N 122 3 E
Horsham Australia 128 36 44S 142 13 E
Horton, R. Canada 140 69 56N 126 52W
Hoshangabad India 114 22 46N 77 45 E
Hoshiarpur India 114 31 32N 75 57 E
Hospet India 114 15 16N 76 26 E
Hoste I. Chile 148 55 0S 69 0W
Hot Springs AR, USA 143 34 31N 93 3W
Hot Springs SD, USA 142 43 26N 103 29W
Hotan China 108 37 25N 79 55 E
Houghton USA 144 47 7N 88 34W
Houghton, L. USA 144 44 21N 84 44W
Houhora New Zealand 132 34 49S 173 9 E
Houlton USA 143 46 8N 67 51W
Houma USA 143 29 36N 90 43W
Houston USA 143 29 46N 95 22W
Hovd Mongolia 108 48 2N 91 37 E
Hövsgöl Nuur, L. Mongolia 108 51 0N 100 30 E
Howe, C. Australia 128 37 30S 150 0 E
Howell USA 144 42 36N 83 56W
Howick New Zealand 132 36 54S 174 48 E
Howland I. Pacific Ocean 133 0 48N 176 38W
Hoy UK 89 58 50N 3 15W
Høyanger Norway 91 61 13N 6 4 E
Hradec Králové Czech Rep. 92 50 15N 15 50 E
Hrodna Belarus 93 53 42N 23 52 E
Hron, R. Slovakia 93 47 49N 18 45 E
Hsinchu Taiwan 109 24 48N 120 58 E
Huacho Peru 149 11 10S 77 35W
Huai He, R. China 109 33 0N 118 30 E
Huainan China 109 32 38N 116 58 E
Huallaga, R. Peru 148 5 15S 75 30W
Huambo Angola 126 12 42S 15 54 E
Huancayo Peru 149 12 5S 75 12W
Huangshan China 109 29 42N 118 25 E
Huangshi China 109 30 10N 115 3 E
Huánuco Peru 149 9 55S 76 15W
Huaraz Peru 149 9 30S 77 32W
Huascaran Peru 148 9 8S 77 36W
Huasco Chile 149 28 30S 71 15W
Huatabampo Mexico 146 26 50N 109 50W
Hubei China 109 31 0N 112 0 E
Hubli India 114 15 20N 75 12 E
Huddersfield UK 89 53 39N 1 47W
Hudiksvall Sweden 91 61 43N 17 10 E
Hudson Bay Canada 141 60 0N 86 0W
Hudson R. USA 143 40 42N 74 2W
Hudson Strait Canada 141 62 0N 70 0W
Huelva Spain 95 37 18N 6 57W
Huesca Spain 95 42 8N 0 25W
Hughenden Australia 128 20 52S 144 10 E
Hugli R. India 115 21 56N 88 4 E
Huiarau Ra. N. Zealand 132 38 45S 176 55 E
Huila Colombia 148 3 0N 76 0W
Huize China 108 26 24N 103 15 E
Hull Canada 141 45 25N 75 44W
Humacoa Puerto Rico 147 18 9N 65 50W
Humaitá Brazil 149 7 35S 63 1W
Humber UK 89 53 42N 0 27W
Humboldt Canada 140 52 15N 105 9W
Humboldt, R. USA 142 39 59N 118 36W
Humphreys Pk. USA 142 35 21N 111 41W
Hunan China 109 27 30N 112 0 E
HUNGARY Europe 93 47 20N 19 20 E
Hungnam North Korea 109 39 49N 127 45 E
Hunsrück Germany 92 49 56N 7 27 E
Hunter Hills, The New Zealand 132 44 26S 170 46 E
Hunter, R. New Zealand 132 44 21S 169 27 E
Huntington IN, USA 144 40 53N 85 30W
Huntington WV, USA 144 38 25N 82 27W
Huntly UK 89 57 27N 2 47W
Huntly New Zealand 132 37 34S 175 11 E
Huntsville Canada 141 45 20N 79 14W
Huntsville IN, USA 143 34 44N 86 35W
Huntsville TX, USA 143 30 43N 95 33W
Huron USA 142 44 22N 98 13W
Huron, L. USA 144 44 30N 82 40W
Hurunui, R. N. Zealand 132 42 54S 173 18 E
Húsavík Iceland 91 66 3N 17 21W
Hutchinson USA 142 38 5N 97 56W
Hwachon-chosuji South Korea 110 38 5N 127 50 E
Hwange Zimbabwe 126 18 18S 26 30 E
Hwang-ho, R. China 109 37 55N 118 50 E
Hyargas Nuur, L. Mongolia 108 49 0N 93 0 E
Hyderabad India 114 17 22N 78 29 E
Hyderabad Pakistan 114 25 23N 68 24 E
Hyères France 94 43 8N 6 9 E
Hyères, Is. d' France 94 43 0N 6 20 E
Hyndman Pk. USA 142 43 45N 114 8W

I

Ialomita, R. Romania 93 44 42N 27 51 E
Iasi Romania 93 47 10N 27 40 E
Ibague Colombia 149 4 20N 75 20W
Ibarra Ecuador 149 0 21N 78 7W
Iberian Pen. Europe 82 40 0N 5 0W
Ibiza Spain 82 38 54N 1 26 E
Ica Peru 149 14 0S 75 48W
Içá, R. Brazil 148 2 55S 67 58W
Iceland Europe 91 64 45N 19 0W
Ichihara Japan 111 35 28N 140 5 E
Ichinomiya Japan 111 35 18N 136 48 E
Ich'on South Korea 110 37 17N 127 27 E
Idaho USA 142 45 0N 115 0W
Idaho Falls USA 142 43 30N 112 2W
Idar-Oberstein Germany 92 49 43N 7 16 E
Idlib Syria 116 35 55N 36 36 E
Ieper Belgium 90 50 51N 2 53 E
Ife Nigeria 124 7 30N 4 31 E
Iglésias Italy 96 39 19N 8 32 E
Igloolik Canada 141 69 20N 81 49W
Iguaçu, R. Brazil 148 25 36S 54 36W
Iguala Mexico 146 18 20N 99 40W
Iguatu Brazil 149 6 20S 39 18W
Iisalmi Finland 91 63 32N 27 10 E
Ijsselmeer Neths. 90 52 45N 5 20 E
Ikeda Japan 111 34 1N 133 48 E
Ilagan Philippines 113 17 7N 121 53 E
Ilam Iran 116 33 36N 46 36 E
Ilebo DRC 126 4 17S 20 55 E
Île-de-France France 94 49 0N 2 20 E
Ili, R. Kazakhstan 106 45 53N 77 10 E
Iliamna, L. USA 142 59 30N 155 0W
Iligan Philippines 113 8 12N 124 13 E
Illapel Chile 149 32 0S 71 10W
Iller, R. Germany 92 48 23N 9 58 E
Illimani Pk. Bolivia 148 16 30S 67 50W
Illinois USA 143 40 15N 89 30W
Illinois R. USA 143 38 58N 90 28W
Ilmen, L. Russia 98 58 15N 31 10 E
Iloilo Philippines 113 10 45N 122 33 E
Ilorin Nigeria 124 8 30N 4 35 E
Imabari Japan 111 34 4N 133 0 E
Imandra, L. Russia 98 67 30N 33 0 E
Imperatriz Brazil 149 5 30S 47 29W
Imphal India 115 24 44N 93 58 E
In Salah Algeria 124 27 10N 2 32 E
Inari Finland 91 68 54N 27 5 E
Inarijärvi, L. Finland 91 69 0N 28 0 E
Ince Burun Turkey 99 42 7N 34 56 E
Inch'on South Korea 109 37 27N 126 40 E
Incomáti, R. Mozambique 126 25 46S 32 43 E
Indalsälven, R. Sweden 91 62 36N 17 30 E
INDIA Asia 114 20 0N 78 0 E
Indian Ocean 100 5 0S 75 0 E
Indiana USA 144 40 0N 86 0W
Indianapolis USA 144 39 46N 86 9W
Indigirka, R. Russia 107 70 48N 148 54 E
Indira Gandhi Canal India 114 28 0N 72 0 E
INDONESIA Asia 112 5 0S 115 0 E
Indore India 114 22 42N 75 53 E
Indre, R. France 94 47 16N 0 11 E
Indus, R. India 114 33 0N 79 0 E
Indus, R. Pakistan 114 24 20N 67 47 E
Inebolu Turkey 99 41 55N 33 40 E
Ingolstadt Germany 92 48 46N 11 26 E
Ingraj Bazar India 115 24 58N 88 10 E
Ingushetia Russia 99 43 20N 44 50 E
Inland Sea Japan 111 34 20N 133 30 E
Inn, R. Austria 92 48 35N 13 28 E
Inner Hebrides UK 89 57 0N 6 30W
Inner Mongolia China 109 42 0N 112 0 E
Innsbruck Austria 92 47 16N 11 23 E
Inowroclaw Poland 93 52 50N 18 12 E
Insein Myanmar 115 16 50N 96 5 E
Inta Russia 98 66 5N 60 8 E
Interlaken Switzerland 92 46 14N 7 50 E
Inukjuak Canada 141 58 25N 78 15W
Inuvik Canada 140 68 16N 133 40W
Invercargill N. Zealand 129 46 24S 168 24 E
Invergordon UK 89 57 41N 4 10W
Inverness UK 89 57 29N 4 13W
Inverurie UK 89 57 17N 2 23W
Ionia USA 144 42 59N 85 4W
Ionian Is. Greece 97 38 40N 20 0 E
Ionian Sea Medit. Sea 97 37 30N 17 30 E
Iowa USA 143 42 18N 93 30W
Ipoh Malaysia 112 4 35N 101 5 E
Ipswich Australia 128 27 35S 152 40 E
Ipswich UK 89 52 4N 1 10 E
Iqaluit Canada 141 63 44N 68 31W
Iquique Chile 149 20 19S 70 5W
Iquitos Peru 149 3 45S 73 10W
Iráklion Greece 97 35 20N 25 12 E
IRAN Asia 117 33 0N 53 0 E
Irapuato Mexico 146 20 40N 101 30W
IRAQ Asia 116 33 0N 44 0 E
Irbil Iraq 116 36 15N 44 5 E
IRELAND Europe 89 53 50N 7 52W
Iri South Korea 110 35 59N 127 0 E
Iringa Tanzania 126 7 48S 35 43 E
Irish Sea UK 89 53 38N 4 48W
Irkutsk Russia 107 52 18N 104 20 E
Iron Mountain USA 144 45 49N 88 4W
Ironton USA 144 38 32N 82 41W
Ironwood USA 143 46 27N 90 9W
Irrawaddy, R. Myanmar 115 15 50N 95 6 E
Irtysh, R. Russia 106 61 4N 68 52 E
Isabela Puerto Rico 147 18 30N 67 2W
Ísafjördur Iceland 91 66 5N 23 9W
Isar, R. Germany 92 48 48N 12 57 E
Isère, R. France 94 44 59N 4 51 E
Ishinomaki Japan 110 38 32N 141 20 E
Ishpeming USA 144 46 29N 87 40W
Iskenderun Turkey 99 36 32N 36 10 E
Islamabad Pakistan 114 33 40N 73 10 E
Island, L. Canada 140 53 47N 94 25W
Island Pond USA 145 44 49N 71 53W
Islay UK 89 55 46N 6 10W
Isles of Scilly UK 89 49 56N 6 22W
Ismail Samani Pk. Tajikistan 106 39 0N 72 2 E
Ismâ'ilîya Egypt 125 30 37N 32 18 E
Isparta Turkey 99 37 47N 30 30 E
ISRAEL Asia 116 32 0N 34 50 E
Istanbul Turkey 97 41 0N 29 0 E
Istra Croatia 96 45 10N 14 0 E
Istres France 94 43 31N 4 59 E
Itabira Brazil 149 19 37S 43 13W
Itabuna Brazil 149 14 48S 39 16W
Itacoatiara Brazil 149 3 8S 58 25W
Itajaí Brazil 149 27 50S 48 39W
ITALY Europe 96 42 0N 13 0 E
Itanagar India 115 27 8N 93 40 E
Itapicuru, R. Brazil 148 11 47S 37 32W
Ithaca USA 144 42 27N 76 30W
Ivanava Belarus 93 52 7N 25 29 E
Ivano-Frankivsk Ukraine 93 48 40N 24 40 E
Ivanovo Russia 98 57 5N 41 0 E
IVORY COAST Africa 118 7 30N 5 0W
Ivujivik Canada 141 62 24N 77 55W
Iwaki Japan 111 37 3N 140 55 E
Iwakuni Japan 111 34 15N 132 8 E
Iwo Nigeria 124 7 39N 4 9 E
Iyssyk Kul Kyrgyzstan 100 42 25N 77 15 E
Izhevsk Russia 98 56 51N 53 14 E
Izmayil Ukraine 99 45 22N 28 46 E
Izmir (Smyrna) Turkey 99 38 25N 27 8 E
Iznik Gölü Turkey 99 40 27N 29 30 E
Izumi-Sano Japan 111 34 23N 135 18 E

J

Jabalpur India 114 23 9N 79 58 E
Jaboatao Brazil 149 8 7S 35 1W
Jackson Barbados 147 13 7N 59 36W
Jackson Bay N. Zealand 132 43 58S 168 42 E
Jackson, C. N. Zealand 132 40 59S 174 20 E
Jackson KY, USA 144 37 33N 83 23W
Jackson MI, USA 144 42 15N 84 24W
Jackson MS, USA 143 32 18N 90 12W
Jackson TN, USA 143 35 37N 88 49W
Jacksonville USA 144 30 20N 81 39W
Jacmel Haiti 147 18 14N 72 32W
Jacobabad Pakistan 114 28 20N 68 29 E
Jaén Spain 95 37 44N 3 43W
Jaffna Sri Lanka 114 9 45N 80 2 E
Jagdalpur India 115 19 05N 82 04 E
Jahrom Iran 117 28 30N 53 31 E
Jaipur India 114 27 0N 75 50 E
Jaisalmer India 114 26 55N 70 57 E
Jakarta Indonesia 112 6 9S 106 49 E
Jalalabad Afghanistan 114 34 30N 70 29 E
Jalgaon India 114 21 0N 75 42 E
Jalna India 114 19 48N 75 38 E
Jalor India 114 25 22N 72 58 E
Jalpaiguri India 115 26 32N 88 46 E
Jaluit I. Marshall Is. 133 6 0N 169 30 E
JAMAICA West Indies 135 18 10N 77 30W
Jamalpur Bangladesh 115 24 52N 89 56 E
Jambi Indonesia 112 1 38S 103 30 E
James Bay Canada 141 54 0N 80 0W
James R. USA 143 42 52N 97 18W
Jamestown ND, USA 142 46 54N 98 42W
Jamestown NY, USA 144 42 6N 79 14W
Jammu India 114 32 43N 74 54 E
Jammu & Kashmir India 114 34 25N 77 0 E
Jamnagar India 114 22 30N 70 6 E
Jamshedpur India 115 22 44N 86 12 E
Jane Pk. New Zealand 132 45 15S 168 20 E
Janesville USA 143 42 41N 89 1W
Januária Brazil 149 15 25S 44 25W
JAPAN Asia 111 36 0N 136 0 E
Japan Trench Pacific Ocean 100 32 0N 142 0 E
Japan, Sea of Asia 110 40 0N 135 0 E
Jarvis I. Pacific Ocean 133 0 15S 160 5W
Jask Iran 117 25 38N 57 45 E
Jasper Canada 140 52 55N 118 5W
Jaunpur India 115 25 46N 82 44 E
JAVA Indonesia 112 7 0S 110 0 E
Java Sea Indonesia 112 4 35S 107 15 E
Java Trench Indian Ocean 112 9 0S 105 0 E
Jaya, Puncak Indonesia 113 3 57S 137 17 E
Jaynagar India 115 26 35N 86 9 E
Jedburgh UK 89 55 29N 2 33W
Jedda Saudi Arabia 116 21 29N 39 10 E
Jeffersonville USA 144 38 17N 85 44W
Jelenia Góra Poland 92 50 50N 15 45 E
Jelgava Latvia 98 56 41N 23 49 E
Jena Germany 92 50 54N 11 35 E
Jequie Brazil 149 13 51S 40 5W
Jérémie Haiti 147 18 40N 74 10W
Jerez de la Frontera Spain 95 36 41N 6 7W
Jersey UK 89 49 11N 2 7W
Jersey City USA 145 40 44N 74 4W
Jerusalem Israel 116 31 47N 35 10 E
Jessore Bangladesh 115 23 10N 89 10 E
Jhang Maghiana Pakistan 114 31 15N 72 22 E
Jhansi India 114 25 30N 78 36 E
Jharkhand India 115 24 0N 85 50 E
Jhelum Pakistan 114 33 0N 73 45 E
Jhelum, R. Pakistan 114 31 20N 72 10 E
Jiamusi China 109 46 40N 130 26 E
Ji'an China 109 27 6N 114 59 E
Jiangmen China 109 22 32N 113 0 E
Jiangsu China 109 33 0N 120 0 E
Jiangxi China 109 27 6N 114 59 E
Jiaxing China 109 30 49N 120 45 E
Jihlava, R. Czech Rep. 92 48 55N 16 36 E
Jilin China 109 44 0N 127 0 E
Jilin City China 109 43 44N 126 30 E
Jiménez Mexico 146 27 10N 104 54W
Jinan China 109 36 38N 117 1 E
Jinchang China 108 38 30N 102 10 E
Jingdezhen China 109 29 20N 117 11 E
Jinggu China 108 23 35N 100 41 E
Jinhua China 109 29 8N 119 38 E
Jining Shandong, China 109 35 22N 116 34 E
Jinzhou China 109 41 5N 121 3 E
Jiujiang China 109 29 42N 115 58 E
Jixi China 109 45 20N 130 50 E
Jizzakh Uzbekistan 117 40 6N 67 50 E
Joao Pessoa Brazil 149 7 10S 34 52W
Jodhpur India 114 26 23N 73 8 E
Johannesburg S. Africa 126 26 10S 28 2 E
John Day R. USA 142 45 44N 120 39W
John O'Groats UK 89 58 38N 3 4W
Johnson City TN, USA 143 36 19N 82 21W
Johnston I. Pacific Ocean 133 17 10N 169 8W
Johnstown USA 144 40 20N 78 55W
Johor Baharu Malaysia 112 1 28N 103 46 E
Joliet USA 144 41 32N 88 5W
Joliette Canada 141 46 3N 73 24W
Jolo Philippines 113 6 0N 121 0 E
Jonesboro USA 143 35 50N 90 42W
Jönköping Sweden 91 57 45N 14 8 E
Jonquière Canada 141 48 27N 71 14W
Joplin USA 143 37 6N 94 31W
JORDAN Asia 116 31 0N 36 0 E
Jordan, R. Asia 116 31 48N 35 32 E
Jorhat India 115 26 46N 94 16 E
Jos Nigeria 124 9 53N 8 51 E
Jost Van Dyke Br. Virgin Is. 147 18 29N 64 47W
Jotunheimen Norway 91 61 35N 8 25 E
Jowzjan Afghanistan 117 36 10N 66 0 E
Juan De Fuca Str. Canada 140 48 15N 124 0W
Juàzeiro Do Norte Brazil 149 7 10S 39 18W
Juba Sudan 125 4 50N 31 35 E
Juchitán Mexico 146 16 27N 95 5W
Juiz De Fora Brazil 149 21 43S 43 19W
Juliaca Peru 149 15 25S 70 10W
Julianatop Suriname 148 3 40N 56 30W
Jullundur India 114 31 20N 75 40 E
Junagadh India 114 21 30N 70 30 E
Juneau USA 142 58 18N 134 25W
Junin Argentina 149 34 33S 60 57W
Jura UK 89 56 0N 5 50W
Jura Europe 92 46 40N 6 5 E
Jutland Denmark 91 56 25N 9 30 E
Juventud, I. de la Cuba 147 21 40N 82 40W
Jyväskylä Finland 91 62 14N 25 50 E

K

K2 Pakistan 114 35 58N 76 32 E
Kabardino-Balkaria Russia 99 43 30N 43 30 E
Kabul Afghanistan 114 34 28N 69 11 E
Kabwe Zambia 126 14 30S 28 29 E
Kachchh, Gulf of India 114 22 50N 69 15 E
Kachin Myanmar 115 26 0N 97 30 E
Kaçkar Turkey 99 40 45N 41 10 E
Kadoma Zimbabwe 126 18 20S 29 52 E
Kaeo New Zealand 132 35 6S 173 49 E
Kaesong North Korea 109 37 58N 126 35 E
Kafue, R. Zambia 126 15 30S 29 0 E
Kagoshima Japan 111 31 35N 130 33 E
Kahoolawe USA 142 20 33N 156 37W
Kahramanmaras Turkey 99 37 37N 36 53 E
Kahurangi Pt. New Zealand 132 40 50S 172 10 E
Kaieteur Falls Brazil 148 5 1N 59 10W
Kaifeng China 109 34 48N 114 21 E
Kaikoura New Zealand 132 42 25S 173 43 E
Kaikoura Pen. New Zealand 132 42 25S 173 43 E
Kailua Kona USA 142 19 39N 155 59W
Kainji Res. Nigeria 124 10 1N 4 40 E
Kaipara Harbour New Zealand 132 36 25S 174 14 E
Kairouan Tunisia 125 35 45N 10 5 E
Kaiserslautern Germany 92 49 26N 7 45 E
Kaitaia New Zealand 129 35 8S 173 17 E
Kaitangata N. Zealand 132 46 17S 169 51 E
Kaitania New Zealand 132 35 8S 173 17 E
Kajaani Finland 91 64 17N 27 46 E
Kajabbi Australia 128 20 0S 140 1 E
Kakamega Kenya 126 0 20N 34 46 E
Kakanui Mts. New Zealand 132 45 10S 170 30 E
Kakinada India 115 16 57N 82 11 E
Kalaallit Nunaat (Greenland) North America 80 66 0N 45 0W
Kalahari Africa 126 24 0S 21 30 E
Kalamazoo USA 143 42 17N 85 35W
Kalamazoo, R. USA 144 42 40N 86 10W
Kalemie DRC 126 5 55S 29 9 E
Kalgoorlie Baulder Australia 128 30 40S 121 22 E
Kalimantan Indonesia 112 0 0 114 0 E
Kaliningrad Russia 98 54 42N 20 32 E
Kalispell USA 142 48 12N 114 19W
Kalisz Poland 93 51 45N 18 8 E
Kalkaska USA 144 44 44N 85 11W
Kalmar Sweden 91 56 40N 16 20 E
Kalmykia Russia 99 46 5N 46 1 E
Kaluga Russia 98 54 35N 36 10 E
Kalutara Sri Lanka 114 6 35N 80 0 E
Kalyan India 114 19 15N 73 9 E
Kama, R. Russia 98 55 45N 52 0 E
Kamchatka Pen. Russia 107 57 0N 160 0 E
Kamina DRC 126 8 45S 25 0 E
Kamloops Canada 140 50 40N 120 20W
Kampala Uganda 126 0 20N 32 30 E
Kamyanets-Podilskyy Ukraine 93 48 45N 26 40 E
Kanaaupscow, R. Canada 141 53 39N 77 9W
Kananga DRC 126 5 55S 22 18 E
Kanash Russia 98 55 30N 47 32 E
Kanawha, R. USA 144 38 50N 82 9W
Kanazawa Japan 111 36 30N 136 38 E
Kanchenjunga Nepal 115 27 50N 88 10 E
Kanchipuram India 114 12 52N 79 45 E
Kandalaksha Russia 98 67 9N 32 30 E
Kandanghaur Indonesia 112 6 21S 108 6 E
Kandavu Fiji 129 19 0S 178 15 E
Kandla India 114 23 0N 70 10 E
Kandy Sri Lanka 114 7 18N 80 43 E
Kane USA 144 41 40N 78 49W
Kaneohe USA 142 21 25N 157 48W
Kangaroo I. Australia 128 35 45S 137 0 E
Kanghwa South Korea 110 37 45N 126 30 E
Kangiqsualujjuaq Canada 141 58 30N 65 59W

LIANYUNGANG–MERIDIAN

NORTH SASKATCHEWAN R.–POCATELLO

171

POCOS DE CALDAS–SAAR, R.

ços de Caldas *Brazil* 149 21 50S 46 33W
dgorica *Montenegro* 97 42 30N 19 19 E
dolsk *Russia* 98 55 25N 37 30 E
hang *South Korea* 110 36 1N 129 23 E
inte Allègre *Guadeloupe*
146 16 22N 61 46W
inte-à-Pitre *Guadeloupe*
146 16 10N 61 32W
inte-Noire *Congo* 126 4 48S 11 53 E
inte-Noire *Guadeloupe*
146 16 14N 61 47W
int Hope *USA* 142 68 21N 166 47W
int, L. *Canada* 140 65 15N 113 4W
int Pleasant *USA* 144 38 51N 82 8W
itiers *France* 94 46 35N 0 20 E
itou *France* 94 46 40N 0 10W
karan *India* 114 26 55N 71 58 E
LAND *Europe* 93 52 0N 20 0 E
latsk *Belarus* 98 55 30N 28 50 E
levskoy *Russia* 98 56 26N 60 1 E
lgyo-ri *South Korea* 110 34 51N 127 21 E
llachi *India* 114 10 39N 77 3 E
ltava *Ukraine* 99 49 35N 34 35 E
lynesia *Pacific Ocean* 133 10 0S 162 0W
nca City *USA* 143 36 42N 97 5W
nce *Puerto Rico* 147 18 1N 66 37W
nd Inlet *Canada* 141 72 40N 77 0W
nnani *India* 114 10 47N 75 58 E
nta Grossa *Brazil* 149 25 7S 50 10W
ntchartrain, L. *USA* 143 30 5N 90 5W
ntevedra *Spain* 95 42 26N 8 40W
ntiac *USA* 144 42 38N 83 18W
ntianak *Indonesia* 112 0 3S 109 15 E
ntine Mts. *Turkey* 99 41 30N 35 0 E
ntivy *France* 94 48 5N 2 58W
ole *UK* 89 50 43N 1 59W
opó, L. de *Bolivia* 148 18 30S 67 35W
or Knights Is. *New Zealand*
132 35 29S 174 43 E
payán *Colombia* 149 2 27N 76 36W
plar Bluff *USA* 143 36 46N 90 24W
pocatépetl Pk. *Mexico*
146 19 2N 98 38W
rangahau *New Zealand*
132 40 17S 176 37 E
rbandar *India* 114 21 44N 69 43 E
rcupine, R. *USA* 142 66 34N 145 19W
ri *Finland* 91 61 29N 21 48 E
rtadown *UK* 89 54 25N 6 27W
rtage La Prairie *Canada*
140 49 58N 98 18W
rt Alberni *Canada* 140 49 14N 124 50W
rt Antonio *Jamaica* 146 18 10N 76 30W
rt Arthur *USA* 143 29 54N 93 56W
rt Augusta *Australia* 128 32 30S 137 50 E
rt-Au-Prince *Haiti* 147 18 40N 72 20W
rt-Cartier *Canada* 141 50 2N 66 50W
rt-de-Paix *Haiti* 147 19 50N 72 50W
rt Elizabeth *South Africa*
126 33 58S 25 40 E
rt Gentil *Equatorial Guinea*
126 0 40S 8 50 E
rt Harcourt *Nigeria* 124 4 40N 7 10 E
rt Hawkesbury *Canada*
141 45 36N 61 22W
rt Hedland *Australia* 128 20 25S 118 35 E
rt Hope Simpson *Canada*
141 52 33N 56 18W
rt Huron *USA* 144 42 58N 82 26W
rtland *OR, USA* 142 45 32N 122 37W
rtland *ME, USA* 143 43 39N 70 16W
rtland Bight *Jamaica* 146 17 52N 77 5W
rtland I. *New Zealand* 132 39 20S 177 51 E
rtland Point *Jamaica* 146 17 42N 77 11W
rt-Louis *Guadeloupe* 146 16 28N 61 32W
rt Lincoln *Australia* 128 34 42S 135 52 E
rt Macquarie *Australia*
128 31 25S 152 25 E
rt Maria *Jamaica* 146 18 25N 76 55W
rt McNeill *Canada* 140 50 35N 127 6W
rt Morant *Jamaica* 146 17 54N 76 19W
rtmore *Jamaica* 146 17 53N 77 33W
rt Moresby *Papua New Guinea*
128 9 24S 147 8 E
rt Nolloth *South Africa*
126 29 17S 16 52 E
rto *Portugal* 95 41 9N 8 49W
rt of Spain *Trinidad & Tobago*
149 10 40N 61 31W
rto Alegre *Brazil* 149 30 5S 51 10W
rto Seguro *Brazil* 149 16 26S 39 5W
rto Velho *Brazil* 149 8 46S 63 54W
rto-Vecchio *Corsica* 94 41 35N 9 16 E
rt Pegasus *New Zealand*
132 47 12S 167 41 E
rt Pirie *Australia* 128 33 10S 138 1 E
rtree *UK* 89 57 25N 6 12W
rt Said *Egypt* 125 31 16N 32 18 E
rt Shepstone *South Africa*
126 30 44S 30 28 E
rtsmouth *UK* 89 50 48N 1 6W
rtsmouth *NH, USA* 145 43 5N 70 45W
rtsmouth *OH, USA* 144 38 44N 82 57W
rt Sudan *Sudan* 125 19 32N 37 9 E
rt Talbot *UK* 89 51 35N 3 47W
rttipahtan Tekojärvi *Finland*
91 68 5N 26 40 E
rttipahtantekojärvi, L. *Finland*
98 68 5N 26 40 E
rt Vila *Vanuatu* 133 17 45S 168 18 E
rt Washington *USA* 144 43 23N 87 53W
RTUGAL *Europe* 95 40 0N 8 0W
song *South Korea* 110 34 46N 129 5 E
stmansburg *S. Africa* 126 28 18S 23 5 E
tchefstroom *S. Africa* 126 26 41S 27 7 E
tenza *Italy* 96 40 38N 15 48 E
teriteri, L. *N. Zealand* 132 46 5S 167 10 E
ti *Georgia* 116 42 10N 41 38 E
tomac, R. *USA* 144 38 0N 76 23W
tosí *Bolivia* 149 19 38S 65 50W
tsdam *Germany* 92 52 25N 13 4 E
ttstown *USA* 145 40 15N 75 39W
ttsville *USA* 145 40 41N 76 12W
ttuvil *Sri Lanka* 114 6 55N 81 50 E
ughkeepsie *USA* 145 41 42N 73 56W

Poverty Bay *N. Zealand* 132 38 43S 178 2 E
Powder, R. *USA* 142 46 45N 105 26W
Powell, L. *USA* 142 36 57N 111 29W
Powell River *Canada* 140 49 50N 124 35W
Powers *USA* 144 45 41N 87 32W
Poyang Hu, L. *China* 109 29 5N 116 20 E
Poza Rica *Mexico* 146 20 33N 97 27W
Poznan *Poland* 93 52 25N 16 55 E
Prague *Czech Rep.* 91 50 5N 14 22 E
Prato *Italy* 96 43 53N 11 6 E
Pratt *USA* 142 37 39N 98 44W
Praya *Indonesia* 113 8 39S 116 17 E
Prescott *USA* 142 34 33N 112 28W
Prescott *Canada* 146 44 45N 75 30W
Presidente *Brazil* 149 22 5S 51 25W
Presidio *USA* 142 29 34N 104 22W
Prespa, L. *Macedonia* 97 40 55N 21 0 E
Presque Isle *USA* 145 46 41N 68 1W
Preston *USA* 142 42 6N 111 53W
Pretoria *South Africa* 126 25 44S 28 12 E
Pribilof Is. *USA* 142 57 0N 170 0W
Price *USA* 142 39 36N 110 49W
Prieska *South Africa* 126 29 40S 22 42 E
Prince Albert *Canada* 140 53 15N 105 50W
Prince Albert Pen. *Canada*
140 72 30N 116 0W
Prince Charles I. *Canada*
141 67 47N 76 12W
Prince George *Canada* 140 53 55N 122 50W
Prince of Wales I. *Canada*
140 73 0N 99 0W
Prince Patrick I. *Canada*
80 77 0N 120 0W
Prince Rupert *Canada* 140 54 20N 130 20W
Princeton *IN, USA* 144 38 21N 87 34W
Princeton *KY, USA* 144 37 7N 87 53W
Princeton *WV, USA* 144 37 22N 81 6W
Príncipe *Atlantic Ocean* 118 1 37N 7 27 E
Pripet Marshes *Europe* 93 52 10N 28 10 E
Pripet, R. *Europe* 93 51 20N 30 15 E
Pristina *Kosovo* 97 42 40N 21 13 E
Privas *France* 94 44 45N 4 37 E
Prizren *Kosovo* 97 42 13N 20 45 E
Probolinggo *Indonesia* 112 7 46S 113 13 E
Progreso *Mexico* 146 21 20N 89 40W
Prome *Myanmar* 115 18 49N 95 13 E
Providence *USA* 143 41 49N 71 24W
Providence, C. *New Zealand*
132 45 59S 166 29 E
Provins *France* 94 48 33N 3 15 E
Provo *USA* 142 40 14N 111 39W
Prudhoe Bay *USA* 142 70 18N 148 22W
Prut, R. *Romania* 93 45 28N 28 10 E
Pryluky *Ukraine* 99 50 30N 32 24 E
Przemysl *Poland* 93 49 50N 22 45 E
Pskov *Russia* 98 57 50N 28 25 E
Puan *South Korea* 110 35 44N 126 7 E
Puducherry (Pondicherry) *India*
114 11 59N 79 50 E
Pudukkottai *India* 114 10 23N 78 52 E
Puebla *Mexico* 146 19 3N 98 12W
Pueblo *USA* 142 38 16N 104 37W
Puerto Aisen *Chile* 149 45 27S 73 0W
Puerto Barrios *Guatemala*
146 15 40N 88 32W
Puerto Cabello *Venezuela*
149 10 28N 68 1W
Puerto Cabezas *Nicaragua*
147 14 0N 83 30W
Puerto Carreño *Colombia*
149 6 12N 67 22W
Puerto Cortés *Honduras* 146 15 51N 88 0W
Puerto Deseado *Argentina*
149 47 55S 66 0W
Puerto La Cruz *Venezuela*
149 10 13N 64 38W
Puerto Madryn *Argentina*
149 42 48S 65 4W
Puerto Maldonado *Peru* 149 12 30S 69 10W
Puerto Montt *Chile* 149 41 28S 73 0W
Puerto Plata *Dominican Rep.*
147 19 48N 70 45W
Puerto Princesa *Philippines*
113 9 46N 118 45 E
Puerto San Julián *Argentina*
149 49 18S 67 43W
Puerto Suárez *Bolivia* 149 18 58S 57 52W
Puget Sound *USA* 142 47 60N 122 30W
Pukaki, L. *New Zealand* 132 44 4S 170 1 E
Pukapuka I. *Cook Is.* 133 10 53S 165 49W
Pukearuhe *New Zealand* 132 38 55S 174 31 E
Pukekohe *New Zealand* 132 37 12S 174 55 E
Puketeraki Ra. *New Zealand*
132 42 58S 172 13 E
Pukeuri *New Zealand* 132 45 4S 171 2 E
Pulacaya *Bolivia* 149 20 25S 66 41W
Pulaski *USA* 143 37 3N 80 47W
Pullman *USA* 142 46 44N 117 10W
Pune *India* 114 18 29N 73 57 E
Punjab *India* 114 31 0N 76 0 E
Punjab *Pakistan* 114 32 0N 72 30 E
Punta Arenas *Chile* 149 53 10S 71 0W
Punxsutawney *USA* 144 40 57N 78 59W
Puri *India* 115 19 50N 85 58 E
Purnia *India* 115 25 45N 87 31 E
Puruliya *India* 115 23 17N 86 24 E
Pusan *South Korea* 109 35 5N 129 0 E
Putorino *New Zealand* 132 39 4S 177 9 E
Puttalam *Sri Lanka* 114 8 1N 79 55 E
Putumayo, R. *South America*
148 3 7S 67 58W
Puvirnituq *Canada* 141 60 2N 77 10W
Puy-de-Dôme *France* 94 45 46N 2 57 E
Pyatigorsk *Russia* 99 44 2N 43 6 E
Pyongtaek *South Korea* 110 37 1N 127 4 E
P'yongyang *N. Korea* 109 39 0N 125 30 E
Pyramid, L. *USA* 142 40 1N 119 35W
Pyrénées *France* 94 42 45N 0 18 E

Q

Qaanaaq (Thule) *Greenland*
80 77 40N 69 0W
Qa'emshahr *Iran* 117 36 30N 52 53 E
Qaidam Basin *China* 108 37 0N 95 0 E
Qandahar *Afghanistan* 114 31 32N 65 43 E
Qaquortoq *Greenland* 141 60 43N 46 0W
Qarqan He, R. *China* 108 39 30N 88 30 E
Qarshi *Uzbekistan* 117 38 53N 65 48 E
QATAR *Asia* 117 25 30N 51 15 E
Qattara Depression *Egypt*
118 29 30N 27 30 E
Qena *Egypt* 125 26 10N 32 43 E
Qeqertarsuaq *Greenland*
80 69 45N 53 30W
Qeqertatsuaq *Greenland*
141 69 15N 53 38W
Qeshm *Iran* 117 26 55N 56 10 E
Qikiqtarjuaq *Canada* 141 67 33N 63 0W
Qilian Shan *China* 108 38 30N 96 0 E
Qingdao *China* 109 36 5N 120 20 E
Qinghai *China* 108 36 0N 98 0 E
Qinghai Hu *China* 108 36 40N 100 10 E
Qinhuangdao *China* 109 39 56N 119 30 E
Qiqihar *China* 109 47 26N 124 0 E
Qitai *China* 108 44 2N 89 35 E
Qom *Iran* 117 34 40N 51 0 E
Qonduz *Afghanistan* 117 36 50N 68 50 E
Quanzhou *China* 109 24 55N 118 34 E
Quaqtaq *Canada* 141 60 55N 69 40W
Québec City *Canada* 141 48 0N 74 0W
Queen Charlotte Is. *Canada*
140 53 20N 132 10W
Queen Maud Land *Canada*
140 68 15N 102 30W
Queensland *Australia* 128 22 0S 142 0 E
Queenstown *New Zealand*
129 45 1S 168 40 E
Queenstown *South Africa*
126 31 52S 26 52 E
Quelimane *Mozambique* 126 17 53S 36 58 E
Querétaro *Mexico* 146 20 36N 100 23W
Quesnel *Canada* 140 53 0N 122 30W
Quesnel, L. *Canada* 140 52 30N 121 20W
Quetta *Pakistan* 117 30 15N 66 55 E
Quetzaltenango *Guatemala*
146 14 50N 91 30W
Quezon City *Philippines*
113 14 38N 121 0 E
Quilán, C. *Chile* 148 43 15S 74 30W
Quilpie *Australia* 128 26 35S 144 11 E
Quimper *France* 94 48 0N 4 9W
Quincy *IL, USA* 143 39 56N 91 23W
Quincy *MA, USA* 145 42 15N 71 0W
Quito *Ecuador* 149 0 15S 78 35W
Qunghirot *Uzbekistan* 117 43 6N 58 54 E
Quzhou *China* 109 28 57N 118 54 E

R

Rhode Island *USA* 143 41 40N 71 30W
Raahe *Finland* 91 64 40N 24 28 E
Raba *Indonesia* 113 8 36S 118 55 E
Rabaul *Papua New Guinea*
128 4 24S 152 18 E
Rabigh *Saudi Arabia* 116 22 50N 39 5 E
Race, C. *Canada* 141 46 40N 53 5W
Racine *USA* 144 42 41N 87 51W
Radford *USA* 144 37 8N 80 34W
Radom *Poland* 93 51 23N 21 12 E
Rae *Canada* 140 62 50N 116 3W
Rae Bareli *India* 115 26 18N 81 20 E
Rafaela *Argentina* 149 31 10S 61 30W
Rafsanjan *Iran* 117 30 30N 56 5 E
Ragged Pt. *Barbados* 147 13 10N 59 10W
Raglan Harb. *New Zealand*
132 37 55S 174 55 E
Ragusa *Italy* 96 36 55N 14 44 E
Rahimyar Khan *Pakistan*
114 28 30N 70 25 E
Rahotu *New Zealand* 132 39 20S 173 49 E
Raichur *India* 114 16 10N 77 20 E
Raigarh *India* 115 21 54N 83 26 E
Rainbow Lake *Canada* 140 58 30N 119 23W
Rainier, Mt. *USA* 142 46 52N 121 46W
Rainy, L. *Canada* 140 48 42N 93 10W
Raipur *India* 115 21 17N 81 45 E
Raj Nandgaon *India* 115 21 5N 81 5 E
Rajahmundry *India* 115 17 1N 81 48 E
Rajapalaiyam *India* 114 9 25N 77 35 E
Rajasthan *India* 114 26 45N 73 30 E
Rajgarh *India* 115 21 54N 83 26 E
Rajkot *India* 114 22 15N 70 56 E
Rajshahi *Bangladesh* 115 25 0N 89 0 E
Rajshahi *Bangladesh* 115 24 22N 88 39 E
Rakaia *New Zealand* 132 43 45S 172 1 E
Rakaia, R. *New Zealand* 132 43 26S 171 47 E
Raleigh *USA* 143 35 47N 78 39W
Ramanathapuram *India*
114 9 22N 78 52 E
Ramgarh *India* 115 23 38N 85 34 E
Râmnicu Vâlcea *Romania*
93 45 9N 24 21 E
Rampur *India* 114 28 50N 79 5 E
Ramree I. *Myanmar* 115 19 0N 93 40 E
Ranchi *India* 115 23 23N 85 23 E
Randers *Denmark* 91 56 29N 10 1 E
Rangaunu Bay *New Zealand*
132 34 51S 173 15 E
Rangitaiki, R. *New Zealand*
132 37 54S 176 49 E
Rangitikei, R. *New Zealand*
132 40 17S 175 15 E
Rangitoto Ra. *New Zealand*
132 38 25S 175 35 E
Rangpur *Bangladesh* 115 25 42N 89 22 E
Rankin Inlet *Canada* 140 62 30N 93 0W
Rann of Kachchh *India* 114 24 0N 70 0 E
Rantoul *USA* 144 40 19N 88 9W
Rapa *Pacific Ocean* 133 27 35S 144 20W
Raper, C. *Canada* 141 69 44N 67 6W
Rapid City *USA* 142 44 5N 103 14W
Rarotonga *Cook Is.* 133 21 30S 160 0W
Ra's al Khaymah *UAE* 117 25 50N 55 59 E
Rasht *Iran* 116 37 20N 49 40 E
Rat Is. *USA* 142 52 0N 178 0 E
Ratangarh *India* 114 28 5N 74 35 E
Ratlam *India* 114 23 20N 75 0 E
Ratnagiri *India* 114 16 57N 73 18 E
Raton *USA* 142 36 54N 104 24W
Raukumara Ra. *New Zealand*
132 38 5S 177 55 E
Raurkela *India* 115 22 14N 84 50 E
Ravenna *Italy* 96 44 25N 12 12 E
Ravi, R. *Pakistan* 114 30 35N 71 49 E
Rawalpindi *Pakistan* 114 33 38N 73 8 E
Rawanduz *Iraq* 116 36 40N 44 30 E
Rawlins *USA* 142 41 47N 107 14W
Rawson *Argentina* 149 43 15S 65 5W
Ray, C. *Canada* 141 47 33N 59 15W
Rayagada *India* 115 19 9N 83 27 E
Raz, Pointe du *France* 94 48 2N 4 47W
Ré, I. de *France* 94 46 12N 1 30W
Reading *USA* 143 40 20N 75 56W
Reading *UK* 89 51 27N 0 58W
Recife *Brazil* 149 8 0S 35 0W
Reconquista *Argentina* 149 29 10S 59 45W
Redding *USA* 142 40 35N 122 24W
Red Bluff *USA* 142 40 11N 122 15W
Red Deer *Canada* 140 52 20N 113 50W
Red Lake *Canada* 140 51 3N 93 49W
Red Oak *USA* 143 41 1N 95 14W
Redon *France* 94 47 40N 2 6W
Red River *LA, USA* 143 31 1N 91 45W
Red River *ND, USA* 142 49 0N 97 15W
Red Sea *Asia* 119 25 0N 36 0 E
Red Wing *USA* 143 44 34N 92 31W
Reefton *New Zealand* 132 42 6S 171 51 E
Reese, R. *USA* 142 40 48N 117 4W
Regensburg *Germany* 92 49 1N 12 6 E
Réggio di Calábria *Italy* 96 38 6N 15 39 E
Réggio nell'Emília *Italy* 96 44 43N 10 36 E
Regina *Canada* 140 50 27N 104 35W
Reichenbach *Germany* 92 50 37N 12 17 E
Reims *France* 94 49 15N 4 1 E
Reindeer L. *Canada* 140 57 15N 102 15W
Reinga, C. *New Zealand* 132 34 25S 172 43 E
Remscheid *Germany* 90 51 11N 7 12 E
Rennell I. *Solomon Is.* 129 11 40S 160 10 E
Rennes *France* 94 48 7N 1 41W
Reno *USA* 142 39 31N 119 48W
Republican R. *USA* 142 39 4N 96 48W
Repulse Bay *Canada* 141 66 30N 86 30W
Resistencia *Argentina* 149 27 30S 59 0W
Resolution I. *New Zealand*
132 45 40S 166 40 E
Resolution I. *Canada* 141 61 30N 65 0W
Réthímnon *Greece* 97 35 18N 24 30 E
Réunion *Indian Ocean* 118 21 0S 56 0 E
Revda *Russia* 98 56 48N 59 57 E
Revelstake *Canada* 140 51 0N 118 10W
Rewa *India* 115 24 33N 81 25 E
Rewari *India* 114 28 12N 76 40 E
Rexburg *USA* 142 43 49N 111 47W
Rey Malabo *Eq. Guinea* 126 3 45N 8 50 E
Reykjavík *Iceland* 91 64 10N 21 57W
Reynosa *Mexico* 146 26 5N 98 18W
Rezekne *Latvia* 98 56 30N 27 17 E
Rheine *Germany* 92 52 17N 7 26 E
Rheinland-Pfalz *Germany*
92 50 0N 7 0 E
Rhine, R. *Europe* 90 51 52N 6 2 E
Rhinelander *USA* 143 45 38N 89 25W
Rhodes *Greece* 97 36 15N 28 10 E
Rhodope Mts. *Bulgaria* 97 41 40N 24 20 E
Rhondda *UK* 89 51 39N 3 31W
Rhône, R. *France* 94 43 28N 4 42 E
Rhum *UK* 89 57 0N 6 20W
Riau Kepulauan *Indonesia*
112 0 30N 104 20 E
Ribble, R. *UK* 89 53 52N 2 25W
Riccarton *New Zealand* 132 43 32S 172 37 E
Richards Bay *South Africa*
126 28 48S 32 6 E
Richardson Mts. *New Zealand*
132 44 49S 168 34 E
Richfield *USA* 142 38 46N 112 5W
Richland *USA* 142 46 17N 119 18W
Richlands *USA* 144 37 6N 81 48W
Richmond Ra. *New Zealand*
132 41 32S 173 22 E
Richmond *IN, USA* 144 39 50N 84 53W
Richmond *KY, USA* 144 37 45N 84 18W
Richmond *VA, USA* 144 37 33N 77 27W
Ridgecrest *USA* 142 35 38N 117 40W
Ridgway *USA* 144 41 25N 78 44W
Riga *Latvia* 98 56 53N 24 8 E
Riga, G. of *Latvia* 98 57 40N 23 45 E
Rigestan *Afghanistan* 117 30 15N 65 0 E
Rigolet *Canada* 141 54 10N 58 23W
Rijeka *Croatia* 92 45 20N 14 21 E
Rímini *Italy* 96 44 3N 12 33 E
Rimouski *Canada* 141 48 27N 68 30W
Rio Branco *Brazil* 149 9 58S 67 49W
Rio De Janeiro *Brazil* 149 23 0S 43 12W
Río Gallegos *Argentina* 149 51 35S 69 15W
Río Grande *Puerto Rico* 147 18 23N 65 50W
Rio Grande *USA* 149 25 58N 97 9W
Rio Grande *Brazil* 149 32 0S 52 20W
Río Grande *Nicaragua* 147 12 54N 83 33W
Rio Grande de Santiago *Mexico*
146 21 36N 105 26W
Rio Grande Do Sul *Brazil*
149 30 0S 53 0W
Río Muni *Eq. Guinea* 126 1 30N 10 0 E
Ripon *USA* 144 43 51N 88 50W
Rivera *Uruguay* 149 31 0S 55 50W
Riverside *USA* 142 33 59N 117 22W
Riverton *USA* 142 43 2N 108 23W
Rivière-du-Loup *Canada*
141 47 50N 69 30W
Rivière-Pilote *Martinique*
146 14 26N 60 53W
Rivière-Salée *Martinique*
146 14 31N 61 0W
Rivne *Ukraine* 93 50 40N 26 10 E
Riyadh *Saudi Arabia* 116 24 41N 46 42 E
Rize *Turkey* 99 41 0N 40 30 E
Road Town *Br. Virgin Is.* 147 18 27N 64 37W
Roanne *France* 94 46 3N 4 4 E
Roanoke *USA* 144 37 16N 79 56W
Roanoke R. *USA* 143 35 57N 76 42W
Roberval *Canada* 141 48 32N 72 15W
Robson, Mt. *Canada* 140 53 10N 119 10W
Roca, C. da *Portugal* 95 38 40N 9 31W
Rocha *Uruguay* 149 34 30S 54 25W
Rochefort *France* 94 45 56N 0 57W
Rochester *IN, USA* 144 41 4N 86 13W
Rochester *MN, USA* 143 44 1N 92 28W
Rochester *NH, USA* 145 43 18N 70 59W
Rochester *NY, USA* 144 43 10N 77 37W
Rockall *Atlantic Ocean* 82 57 37N 13 42W
Rockford *USA* 143 42 16N 89 6W
Rockhampton *Australia* 128 23 22S 150 32 E
Rock Hills *USA* 143 34 56N 81 1W
Rock Island *USA* 143 41 30N 90 34W
Rock Springs *USA* 142 41 35N 109 14W
Rocky Mount *USA* 143 35 57N 77 48W
Rodez *France* 94 44 21N 2 33 E
Rodney, C. *N. Zealand* 132 36 17S 174 50 E
Roes Welcome Sound *Canada*
141 65 0N 87 0W
Roeselare *Belgium* 90 50 57N 3 7 E
Rogers City *USA* 144 45 25N 83 49W
Rohri *Pakistan* 114 27 45N 68 51 E
Rohtak *India* 114 28 54N 76 38 E
Rojo, C. *Mexico* 146 21 33N 97 20W
Rolla *USA* 143 37 57N 91 46W
Romaine, R. *Canada* 141 50 18N 63 47W
ROMANIA *Europe* 93 46 0N 25 0 E
Romans- sur-Isére *France*
94 45 3N 5 3 E
Rome *Italy* 96 41 54N 12 29 E
Rome *GA, USA* 143 34 15N 85 10W
Romney *USA* 144 39 21N 78 45W
Romorantin-Lanthenay *France*
94 47 21N 1 45 E
Roncador Serra do *Brazil*
148 12 30S 52 30W
Rondonia *Brazil* 149 11 0S 63 0W
Ronne Ice Shelf *Antarctica*
81 78 0S 60 0W
Ronse *Belgium* 90 50 45N 3 35 E
Roosendaal *Neths.* 90 51 32N 4 29 E
Roraima *Brazil* 149 2 0N 61 30W
Rosario *Mexico* 146 23 0N 105 52W
Rosario *Argentina* 149 33 0S 60 40W
Roscommon *Ireland* 89 53 38N 8 11W
Roseau *Dominica* 147 16 20N 61 24W
Roseburg *USA* 142 43 13N 123 20W
Rosetown *Canada* 140 51 35N 107 59W
Roseville *USA* 142 38 45N 121 17W
Roslavl *Russia* 98 53 57N 32 55 E
Ross Ice Shelf *Antarctica*
81 80 0S 180 0 E
Ross River *Canada* 140 62 30N 131 30W
Ross Sea *Antarctica* 81 74 0S 178 0 E
Rossignol, L. *Canada* 146 44 12N 65 10W
Rosslare *Ireland* 89 52 17N 6 24W
Rossosh *Russia* 99 50 15N 39 28 E
Rostock *Germany* 91 54 5N 12 8 E
Rostov *Russia* 99 47 15N 39 45 E
Roswell *USA* 142 33 24N 104 32W
Rotaruc *New Zealand* 129 38 9S 176 16 E
Rotherham *UK* 89 53 26N 1 20W
Rotoehu, L. *New Zealand*
132 38 1S 176 32 E
Rotoiti, L. *New Zealand* 132 41 51S 172 49 E
Rotoma, L. *New Zealand* 132 38 2S 176 35 E
Rotorua *New Zealand* 132 38 9S 176 16 E
Rotoroa, L. *New Zealand* 132 41 55S 172 39 E
Rotorua, L. *New Zealand* 132 38 5S 176 18 E
Rotterdam *Neths.* 90 51 55N 4 30 E
Rotuma *Fiji* 129 12 25S 177 5 E
Roubaix *France* 94 50 40N 3 10 E
Rouen *France* 94 49 27N 1 4 E
Rough Ridge *New Zealand*
132 45 10S 169 55 E
Roussillon *France* 94 42 30N 2 35 E
Rouyn-Noranda *Canada*
141 48 20N 79 0W
Rovaniemi *Finland* 91 66 29N 25 41 E
Roxas *Philippines* 113 11 36N 122 49 E
Roxburgh *New Zealand* 132 45 33S 169 19 E
Royale Isle *USA* 144 48 0N 88 54W
Royan *France* 94 45 37N 1 2W
Ruahine Ra. *New Zealand*
132 39 55S 176 2 E
Ruapehu *New Zealand* 132 39 17S 175 35 E
Ruapuke I. *New Zealand*
132 46 46S 168 31 E
Rub' Al Khali, Mt. *Saudi Arabia*
100 19 0N 48 0 E
Ruby, L. *USA* 142 40 10N 115 28W
Rufiji, R. *Tanzania* 126 7 50S 39 15 E
Rufling Pt. *Br. Virgin Is.* 147 18 44N 64 27W
Rugby *UK* 89 52 23N 1 16W
Rügen *Germany* 92 54 22N 13 24 E
Ruhr, R. *Germany* 92 51 27N 6 43 E
Rumford *USA* 145 44 33N 70 33W
Runaway Bay *Jamaica* 146 18 27N 77 20W
Runaway, C. *New Zealand*
132 37 32S 178 2 E
Rundu *Namibia* 126 17 52S 19 43 E
Rungwe *Tanzania* 118 9 11S 33 32 E
Ruoqiang *China* 108 38 55N 88 10 E
Rupert *USA* 142 42 37N 113 41W
Rupert R. *Canada* 141 51 29N 78 45W
Ruse *Bulgaria* 97 43 48N 25 59 E
Rushville *USA* 144 39 37N 85 27W
Russellville *USA* 143 35 17N 93 8W
RUSSIA *Eurasia* 106 62 0N 105 0 E
Rustavi *Georgia* 116 41 30N 45 0 E
Rustenburg *S. Africa* 126 25 41S 27 14 E
Ruvuma, R. *Tanzania* 126 10 29S 40 28 E
Ruwenzori *Africa* 118 0 30N 29 55 E
Ryazan *Russia* 98 54 40N 39 40 E
Rybinsk *Russia* 98 58 5N 38 50 E
Rybinsk Res. *Russia* 98 58 30N 38 25 E
Ryukyu Is. *Japan* 109 26 0N 126 0 E
Rzeszów *Poland* 93 50 5N 21 58 E
Rzhev *Russia* 98 56 20N 34 20 E

S

Saale, R. *Germany* 92 51 56N 11 54 E
Saar, R. *Europe* 90 49 41N 6 32 E

173
SOLOMON IS.–TOTTORI

LOMON IS. Pacific Ocean
133 6 0S 155 0 E
lomon Sea Papua New Guinea
128 7 0S 150 0 E
lon China 109 46 32N 121 10 E
lothurn Switzerland 92 47 13N 7 32 E
mali Pen. Africa 118 7 0N 46 0 E
MALI REP. Africa 127 7 0N 47 0 E
mbrerete Mexico 146 23 40N 103 40W
merset USA 144 37 5N 84 36W
merset I. Canada 140 73 30N 93 0W
mme, R. France 94 50 11N 1 38 E
nepur India 115 20 51N 83 59 E
nghua Jiang, R. China
109 47 45N 132 30 E
ngjongni South Korea 110 35 8N 126 47 E
ngnim South Korea 110 38 45N 125 39 E
ngpan China 108 32 40N 103 30 E
nora, R. Mexico 146 28 50N 111 33W
noran Desert USA 142 33 40N 114 15W
nsan South Korea 110 36 14N 128 17 E
nsonate El Salvador 146 13 43N 89 44W
pot Poland 93 54 27N 18 31 E
rocaba Brazil 149 23 31S 47 27W
røya Norway 91 70 40N 22 30 E
snowiec Poland 93 50 20N 19 10 E
ufrière Guadeloupe 146 16 5N 61 40W
ufrière Bay St Lucia 147 13 51N 61 4W
usse Tunisia 125 35 50N 10 38 E
uth Australia Australia
128 32 0S 139 0 E
UTH AFRICA Africa
119 32 0S 23 0 E
uthampton I. Canada 141 64 30N 84 0W
uth Bend USA 144 41 41N 86 15W
uth Br. Ashburton, R. New Zealand
132 43 30S 171 15 E
uth Carolina USA 143 34 0N 81 0W
uth Charleston USA 144 38 22N 81 44W
uth China Sea Asia 112 10 0N 113 0 E
uth Dakota USA 142 44 15N 100 0W
uthend on Sea UK 89 51 32N 0 44 E
uthern Alps New Zealand
129 43 41S 170 11 E
uthern Indian L. Canada
140 57 10N 98 30W
uthern Ocean Antarctica
81 62 0S 60 0 E
uthern Uplands UK 89 55 28N 3 52W
uth Georgia Antarctica
81 54 30S 37 0W
uth Honshu Ridge Pacific Ocean
133 23 0N 143 0 E
uth I. New Zealand 129 44 0S 170 0 E
UTH KOREA Asia 109 36 0N 128 0 E
uth Magnetic Pole Antarctica
81 64 8S 138 8 E
uth Nahanni R. Canada
140 61 3N 123 21W
uth Negril Pt. Jamaica
146 18 14N 78 30W
uth Orkney Is. Antarctica
81 63 0S 45 0W
uth Platte R. USA 142 41 7N 100 42W
uthport UK 89 53 39N 3 0W
uth Pt. Barbados 147 13 2N 59 32W
uth Sandwich Is. Antarctica
81 57 0S 27 0W
uth Saskatchewan R. Canada
140 53 15N 105 5W
uth Shetland Is. Antarctica
81 62 0S 59 0W
uth Shields UK 89 55 0N 1 25W
uth Taranaki Bight New Zealand
132 39 40S 174 5 E
uth West, Cape New Zealand
132 47 16S 167 31 E
vetsk Russia 98 55 6N 21 50 E
weto South Africa 126 26 14S 27 54 E
AIN Europe 95 39 0N 4 0W
anish Town Br. Virgin Is.
147 17 43N 64 26W
anish Town Jamaica 146 18 0N 76 57W
arks USA 142 39 32N 119 45W
artanburg USA 143 34 56N 81 57W
artivento, C. Italy 96 37 55N 16 4 E
eightstown Barbados 147 13 15N 59 39W
encer USA 143 43 9N 95 9W
encer Gulf Australia 128 34 0S 137 20 E
enser Mts. New Zealand
132 42 15S 172 45 E
ey, R. UK 89 57 40N 3 6W
lit Croatia 96 43 31N 16 26 E
okane USA 142 47 40N 117 24W
ratly Is. S. China Sea 112 8 20N 112 0 E
ree, R. Germany 92 52 32N 13 13 E
ring Hall Barbados 147 13 18N 59 36W
ringburn New Zealand
132 43 40S 171 32 E
ringfield IL, USA 143 39 48N 89 39W
ringfield MA, USA 145 42 6N 72 35W
ringfield MO, USA 143 37 13N 93 17W
ringfield OH, USA 144 39 55N 83 49W
ringfield OR, USA 142 44 3N 123 1W
ringhill Canada 146 45 40N 64 4W
rings South Africa 126 26 13S 28 25 E
ebrenica Bosnia & Herzegovina
97 44 6N 19 18 E
edinny Ra. Russia 106 57 0N 160 0 E
ikakulam India 115 18 17N 83 57 E
I LANKA Asia 114 7 30N 80 50 E
inagar India 114 34 5N 74 50 E
afford UK 89 52 49N 2 7W
akhanov Ukraine 99 48 35N 38 40 E
amford USA 145 41 3N 73 32W
andish USA 144 43 59N 83 57W
anovoy Ra. Russia 107 55 0N 130 0 E
ara Zagora Bulgaria 97 42 26N 25 39 E
araya Russa Russia 98 57 58N 31 23 E
arbuck I. Kiribati 133 5 37S 155 55W
art Pt. UK 89 50 13N 3 39N
aryy Oskol Russia 99 51 19N 37 55 E
ate College USA 144 40 48N 77 52W
aunton USA 144 38 9N 79 4W
avanger Norway 91 58 57N 5 40 E
Stavropol Russia 99 45 5N 42 0 E
Steiermark Austria 92 47 26N 15 0 E
Steinkjer Norway 91 64 1N 11 31 E
Stellarton Canada 146 45 32 62 30W
Stephens I. New Zealand
132 40 40S 174 1 E
Steppe Asia 100 50 0N 50 0 E
Sterling USA 142 40 37N 103 13W
Sterlitamak Russia 98 53 40N 56 0 E
Stettler Canada 140 52 19N 112 40W
Steubenville USA 144 40 22N 80 37W
Stevens Point USA 144 44 31N 89 34W
Steward I. New Zealand 129 46 58S 167 54 E
Stewart Canada 140 55 56N 129 57W
Stewart, R. Canada 140 63 19N 139 26W
Steyr Austria 92 48 3N 14 25 E
Stikine, R. Canada 140 56 40N 132 30W
Stillwater USA 143 36 7N 97 4W
Stirling UK 89 56 8N 3 57W
Stockholm Sweden 91 59 20N 18 3 E
Stockport UK 89 53 25N 2 9W
Stockton USA 142 37 58N 121 17W
Stockton on Tees UK 89 54 35N 1 19W
Stonehaven UK 89 56 59N 2 12W
Stora Lulevatten Sweden
91 67 10N 19 30 E
Storavan Sweden 91 65 45N 18 10 E
Store Bælt Finland 91 55 20N 11 0 E
Stornoway UK 89 58 13N 6 23W
Storsjön Sweden 91 63 9N 14 30 E
Storuman Sweden 91 65 5N 17 10 E
Strait of Karimata Indonesia
112 2 0S 108 40 E
Strait of Malacca Indonesia
112 3 0N 101 0 E
Stralsund Germany 92 54 18N 13 4 E
Stranraer UK 89 54 54N 5 1W
Strasbourg France 94 48 35N 7 42 E
Strómboli Italy 96 38 47N 15 13 E
Stuart, L. Canada 140 54 30N 124 30W
Stuart, Mt. New Zealand 132 45 2S 169 31 E
Sturgeon Bay USA 144 44 50N 87 23W
Stuttgart Germany 92 48 48N 9 11 E
Stuttgart USA 143 34 30N 91 33W
Su
Suakin Sudan 125 19 8N 37 20 E
Suan South Korea 110 38 42N 126 22 E
Subotica Serbia 97 46 6N 19 39 E
Suceava Romania 93 47 38N 26 16 E
Sucre Bolivia 149 19 0S 65 15W
SUDAN Africa 119 15 0N 30 0 E
Sudbury Canada 141 46 30N 81 0W
Sûdd Sudan 125 8 20N 30 0 E
Sudetes Poland 82 50 20N 16 45 E
Suez Egypt 125 29 58N 32 31 E
Suez Canal Egypt 125 31 0N 32 20 E
Suez, G. of Egypt 125 28 40N 33 0 E
Suhar Oman 117 24 20N 56 40 E
Suihua China 109 46 32N 126 55 E
Suir, R. Ireland 89 52 16N 7 9W
Sukabumi Indonesia 112 6 56S 106 50 E
Sukhona, R. Russia 98 61 15N 46 39 E
Sukkur Pakistan 114 27 42N 68 54 E
Sulamain Ra. Pakistan 114 30 30N 69 50 E
Sulawesi Indonesia 113 2 0S 120 0 E
Sullana Peru 149 4 52S 80 39W
Sultanpur India 115 26 16N 82 7 E
Sulu Sea East Indies 113 8 0N 120 0 E
Sulu Arch. Philippines 113 6 0N 121 0 E
SUMATRA Indonesia 112 0 40N 100 20 E
Sumba Indonesia 113 9 45S 119 35 E
Sumbawa Indonesia 113 8 26S 117 30 E
Sumenep Indonesia 112 1 1S 113 52 E
Summer, L. USA 142 42 50N 120 45W
Summerside Canada 141 46 24N 63 47W
Sumner, L. New Zealand 132 42 42S 172 15 E
Sumqayit Azerbaijan 116 40 34N 49 38 E
Sumter USA 143 33 55N 80 21W
Sumy Ukraine 99 50 57N 34 50 E
Sun Valley USA 142 43 42N 114 21W
Sunbury USA 144 40 52N 76 48W
Sunchon South Korea 110 34 52N 127 31 E
Sunda Is. Indonesia 100 5 0S 105 0 E
Sundarbans ASIA 115 22 0N 89 0 E
Sundargarh India 115 21 6N 84 0 E
Sundsvall Sweden 91 62 23N 17 17 E
Sungaipenuh Indonesia 112 2 1S 101 20 E
Superior USA 144 46 44N 92 5W
Superior, L. N. America 145 47 0N 87 0W
Sur Lebanon 116 33 19N 35 16 E
Sura, R. Russia 98 56 6N 46 0 E
Surabaya Indonesia 112 7 17S 112 45 E
Surakarta Indonesia 112 7 35S 110 48 E
Surat India 114 21 12N 72 55 E
Suratgarh India 114 29 19N 73 57 E
Surgut Russia 106 61 14N 73 20 E
SURINAME South America
149 4 0N 56 0W
Surt Libya 125 31 11N 16 39 E
Sussex Canada 146 45 45N 65 37W
Sutlej, R. Pakistan 114 29 23N 71 3 E
Suva Fiji 129 18 6S 178 30 E
Suwalki Poland 93 54 8N 22 59 E
Suwon South Korea 110 37 17N 127 1 E
Suzhou China 109 31 19N 120 38 E
Svalbard Arctic Ocean 100 78 0N 0 0 E
Svealand Sweden 91 60 20N 15 0 E
Sverdrup Is. Canada 80 79 0N 97 0W
Svir, R. Russia 98 60 30N 32 48 E
Sw
Swakopmund Namibia 126 22 37S 14 30 E
Swan Hill Australia 128 35 20S 143 33 E
Swan River Canada 140 52 10N 101 16W
Swansea UK 89 51 37N 3 57W
SWAZILAND Africa 119 26 30S 31 30 E
SWEDEN Europe 91 57 0N 15 0 E
Sweetwater USA 142 32 28N 100 25W
Swellenbdam South Africa
126 34 1S 20 26 E
Swift Current Canada 140 50 20N 107 45W
Swindon UK 89 51 34N 1 46W
SWITZERLAND Europe
126 46 30N 8 0 E
Sydney Australia 128 33 53S 151 10 E
Sydney Canada 141 46 7N 60 7W
Syktyvkar Russia 98 61 45N 50 40 E
Sylhet Bangladesh 115 24 50N 91 50 E
Syracuse USA 145 43 3N 76 9W
Syrdarya, R. Kazakhstan 106 46 3N 61 0 E
SYRIA Asia 101 35 0N 38 0 E
Syrian Desert Asia 116 32 0N 40 0 E
Syzran Russia 98 53 12N 48 30 E
Szczecin Poland 92 53 27N 14 27 E
Szeged Hungary 93 46 16N 20 10 E
Székesfehérvár Hungary
93 47 15N 18 25 E
Szekszárd Hungary 93 46 22N 18 42 E
Szolnok Hungary 93 47 10N 20 15 E
Szornbathely Hungary 93 47 14N 16 38 E

T

Tabas Iran 117 33 35N 56 55 E
Tablas I. Philippines 113 12 25N 122 2 E
Table Bay South Africa 126 33 35S 18 25 E
Table Mt. South Africa 126 34 0S 18 22 E
Tabriz Iran 116 38 7N 46 20 E
Tabuaeran Kiribati 133 3 51N 159 22W
Tacheng China 108 46 40N 82 58 E
Tacloban Philippines 113 11 15N 124 58 E
Tacna Peru 149 18 0S 70 20W
Tacoma USA 142 47 14N 122 26W
Taechonni South Korea 110 36 21N 126 36 E
Taegu South Korea 109 35 50N 128 37 E
Taejon South Korea 110 36 20N 127 28 E
Taganrog Russia 99 47 12N 38 50 E
Taguatinga Brazil 149 12 16S 42 26W
Tagus, R. Europe 95 38 40N 9 24W
Tahakopa New Zealand 132 46 30S 169 23 E
Tahiti I. Pacific Ocean 133 17 37S 149 27W
Tahoe, L. USA 142 39 6N 120 2W
Tahora New Zealand 132 39 2S 174 49 E
T'aichung Taiwan 109 24 9N 120 37 E
Taieri, R. New Zealand 132 46 3S 170 12 E
Taimyr Pen. Russia 109 75 0N 100 0 E
T'ainan Taiwan 109 23 0N 120 10 E
Taipei Taiwan 109 25 2N 121 30 E
Taiping Malaysia 112 4 51N 100 44 E
Taitao, Pen. de Chile 148 46 30S 75 0W
T'aitung Taiwan 109 22 43N 121 4 E
TAIWAN Asia 101 23 30N 121 0 E
Taiyuan China 109 37 52N 112 33 E
TAJIKISTAN Asia 106 38 30N 70 0 E
Tak Thailand 115 16 52N 99 0 E
Takamatsu Japan 111 34 20N 134 5 E
Takaoka Japan 111 36 47N 137 0 E
Takasaki Japan 111 36 20N 139 0 E
Takhar Afghanistan 114 36 40N 70 0 E
Takla Makan China 108 38 0N 83 0 E
Talara Peru 149 4 38S 81 18W
Talaud Kepulauan Indonesia
113 4 30N 126 50 E
Talca Chile 149 35 28S 71 40W
Talcahuano Chile 149 36 40S 73 10W
Taldyqerghan Kazakhstan
106 45 10N 78 45 E
Taliabu Indonesia 113 1 50S 125 0 E
Tallahassee USA 143 30 27N 84 17W
Tallinn Estonia 98 59 22N 24 48 E
Taloypoak Canada 140 69 32N 93 32W
Tamale Ghana 124 9 22N 0 50W
Tamana Kiribati 129 2 30S 175 59 E
Tamar, R. UK 89 50 27N 4 15W
Tambov Russia 98 52 45N 41 28 E
Tamil Nadu India 114 11 0N 77 0 E
Tampa USA 143 27 57N 82 27W
Tampa Bay USA 143 27 50N 82 30W
Tampere Finland 91 61 30N 23 50 E
Tampico Mexico 146 22 20N 97 50W
Tamworth Australia 128 31 7S 150 58 E
Tana, L. Ethiopia 118 13 5N 37 30 E
Tana, R. Kenya 126 2 32S 40 31 E
Tana, R. Norway 91 70 30N 28 14 E
Tanami Desert Australia
128 18 50S 132 0 E
Tandil Argentina 149 37 15S 59 6W
Tane-ga-shima Japan 109 36 47N 137 0 E
Tanga Tanzania 126 5 5S 39 2 E
Tanganyika, L. Africa 118 6 40S 30 0 E
Tanggula Shan China 108 32 40N 92 10 E
Tangier Morocco 124 35 50N 5 49W
Tangshan China 109 39 38N 118 10 E
Tanjungbalai Indonesia 112 2 55N 99 44 E
Tanjungkarang Telukbetung (Bandar Lampung)
112 5 20S 105 10 E
Tanjungpandan Indonesia
112 2 43S 107 38 E
Tanjungredeb Indonesia 113 2 9N 117 29 E
TANZANIA Africa 119 6 0S 34 0 E
Taolanaro Madagascar 126 25 2S 47 0 E
Taos USA 142 36 24N 105 35W
Tapachula Mexico 146 14 54N 92 17W
Tapajés, R. Brazil 148 2 24S 54 41W
Tapanu New Zealand 132 45 56S 169 18 E
Tapti, R. India 114 21 8N 72 41 E
Tapuaenuku, Mt. New Zealand
132 41 55S 173 50 E
Tarakan Indonesia 113 3 20N 117 35 E
Taranaki New Zealand 132 39 5S 174 51 E
Táranto, G. di Italy 96 40 8N 17 20 E
Tararua Ra. New Zealand
132 40 45S 175 25 E
Tarawa Kiribati 133 1 30N 173 0 E
Tarawera, L. New Zealand
132 38 13S 176 27 E
Tarawera, Mt. New Zealand
132 38 14S 176 32 E
Taraz Kazakhstan 117 42 54N 71 22 E
Tarbagati Ra. Kazakhstan
106 48 0N 83 0 E
Tarbes France 94 43 15N 0 3 E
Tarcoola Australia 128 30 44S 134 36 E
Taree Australia 128 31 50S 152 30 E
Tarfaya Morocco 124 27 55N 12 55W
Târgoviste Romania 93 44 55N 25 27 E
Târgu Mures Romania 93 46 31N 24 38 E
Târgu-Jiu Romania 93 45 5N 23 19 E
Tarija Bolivia 149 21 30S 64 40W
Tarim Basin China 108 40 0N 84 0 E
Tarim He, R. China 108 39 30N 88 30 E
Tarn, R. France 94 44 5N 1 6 E
Tarnów Poland 93 50 3N 21 0 E
Taroudannt Morocco 124 30 30N 8 52W
Tarragona Spain 95 41 5N 1 17 E
Tarsus Turkey 99 36 58N 34 55 E
Tartu Estonia 98 58 20N 26 44 E
Tashkent Uzbekistan 106 41 20N 69 10 E
Tasikmalaya Indonesia 112 7 18S 108 12 E
Tasman Bay New Zealand
132 40 59S 173 25 E
Tasman, Mt. New Zealand
132 43 34S 170 12 E
Tasman Mts. New Zealand
132 41 3S 172 25 E
Tasman Sea Pacific Ocean
129 36 0S 160 0 E
Tasmania Australia 128 42 0S 146 30 E
Tassili n Ajjer Algeria 124 25 47N 8 1 E
Tatarstan Russia 98 55 30N 51 30 E
Tatnam, C. Canada 141 57 16N 91 0W
Tatta Pakistan 114 24 42N 67 55 E
Tatvan Turkey 99 38 31N 42 15 E
Taumarunui New Zealand
132 38 53S 175 15 E
Taunton USA 145 41 54N 71 6W
Taunton UK 89 51 1N 3 5W
Taunus Germany 92 50 13N 8 34 E
Taupo, L. New Zealand 132 38 46S 175 55 E
Taurus Mts. Turkey 99 37 0N 32 30 E
Taw, R. UK 89 51 4N 4 4W
Tawas City USA 144 44 16N 83 31W
Tawau Malaysia 113 4 20N 117 55 E
Tay, R. UK 89 56 37N 3 38W
Taylor, Mt. USA 142 35 14N 107 37W
Taza Morocco 124 34 16N 4 6W
Tbilisi Georgia 99 41 43N 44 50 E
Te
Te Araroa New Zealand 132 37 39S 178 25 E
Te Awamutu New Zealand
132 38 1S 175 20 E
Te Karaka New Zealand 132 38 26S 177 53 E
Te Puke New Zealand 132 37 46S 176 22 E
Te Waewae Bay New Zealand
132 46 13S 167 33 E
Tebessa Algeria 124 35 22N 8 8 E
Tees, R. UK 89 54 37N 1 10W
Tegal Indonesia 112 6 52S 109 8 E
Tegucigalpa Honduras 146 14 5N 87 14W
Tehran Iran 117 35 44N 51 30 E
Tehuantepec Mexico 146 16 21N 95 13W
Tehuantepec, G. de Mexico
146 15 50N 95 12W
Tejen Turkmenistan 117 37 23N 60 31 E
Tekapo, L. New Zealand 132 43 53S 170 33 E
Tekirdag Turkey 99 40 58N 27 30 E
Tel Aviv-Jaffa Israel 116 32 4N 34 48 E
Tela Honduras 146 15 40N 87 28W
Telegraph Creek Canada
140 58 0N 131 10W
Teles Pires, R. Brazil 148 7 21S 58 3W
Telford UK 89 52 40N 2 27W
Tell City USA 144 37 57N 86 46W
Tellicherry India 114 11 45N 75 30 E
Telpos Iz Russia 98 63 16N 59 13 E
Teluk Intan Malaysia 112 4 3N 101 0 E
Tema Ghana 124 5 41N 0 0W
Temple USA 143 31 6N 97 21W
Temuco Chile 149 38 45S 72 40W
Temuka New Zealand 132 44 14S 171 17 E
Tenerife Canary Is. 124 28 15N 16 35W
Tengchong China 108 25 0N 98 28 E
Tenkasi India 114 8 58N 77 21 E
Tennant Creek Australia
128 19 30S 134 15 E
Tennessee USA 143 36 0N 86 30W
Tennessee R. USA 143 37 4N 88 34W
Teófilo Otoni Brazil 149 17 50S 41 30W
Tepic Mexico 146 21 30N 104 54W
Teraina I. Kiribati 133 4 43N 160 25W
Teresina Brazil 149 5 9S 42 45W
Ternate Indonesia 113 0 45N 127 25 E
Terni Italy 96 42 34N 12 37 E
Ternopil Ukraine 99 49 30N 25 40 E
Terrace Canada 140 54 30N 128 35W
Terrassa Spain 95 41 34N 2 1 E
Terre Haute USA 144 39 28N 87 25W
Teruel Spain 95 40 22N 1 8W
Tesiyn Gol, R. Mongolia 108 50 40N 93 20 E
Teslin Canada 140 60 10N 132 43W
Tete Mozambique 126 16 13S 33 33 E
Tétouan Morocco 124 35 35N 8 21W
Tetovo Macedonia 97 42 1N 20 59 E
Teuco, R. Argentina 148 25 35S 60 11W
Teutoburger Wald Germany
92 52 5N 8 22 E
Texarkana USA 143 33 26N 94 3W
Texas USA 142 31 40N 98 30W
Texel Neths. 90 53 5N 4 50 E
Tezpur India 115 26 40N 92 45 E
Th
Thabana Ntlenyana Lesotho
126 29 30S 29 16 E
Thabazimbi South Africa
126 24 40S 27 21 E
THAILAND Asia 101 16 0N 102 0 E
Thailand, G. of Asia 100 11 30N 101 0 E
Thal Desert Pakistan 114 31 10N 71 30 E
Thame, R. UK 82 51 39N 1 9W
Thames, R. UK 89 51 29N 0 34 E
Thane India 114 19 12N 72 59 E
Thanjavur India 114 10 48N 79 12 E
Thar Desert India 114 28 0N 72 0 E
Thargomindah Australia
128 27 58S 143 46 E
The Crane Barbados 147 13 6N 59 27W
The Dalles USA 142 45 36N 121 10W
THE GAMBIA Africa 119 13 25N 16 0W
The Gulf Asia 100 27 0N 50 0 E
The Pas Canada 140 53 45N 101 15W
The Settlement Br. Virgin Is.
147 18 43N 64 22W
Thebes Egypt 125 25 40N 32 35 E
Thelon, R. Canada 140 64 16N 96 4W
Thermopolis USA 142 43 39N 108 13W
Thessaloníki Greece 97 40 38N 22 58 E
Thetford Mines Canada
141 46 8N 71 18W
Thiers France 94 45 52N 3 33 E
Thiès Senegal 124 14 50N 16 54W
Thika Kenya 126 1 1S 37 5 E
Thimphu Bhutan 115 27 31N 89 45 E
Thionville France 94 49 20N 6 10 E
Thíra I. Greece 97 36 23N 25 27 E
Thiruvananthapuram India
114 8 29N 76 59 E
Thlewiaza, R. Canada 140 60 29N 94 40W
Thomasville USA 143 30 50N 83 59W
Thompson Canada 140 55 45N 97 52W
Thunder Bay Canada 141 48 20N 89 15W
Thüringer Wald Germany
92 50 35N 11 0 E
Ti
Thurso UK 89 58 36N 3 32W
Tian Shan Asia 108 40 30N 76 0 E
Tianjin China 109 39 8N 117 10 E
Tianshui China 108 34 32N 105 40 E
Tiaret Algeria 124 35 20N 1 21 E
Tiber, R. Italy 96 41 44N 12 14 E
Tibesti Chad 125 21 0N 17 30 E
Tibet China 108 32 0N 88 0 E
Tibet, Plateau of Asia 100 32 0N 86 0 E
Ticino, R. Italy 92 45 9N 9 14 E
Ticonderoga USA 145 43 51N 73 26W
Tiffin USA 144 41 7N 83 11W
Tighina Moldova 99 46 50N 29 30 E
Tignish Canada 146 46 58N 64 2W
Tigris, R. Asia 116 31 0N 47 25 E
Tijuana Mexico 146 32 30N 117 10W
Tikamgarh India 114 24 45N 78 53 E
Tikhoretsk Russia 99 45 56N 40 5 E
Tikhvin Russia 98 59 35N 33 30 E
Tikrit Iraq 116 34 35N 43 37 E
Tiksi Russia 107 71 40N 128 45 E
Tilburg Neths. 90 51 31N 5 6 E
Timaru New Zealand 129 44 23S 171 14 E
Timisoara Romania 93 45 43N 21 15 E
Timmins Canada 141 48 28N 81 25W
Timor Indonesia 113 9 0S 125 0 E
Timor Sea Indian Ocean
113 12 0S 127 0 E
Tinu New Zealand 132 40 52S 176 5 E
Tipperary Ireland 89 52 28N 8 10W
Tirana Albania 97 41 18N 19 49 E
Tiraspol Moldova 93 46 55N 29 35 E
Tirebolu Turkey 99 40 58N 38 45 E
Tiree UK 89 56 31N 6 55W
Tirich Mir Pk. Pakistan 114 36 15N 71 55 E
Tirol Tauern Austria 92 47 3N 10 43 E
Tirua New Zealand 132 38 25S 174 40 E
Tiruchchirappalli India 114 10 45N 78 45 E
Tirunelveli India 114 8 45N 77 45 E
Tirupati India 114 13 40N 79 20 E
Tiruppur India 114 11 5N 77 22 E
Tiruvannamalai India 114 12 15N 79 7 E
Tisa, R. Serbia 97 45 15N 20 17 E
Tisdale Canada 140 52 50N 104 0W
Titicaca, L. S. America 148 15 30S 69 30W
Titusville USA 144 41 38N 79 41W
Tizi-Ouzou Algeria 124 36 42N 4 3 E
To
Tlaxiaco Mexico 146 17 18N 97 40W
Tlemcen Algeria 124 34 52N 1 21W
Toamasina Madagascar 126 18 10S 49 25 E
Toba, Danau Indonesia 112 2 30N 97 30 E
Tobago Trinidad & Tobago
147 11 10N 60 30W
Tobermory UK 89 56 38N 6 5W
Tocantins, R. Brazil 148 1 45S 49 10W
Todos os Santos, Baía de Brazil
148 12 48S 38 38W
Togliatti Russia 98 53 32N 49 24 E
TOGO Africa 119 8 30N 1 35 E
Tok USA 142 63 20N 142 59W
Tokanui New Zealand 132 46 34S 168 56 E
Tokarahi New Zealand 132 44 56S 170 39 E
Tokat Turkey 99 40 22N 36 35 E
Tokelau Is. Pacific Ocean
129 9 0S 171 45W
Tokomaru Bay New Zealand
132 38 8S 178 22 E
Tokushima Japan 111 34 4N 134 34 E
Tokuyama Japan 111 34 3N 131 50 E
Tokyo Japan 111 35 45N 139 45 E
Tolaga Bay New Zealand
132 38 21S 178 20 E
Toledo Spain 95 39 50N 4 2W
Toledo USA 144 41 39N 83 33W
Toliara Madagascar 126 23 21S 43 40 E
Tolima Pk. Colombia 148 4 40N 75 19W
Toluca Mexico 146 19 20N 99 40W
Tomakomai Japan 110 42 38N 141 36 E
Tomaszów Mazowiecki Poland
93 51 30N 20 2 E
Tombador, Serra do Brazil
148 12 0S 58 0W
Tombigbee R. USA 143 31 8N 87 57W
Tombouctou Mali 124 16 50N 3 0W
Tomsk Russia 106 56 30N 85 5 E
TONGA Pacific Ocean 129 19 50S 174 30W
Tonga Trench Pacific Ocean
133 18 0S 173 0W
Tongareva I. Cook Is. 133 9 0S 158 0W
Tongatapu Group Tonga
129 21 0S 175 0W
Tonghua China 109 41 42N 125 58 E
Tongue R. USA 142 46 25N 105 52W
Tonk India 114 26 6N 75 54 E
Tonkin, G. of Asia 108 20 0N 108 0 E
Tonopah USA 142 38 4N 117 14W
Toowoomba Australia 128 27 32S 151 56 E
Topeka USA 143 39 3N 95 40W
Topolobampo Mexico 146 25 40N 109 4W
Torbay UK 89 50 26N 3 31W
Torne Älv, R. Sweden 91 65 50N 24 12 E
Torneträsk Sweden 91 68 24N 19 15 E
Tornio Finland 91 65 50N 24 12 E
Torre del Greco Italy 96 40 47N 14 22 E
Torrens, L. Australia 128 31 0S 137 50 E
Torreón Mexico 146 25 33N 103 26W
Torres Str. Australia 128 9 50S 142 20 E
Tortola Br. Virgin Is. 147 18 19N 64 45W
Tortosa Spain 95 40 49N 0 31 E
Torun Poland 91 53 2N 18 39 E
Toscana Italy 96 43 25N 11 0 E
Tottori Japan 111 35 30N 134 15 E

174 INDEX

TOUBHAL, DJEBEL–WHITE NILE, R.

Toubhal, Djebel *Morocco* 124 31 0N 8 0W
Touggourt *Algeria* 124 33 6N 6 4 E
Toul *France* 94 48 40N 5 53 E
Toulon *France* 94 43 10N 5 55 E
Toulouse *France* 94 43 37N 1 27 E
Touraine *France* 94 47 20N 0 30 E
Tournai *Belgium* 90 50 35N 3 25 E
Tournon sur-Rhône *France* 94 45 4N 4 50 E
Tours *France* 94 47 22N 0 40 E
Towanda *USA* 144 41 46N 76 27W
Townsville *Australia* 128 19 15S 146 45 E
Towraghondi *Afghanistan* 114 35 13N 62 16 E
Toyama *Japan* 111 36 40N 137 15 E
Toyohashi *Japan* 111 34 45N 137 25 E
Toyooka *Japan* 111 35 35N 134 55 E
Toyota *Japan* 111 35 3N 137 7 E
Tr
Trabzon *Turkey* 99 41 0N 39 45 E
Trafalgar, C. *Spain* 95 36 10N 6 2W
Trail *Canada* 140 49 5N 117 40W
Tralee *Ireland* 89 52 16N 9 42W
Transantarctic Mts. *Antarctica* 81 85 0S 170 0W
Transylvania *Romania* 93 46 30 24 0 E
Trápani *Italy* 96 38 1N 12 29 E
Traverse City *USA* 144 44 46N 85 38W
Treinta Tres *Uruguay* 149 33 16S 54 17W
Trent, R. *UK* 82 53 41N 0 42W
Trento *Italy* 96 46 4N 11 8 E
Trenton *USA* 145 40 14N 74 46W
Tres Arrayos *Argentina* 149 38 26S 60 20W
Três Lagoas *Brazil* 149 20 50S 51 43W
Tres Puntas, C. *Argentina* 148 47 0S 66 0W
Tribal Areas *Pakistan* 114 33 0N 70 0 E
Trichur *India* 114 10 30N 76 18 E
Trier *Germany* 92 49 45N 6 38 E
Trieste *Slovenia* 96 45 40N 13 46 E
Trincomalee *Srilanka* 114 8 38N 81 15 E
Trinidad *Bolivia* 149 14 46S 64 50W
Trinidad *Cuba* 147 21 48N 80 0W
Trinidad *USA* 142 37 10N 104 31W
TRINIDAD & TOBAGO *West Indies* 149 10 30N 61 20W
Trinity Bay *Canada* 141 48 20N 53 10W
Trinity Is. *USA* 142 56 33N 154 25W
Trinity, R. *USA* 143 29 45N 94 43W
Tripoli *Lebanon* 116 34 31N 35 50 E
Tripoli *Libya* 125 32 49N 13 7 E
Tripolitania *N. Africa* 125 31 0N 13 0 E
Tripura *India* 115 24 0N 92 0 E
Trnava *Slovakia* 93 48 23N 17 35 E
Trois-Rivières *Canada* 141 46 25N 72 34W
Trois-Rivières *Guadeloupe* 146 15 57N 61 40W
Trollhättan *Sweden* 91 58 17N 12 20 E
Trombetas, R. *Brazil* 148 1 55S 55 35W
Tromsø *Norway* 91 69 40N 18 56 E
Tronador Pk. *Argentina* 148 41 10S 71 50W
Trondheim *Norway* 91 63 36N 10 25 E
Trondheimsfjorden *Norway* 91 63 35N 10 30 E
Trou Gras Pt. *St Lucia* 147 13 54N 60 53W
Trout, L. *ON, Canada* 140 51 20N 93 15W
Trout L. *NT, Canada* 140 60 40N 121 14W
Troy *Turkey* 99 39 57N 26 12 E
Troy *AL, USA* 143 31 48N 85 58W
Troy *NY, USA* 145 42 44N 73 41W
Troy *OH, USA* 144 40 2N 84 12W
Troyes *France* 94 48 19N 4 3 E
Trujillo *Peru* 149 8 6S 79 0W
Trujillo *Honduras* 146 16 0N 86 0W
Truk *Micronesia* 133 7 25N 151 46 E
Truro *Canada* 141 45 21N 63 14W
Tsiigehtchic *Canada* 140 67 15N 134 0W
Tsimlyansk Res. *Russia* 99 48 0N 43 0 E
Tskhinvali *Georgia* 116 42 14N 44 1 E
Tsuchiura *Japan* 111 36 5N 140 15 E
Tsugaru Strait *Japan* 110 41 35N 141 0 E
Tsuruoka *Japan* 110 38 44N 139 50 E
Tsushima *Japan* 109 34 20N 129 20 E
Tu
Tuapse *Russia* 99 44 5N 39 10 E
Tuatapere *New Zealand* 132 46 8S 167 41 E
Tubuai Is. *Pacific Ocean* 133 25 0S 150 0W
Tucson *USA* 142 32 13N 110 58W
Tucumcari *USA* 142 35 10N 103 44W
Tucupita *Venezuela* 149 9 2N 62 3W
Tucuruí *Brazil* 149 3 42S 49 44W
Tuktoyaktuk *Canada* 140 69 27N 133 2W
Tula *Russia* 98 54 13N 37 38 E
Tulare *USA* 142 36 13N 119 21W
Tulcán *Ecuador* 149 0 48N 77 43W
Tulcea *Romania* 93 45 13N 28 46 E
Tulita *Canada* 140 64 57N 125 30W
Tullamore *Ireland* 89 53 16N 7 31W
Tulle *France* 94 45 16N 1 46 E
Tulsa *USA* 143 36 10N 95 55W
Tumaco *Colombia* 149 1 50N 78 45W
Tumucumaque Serra *Brazil* 148 2 0N 55 0W
Tunis *Tunisia* 125 36 50N 10 11 E
TUNISIA *Africa* 119 33 30N 9 10 E
Tunja *Colombia* 149 5 33N 73 25W
Tupelo *USA* 143 34 16N 88 43W
Turfan Depression *China* 100 42 40N 89 25 E
Turgutlu *Turkey* 99 38 30N 27 43 E
Turkana, L. *Africa* 118 3 30N 36 5 E
TURKEY *Eurasia* 99 39 0N 36 0 E
Türkmenbashi *Turkmenistan* 99 40 5N 53 5 E
TURKMENISTAN *Asia* 106 39 0N 59 0 E
Turks & Caicos Is. *W. Indies* 147 21 20N 71 20W
Turku *Finland* 91 60 30N 22 19 E
Turnagain, C. *New Zealand* 132 40 28S 176 38 E
Turneffe Is. *Belize* 146 17 20N 87 50W
Turpan *China* 108 43 58N 89 10 E
Tuscaloosa *USA* 143 33 12N 87 34W
Tuticorin *India* 114 8 50N 78 12 E
Tutuila *American Samoa* 129 14 19S 170 50W
Tutume *Botswana* 126 20 30S 27 5 E
Tuvalu *Pacific Ocean* 129 8 0S 178 0 E
Tuxpan *Mexico* 146 20 58N 97 23W
Tuxtla Gutiérrez *Mexico* 146 16 50N 93 10W
Tuz Gölü *Turkey* 99 38 42N 33 18 E
Tuzla *Bosnia-Herz.* 97 44 34N 18 41 E
Tver *Russia* 98 56 55N 35 55 E
Tweed, R. *UK* 89 55 45N 2 0W
Twin Falls *USA* 142 42 34N 114 28W
Two Harbors *USA* 143 47 2N 91 40W
Two Rivers *USA* 144 44 9N 87 34W
Two Thumb Ra. *New Zealand* 132 43 45S 170 44 E
Tychy *Poland* 93 50 9N 18 59 E
Tyler *USA* 143 32 21N 95 18W
Tyrrhenian Sea *Mediterranean Sea* 96 40 0N 12 30 E
Tyumen *Russia* 106 57 11N 65 29 E
Tzaneen *South Africa* 126 23 47S 30 9 E

U

Uaupés, R. *Brazil* 148 0 2N 67 16W
Ube *Japan* 111 33 56N 131 15 E
Uberaba *Brazil* 149 19 50S 47 55W
Uberlândia *Brazil* 149 19 0S 48 20W
Ucayali, R. *Peru* 148 4 30S 73 30W
Udagamandalam *India* 114 11 30N 76 44 E
Udaipur *India* 114 24 36N 73 44 E
Udhampur *India* 114 32 55N 75 9 E
Údine *Italy* 96 46 3N 13 14 E
Udmurtia *Russia* 98 57 30N 52 30 E
Udupi *India* 114 13 25N 74 42 E
Uele, R. *D.R. Congo* 126 3 45N 24 45 E
Ufa *Russia* 98 54 45N 55 55 E
UGANDA *Africa* 119 2 0N 32 0 E
Uinta Mts. *USA* 142 40 45N 110 30W
Uitenhage *South Africa* 126 33 40S 25 28 E
Ujjain *India* 114 23 9N 75 43 E
Ujung Pandang *Indonesia* 112 5 10S 119 20 E
Ukhta *Russia* 98 63 34N 53 41 E
Ukiah *USA* 142 39 9N 123 13W
Ul
UKRAINE *Europe* 99 49 0N 32 0 E
Ulaangom *Mongolia* 108 50 5N 92 10 E
Ulaanjirem *Mongolia* 108 45 5N 105 30 E
Ulan Bator *Mongolia* 101 47 55N 106 53 E
Ulan Ude *Russia* 106 51 45N 107 40 E
Ulasnagar *India* 114 19 15N 73 10 E
Ullapool *UK* 89 57 54N 5 9W
Ulm *Germany* 92 48 23N 9 58 E
Ulster *UK* 89 54 35N 6 30W
Ulungur He, R. *China* 108 47 1N 87 24 E
Ulyasutay *Mongolia* 108 47 56N 97 28 E
Uman *Ukraine* 99 48 40N 30 12 E
Umbrella, Mt. *New Zealand* 132 45 35S 169 5 E
Ume Älv, R. *Sweden* 91 63 45N 20 20 E
Umeå *Sweden* 91 63 45N 20 20 E
Umlazi *South Africa* 126 29 59S 30 54 E
Umnak I. *USA* 142 53 15N 168 20W
Umtata *South Africa* 126 31 36S 28 49 E
Umuarama *Brazil* 149 23 45S 53 20W
Unalakleet *USA* 142 63 52N 160 47W
Unalaska *USA* 142 53 53N 166 32W
Unalaska I. *USA* 142 53 35N 166 50W
Ungava Bay *Canada* 141 59 30N 67 30W
Ungava Pen. *Canada* 141 60 0N 74 0W
Unimak I. *USA* 142 54 45N 164 0W
Uniontown *USA* 144 39 54N 79 44W
UNITED ARAB EMIRATES *Asia* 101 23 50N 54 0 E
UNITED KINGDOM *Europe* 83 53 0N 2 0W
Unnao *India* 115 26 48N 80 43 E
Upington *South Africa* 126 28 25S 21 15 E
Upolu *Samoa* 129 13 58S 172 0W
Upper Klamath L. *USA* 142 42 25N 121 55W
Uppsala *Sweden* 91 59 53N 17 38 E
Ur
Ur *Iraq* 116 30 55N 46 25 E
Ural Mts. *Eurasia* 98 60 0N 59 0 E
Ural, R. *Kazakhstan* 99 47 0N 51 48 E
Uranium City *Canada* 140 59 34N 108 37W
Urbana *IL, USA* 144 40 7N 88 12W
Urbana *OH, USA* 144 40 7N 83 45W
Ure, R. *UK* 89 54 5N 1 20W
Urganch *Uzbekistan* 117 41 40N 60 41 E
Urmia *Iran* 116 37 40N 45 0 E
Urmia, L. *Iran* 116 37 50N 45 30 E
Uruapan *Mexico* 146 19 30N 102 0W
Urubamba, R. *Peru* 148 10 43S 73 48W
Uruguai, R. *Brazil* 148 26 0S 53 30W
Uruguaiana *Brazil* 149 29 50S 57 0W
URUGUAY *South America* 149 32 30S 56 30W
Ürümqi *China* 108 43 45N 87 45 E
Usa, R. *Russia* 98 66 16N 59 49 E
Usak *Turkey* 99 38 43N 29 28 E
Usakos *Namibia* 126 21 54S 15 31 E
Ushant *France* 82 48 28N 5 6W
Ushuaia *Argentina* 149 54 50S 68 23W
Üsküdar *Turkey* 116 41 0N 29 5 E
Ustí nad Labem *Czech Rep.* 92 50 41N 14 3 E
Ust-Ilimsk *Russia* 107 58 3N 102 39 E
Ustyurt Plateau *Asia* 106 44 0N 55 0 E
Usu *China* 108 44 27N 84 40 E
Usumacinta, R. *Mexico* 146 17 0N 91 0W
Utah *USA* 142 39 20N 111 30W
Utah, L. *USA* 142 40 10N 111 58W
Utica *USA* 145 43 6N 75 14W
Utrecht *Neths.* 90 52 5N 5 8 E
Utsunomiya *Japan* 111 36 30N 139 50 E
Uttar Pradesh *India* 114 27 0N 80 0 E
Uttarakhand *India* 114 30 0N 79 30 E
Utuado *Puerto Rico* 147 18 16N 66 42W
Uusikaupunki *Finland* 91 60 47N 21 25 E
Uvalde *USA* 142 29 13N 99 47W
Uvs Nuur L. *Mongolia* 108 50 20N 92 30 E
UZBEKISTAN *Asia* 106 41 30N 65 0 E
Uzhhorod *Ukraine* 93 48 36N 22 18 E

V

Vaal, R. *South Africa* 126 29 4S 23 38 E
Vaasa *Finland* 91 63 6N 21 38 E
Vadodara *India* 114 22 20N 73 10 E
Vadsø *Norway* 91 70 3N 29 50 E
Vaduz *Liechtenstein* 92 47 8N 9 31 E
Váh, R. *Slovak Rep.* 93 47 43N 18 7 E
Vail *USA* 142 39 40N 106 20W
Valahia *Romania* 93 44 35N 25 0 E
Valdai Hills *Russia* 98 57 0N 33 30 E
Valdés, Pen. *Argentina* 148 42 30S 63 45W
Valdez *USA* 142 61 7N 146 16W
Valdivia *Chile* 149 39 50S 73 14W
Val-d'or *Canada* 141 48 7N 77 47W
Valdosta *USA* 143 30 50N 83 17W
Valence *France* 94 44 57N 4 54 E
Valencia *Venezuela* 149 10 11N 68 0W
Valencia *Spain* 95 39 27N 0 23 W
Valenciennes *France* 94 50 20N 3 34 E
Valladolid *Mexico* 146 20 40N 88 11W
Valladolid *Spain* 95 41 38N 4 43W
Valletta *Malta* 96 35 54N 14 31 E
Valley City *USA* 142 46 55N 98 0W
Valsad *India* 114 20 36N 72 59 E
Van *Turkey* 99 38 30N 43 20 E
Van, L. *Turkey* 99 38 30N 43 0 E
Van Wert *USA* 144 40 52N 84 35W
Vancouver *USA* 142 45 38N 122 40W
Vancouver *Canada* 140 49 15N 123 10W
Vancouver I. *Canada* 140 49 50N 126 0W
Vanderhoof *Canada* 140 54 0N 124 0W
Vänern *Sweden* 82 58 25N 14 30 E
Vänern *Sweden* 91 58 47N 13 30 E
Vanino *Russia* 107 48 50N 140 5 E
Vännäs *Sweden* 91 63 58N 19 48 E
Vannes *France* 94 47 40N 2 47W
Vanrhynsdorp *South Africa* 126 31 36S 18 44 E
Vanua Levu *Fiji* 129 16 33S 179 15 E
VANUATU *Pacific Ocean* 133 15 0S 168 0 E
Varanasi *India* 115 25 22N 83 0 E
Varangerfjorden *Norway* 91 70 3N 29 25 E
Varberg *Sweden* 91 57 6N 12 20 E
Vardak *Afghan.* 117 34 0N 68 0 E
Varna *Bulgaria* 97 43 13N 27 56 E
Västerås *Sweden* 91 59 37N 16 38 E
Västervik *Sweden* 91 57 43N 16 33 E
Vatican City *Europe* 96 41 54N 12 27 E
Vättern *Sweden* 91 58 25N 14 30 E
Ve
Vaughn *USA* 142 34 36N 105 13W
Vava'u Group *Tonga* 129 18 40S 174 0W
Vega *Norway* 91 65 40N 11 55 E
Vega Baja *Puerto Rico* 147 18 27N 66 23W
Vegreville *Canada* 140 53 30N 112 5W
Velikiye Luki *Russia* 98 56 25N 30 32 E
Vellore *India* 114 12 57N 79 10 E
Velsk *Russia* 98 61 10N 42 5 E
Vendôme *France* 94 47 47N 1 3 E
VENEZUELA *South America* 149 8 0N 66 0W
Venezuela, G. de *Venezuela* 148 11 30N 71 0W
Vengurla *India* 114 15 53N 73 45 E
Venice *Italy* 96 45 27N 12 21 E
Venlo *Neths.* 90 51 22N 6 11 E
Ventoux, Mt. *France* 94 44 10N 5 17 E
Ventspils *Latvia* 98 57 25N 21 32 E
Veracruz *Mexico* 146 19 10N 96 10W
Veraval *India* 114 20 53N 70 27 E
Verde, R. *USA* 142 33 33N 111 40W
Verdun *France* 94 49 9N 5 24 E
Vereeniging *South Africa* 126 26 38S 27 57 E
Verkhoyansk *Russia* 106 67 35N 133 25 E
Verkhoyansk Ra. *Russia* 107 68 0N 129 0 E
Vermont *USA* 143 44 0N 73 0W
Vernal *USA* 142 40 27N 109 32W
Vernon *USA* 142 34 9N 99 17W
Vernon *Canada* 140 50 20N 119 15W
Verona *Italy* 96 45 27N 10 59 E
Versailles *France* 94 48 48N 2 8 E
Vert, C. *Senegal* 118 14 45N 17 30W
Verviers *Belgium* 90 50 37N 5 52 E
Vesoul *France* 94 47 40N 6 11 E
Vesterålen *Norway* 91 68 45N 15 0 E
Vestfjorden *Norway* 91 67 55N 14 0 E
Vesuvio *Italy* 96 40 49N 14 26 E
Vi
Vicenza *Italy* 96 45 33N 11 33 E
Vichada, R. *Colombia* 148 4 55N 67 50W
Vichy *France* 94 46 9N 3 26 E
Vicksburg *USA* 143 32 21N 90 53W
Victoria *Australia* 128 37 0S 144 0 E
Victoria *Canada* 140 48 30N 123 25W
Victoria *USA* 145 28 48N 97 0W
Victoria de las Tunas *Cuba* 147 20 58N 76 59W
Victoria Falls *Zimbabwe* 126 17 58S 25 52 E
Victoria I. *Canada* 140 71 0N 111 0W
Victoria, L. *Africa* 126 1 0S 33 0 E
Victoria Ld. *Antarctica* 81 75 0S 160 0 E
Victoria Ra. *N. Zealand* 132 42 12S 172 7 E
Victoria Str. *Canada* 140 69 31N 100 30W
Victoriaville *Canada* 146 46 4N 71 56W
Vidisha *India* 114 23 32N 77 51 E
Vienna *Austria* 92 48 12N 16 22 E
Vienne *France* 94 45 31N 4 53 E
Vieques, Isla de *Puerto Rico* 147 18 8N 65 25W
Vierge Pt. *St. Lucia* 147 13 49N 60 53W
Vierzon *France* 94 47 13N 2 5F
VIETNAM *Asia* 101 19 0N 106 0 E
Vieux Fort *St Lucia* 147 13 46N 60 58W
Vigo *Spain* 95 42 12N 8 41W
Vijayawada *India* 115 16 31N 80 39 E
Vikna *Norway* 91 64 56N 10 58 E
Vila Velha *Brazil* 149 20 20S 40 17W
Vilaine, R. *France* 94 47 30N 2 27W
Vilhelmina *Sweden* 91 64 35N 16 39 E
Villach *Austria* 92 46 37N 13 51 E
Villahermosa *Mexico* 146 17 59N 92 55W
Villapuram *India* 114 11 57N 79 32 E
Villeneuve-sur-Lot *France* 94 44 24N 0 42 E
Vilnius *Lithuania* 98 54 38N 25 19 E
Vilyuy, R. *Russia* 107 64 24N 126 26 E
Vilyuysk *Russia* 107 63 40N 121 35 E
Viña Del Mar *Chile* 149 33 0S 71 30W
Vincennes *USA* 144 38 41N 87 32W
Vineland *USA* 145 39 29N 75 2W
Vinnytsya *Ukraine* 93 49 15N 28 30 E
Virden *Canada* 140 49 50N 100 56W
Vire *France* 94 48 50N 0 53W
Vírgenes, C. *Argentina* 148 52 19S 68 21W
Virgin Gorda *Br. Virgin Is.* 147 18 30N 64 26W
Virgin Is. (UK) *W. Indies* 147 18 30N 64 30W
Virgin Is. (US) *W. Indies* 147 18 20N 65 0W
Virginia *USA* 144 37 30N 78 45W
Virginia *MN, USA* 143 47 31N 92 32W
Virudunagar *India* 114 9 35N 77 57 E
Visalia *USA* 142 36 20N 119 18W
Visby *Sweden* 91 57 37N 18 18 E
Vishakhapatnam *India* 115 17 45N 83 20 E
Vistula, R. *Poland* 93 54 22N 18 55 E
Vitebsk *Belarus* 98 55 10N 30 15 E
Viterbo *Italy* 96 42 25N 12 6 E
Viti Levu *Fiji* 129 17 30S 177 30 E
Vitori-Gasteiz *Spain* 95 42 50N 2 41W
Vizianagaram *India* 115 18 6N 83 30 E
Vlaardingen *Neths.* 90 51 55N 4 21 E
Vladikavkaz *Russia* 99 43 0N 44 35 E
Vladimir *Russia* 98 56 15N 40 30 E
Vladivostok *Russia* 107 43 10N 131 53 E
Vlorë *Albania* 97 40 32N 19 28 E
Vltava, R. *Czech Rep.* 92 50 21N 14 30 E
Vo
Vogelkop *Indonesia* 112 1 25S 133 0 E
Vogelsberg Pk. *Germany* 92 50 31N 9 12 E
Vohimena, Tanjon'i (Cape) *Madagascar* 126 25 36S 45 8 E
Voi *Kenya* 126 3 25S 38 32 E
Vojvodina *Serbia* 97 45 20N 20 0 E
Volga Heights *Russia* 99 51 0N 46 0 E
Volga, R. *Russia* 99 46 0N 48 30 E
Volgodonsk *Russia* 99 47 33N 42 5 E
Volgograd *Russia* 99 48 40N 44 25 E
Vologda *Russia* 98 59 10N 39 45 E
Vólos *Greece* 97 39 24N 22 59 E
Volsk *Russia* 98 52 5N 47 22 E
Volta, R. *Ghana* 124 5 46N 0 41 E
Volta, L. *Ghana* 124 7 30N 0 0W
Volzhskiy *Russia* 99 48 56N 44 46 E
Vorkuta *Russia* 98 67 48N 64 20 E
Voronezh *Russia* 99 51 40N 39 10 E
Vosges *France* 94 48 20N 7 10 E
Vostok I. *Kiribati* 133 10 5S 152 23W
Votkinsk *Russia* 98 57 0N 53 55 E
Vryburg *South Africa* 126 26 55S 24 45 E
Vryheid *South Africa* 126 27 45S 30 47 E
Vyazma *Russia* 98 55 10N 34 15 E
Vyborg *Russia* 98 60 43N 28 47 E
Vychegda, R. *Russia* 98 61 18N 46 36 E
Vyshniy Volochek *Russia* 98 57 30N 34 30 E

W

Waal, R. *Neths.* 90 51 37N 5 0 E
Wabasca, R. *Canada* 140 58 22N 115 20W
Wabash *USA* 144 40 48N 85 49W
Wabash, R. *USA* 144 37 48N 88 2W
Waco *USA* 143 31 33N 97 9W
Wâd Medanî *Sudan* 125 14 28N 33 30 E
Wadden Zee *Neths.* 90 53 6N 5 10 E
Waddington, Mt. *Canada* 140 51 23N 125 15W
Wadi Halfa *Sudan* 125 21 53N 31 19 E
Wager Bay *Canada* 141 65 26N 88 40W
Wagga Wagga *Australia* 128 35 7S 147 24 E
Wah *Pakistan* 114 33 45N 72 40 E
Wahiawa *USA* 142 21 30N 158 2W
Waiau *New Zealand* 132 42 39S 173 5 E
Waiau, R. *New Zealand* 132 42 47S 173 22 E
Waigeo *Indonesia* 113 0 20S 130 40 E
Waihao, R. *N. Zealand* 132 44 52S 171 11 E
Waiheke I. *N. Zealand* 132 36 48S 175 6 E
Waihola *New Zealand* 132 46 1S 170 8 E
Waihola, L. *N. Zealand* 132 45 59S 170 8 E
Waikare, L. *N. Zealand* 132 37 26S 175 13 E
Waikaremoana, L. *New Zealand* 132 38 49S 177 9 E
Waikari *New Zealand* 132 42 58S 172 41 E
Waikato, R. *N. Zealand* 132 37 23S 174 43 E
Wailuku *USA* 142 20 53N 156 30W
Waimea Plains *New Zealand* 132 45 55S 168 35 E
Waipapa Pt. *New Zealand* 132 46 40S 168 51 E
Waipara *New Zealand* 132 43 3S 172 46 E
Waipiro *New Zealand* 132 38 2S 176 22 E
Wairakei *New Zealand* 132 38 37S 176 6 E
Wairau, R. *New Zealand* 132 41 32S 174 7 E
Wairoa *New Zealand* 132 39 3S 177 25 E
Wairoa, R. *N. Zealand* 132 36 5S 173 59 E
Waitaki, R. *N. Zealand* 132 44 23S 169 55 E
Waitaki Plains *New Zealand* 132 44 22S 170 0 E
Waitara *New Zealand* 132 38 59S 174 15 E
Waitoa *New Zealand* 132 37 37S 175 35 E
Waitotara *New Zealand* 132 39 49S 174 44 E
Wakatipu, L. *N. Zealand* 132 45 5S 168 33 E
Wakayama *Japan* 111 34 15N 135 15 E
Wake I. *Pacific Ocean* 133 19 18N 166 36 E
Wakefield *Jamaica* 146 18 26N 77 42W
Wakkanai *Japan* 110 45 28N 141 35 E
Walbrzych *Poland* 92 50 45N 16 18 E
Walcheren *Neths.* 90 51 30N 3 35 E
Wales *UK* 89 52 19N 4 43W
Walgett *Australia* 128 30 0S 148 5 E
Walker, L. *USA* 142 38 42N 118 43W
Walla Walla *USA* 142 46 4N 118 20W
Wallacetown *New Zealand* 132 46 21S 168 19 E
Wallachia *Romania* 82 44 35N 25 0 E
Wallis & Futuna Is. *Pacific Ocean* 129 13 18S 176 10W
Walsall *UK* 89 52 35N 1 58W
Walsenburg *USA* 142 37 38N 104 47W
Walvis Bay *Namibia* 126 23 0S 14 28
Wanaka, L. *New Zealand* 132 44 33S 169 7
Wanganui *New Zealand* 129 39 56S 175 3
Wanganui, R. *New Zealand* 132 39 25S 175 4
Wapakoneta *USA* 144 40 34N 84 12W
Warangal *India* 114 17 58N 79 35
Ward *New Zealand* 132 41 49S 174 11
Wardha *India* 114 20 45N 78 39
Warren *PA, USA* 143 41 51N 79 9W
Warren *MI, USA* 144 42 30N 83 0W
Warren *OH, USA* 144 41 14N 80 49W
Warrington *UK* 89 53 24N 2 35W
Warrnambool *Australia* 128 38 25S 142 30
Warsaw *Poland* 93 52 13N 21 0
Warsaw *USA* 144 41 14N 85 61W
Warta, R. *Poland* 92 52 35N 14 39
Wasatch Ra. *USA* 142 40 30N 111 15W
Wash, The *UK* 82 52 58N 0 20
Washim *India* 114 20 5N 77 10
Washington *USA* 142 47 30N 120 30W
Washington, D.C. *USA* 144 38 54N 77 2W
Washington I. *USA* 144 45 23N 86 54W
Washington *IN, USA* 144 38 40N 87 10W
Washington *PA, USA* 144 40 10N 80 15W
Waskaganish *Canada* 141 51 30N 78 40W
Watampone *Indonesia* 113 4 29S 120 25
Waterbury *USA* 145 41 33N 73 3W
Waterloo *USA* 143 42 30N 92 21W
Waterloo *Canada* 145 43 30N 80 32W
Watertown *NY, USA* 145 43 59N 75 55W
Watertown *SD, USA* 143 44 54N 97 7W
Waterville *USA* 145 44 33N 69 38W
Watford *Ireland* 89 51 40N 0 24W
Watrous *Canada* 140 51 40N 105 25W
Watseka *USA* 144 40 47N 87 44W
Watson Lake *Canada* 140 60 6N 128 49W
Waukegan *USA* 144 42 22N 87 50W
Waukesha *USA* 144 43 1N 88 14W
Wausau *USA* 143 44 58N 89 38W
Wauwatosa *USA* 144 43 3N 88 0W
Wâw *Sudan* 125 7 45N 28 1
Wawa *Canada* 141 47 59N 84 47W
Waycross *USA* 143 31 13N 82 21W
Wayne *USA* 144 38 13N 82 27W
Waynesboro *USA* 144 38 4N 78 53W
Waynesburg *USA* 144 39 54N 80 11W
We
Wazirabad *Pakistan* 114 32 30N 74 8
Wear, R. *UK* 89 54 55N 1 23W
Weber *New Zealand* 132 40 24S 176 20
Webster Springs *USA* 144 38 29N 80 25W
Weddell Sea *Antarctica* 81 72 30S 40 0W
Weifang *China* 109 36 44N 119 7
Weipa *Australia* 128 12 40S 141 50
Welch *USA* 144 37 26N 81 35W
Welkom *South Africa* 126 28 0S 26 46
Wellesley Is. *Australia* 128 16 42S 139 30
Wellington *New Zealand* 129 41 19S 174 46
Wellington I. *Chile* 148 49 30S 75 0W
Wellsboro *USA* 144 41 45N 77 18W
Wellsville *USA* 144 42 7N 77 57W
Wels *Austria* 92 48 9N 14 1
Wemindji *Canada* 141 53 0N 78 49W
Wenatchee *USA* 142 47 25N 120 19W
Wensu *China* 108 41 15N 80 10
Wenzhou *China* 109 28 0N 120 38
Weser, R. *Germany* 92 53 36N 8 28
West Bank *Asia* 116 32 6N 35 13
West Bend *USA* 144 43 25N 88 11W
West Bengal *India* 115 23 0N 88 0
West Beskids *Slovak Rep.* 93 49 30N 19 0
Westbrook *USA* 145 43 41N 70 22W
West Dvina R. *Latvia* 98 57 4N 24 3
Western Australia *Australia* 128 25 0S 118 0
Western Ghats *India* 114 14 0N 75 0
WESTERN SAHARA *Africa* 119 25 0N 13 0W
Westerschelde, R. *Neths.* 90 51 25N 3 25
Westerwald *Germany* 92 50 38N 7 56
West Falkland I. *Argentina* 148 51 40S 60 0W
Westland *New Zealand* 132 43 33S 169 59
Westland Bright *New Zealand* 132 42 55S 170 5
Westminster *USA* 144 39 34N 76 59W
Westmoreland *Barbados* 147 13 13N 59 37W
Weston *USA* 144 39 2N 80 28W
Weston-super-Mare *UK* 89 51 21N 2 58W
West Palm Beach *USA* 143 26 43N 80 3W
West Point *USA* 144 37 32N 76 48W
Westport *Ireland* 89 53 48N 9 31W
Westport *New Zealand* 132 41 46S 171 37
West Seneca *USA* 144 42 51N 78 48W
West Siberian Plain *Russia* 100 62 0N 75 0
West Virginia *USA* 144 38 45N 80 30W
Wetar *Indonesia* 113 7 48S 126 30
Wetaskiwin *Canada* 140 52 55N 113 24W
Wewak *Papua New Guinea* 128 3 38S 143 41
Wexford *Ireland* 89 52 20N 6 25W
Weyburn *Canada* 140 49 40N 103 50W
Weymouth *UK* 89 50 37N 2 28W
Wh
Whakatane *New Zealand* 132 37 57S 177 1
Whale Cove *Canada* 140 62 10N 92 34W
Whales, Bay of *Antarctica* 81 78 0S 165 0W
Whangamata *New Zealand* 132 37 12S 175 53
Whangarei *New Zealand* 129 35 43S 174 21
Whatì *Canada* 140 63 8N 117 16W
Wheeler Pk. *USA* 142 38 57N 114 15W
Wheeling *USA* 144 40 4N 80 43W
White I. *New Zealand* 132 37 30S 177 13
White Mts. *USA* 143 44 15N 71 15W
White Nile, R. *Sudan* 125 15 38N 32 31

Illustration credits

Page 8
NASA Earth Observatory

Page 16
USGS

Page 17
after Stanford's *Geological Atlas* by Horace B. Woodward

Page 18
Bottom left: NASA/USGS EDC/Landsat 7
Bottom right: NASA/Aster

Page 19
Top left: Dirk Beyer
Top right: NASA/Aster
Bottom: NASA/JPL/NIMA

Page 20
Top: NASA Earth Observatory/USGS
Bottom left: NASA/JPL/NIMA
Bottom right: USGS

Page 21
Top left: NASA/Earth Observatory
Top right and bottom left: NASA/JPL
Bottom right: USGS

Page 22
left and right: NASA/JPL

Page 23
Top left: NASA/GSFC/MODIS
Top right: NASA/Earth Observatory
Bottom left: NASA/Space Imaging/IKONOS

Page 24
Top left: DigitalGlobe
Top right: US Navy
Bottom: NOAA

Page 27
Top left: NASA/GSFC
Top right: GOES

Page 27
Bottom left: NASA/MODIS/Karl Wurster
Bottom right: DigitalGlobe

Page 29
Top left: NASA
Top right and bottom: NASA/JPL

Page 32
Top: NASA
Middle: NASA/ERBE
Bottom: NASA

Page 33
Top: NASA/GSFC/LaRC/JPL, MISR

Page 34
Top: NASA
Bottom left: NASA/Earth Observatory
Bottom right: Shuttle Radar Topography Mission

Page 35
Top left and right: NASA/Earth Observatory
Bottom: Global Warming Art

Page 36
Top: NASA/Earth Observatory
Bottom left: NASA/Earth Observatory
Bottom right: NASA/JPL

Page 37
NASA/Earth Observatory

Page 38
Top: NASA/Earth Observatory

Page 40
Bottom left: Jacques Descloitres, MODIS Land Rapid Response Team, NASA/GSFC
Bottom right: USGS EROS

Page 41
Bottom: NASA/GSFC/LaRC/JPL, MISR

Flags of the World

Afghanistan

Albania

Algeria

Andorra

Angola

Anguilla

Antigua & Barbuda

Argentina

Armenia

Australia

Austria

Azerbaijan

Bahamas

Bahrain

Bangladesh

Barbados

Belarus

Belgium

Belize

Benin

Bermuda

Bhutan

Bolivia

Bosnia & Herzegovina

Botswana

Brazil

Brunei

Bulgaria

Burkina Faso

Burundi

Cambodia

Cameroon

Canada

Cape Verde

Central African Republic

Chad

Chile

China

Colombia

Comoros

Congo, Democratic Republic

Congo

Cook Islands

Costa Rica

Cote D'Ivoire

Croatia

Cuba

Cyprus

Czech Republic

Denmark

Djibouti

Dominica

Dominican Republic

East Timor

Ecuador

Egypt

El Salvador

Equatorial Guinea

Eritrea

Estonia

Ethiopia

Fiji

Finland

France

Gabon

Gambia

Georgia

Ghana

Gibraltar

Greece

Greenland

Grenada

Guatemala

Guinea

Guinea Bissau

Guyana

Haiti

Honduras

Hungary

Iceland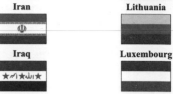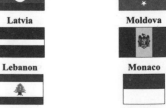

India

Indonesia

Iran

Iraq

Ireland

Israel

Italy

Jamaica

Japan

Jordan

Kazakhstan

Kenya

Kiribati

Kuwait

Kyrgyzstan

Laos

Latvia

Lebanon

Lesotho

Liberia

Libya

Liechtenstein

Lithuania

Luxembourg

Macedonia

Madagascar

Malawi

Malaysia

Maldives

Mali

Malta

Marshall Islands

Mauritania

Mauritius

Mexico

Micronesia

Moldova

Monaco

Mongolia